DAREDEVIL

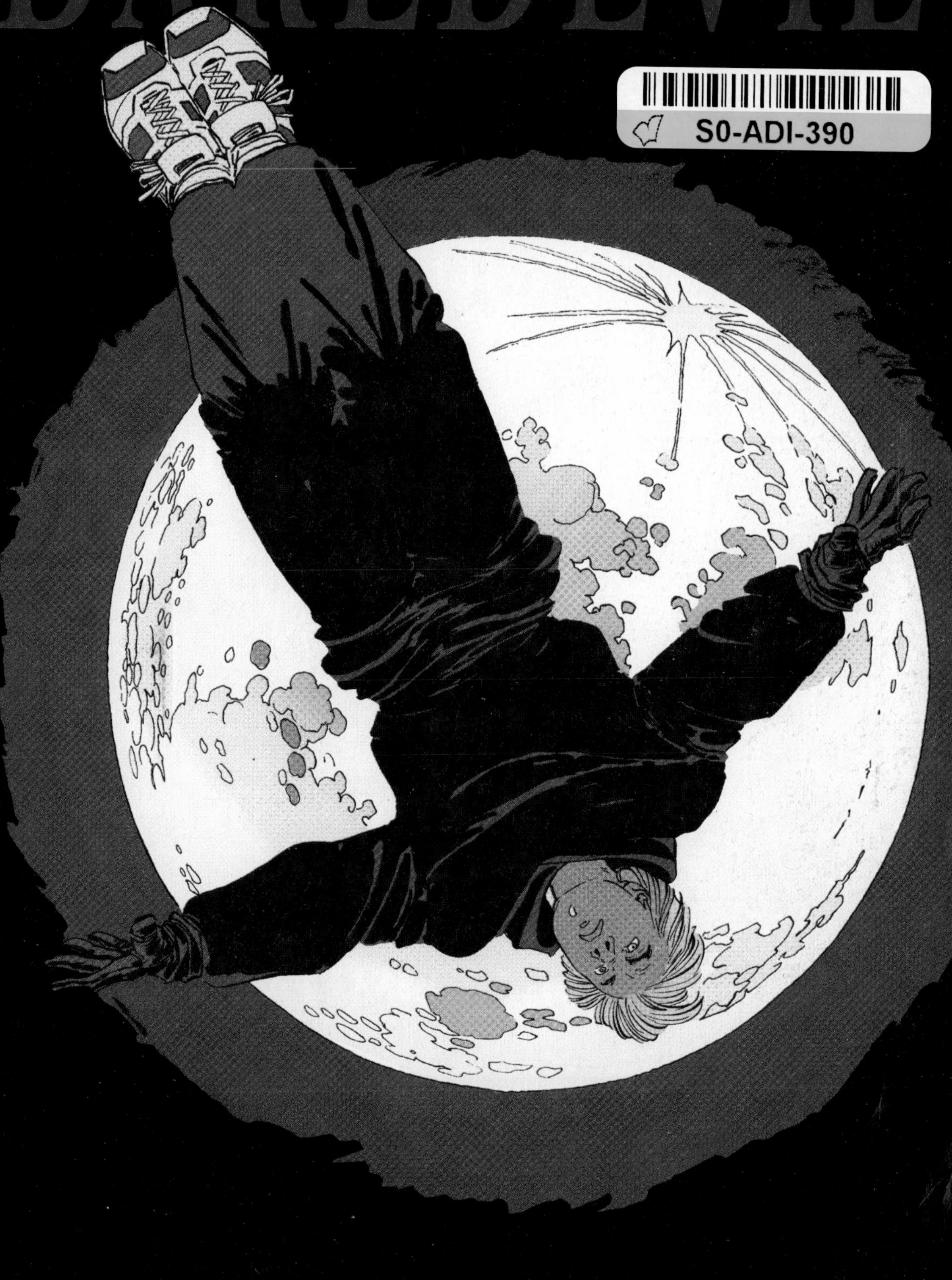

THE MAN WITHOUT FEAR

DAREDEVIL

WRITER

FRANK MILLER

PENCILER

JOHN ROMITA JR.

INKER

AL WILLIAMSON

COLORIST

CHRISTIE SCHEELE

LETTERER

JOE ROSEN

EDITOR

RALPH MACCHIO

COVER ARTIST

JOHN ROMITA JR.

COVER COLORS

RAIN BEREDO

DAREDEVIL: THE MAN WITHOUT FEAR. Contains material originally published in magazine form as DAREDEVIL: THE MAN WITHOUT FEAR #1-5. Second edition. Second printing 2012. ISBN# 978-0-7851-3479-4. Published by MARVEL WORLDWIDE, INC., a subsidiary of MARVEL ENTERTAINMENT, LLC. OFFICE OF PUBLICATION: 135 West 50th Street, New York, NY 10020. Copyright © 1993, 1994 and 2010 Marvel Characters, Inc. All rights reserved. $19.99 per copy in the U.S. and $21.99 in Canada (GST #R127032852); Canadian Agreement #40668537. All characters featured in this issue and the distinctive names and likenesses thereof, and all related indicia are trademarks of Marvel Characters, Inc. No similarity between any of the names, characters, persons, and/or institutions in this magazine with those of any living or dead person or institution is intended, and any such similarity which may exist is purely coincidental. **Printed in the U.S.A.** ALAN FINE, EVP - Office of the President, Marvel Worldwide, Inc. and EVP & CMO Marvel Characters B.V.; DAN BUCKLEY, Publisher & President - Print, Animation & Digital Divisions; JOE QUESADA, Chief Creative Officer; DAVID BOGART, SVP of Business Affairs & Talent Management; TOM BREVOORT, SVP of Publishing; C.B. CEBULSKI, SVP of Creator & Content Development; DAVID GABRIEL, SVP of Publishing Sales & Circulation; MICHAEL PASCIULLO, SVP of Brand Planning & Communications; JIM O'KEEFE, VP of Operations & Logistics; DAN CARR, Executive Director of Publishing Technology; SUSAN CRESPI, Editorial Operations Manager; ALEX MORALES, Publishing Operations Manager; STAN LEE, Chairman Emeritus. For information regarding advertising in Marvel Comics or on Marvel.com, please contact John Dokes, SVP Integrated Sales and Marketing, at jdokes@marvel.com. For Marvel subscription inquiries, please call 800-217-9158. **Manufactured between 2/8/12 and 2/27/12 by R.R. DONNELLEY, INC., SALEM, VA, USA.**

10 9 8 7 6 5 4 3 2

COLLECTION EDITOR
MARK D. BEAZLEY

ASSISTANT EDITORS
NELSON RIBEIRO & ALEX STARBUCK

EDITOR, SPECIAL PROJECTS
JENNIFER GRÜNWALD

SENIOR EDITOR, SPECIAL PROJECTS
JEFF YOUNGQUIST

PRODUCTION
JERRON QUALITY COLOR

SENIOR VICE PRESIDENT OF SALES
DAVID GABRIEL

SVP OF BRAND PLANNING & COMMUNICATIONS
MICHAEL PASCIULLO

EDITOR IN CHIEF
AXEL ALONSO

CHIEF CREATIVE OFFICER
JOE QUESADA

PUBLISHER
DAN BUCKLEY

EXECUTIVE PRODUCER
ALAN FINE

SPECIAL THANKS TO FRANK MILLER, HARRIS MILLER,
HILDY MESNIK, TOM BREVOORT, RALPH MACCHIO,
JODY LEHEUP & MATT MASDEU

THE MAN WITHOUT FEAR

What a way to celebrate your thirtieth anniversary! This volume had its genesis some five years ago when a talented gent by the name of Frank Miller called me and said he was itching to do a *Daredevil* project again. If I remember correctly, he'd been contacted by then – *Daredevil* penciler John Romita Jr., who was anxious to work with the Lanky One on a dressed-to-kill one-shot. Having seen the results of Frank's prior pairings with Bill Sienkiewicz, and David Mazzucchelli, I didn't need too much convincing. Frank and John set out to do the definitive, all-inclusive origin of the Man Without Fear. In a short period, Frank turned around a superb sixty-four page plot that left me panting for more. And so more I requested. Frank and John responded by conceiving whole new sequences, and drastically expanding the existing ones. The mind-wrenching result is a one hundred forty-four page tour de force, sure to stand as a milestone in this beloved character's long and proud history. And when John had completed his herculean drawing labors, the truly extraordinary pages (actually Xeroxes thereof) were sent to Mr. Miller.

Meanwhile, I was busy lining up three other long-time *Daredevil* coconspirators: Al Williamson, Joe Rosen and Christie Scheele. Happily, all were only too pleased to become part of our mammoth undertaking. And while the aforementioned trio sharpened (figuratively) their pens and brushes, Frank Miller completed one of his finest scripts in his more than decade-long association with *Daredevil*. And how could he help but do first-rate scrivening, inspired as he was by John's pencils. Joe Rosen did his usual exceptional lettering. He's one of the unsung heroes of our biz. Top pro Al Williamson lovingly rendered John's matchless pencils, giving the book a look that's the envy of any artist who's come in to see the completed pages (And there've been plenty!). Naturally, Christie Scheele put the icing on the cake, injecting the art with an added dimension of excellence, utilizing an array of color combination as impressive as they are innovative. Thanks to one and all – especially big boss (at the time) Tom DeFalco, for giving us the go-ahead on this monumental venture.

And a special tip of the horned cowl to Matthew Murdock himself, a childhood hero of mine, whose exploits as the supreme swashbuckler in comics afforded me endless hours of entertainment. This is your story, mister, and we're proud as can be to present it. You bet!

Of course, none of this would even exist were it not for the initial creativity of those twin titans, Stan Lee and the late Bill Everett, who first breathed life into the eternally compelling saga of the Man

Without Fear. And thirty years later, their work on *Daredevil* (expanding and embellished though it's been) retains the power and luster only a true classic can possess. More than ever, the world needs heroes; men and women whose courage and compassion let us see through the fog of everyday life to a higher purpose. Let me tell you, they don't come any more courageous, noble – or mortal-than our Matthew Murdock. And it's time you found out why!

Ralph Macchio
1994

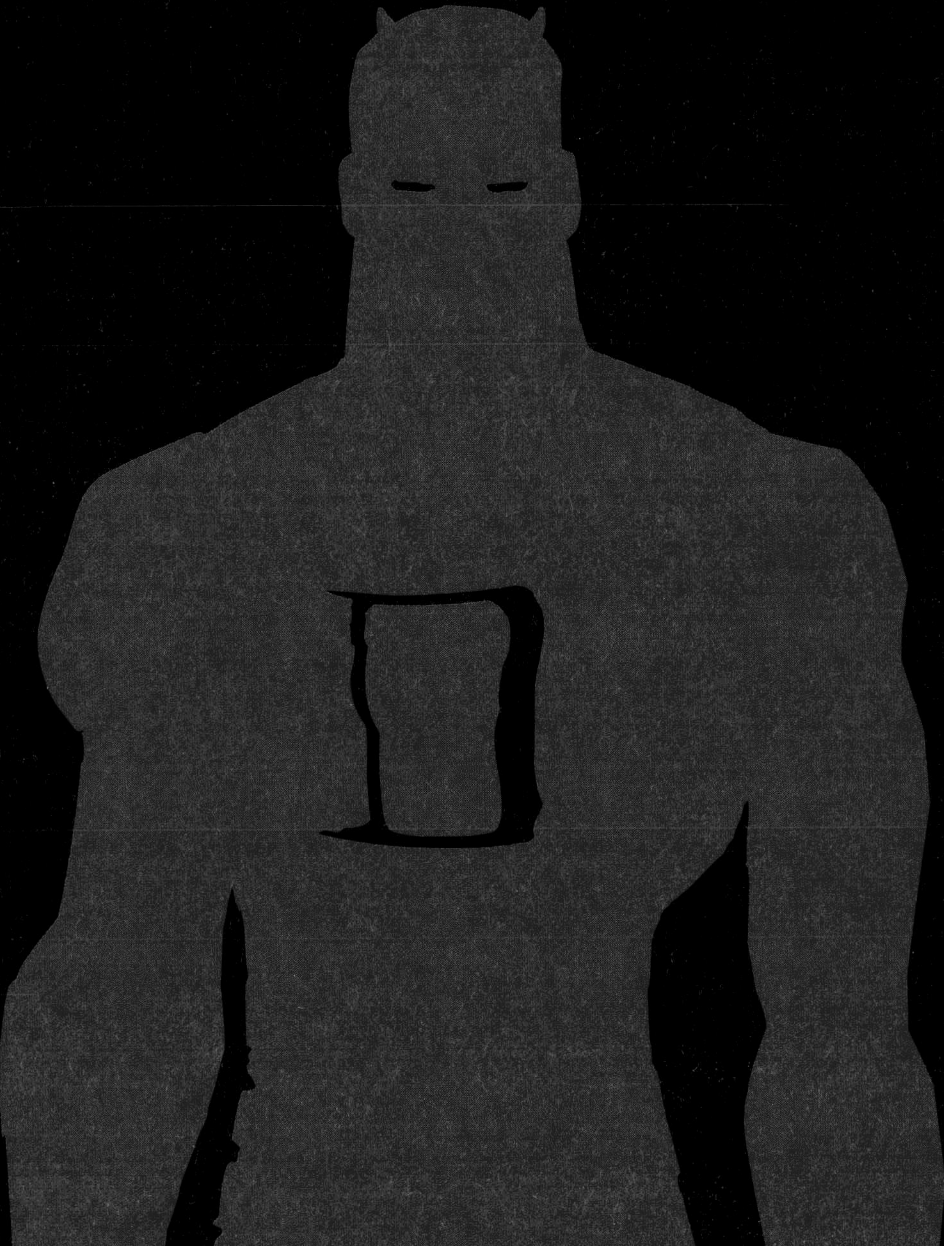

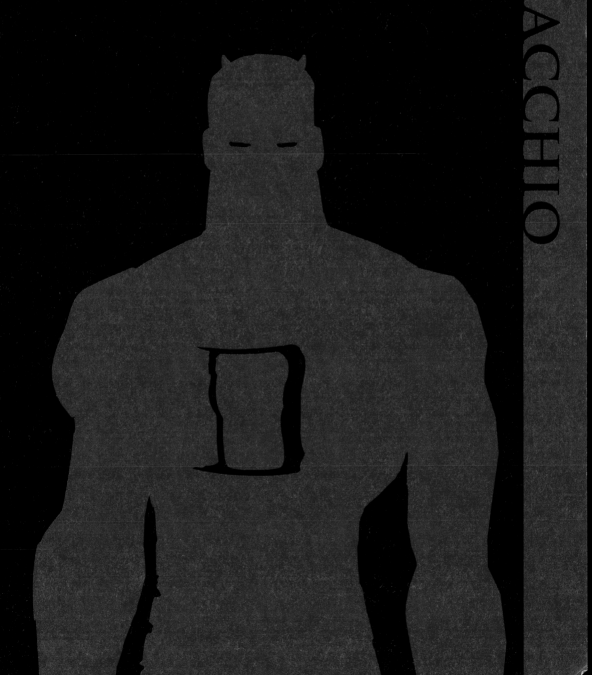

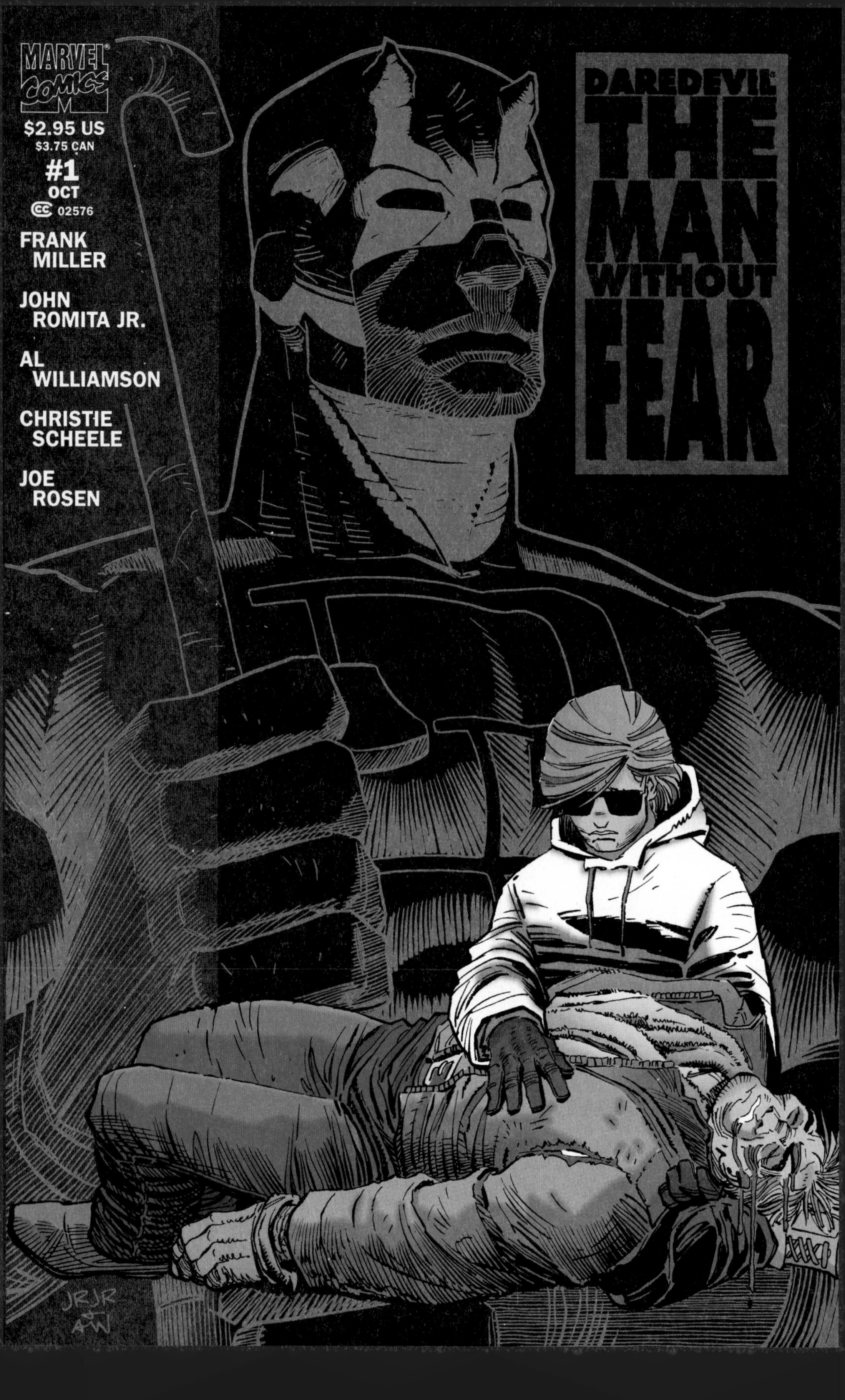
MARVEL COMICS
$2.95 US
$3.75 CAN
#1
OCT
02576
FRANK MILLER
JOHN ROMITA JR.
AL WILLIAMSON
CHRISTIE SCHEELE
JOE ROSEN
DAREDEVIL
THE MAN WITHOUT FEAR

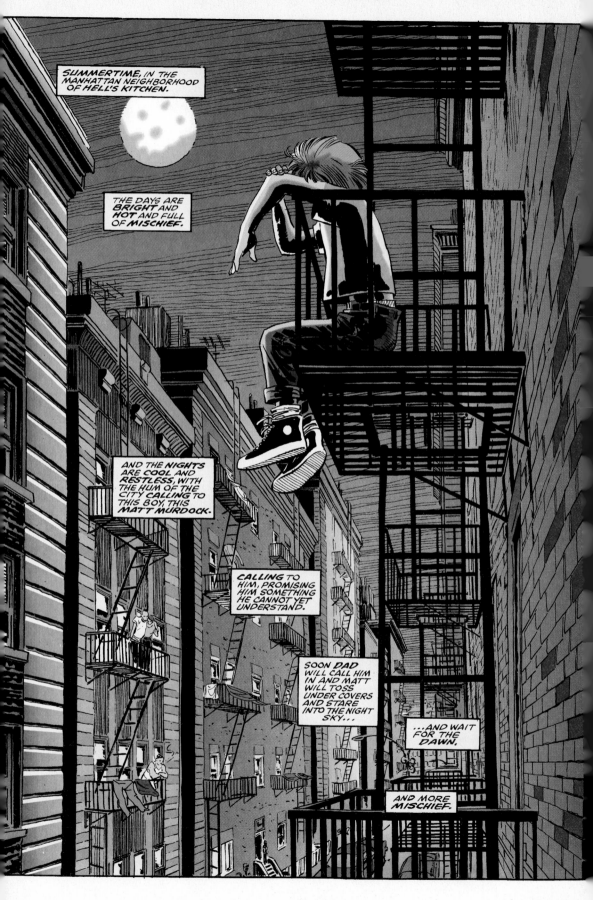

SUMMERTIME, IN THE MANHATTAN NEIGHBORHOOD OF HELL'S KITCHEN.

THE DAYS ARE *BRIGHT* AND *HOT* AND FULL OF *MISCHIEF.*

AND THE *NIGHTS* ARE *COOL* AND *RESTLESS,* WITH THE HUM OF THE CITY *CALLING* TO THIS BOY, THIS *MATT MURDOCK.*

CALLING TO HIM, PROMISING HIM SOMETHING HE CANNOT YET UNDERSTAND.

SOON *DAD* WILL CALL HIM IN AND MATT WILL TOSS UNDER COVERS AND STARE INTO THE NIGHT SKY...

...AND WAIT FOR THE *DAWN.*

AND MORE *MISCHIEF.*

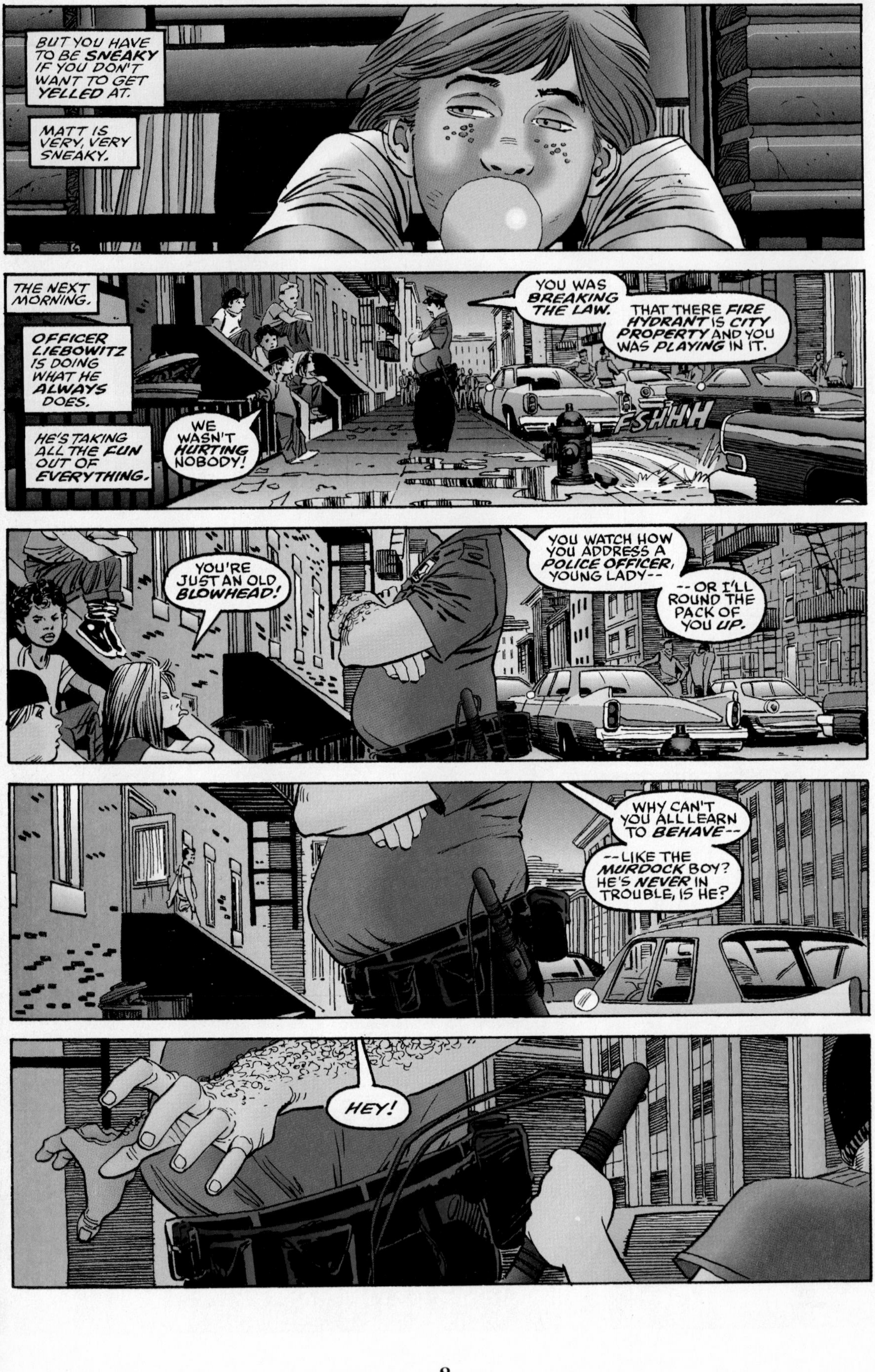
BUT YOU HAVE TO BE SNEAKY IF YOU DON'T WANT TO GET YELLED AT.
MATT IS VERY, VERY SNEAKY.
THE NEXT MORNING.
OFFICER LIEBOWITZ IS DOING WHAT HE ALWAYS DOES.
HE'S TAKING ALL THE FUN OUT OF EVERYTHING.
YOU WAS BREAKING THE LAW.
THAT THERE FIRE HYDRANT IS CITY PROPERTY AND YOU WAS PLAYING IN IT.
FSHHH
WE WASN'T HURTING NOBODY!
YOU'RE JUST AN OLD BLOWHEAD!
YOU WATCH HOW YOU ADDRESS A POLICE OFFICER, YOUNG LADY--
--OR I'LL ROUND THE PACK OF YOU UP.
WHY CAN'T YOU ALL LEARN TO BEHAVE--
--LIKE THE MURDOCK BOY? HE'S NEVER IN TROUBLE, IS HE?
HEY!

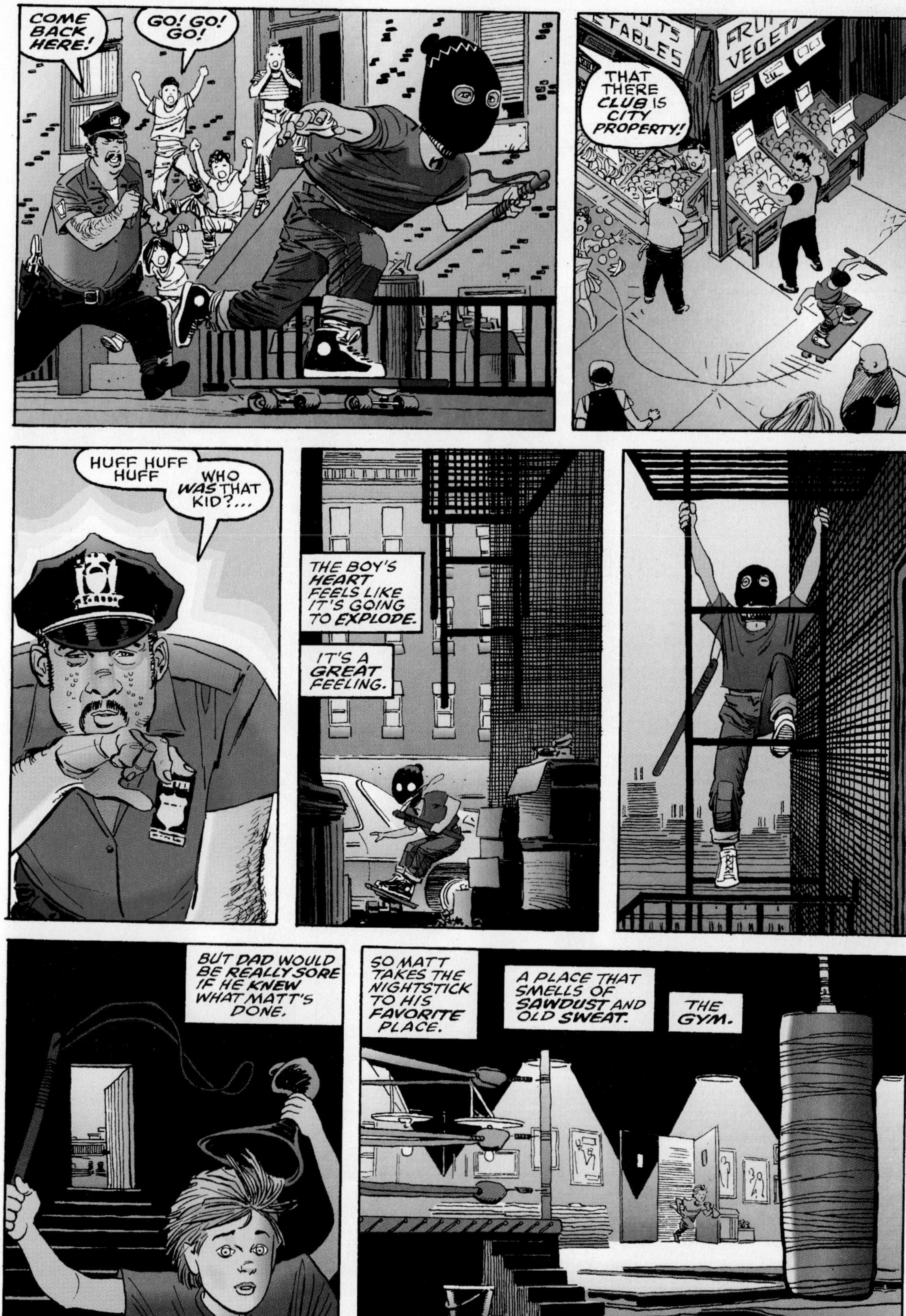
COME BACK HERE!
GO! GO! GO!
FRUITS VEGETABLES
THAT THERE CLUB IS CITY PROPERTY!
HUFF HUFF HUFF
WHO WAS THAT KID?....
THE BOY'S HEART FEELS LIKE IT'S GOING TO EXPLODE.
IT'S A GREAT FEELING.
BUT DAD WOULD BE REALLY SORE IF HE KNEW WHAT MATT'S DONE.
SO MATT TAKES THE NIGHTSTICK TO HIS FAVORITE PLACE.
A PLACE THAT SMELLS OF SAWDUST AND OLD SWEAT.
THE GYM.

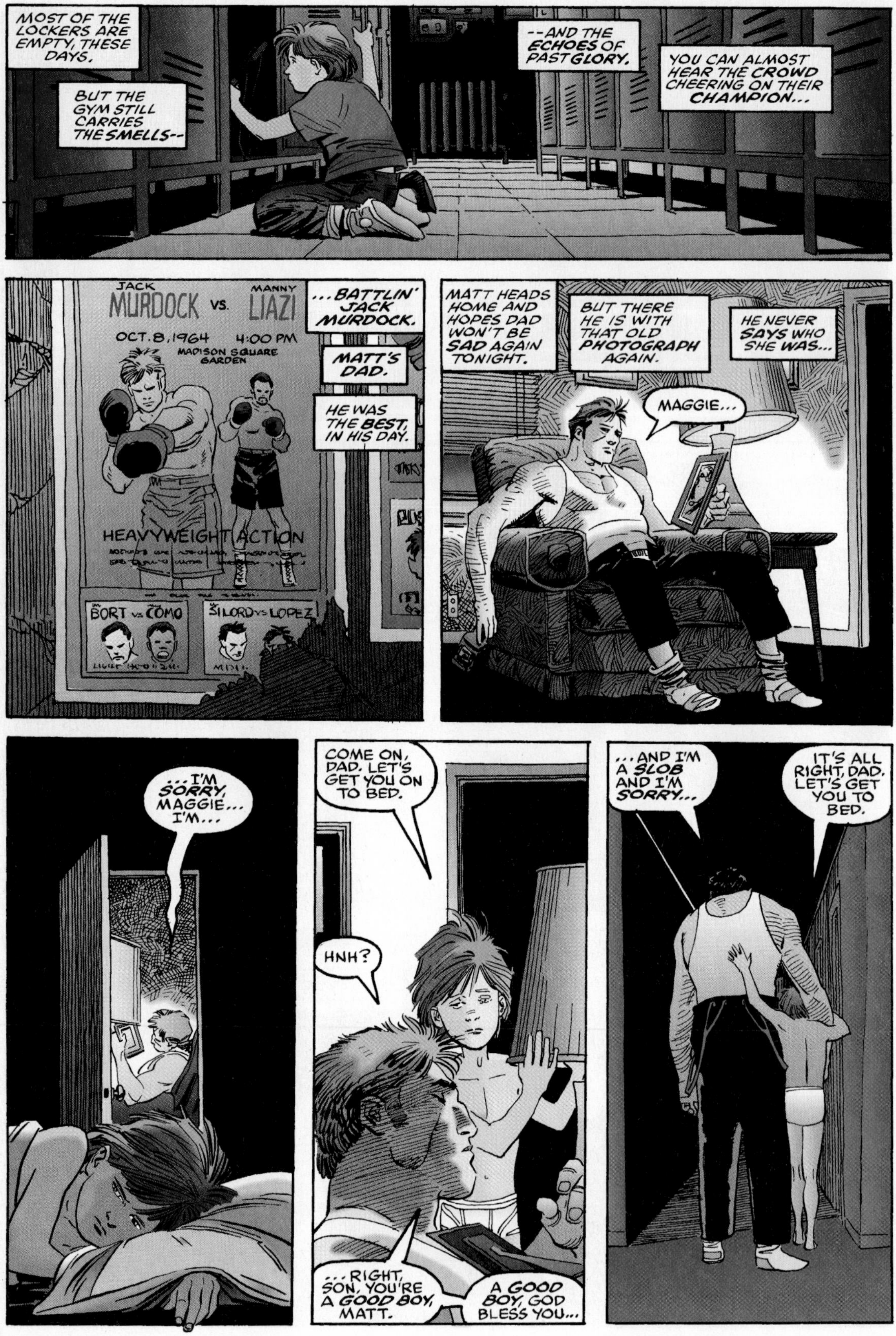

MOST OF THE LOCKERS ARE EMPTY, THESE DAYS.
BUT THE GYM STILL CARRIES THE SMELLS--
--AND THE ECHOES OF PAST GLORY.
YOU CAN ALMOST HEAR THE CROWD CHEERING ON THEIR CHAMPION...
JACK MURDOCK VS. MANNY LIAZI
OCT. 8, 1964 4:00 PM
MADISON SQUARE GARDEN
HEAVYWEIGHT ACTION
BORT vs COMO
SILORD vs LOPEZ
...BATTLIN' JACK MURDOCK.
MATT'S DAD.
HE WAS THE BEST, IN HIS DAY.
MATT HEADS HOME AND HOPES DAD WON'T BE SAD AGAIN TONIGHT.
BUT THERE HE IS WITH THAT OLD PHOTOGRAPH AGAIN.
HE NEVER SAYS WHO SHE WAS...
MAGGIE...
...I'M SORRY, MAGGIE... I'M...
COME ON, DAD. LET'S GET YOU ON TO BED.
HNH?
...RIGHT, SON, YOU'RE A GOOD BOY, MATT.
A GOOD BOY, GOD BLESS YOU...
...AND I'M A SLOB AND I'M SORRY...
IT'S ALL RIGHT, DAD. LET'S GET YOU TO BED.

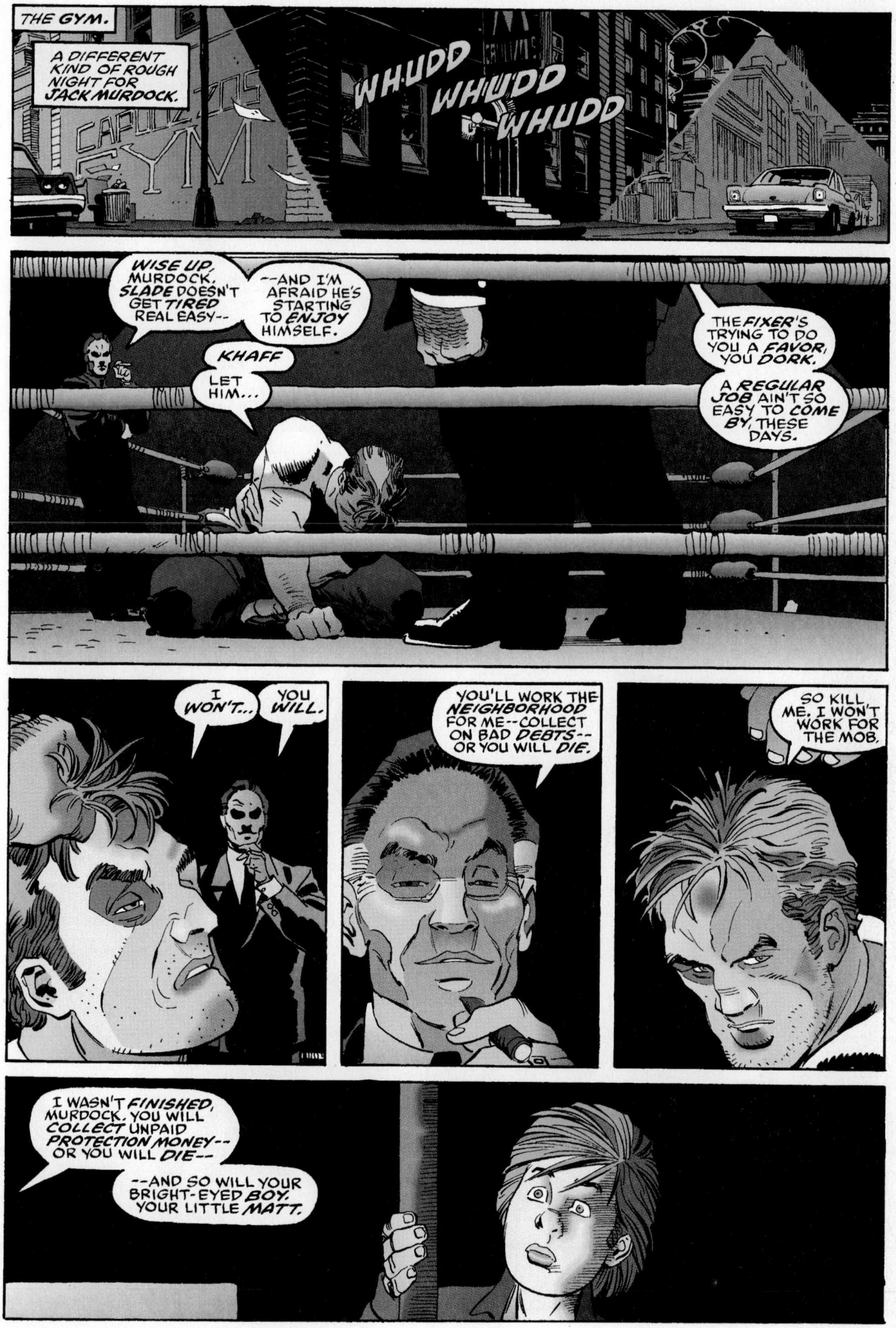
THE GYM.
A DIFFERENT KIND OF ROUGH NIGHT FOR JACK MURDOCK.
CAPOLLI'S GYM
WHUDD WHUDD WHUDD
WISE UP, MURDOCK. SLADE DOESN'T GET TIRED REAL EASY--
--AND I'M AFRAID HE'S STARTING TO ENJOY HIMSELF.
KHAFF
LET HIM...
THE FIXER'S TRYING TO DO YOU A FAVOR, YOU DORK.
A REGULAR JOB AIN'T SO EASY TO COME BY, THESE DAYS.
I WON'T...
YOU WILL.
YOU'LL WORK THE NEIGHBORHOOD FOR ME--COLLECT ON BAD DEBTS--OR YOU WILL DIE.
SO KILL ME. I WON'T WORK FOR THE MOB.
I WASN'T FINISHED, MURDOCK. YOU WILL COLLECT UNPAID PROTECTION MONEY--OR YOU WILL DIE--
--AND SO WILL YOUR BRIGHT-EYED BOY. YOUR LITTLE MATT.

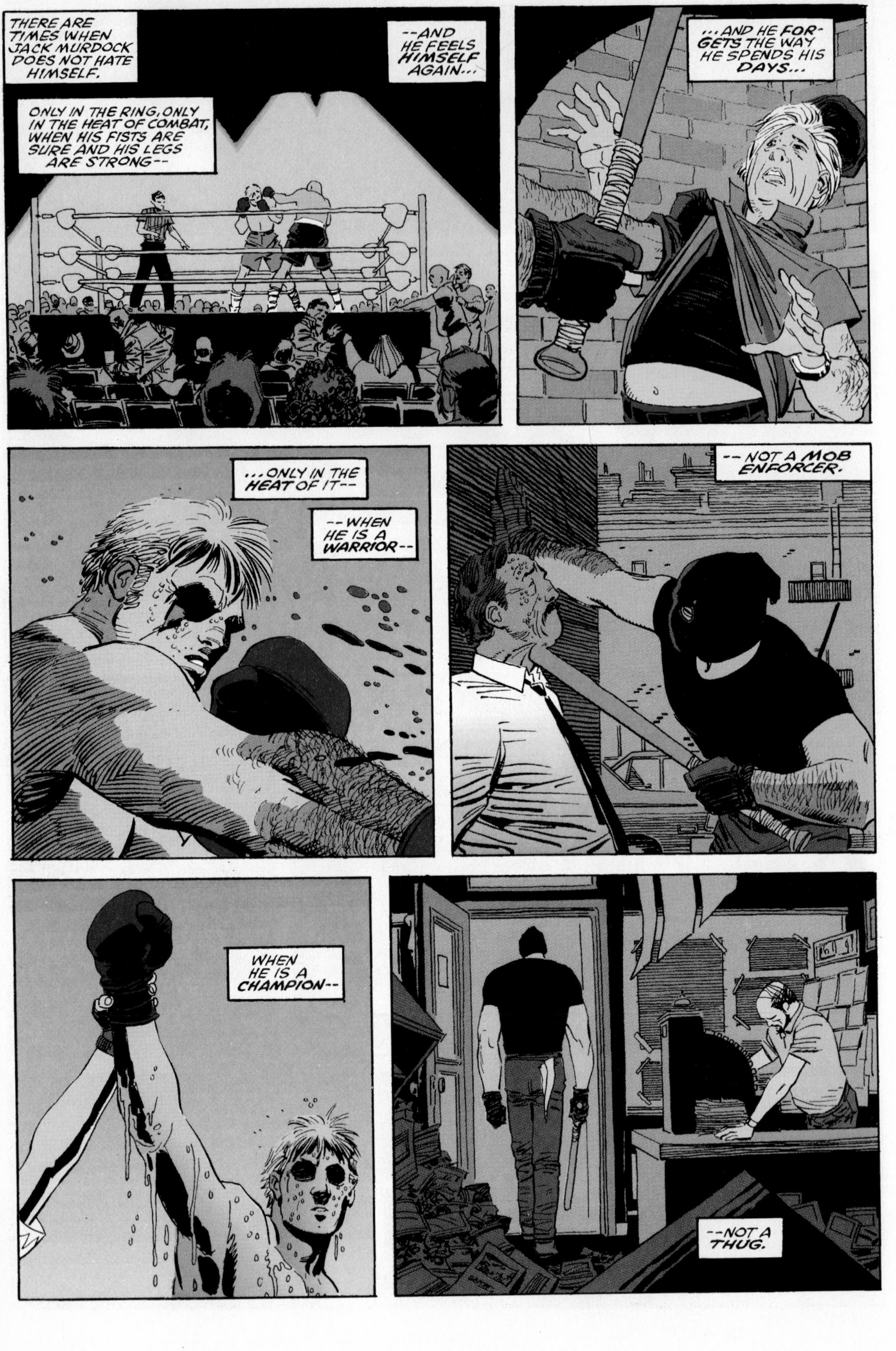
THERE ARE TIMES WHEN JACK MURDOCK DOES NOT HATE HIMSELF.
ONLY IN THE RING, ONLY IN THE HEAT OF COMBAT, WHEN HIS FISTS ARE SURE AND HIS LEGS ARE STRONG--
--AND HE FEELS HIMSELF AGAIN...
...AND HE FORGETS THE WAY HE SPENDS HIS DAYS...
...ONLY IN THE HEAT OF IT--
--WHEN HE IS A WARRIOR--
--NOT A MOB ENFORCER.
WHEN HE IS A CHAMPION--
--NOT A THUG.

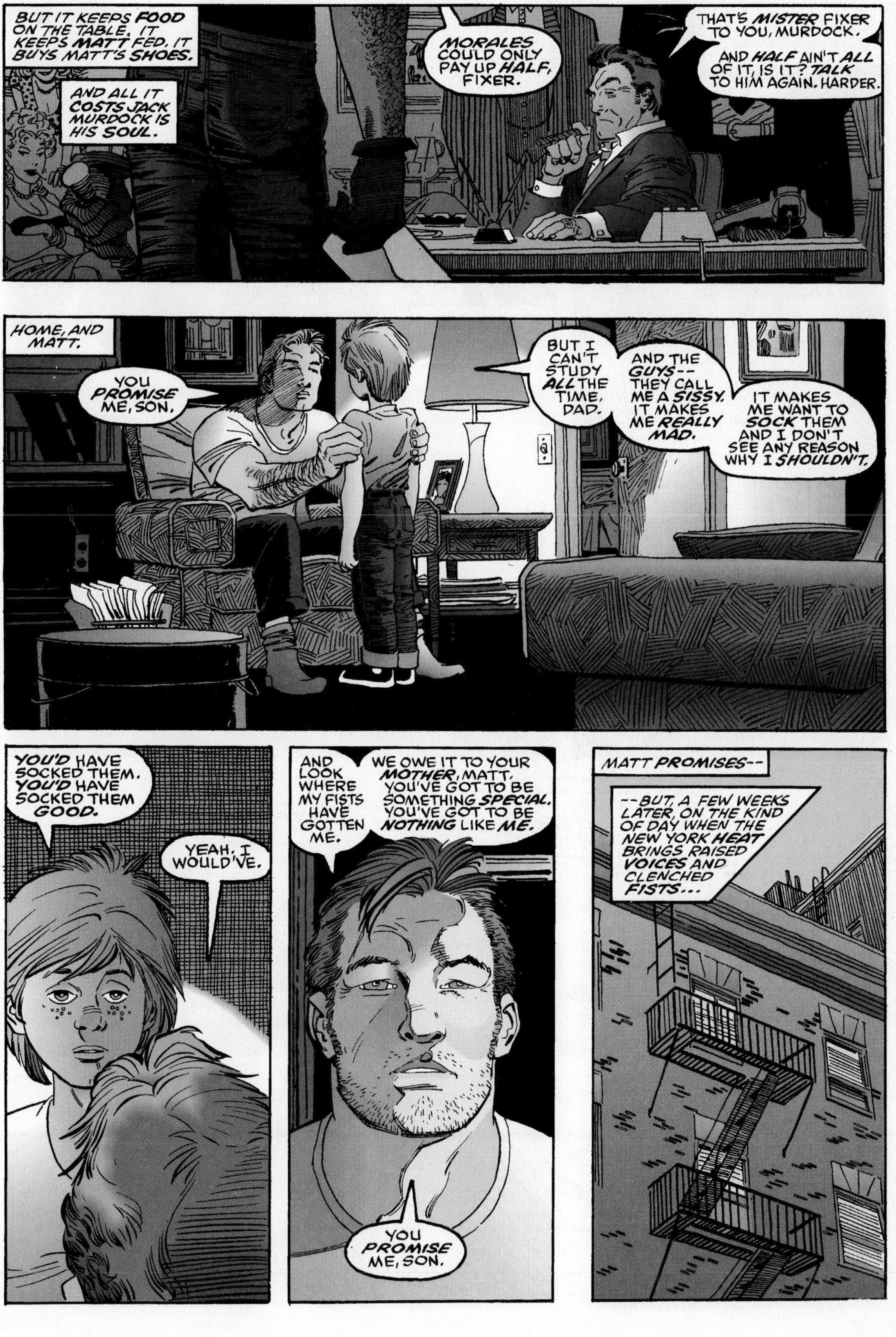
BUT IT KEEPS FOOD ON THE TABLE. IT KEEPS MATT FED. IT BUYS MATT'S SHOES.
AND ALL IT COSTS JACK MURDOCK IS HIS SOUL.
MORALES COULD ONLY PAY UP HALF, FIXER.
THAT'S MISTER FIXER TO YOU, MURDOCK.
AND HALF AIN'T ALL OF IT, IS IT? TALK TO HIM AGAIN. HARDER.
HOME, AND MATT.
YOU PROMISE ME, SON.
BUT I CAN'T STUDY ALL THE TIME, DAD.
AND THE GUYS-- THEY CALL ME A SISSY. IT MAKES ME REALLY MAD.
IT MAKES ME WANT TO SOCK THEM AND I DON'T SEE ANY REASON WHY I SHOULDN'T.
YOU'D HAVE SOCKED THEM. YOU'D HAVE SOCKED THEM GOOD.
YEAH, I WOULD'VE.
AND LOOK WHERE MY FISTS HAVE GOTTEN ME.
WE OWE IT TO YOUR MOTHER, MATT. YOU'VE GOT TO BE SOMETHING SPECIAL. YOU'VE GOT TO BE NOTHING LIKE ME.
YOU PROMISE ME, SON.
MATT PROMISES--
--BUT, A FEW WEEKS LATER, ON THE KIND OF DAY WHEN THE NEW YORK HEAT BRINGS RAISED VOICES AND CLENCHED FISTS...

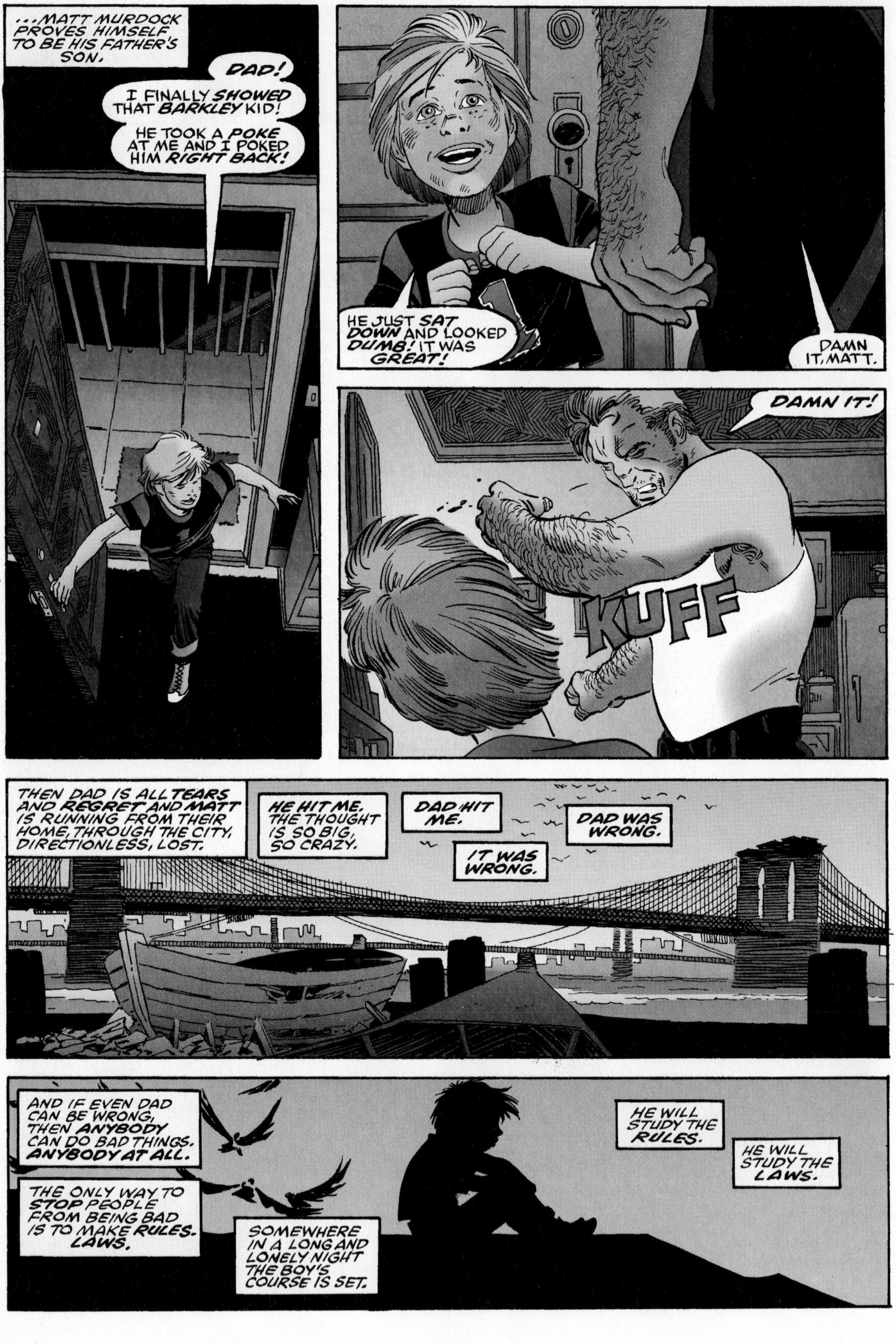

...MATT MURDOCK PROVES HIMSELF TO BE HIS FATHER'S SON.
DAD!
I FINALLY SHOWED THAT BARKLEY KID!
HE TOOK A POKE AT ME AND I POKED HIM RIGHT BACK!
HE JUST SAT DOWN AND LOOKED DUMB! IT WAS GREAT!
DAMN IT, MATT.
DAMN IT!
KUFF
THEN DAD IS ALL TEARS AND REGRET AND MATT IS RUNNING FROM THEIR HOME, THROUGH THE CITY, DIRECTIONLESS, LOST.
HE HIT ME. THE THOUGHT IS SO BIG, SO CRAZY.
DAD HIT ME.
IT WAS WRONG.
DAD WAS WRONG.
AND IF EVEN DAD CAN BE WRONG, THEN ANYBODY CAN DO BAD THINGS. ANYBODY AT ALL.
THE ONLY WAY TO STOP PEOPLE FROM BEING BAD IS TO MAKE RULES. LAWS.
SOMEWHERE IN A LONG AND LONELY NIGHT THE BOY'S COURSE IS SET.
HE WILL STUDY THE RULES.
HE WILL STUDY THE LAWS.

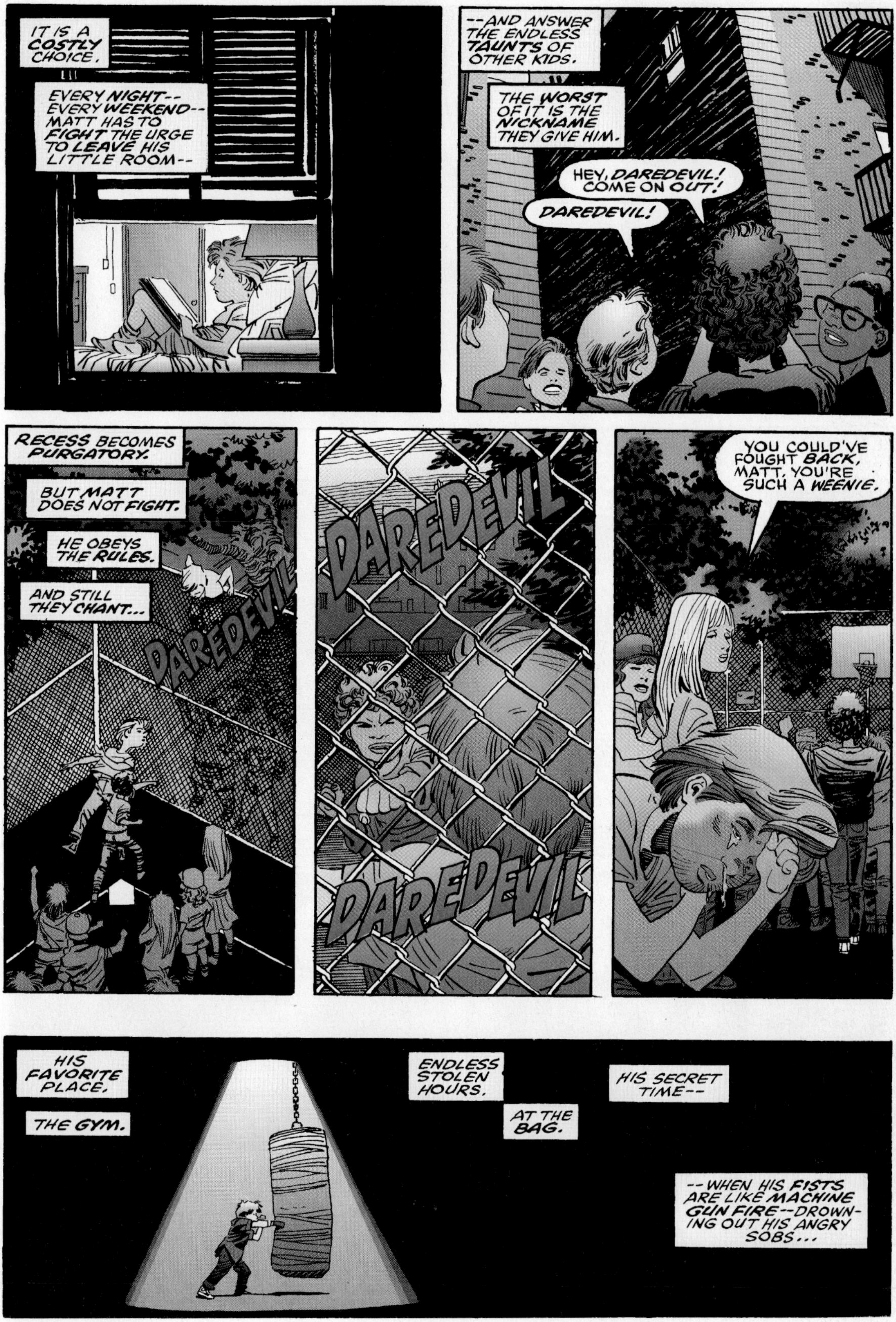
IT IS A COSTLY CHOICE.
EVERY NIGHT-- EVERY WEEKEND-- MATT HAS TO FIGHT THE URGE TO LEAVE HIS LITTLE ROOM--
--AND ANSWER THE ENDLESS TAUNTS OF OTHER KIDS.
THE WORST OF IT IS THE NICKNAME THEY GIVE HIM.
HEY, DAREDEVIL! COME ON OUT!
DAREDEVIL!
RECESS BECOMES PURGATORY.
BUT MATT DOES NOT FIGHT.
HE OBEYS THE RULES.
AND STILL THEY CHANT...
DAREDEVIL
DAREDEVIL
DAREDEVIL
DAREDEVIL
YOU COULD'VE FOUGHT BACK, MATT. YOU'RE SUCH A WEENIE.
HIS FAVORITE PLACE.
THE GYM.
ENDLESS STOLEN HOURS.
AT THE BAG.
HIS SECRET TIME--
--WHEN HIS FISTS ARE LIKE MACHINE GUN FIRE--DROWNING OUT HIS ANGRY SOBS...

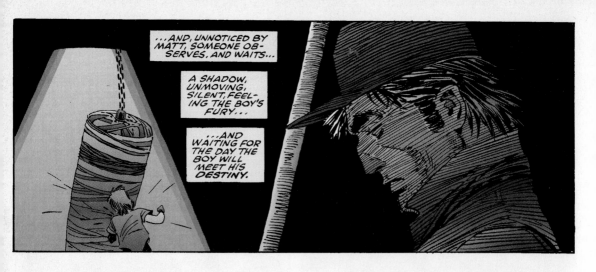

...AND, UNNOTICED BY MATT, SOMEONE OBSERVES, AND WAITS...

A SHADOW, UNMOVING, SILENT, FEELING THE BOY'S FURY...

...AND WAITING FOR THE DAY THE BOY WILL MEET HIS DESTINY.

IT'S A PICTURE PERFECT DAY, ONE MATT WILL NEVER FORGET.

THE LAST HE WILL EVER SEE.

A HELPLESS OLD BLIND MAN-- A CAREENING TRUCK--

--A DECISION MADE FASTER THAN THOUGHT--

--GALLONS OF HORRID, SPEWING MUCK--

--PAIN--

--AND DARKNESS--

--BRAVEST THING I EVER SAW! BUT HIS FACE-- HIS EYES...

MY GOD-- THAT STUFF IN HIS EYES--

--IS IT RADIOACTIVE?

YES...

...YES, IT COURSES THROUGH HIS BLOOD. IT CHANGES HIM.

HIS BLOOD. IT BURNS...

...IT GUSHES THROUGH HIGH POWER HOSES AND SLAMS AGAINST THE BASE OF HIS *SKULL.*

EVERYTHING HURTS.

HE DOESN'T KNOW WHERE HE *IS.*

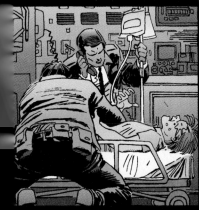

SANDPAPER SCRAPES HIS SKIN EVERY TIME HE MOVES--NO--NOT SANDPAPER--SHEETS-- STARCHED SHEETS--

--AND THE SMELLS... CHEMICAL SMELLS. DISINFECTANTS.

HOSPITAL, HE THINKS. I'M IN A HOSPITAL.

PEOPLE COME AND GO, SMELLING LIKE BATHTUBS FULL OF SWEAT--LIKE EATEN FOOD--LIKE ITALIAN SAUCES AND HALF- DIGESTED *EGGS--*

--THEY STAB HIM WITH NEEDLES AND FILL HIM FULL OF DRUGS BUT DRUGS DON'T FOOL HIM. HE KNOWS THEY CUT HIS FACE.

EVERYTHING HURTS.

ALL HE WANTS IS TO DIE.

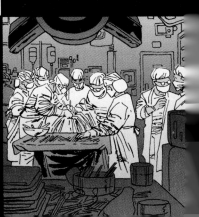

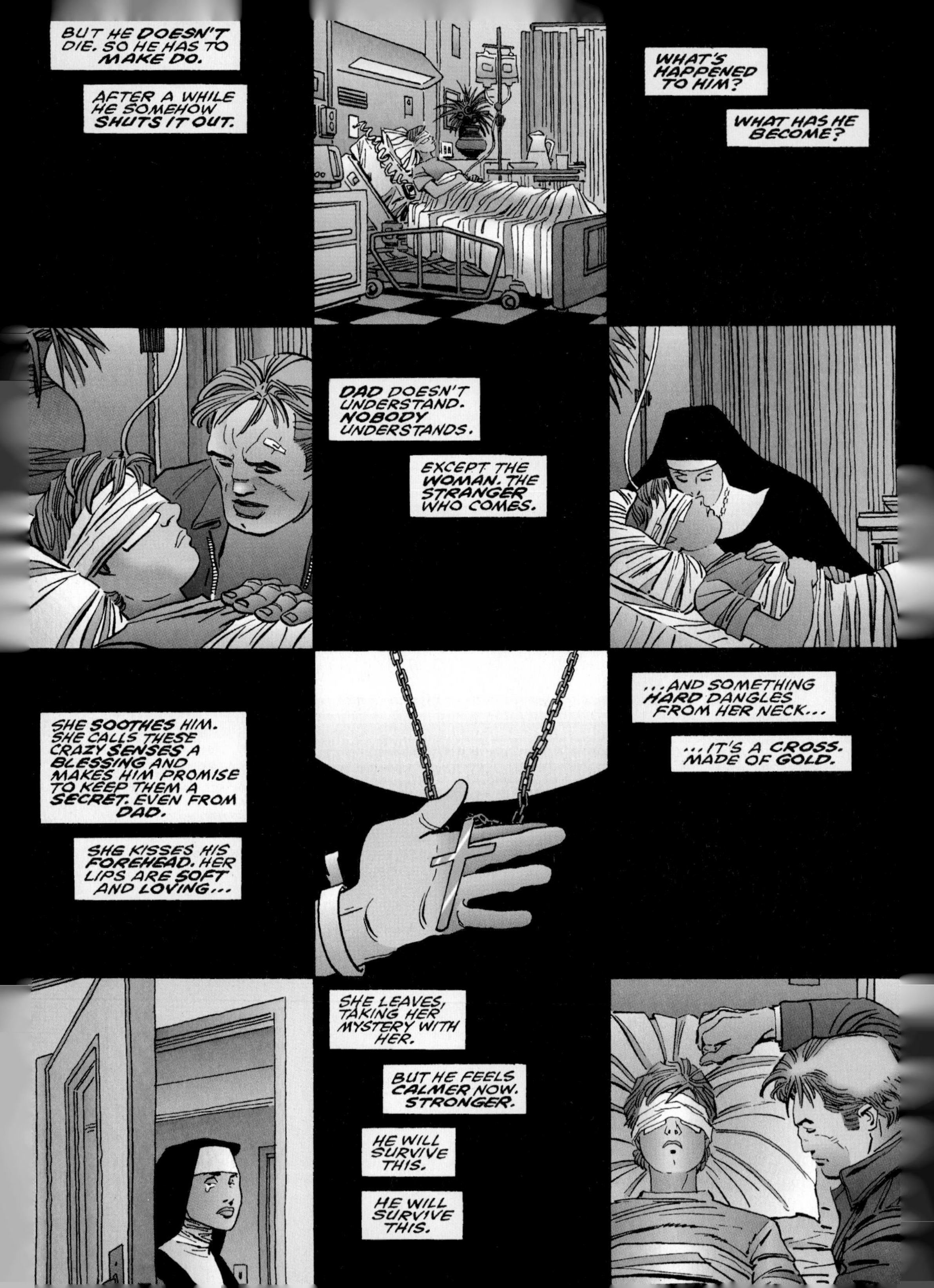

BUT HE DOESN'T DIE. SO HE HAS TO MAKE DO.
AFTER A WHILE HE SOMEHOW SHUTS IT OUT.
WHAT'S HAPPENED TO HIM?
WHAT HAS HE BECOME?
DAD DOESN'T UNDERSTAND. NOBODY UNDERSTANDS.
EXCEPT THE WOMAN. THE STRANGER WHO COMES.
SHE SOOTHES HIM. SHE CALLS THESE CRAZY SENSES A BLESSING AND MAKES HIM PROMISE TO KEEP THEM A SECRET. EVEN FROM DAD.
SHE KISSES HIS FOREHEAD. HER LIPS ARE SOFT AND LOVING...
...AND SOMETHING HARD DANGLES FROM HER NECK...
...IT'S A CROSS. MADE OF GOLD.
SHE LEAVES, TAKING HER MYSTERY WITH HER.
BUT HE FEELS CALMER NOW. STRONGER.
HE WILL SURVIVE THIS.
HE WILL SURVIVE THIS.

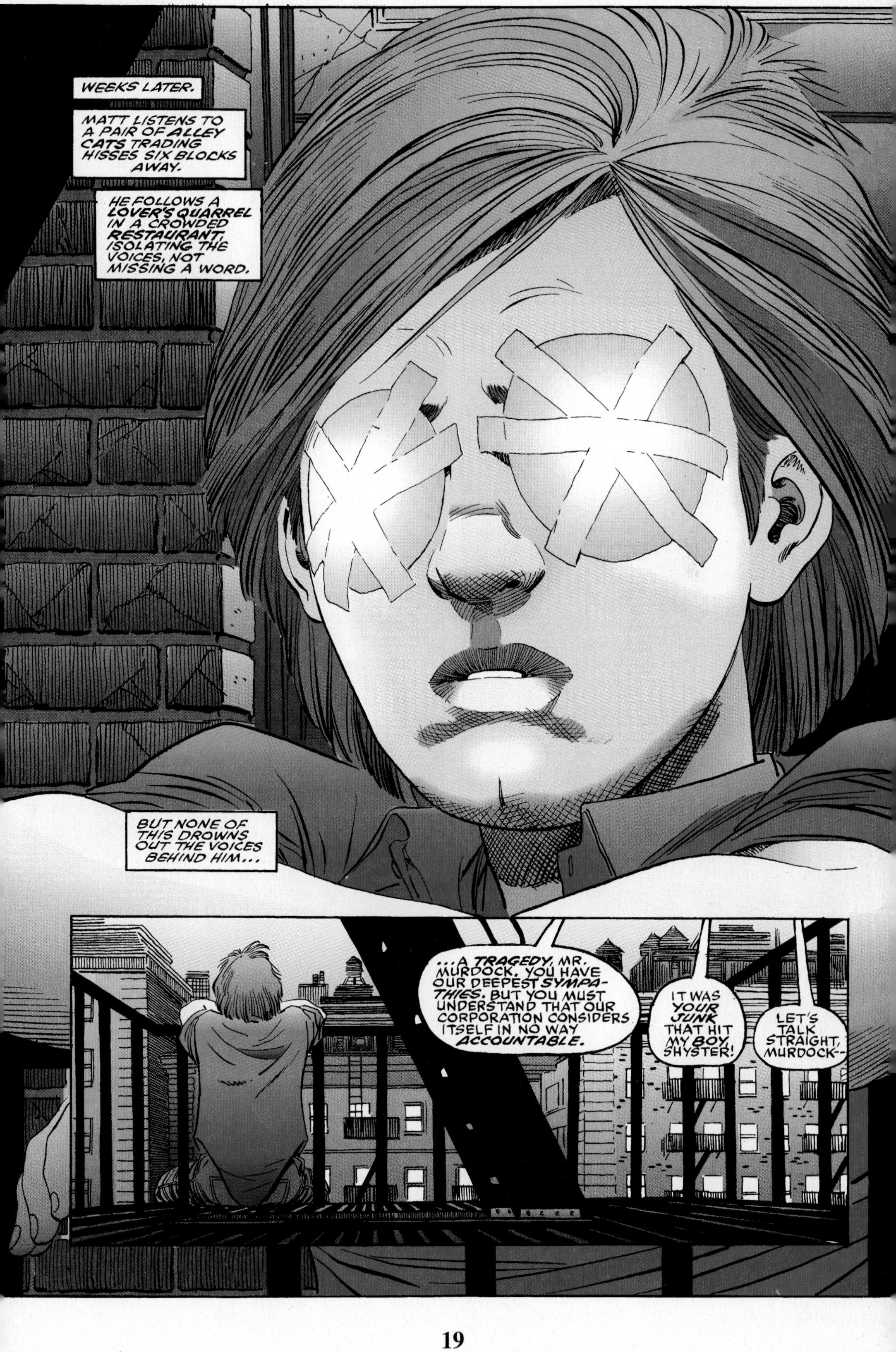
WEEKS LATER.
MATT LISTENS TO A PAIR OF ALLEY CATS TRADING HISSES SIX BLOCKS AWAY.
HE FOLLOWS A LOVER'S QUARREL IN A CROWDED RESTAURANT, ISOLATING THE VOICES, NOT MISSING A WORD.
BUT NONE OF THIS DROWNS OUT THE VOICES BEHIND HIM...
...A TRAGEDY, MR. MURDOCK. YOU HAVE OUR DEEPEST SYMPATHIES. BUT YOU MUST UNDERSTAND THAT OUR CORPORATION CONSIDERS ITSELF IN NO WAY ACCOUNTABLE.
IT WAS YOUR JUNK THAT HIT MY BOY, SHYSTER!
LET'S TALK STRAIGHT, MURDOCK--

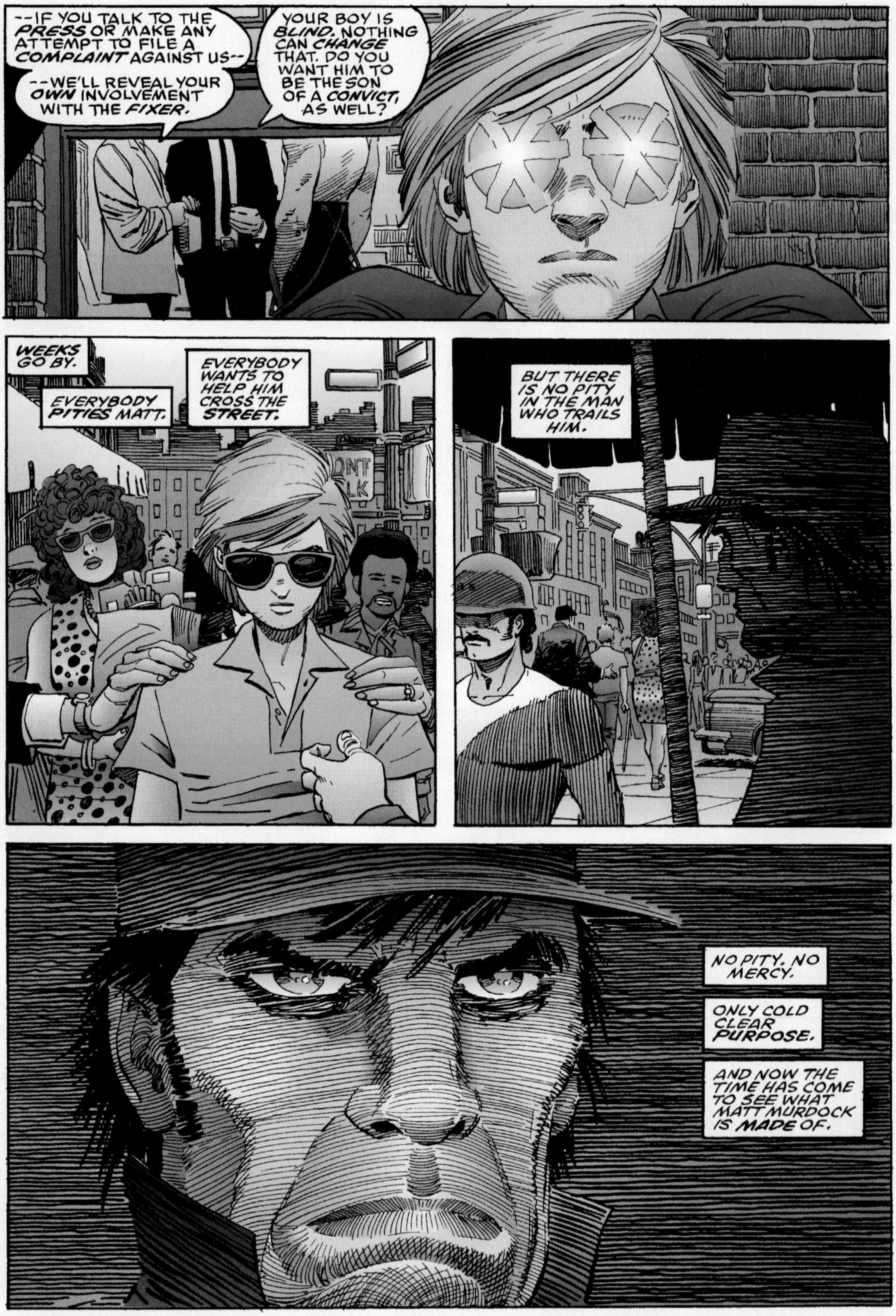
--IF YOU TALK TO THE PRESS OR MAKE ANY ATTEMPT TO FILE A COMPLAINT AGAINST US--
--WE'LL REVEAL YOUR OWN INVOLVEMENT WITH THE FIXER.
YOUR BOY IS BLIND. NOTHING CAN CHANGE THAT. DO YOU WANT HIM TO BE THE SON OF A CONVICT, AS WELL?
WEEKS GO BY.
EVERYBODY PITIES MATT.
EVERYBODY WANTS TO HELP HIM CROSS THE STREET.
BUT THERE IS NO PITY IN THE MAN WHO TRAILS HIM.
NO PITY. NO MERCY.
ONLY COLD CLEAR PURPOSE.
AND NOW THE TIME HAS COME TO SEE WHAT MATT MURDOCK IS MADE OF.

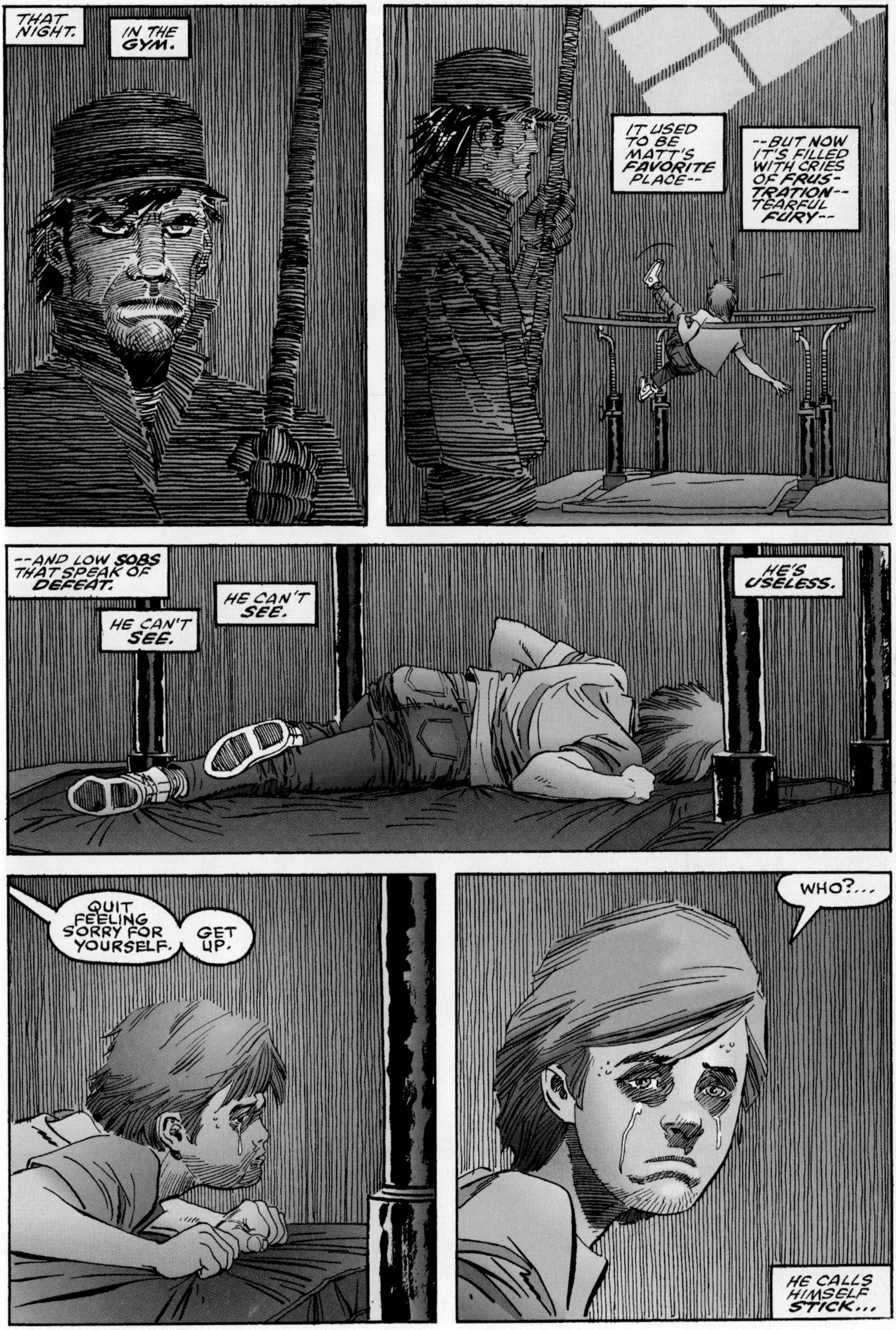
THAT NIGHT.
IN THE GYM.
IT USED TO BE MATT'S FAVORITE PLACE--
--BUT NOW IT'S FILLED WITH CRIES OF FRUSTRATION-- TEARFUL FURY--
--AND LOW SOBS THAT SPEAK OF DEFEAT.
HE CAN'T SEE.
HE CAN'T SEE.
HE'S USELESS.
QUIT FEELING SORRY FOR YOURSELF.
GET UP.
WHO?...
HE CALLS HIMSELF STICK...

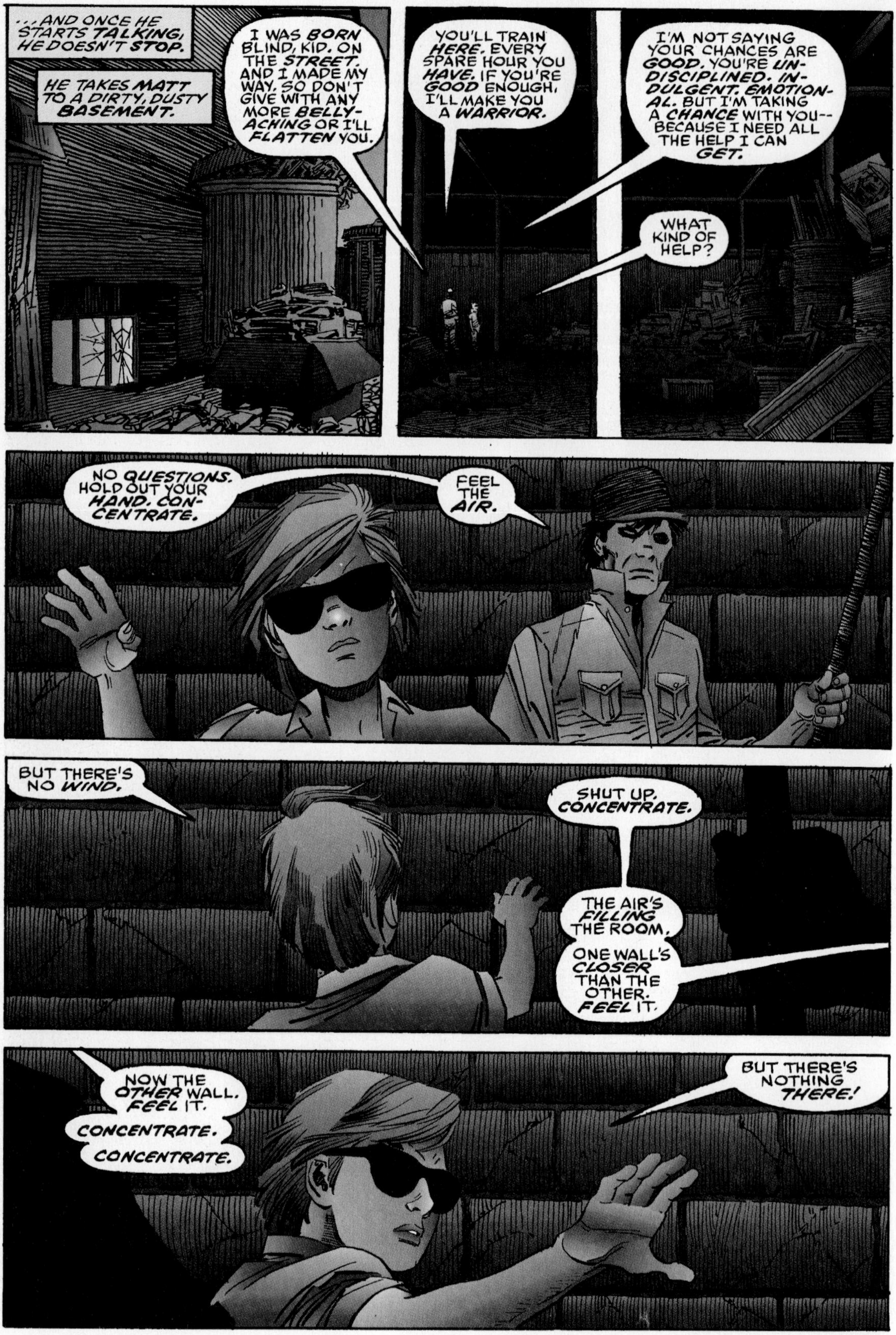
...AND ONCE HE STARTS TALKING, HE DOESN'T STOP.
HE TAKES MATT TO A DIRTY, DUSTY BASEMENT.
I WAS BORN BLIND, KID. ON THE STREET. AND I MADE MY WAY. SO DON'T GIVE WITH ANY MORE BELLY-ACHING OR I'LL FLATTEN YOU.
YOU'LL TRAIN HERE. EVERY SPARE HOUR YOU HAVE. IF YOU'RE GOOD ENOUGH, I'LL MAKE YOU A WARRIOR.
I'M NOT SAYING YOUR CHANCES ARE GOOD. YOU'RE UN-DISCIPLINED. IN-DULGENT. EMOTION-AL. BUT I'M TAKING A CHANCE WITH YOU-- BECAUSE I NEED ALL THE HELP I CAN GET.
WHAT KIND OF HELP?
NO QUESTIONS. HOLD OUT YOUR HAND. CON-CENTRATE.
FEEL THE AIR.
BUT THERE'S NO WIND.
SHUT UP. CONCENTRATE.
THE AIR'S FILLING THE ROOM.
ONE WALL'S CLOSER THAN THE OTHER. FEEL IT.
NOW THE OTHER WALL. FEEL IT.
CONCENTRATE.
CONCENTRATE.
BUT THERE'S NOTHING THERE!

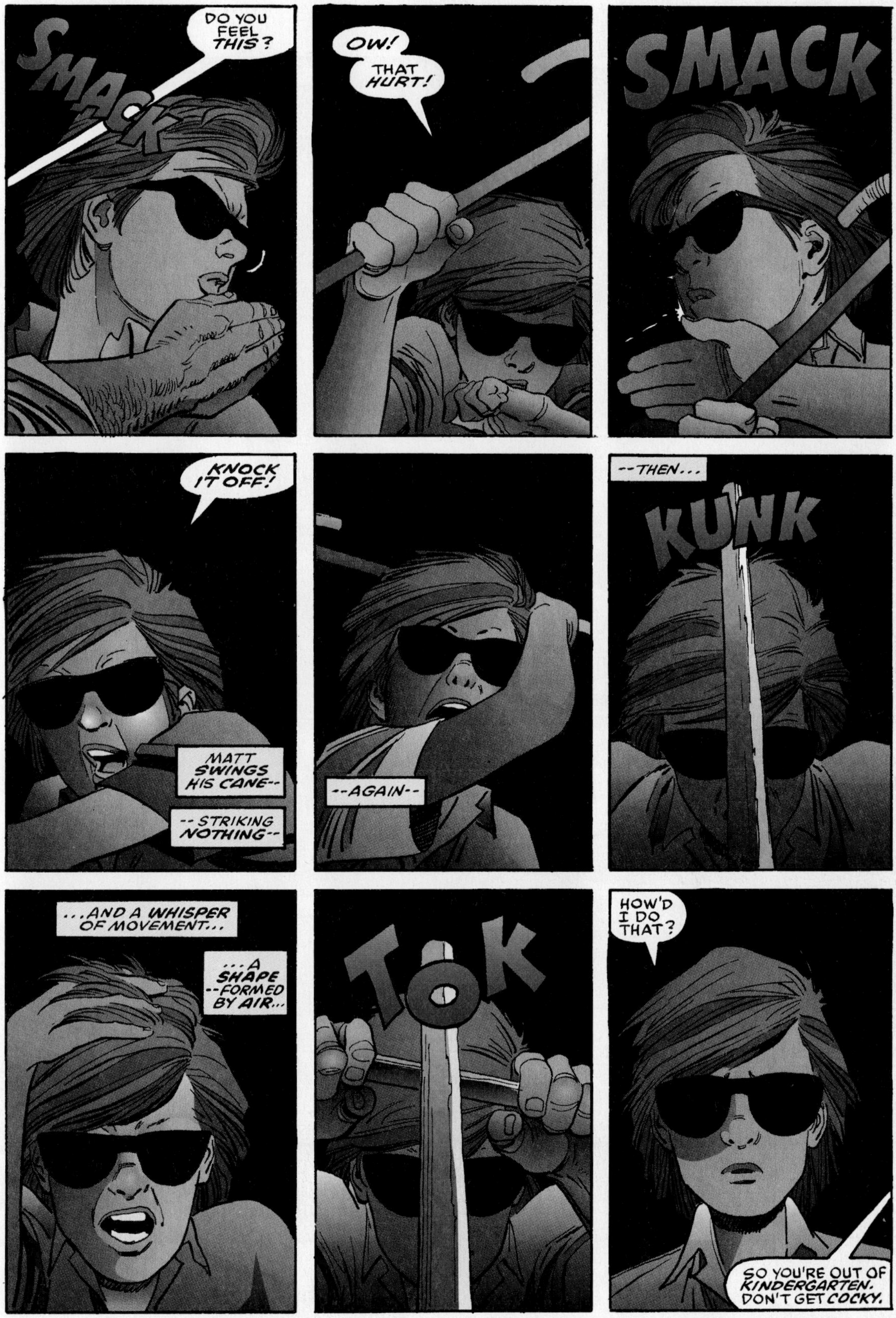
SMACK
DO YOU FEEL THIS?
OW!
THAT HURT!
SMACK
KNOCK IT OFF!
MATT SWINGS HIS CANE--
-- STRIKING NOTHING--
--AGAIN--
--THEN...
KUNK
...AND A WHISPER OF MOVEMENT...
...A SHAPE --FORMED BY AIR...
TOK
HOW'D I DO THAT?
SO YOU'RE OUT OF KINDERGARTEN. DON'T GET COCKY.

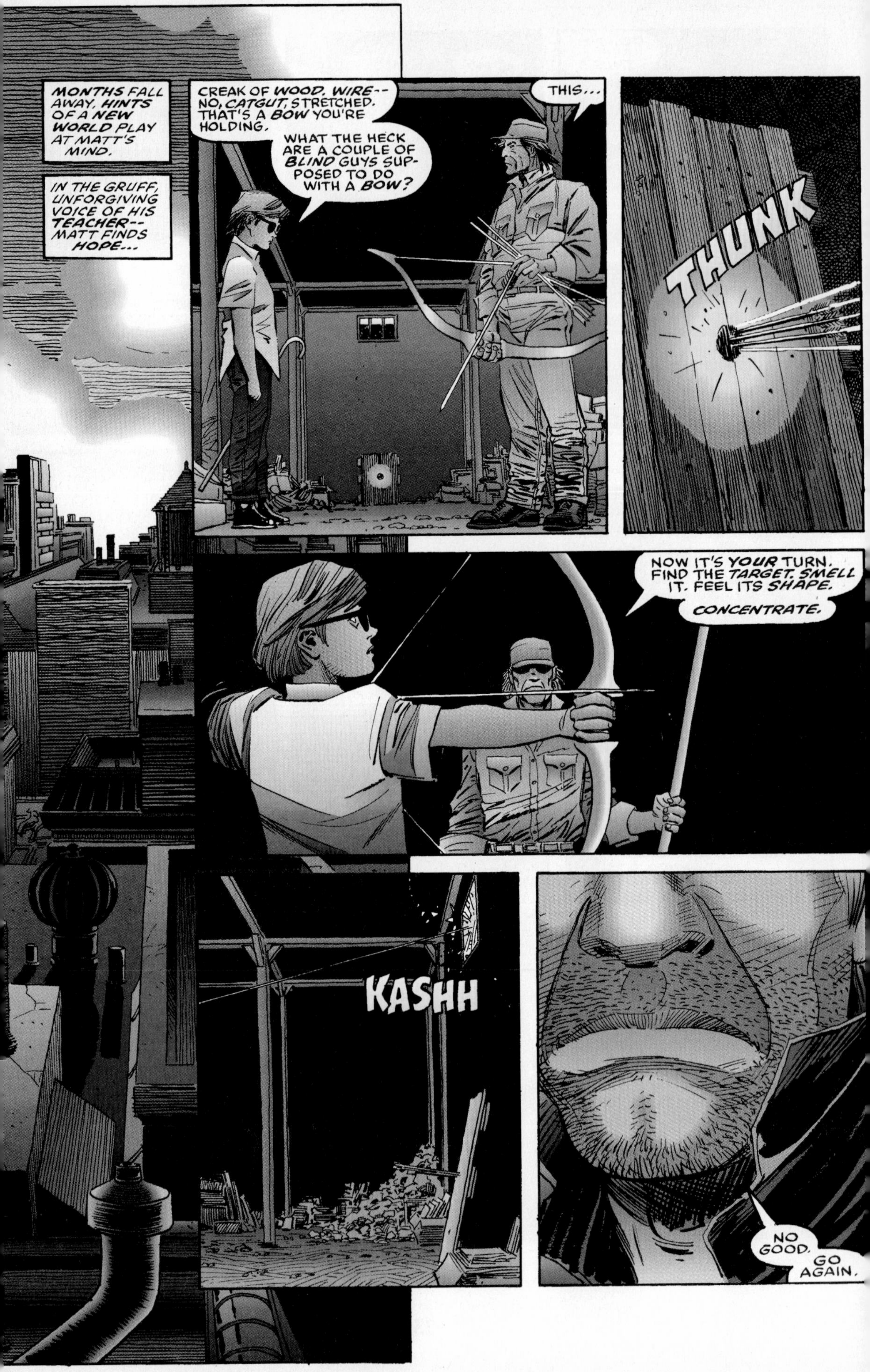
MONTHS FALL AWAY. HINTS OF A NEW WORLD PLAY AT MATT'S MIND.
IN THE GRUFF, UNFORGIVING VOICE OF HIS TEACHER-- MATT FINDS HOPE...
CREAK OF WOOD. WIRE-- NO, CATGUT, STRETCHED. THAT'S A BOW YOU'RE HOLDING.
WHAT THE HECK ARE A COUPLE OF BLIND GUYS SUPPOSED TO DO WITH A BOW?
THIS...
THUNK
NOW IT'S YOUR TURN. FIND THE TARGET. SMELL IT. FEEL ITS SHAPE.
CONCENTRATE.
KASHH
NO GOOD. GO AGAIN.

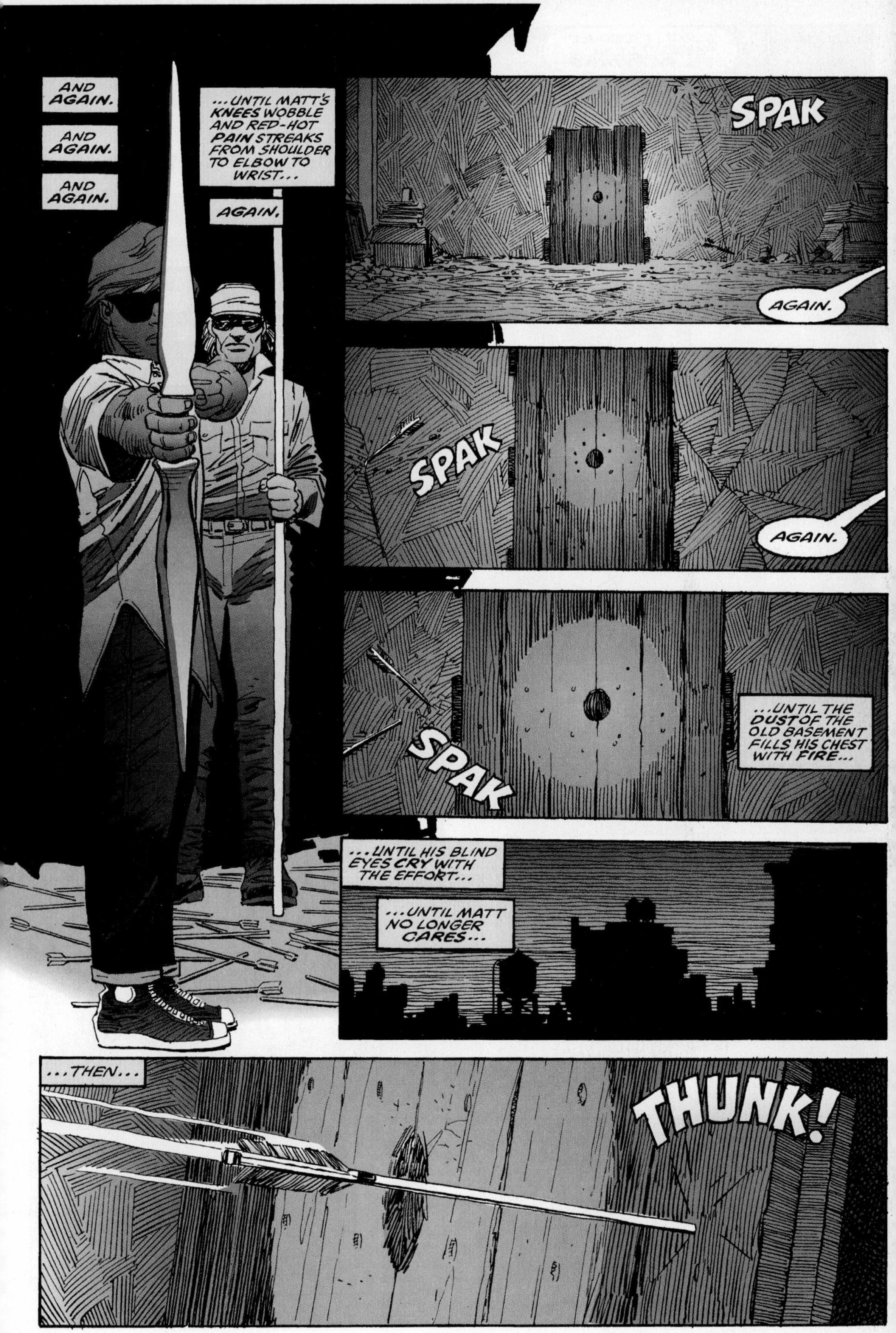
AND AGAIN.
AND AGAIN.
AND AGAIN.
...UNTIL MATT'S KNEES WOBBLE AND RED-HOT PAIN STREAKS FROM SHOULDER TO ELBOW TO WRIST...
AGAIN.
SPAK
AGAIN.
SPAK
AGAIN.
SPAK
...UNTIL THE DUST OF THE OLD BASEMENT FILLS HIS CHEST WITH FIRE...
...UNTIL HIS BLIND EYES CRY WITH THE EFFORT...
...UNTIL MATT NO LONGER CARES...
...THEN...
THUNK!

I DID IT! I COULD FEEL IT! I CAN FEEL EVERYTHING-- OWW!

ANYBODY CAN DO IT ONCE. AGAIN!

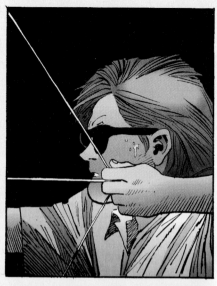

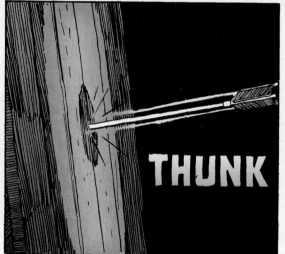

THUNK

SKIKK THUNK

NIGHT AFTER NIGHT, JACK MURDOCK FINDS HIS SON ASLEEP, EXHAUSTED.

A FINE BOY, HE THINKS. STUDYING LIKE A DEMON.

HE'S RIGHT.

BUT MATT'S STUDIES GO FAR BEYOND HISTORY AND GEOGRAPHY AND LAW...

...INTO A REALM OF NEAR-MAGIC.

AND STICK WAITS,

AND HOPES.

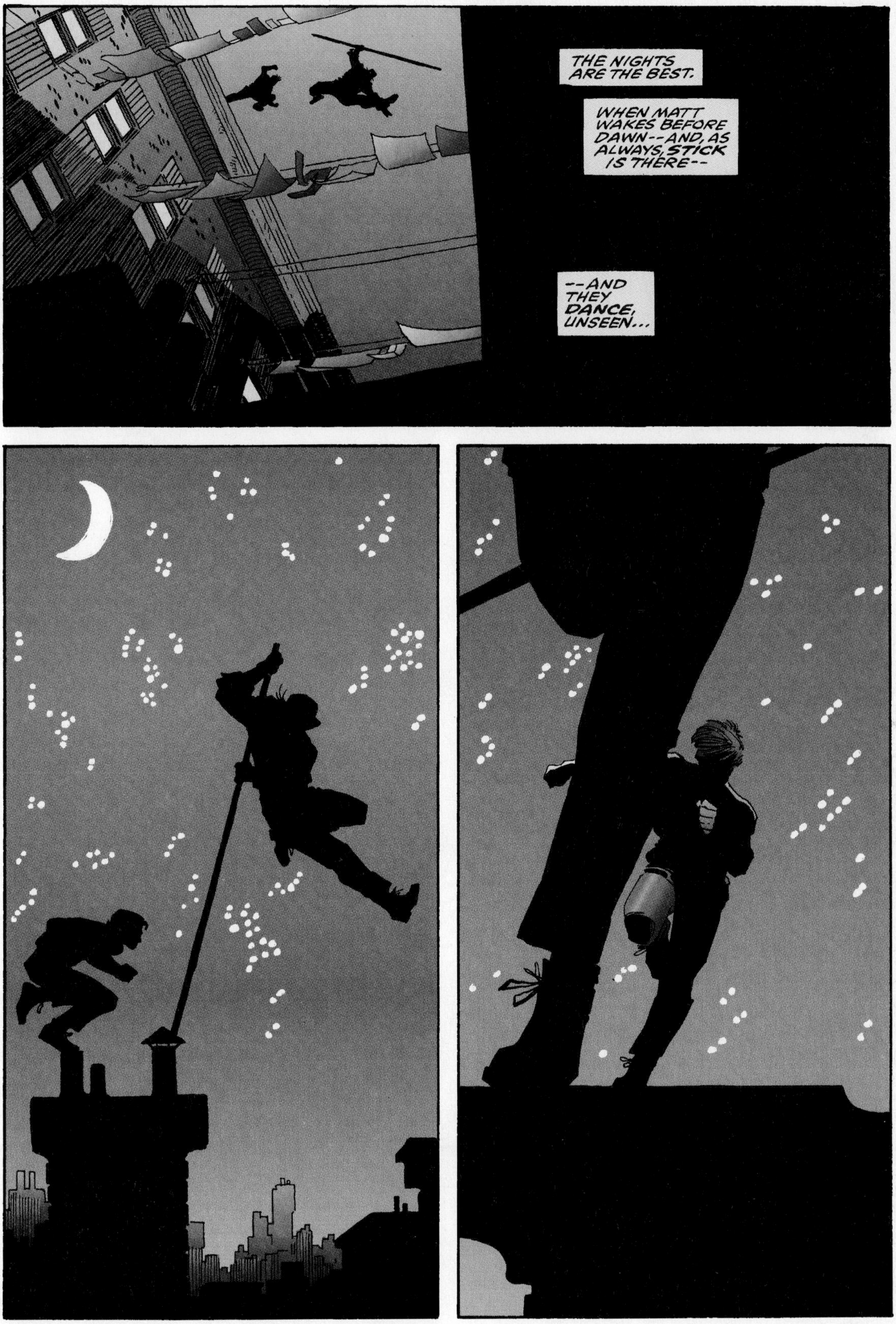
THE NIGHTS ARE THE BEST.
WHEN MATT WAKES BEFORE DAWN--AND, AS ALWAYS, STICK IS THERE--
--AND THEY DANCE, UNSEEN...

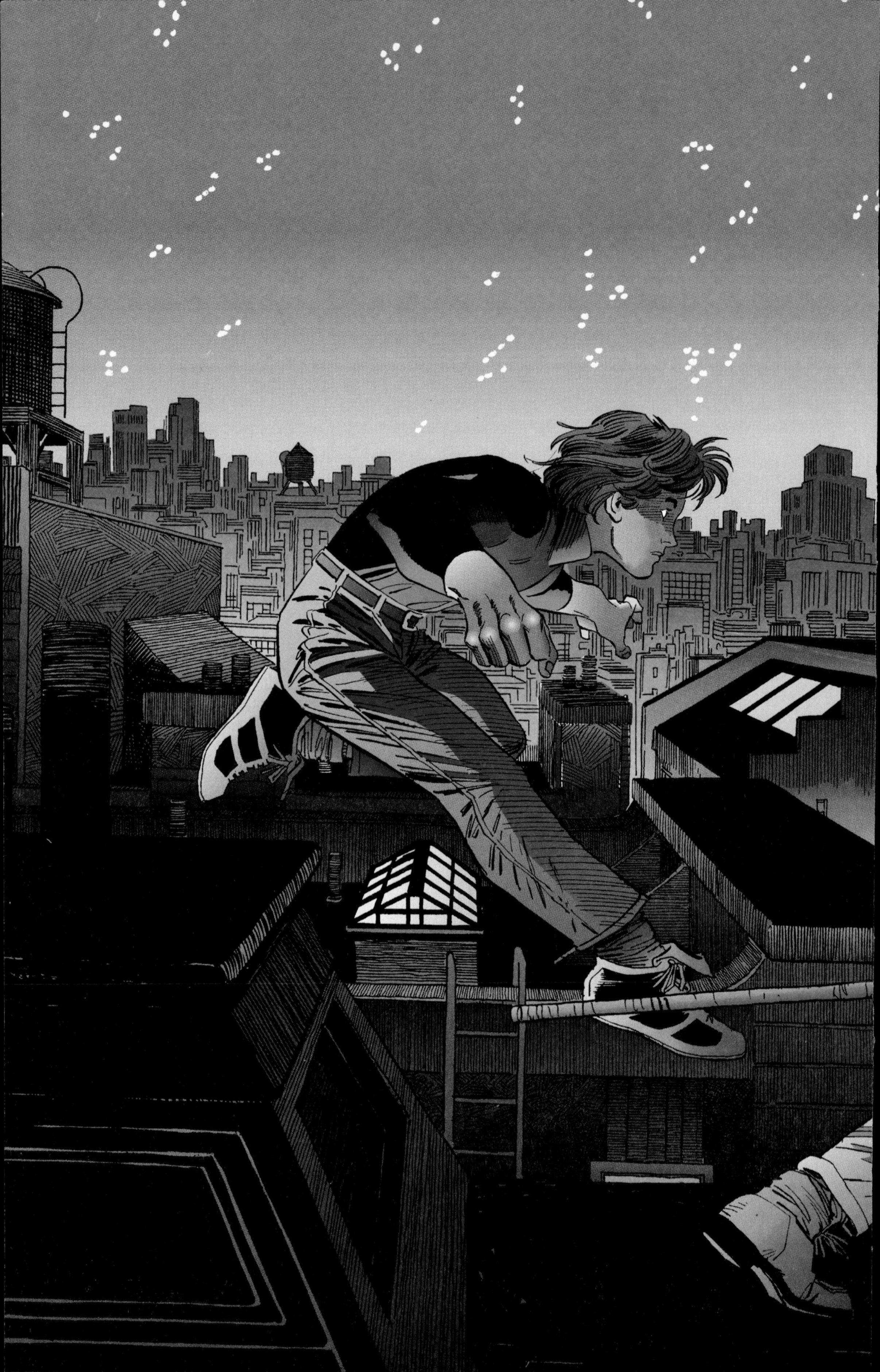

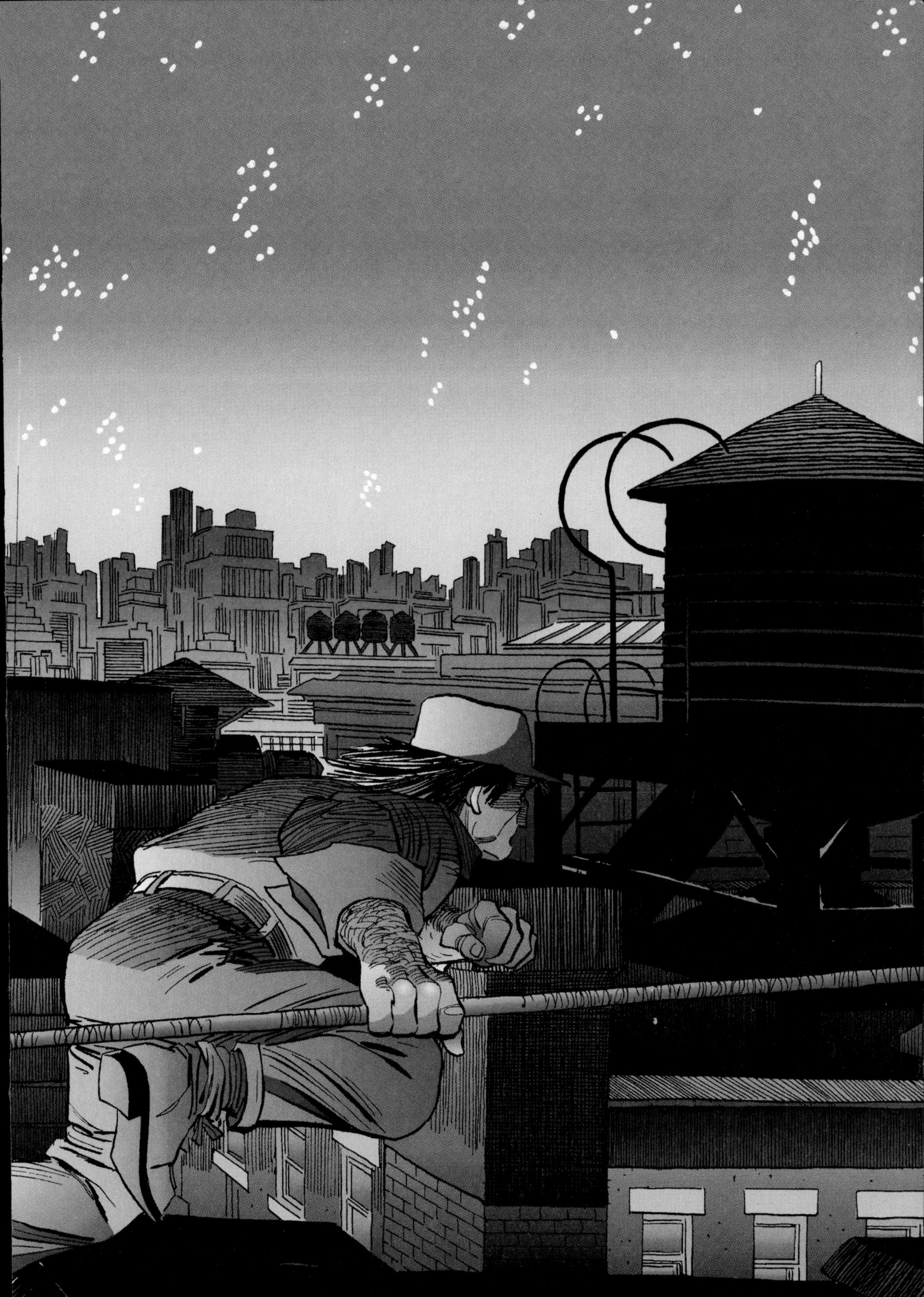

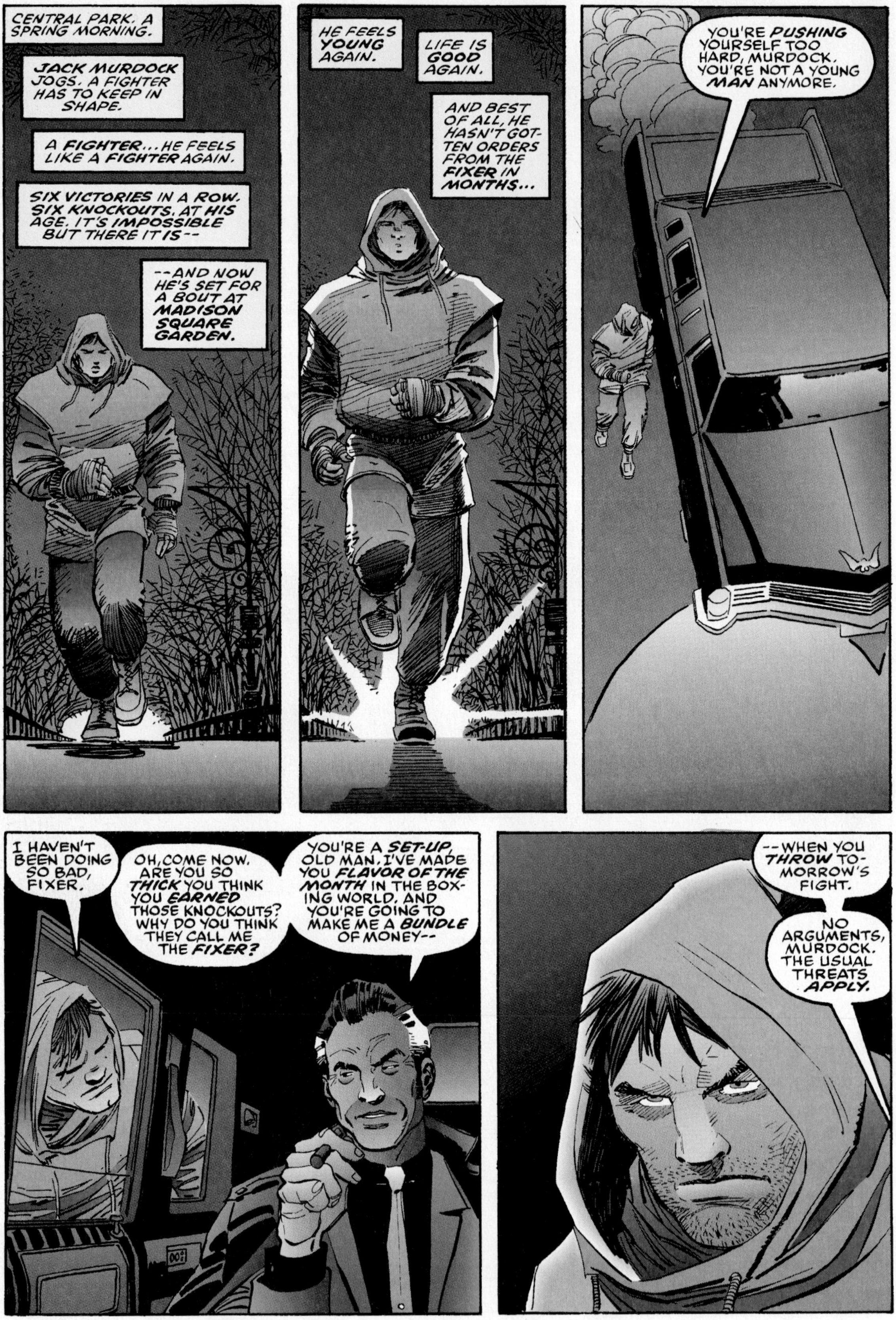
CENTRAL PARK. A SPRING MORNING.
JACK MURDOCK JOGS. A FIGHTER HAS TO KEEP IN SHAPE.
A FIGHTER... HE FEELS LIKE A FIGHTER AGAIN.
SIX VICTORIES IN A ROW. SIX KNOCKOUTS. AT HIS AGE. IT'S IMPOSSIBLE BUT THERE IT IS--
--AND NOW HE'S SET FOR A BOUT AT MADISON SQUARE GARDEN.
HE FEELS YOUNG AGAIN.
LIFE IS GOOD AGAIN.
AND BEST OF ALL, HE HASN'T GOTTEN ORDERS FROM THE FIXER IN MONTHS...
YOU'RE PUSHING YOURSELF TOO HARD, MURDOCK. YOU'RE NOT A YOUNG MAN ANYMORE.
I HAVEN'T BEEN DOING SO BAD, FIXER.
OH, COME NOW. ARE YOU SO THICK YOU THINK YOU EARNED THOSE KNOCKOUTS? WHY DO YOU THINK THEY CALL ME THE FIXER?
YOU'RE A SET-UP, OLD MAN. I'VE MADE YOU FLAVOR OF THE MONTH IN THE BOXING WORLD. AND YOU'RE GOING TO MAKE ME A BUNDLE OF MONEY--
--WHEN YOU THROW TOMORROW'S FIGHT.
NO ARGUMENTS, MURDOCK. THE USUAL THREATS APPLY.

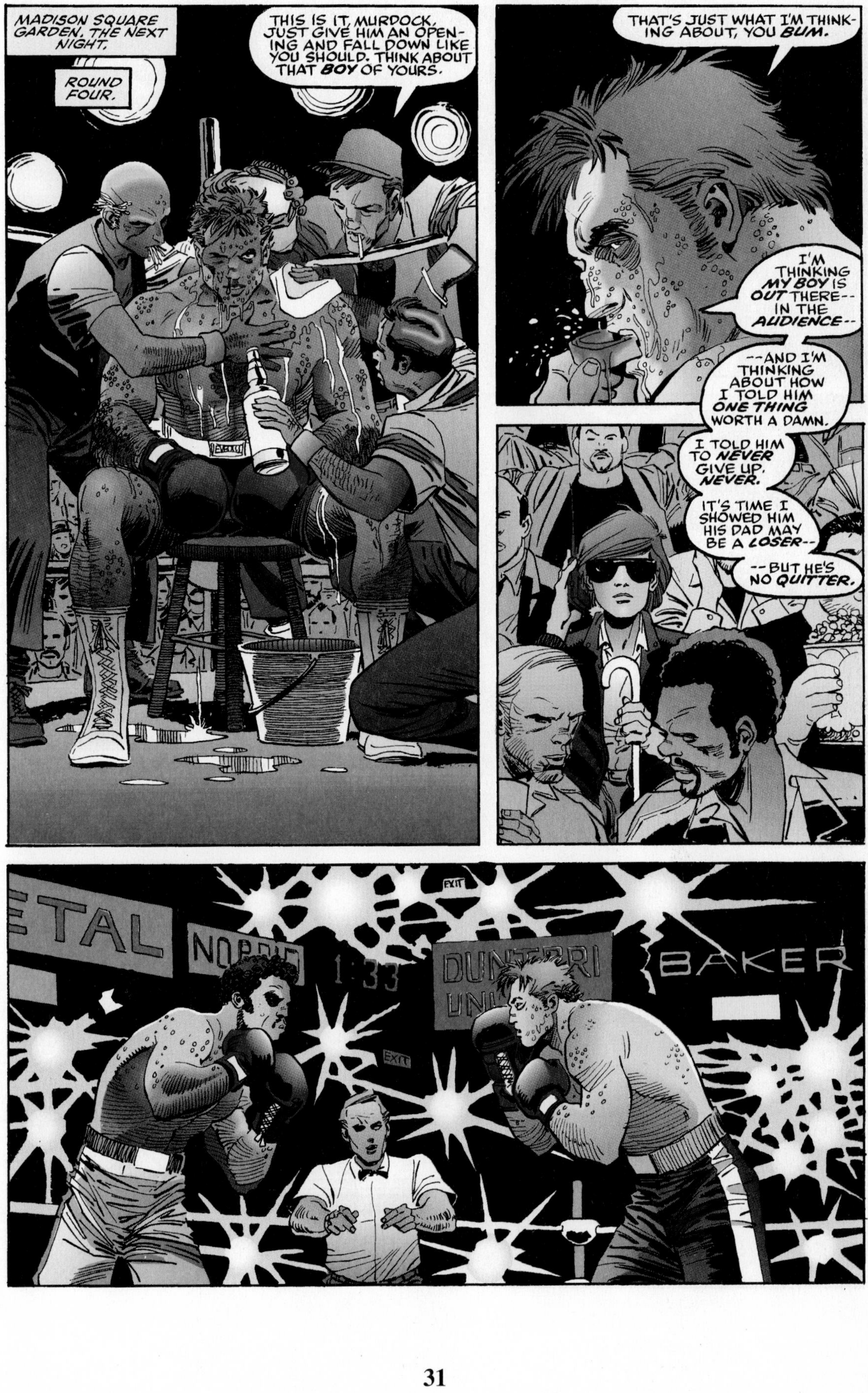

MADISON SQUARE GARDEN, THE NEXT NIGHT.
ROUND FOUR.
THIS IS IT, MURDOCK. JUST GIVE HIM AN OPENING AND FALL DOWN LIKE YOU SHOULD. THINK ABOUT THAT *BOY* OF YOURS.
THAT'S JUST WHAT I'M THINKING ABOUT, YOU *BUM.*
I'M THINKING *MY BOY* IS *OUT* THERE-- IN THE *AUDIENCE*--
--AND I'M THINKING ABOUT HOW I TOLD HIM *ONE THING* WORTH A DAMN.
I TOLD HIM TO *NEVER* GIVE UP. *NEVER.*
IT'S TIME I SHOWED HIM HIS DAD MAY BE A *LOSER*--
--BUT HE'S NO *QUITTER.*
ETAL
EXIT
BAKER
EXIT

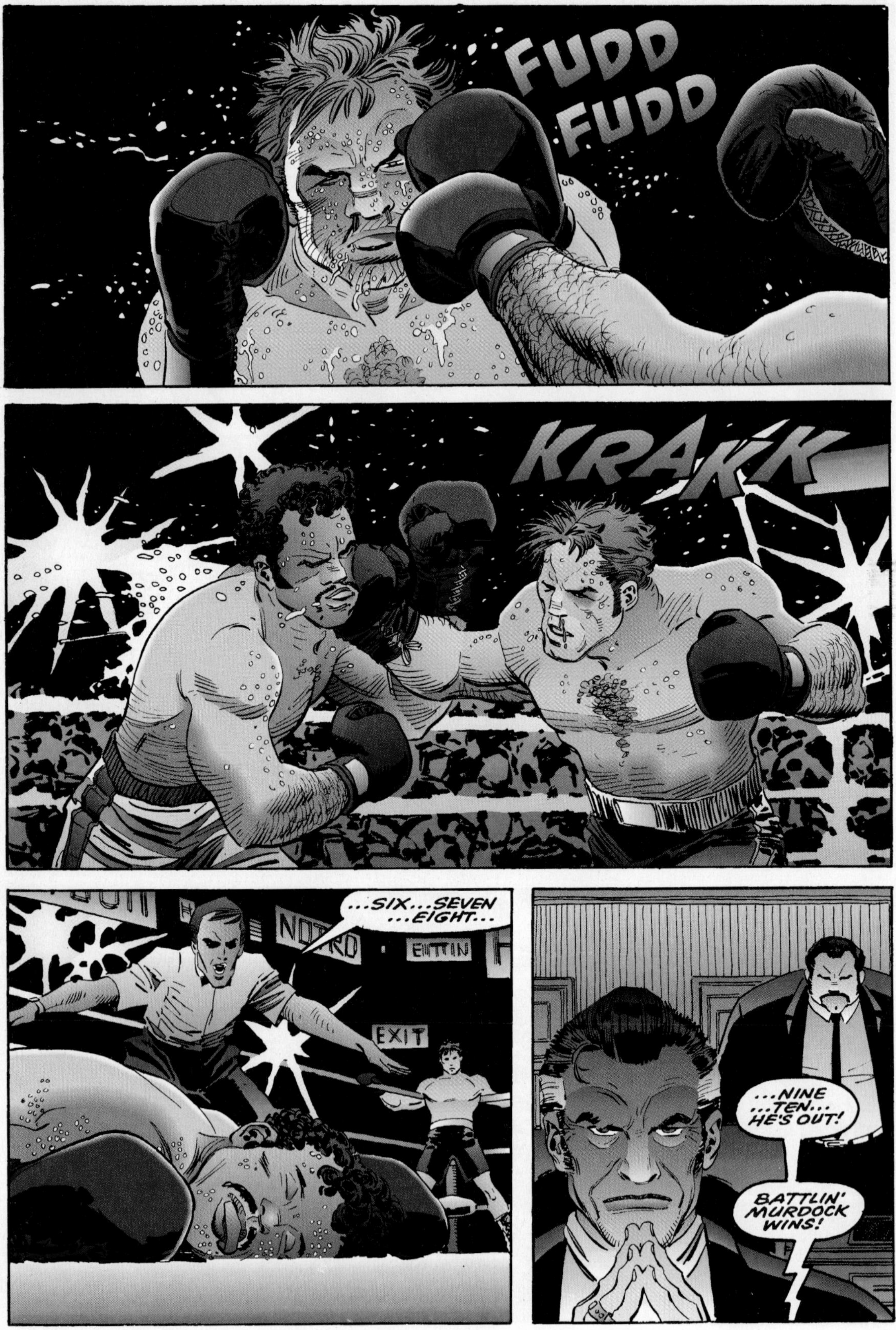
FUDD
FUDD
KRAKK
...SIX...SEVEN ...EIGHT...
EXIT
...NINE ...TEN... HE'S OUT!
BATTLIN' MURDOCK WINS!

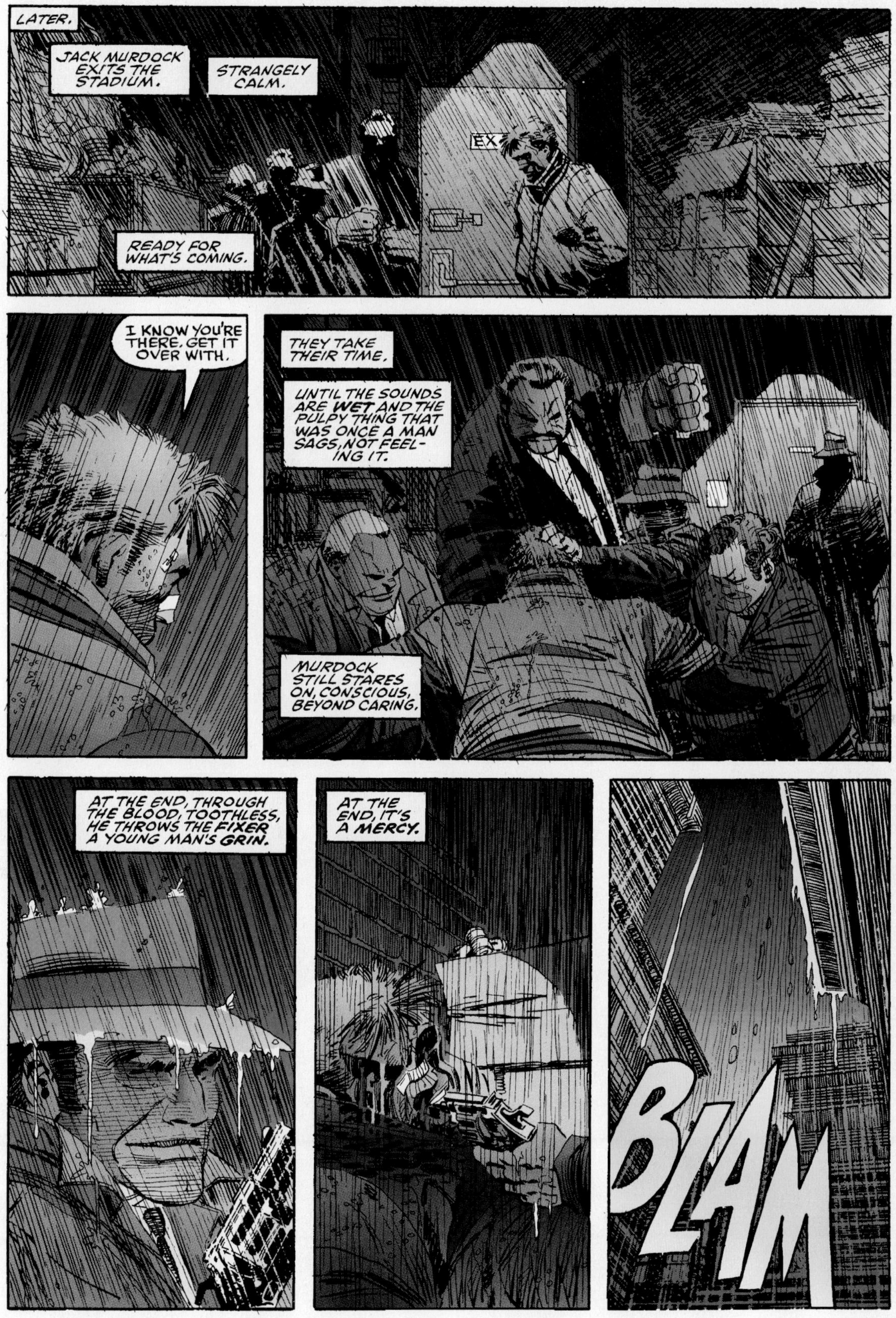
LATER.
JACK MURDOCK EXITS THE STADIUM.
STRANGELY CALM.
READY FOR WHAT'S COMING.
I KNOW YOU'RE THERE. GET IT OVER WITH.
THEY TAKE THEIR TIME.
UNTIL THE SOUNDS ARE WET AND THE PULPY THING THAT WAS ONCE A MAN SAGS, NOT FEEL-ING IT.
MURDOCK STILL STARES ON, CONSCIOUS, BEYOND CARING.
AT THE END, THROUGH THE BLOOD, TOOTHLESS, HE THROWS THE FIXER A YOUNG MAN'S GRIN.
AT THE END, IT'S A MERCY.
BLAM

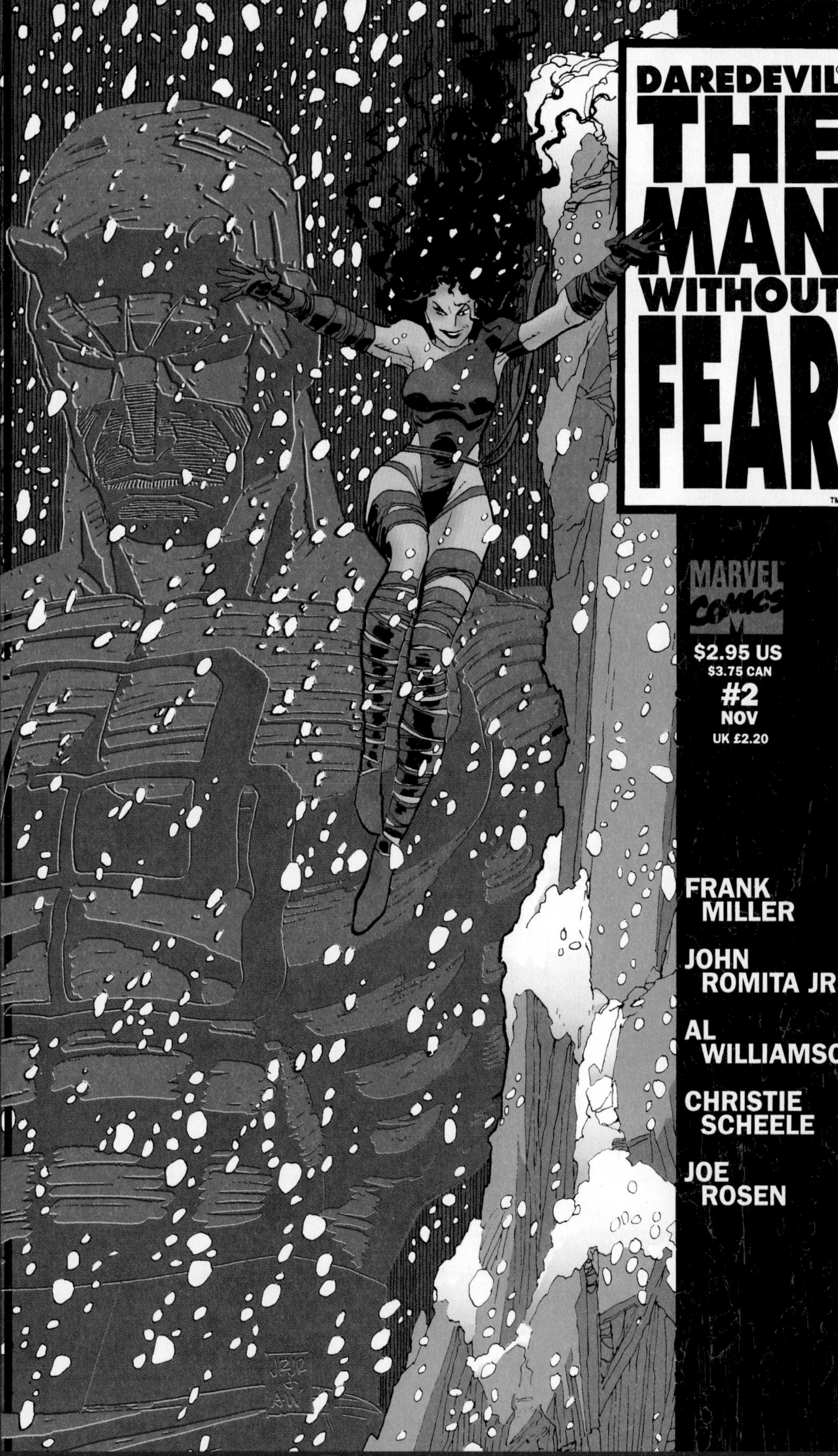
DAREDEVIL®
THE MAN WITHOUT FEAR™
MARVEL COMICS
$2.95 US
$3.75 CAN
#2
NOV
UK £2.20
FRANK MILLER
JOHN ROMITA JR.
AL WILLIAMSON
CHRISTIE SCHEELE
JOE ROSEN

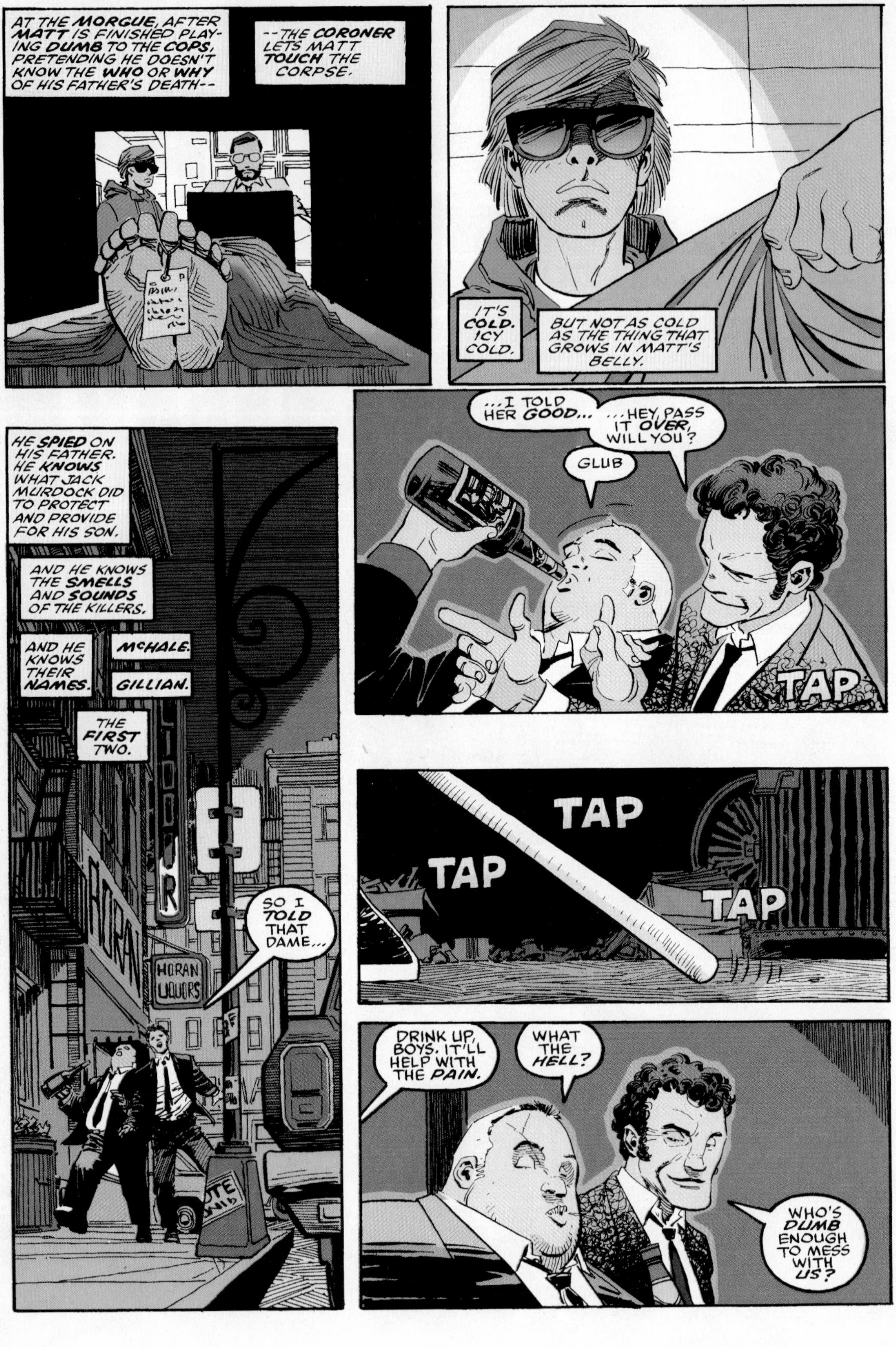
AT THE MORGUE, AFTER MATT IS FINISHED PLAYING DUMB TO THE COPS, PRETENDING HE DOESN'T KNOW THE WHO OR WHY OF HIS FATHER'S DEATH--
--THE CORONER LETS MATT TOUCH THE CORPSE.
IT'S COLD. ICY COLD.
BUT NOT AS COLD AS THE THING THAT GROWS IN MATT'S BELLY.
HE SPIED ON HIS FATHER. HE KNOWS WHAT JACK MURDOCK DID TO PROTECT AND PROVIDE FOR HIS SON.
AND HE KNOWS THE SMELLS AND SOUNDS OF THE KILLERS.
AND HE KNOWS THEIR NAMES.
MCHALE.
GILLIAN.
THE FIRST TWO.
HORAN
HORAN LIQUORS
SO I TOLD THAT DAME...
...I TOLD HER GOOD...
...HEY, PASS IT OVER, WILL YOU?
GLUB
TAP
TAP
TAP
TAP
DRINK UP, BOYS. IT'LL HELP WITH THE PAIN.
WHAT THE HELL?
WHO'S DUMB ENOUGH TO MESS WITH US?

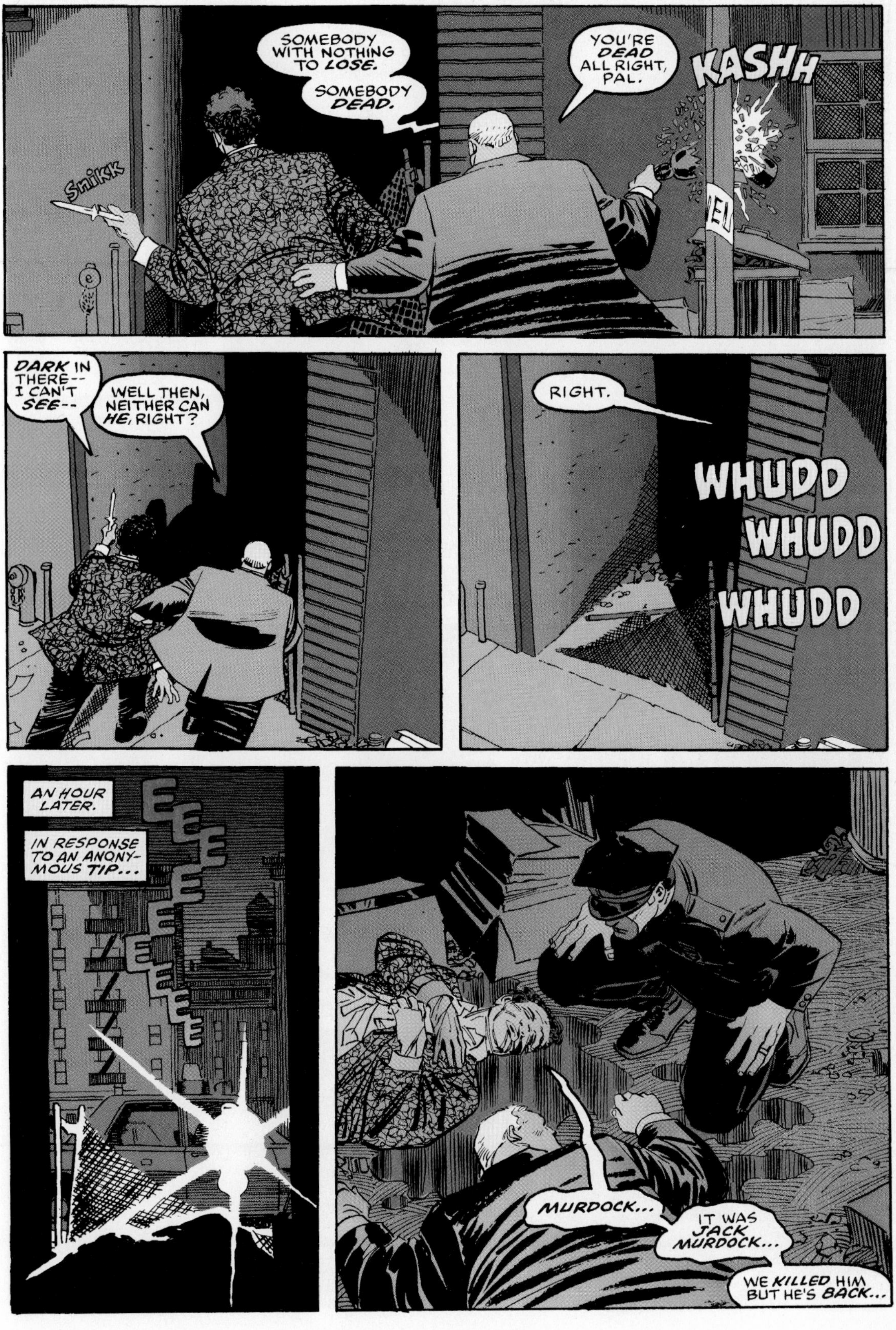
SNIKK
SOMEBODY WITH NOTHING TO LOSE.
SOMEBODY DEAD.
YOU'RE DEAD ALL RIGHT, PAL.
KASHH
DARK IN THERE-- I CAN'T SEE--
WELL THEN, NEITHER CAN HE, RIGHT?
RIGHT.
WHUDD
WHUDD
WHUDD
AN HOUR LATER.
IN RESPONSE TO AN ANONY-MOUS TIP...
EEEEEEEEEE
MURDOCK...
IT WAS JACK MURDOCK...
WE KILLED HIM BUT HE'S BACK...

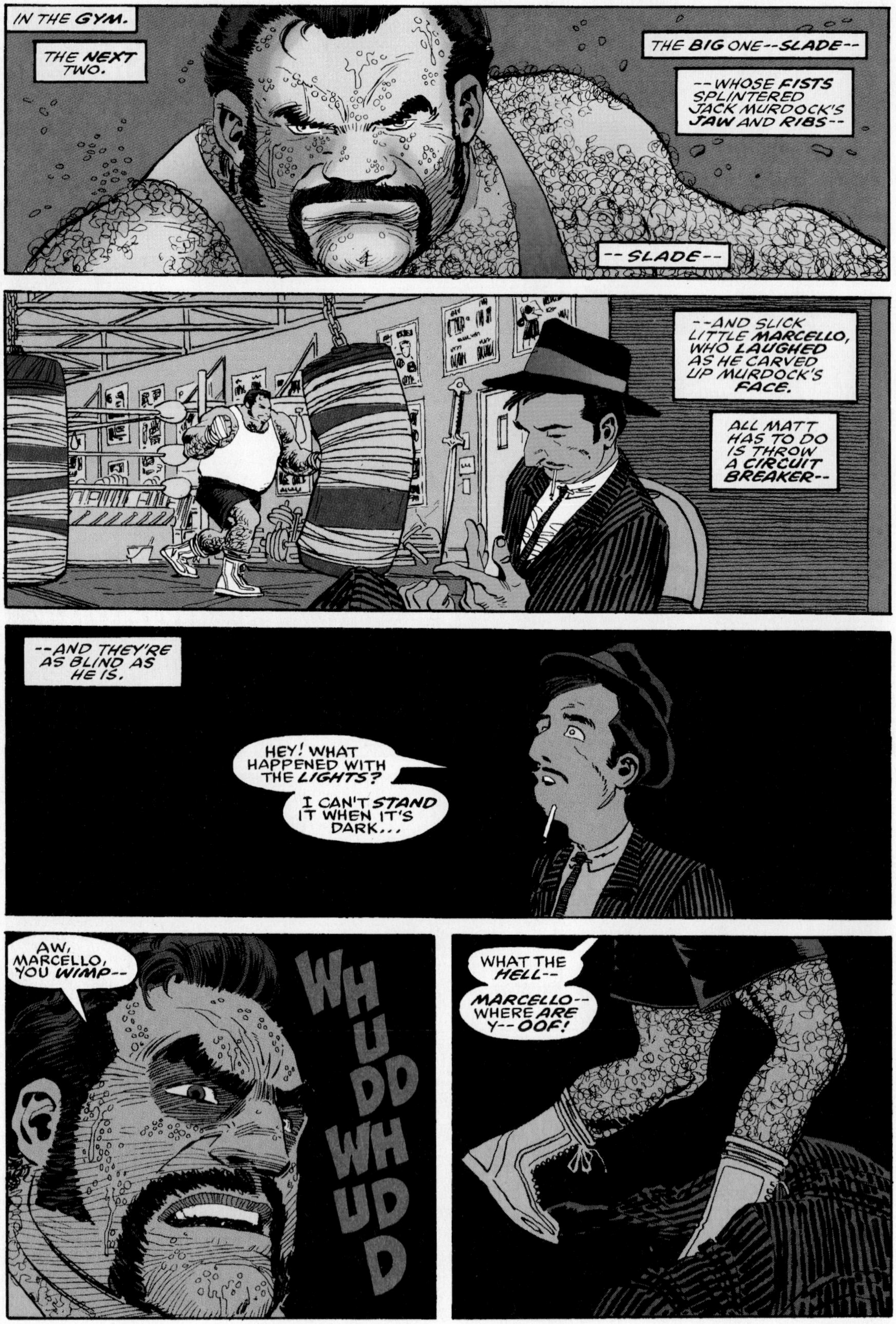
IN THE GYM.
THE NEXT TWO.
THE BIG ONE--SLADE--
--WHOSE FISTS SPLINTERED JACK MURDOCK'S JAW AND RIBS--
--SLADE--
--AND SLICK LITTLE MARCELLO, WHO LAUGHED AS HE CARVED UP MURDOCK'S FACE.
ALL MATT HAS TO DO IS THROW A CIRCUIT BREAKER--
--AND THEY'RE AS BLIND AS HE IS.
HEY! WHAT HAPPENED WITH THE LIGHTS?
I CAN'T STAND IT WHEN IT'S DARK...
AW, MARCELLO, YOU WIMP--
WHUDD WHUD WHUDD
WHAT THE HELL--
MARCELLO--WHERE ARE Y--OOF!

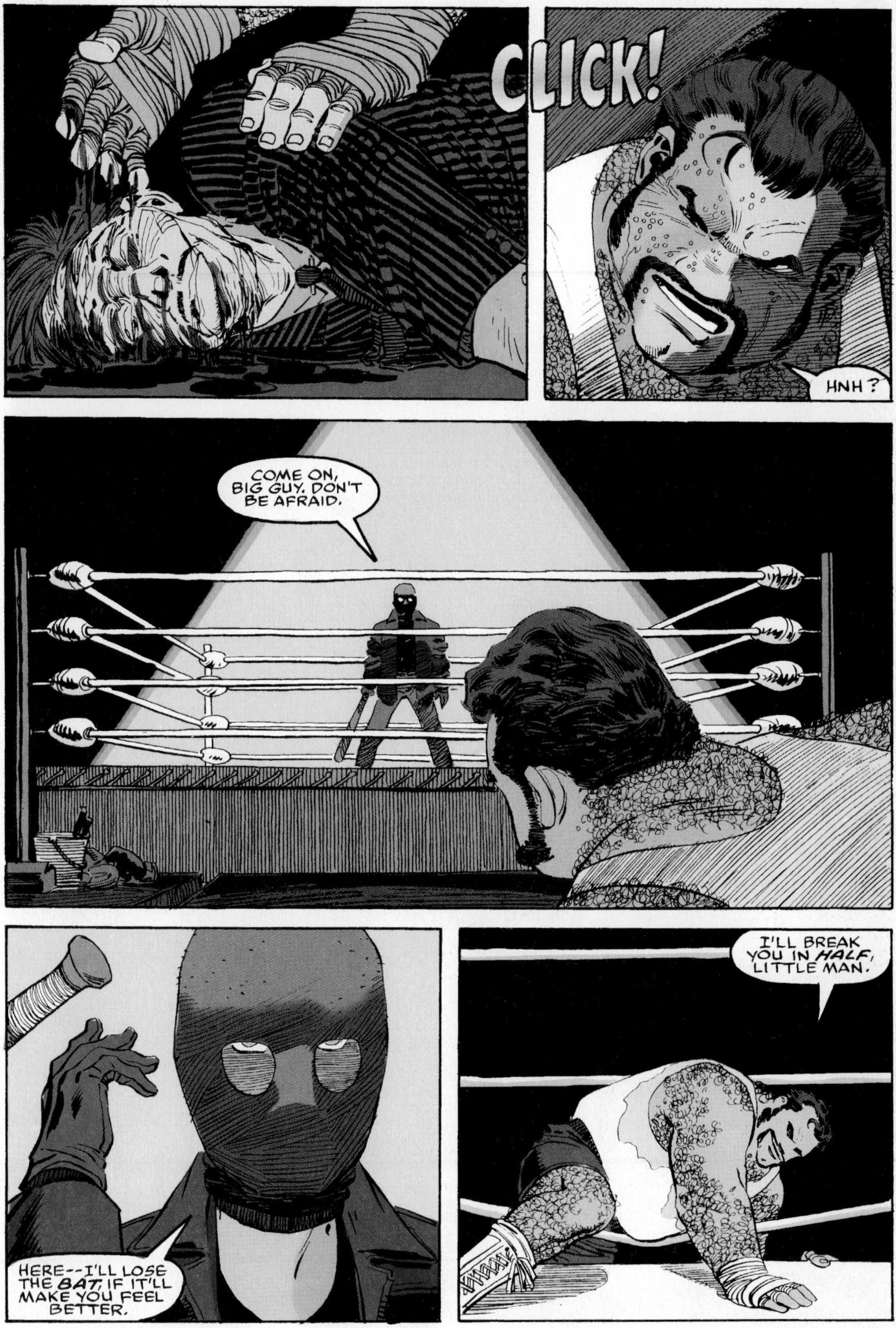
CLICK!
HNH?
COME ON, BIG GUY. DON'T BE AFRAID.
HERE--I'LL LOSE THE BAT, IF IT'LL MAKE YOU FEEL BETTER.
I'LL BREAK YOU IN HALF, LITTLE MAN.

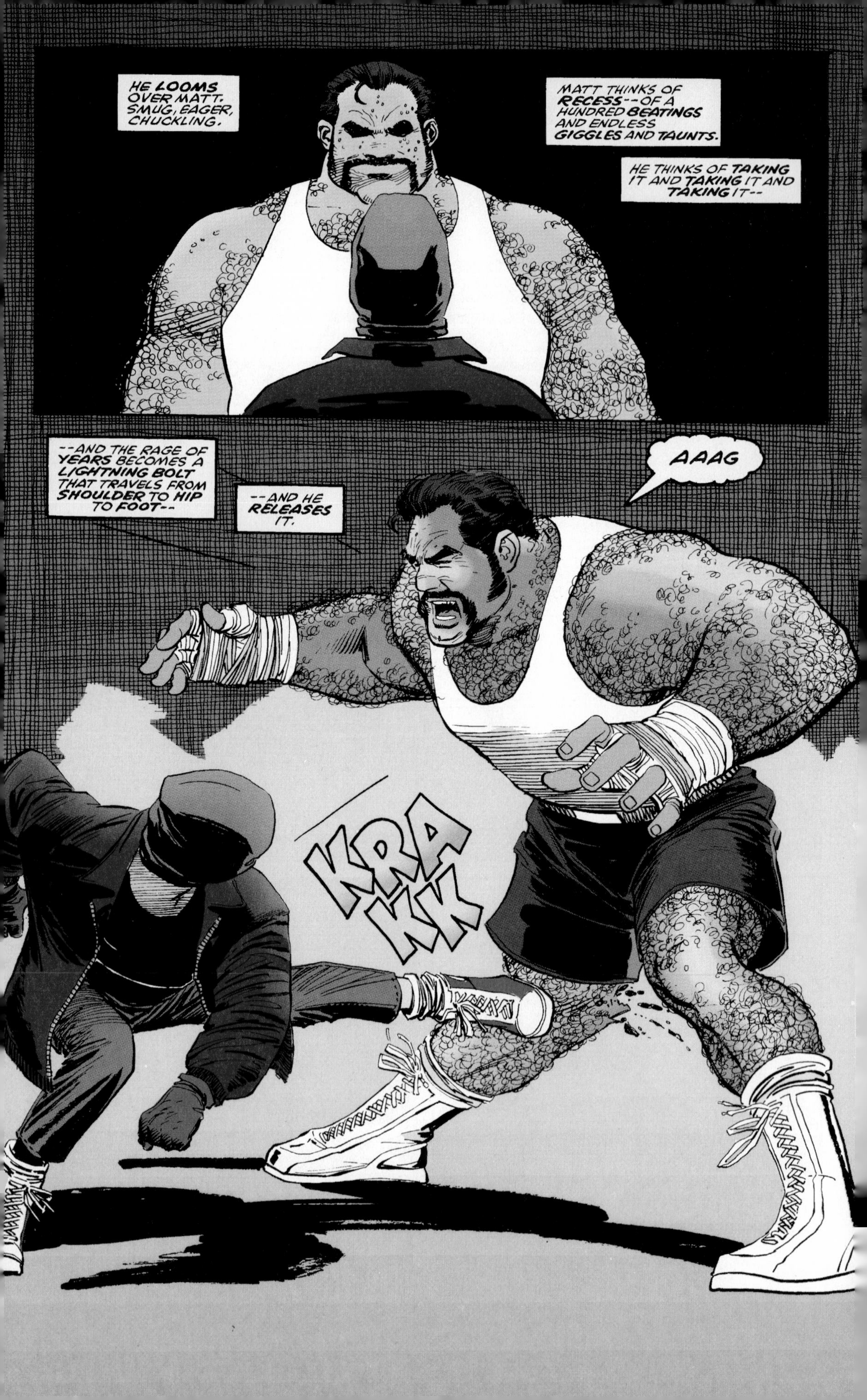
HE LOOMS OVER MATT. SMUG, EAGER, CHUCKLING.
MATT THINKS OF RECESS--OF A HUNDRED BEATINGS AND ENDLESS GIGGLES AND TAUNTS.
HE THINKS OF TAKING IT AND TAKING IT AND TAKING IT--
--AND THE RAGE OF YEARS BECOMES A LIGHTNING BOLT THAT TRAVELS FROM SHOULDER TO HIP TO FOOT--
--AND HE RELEASES IT.
AAAG
KRAKK

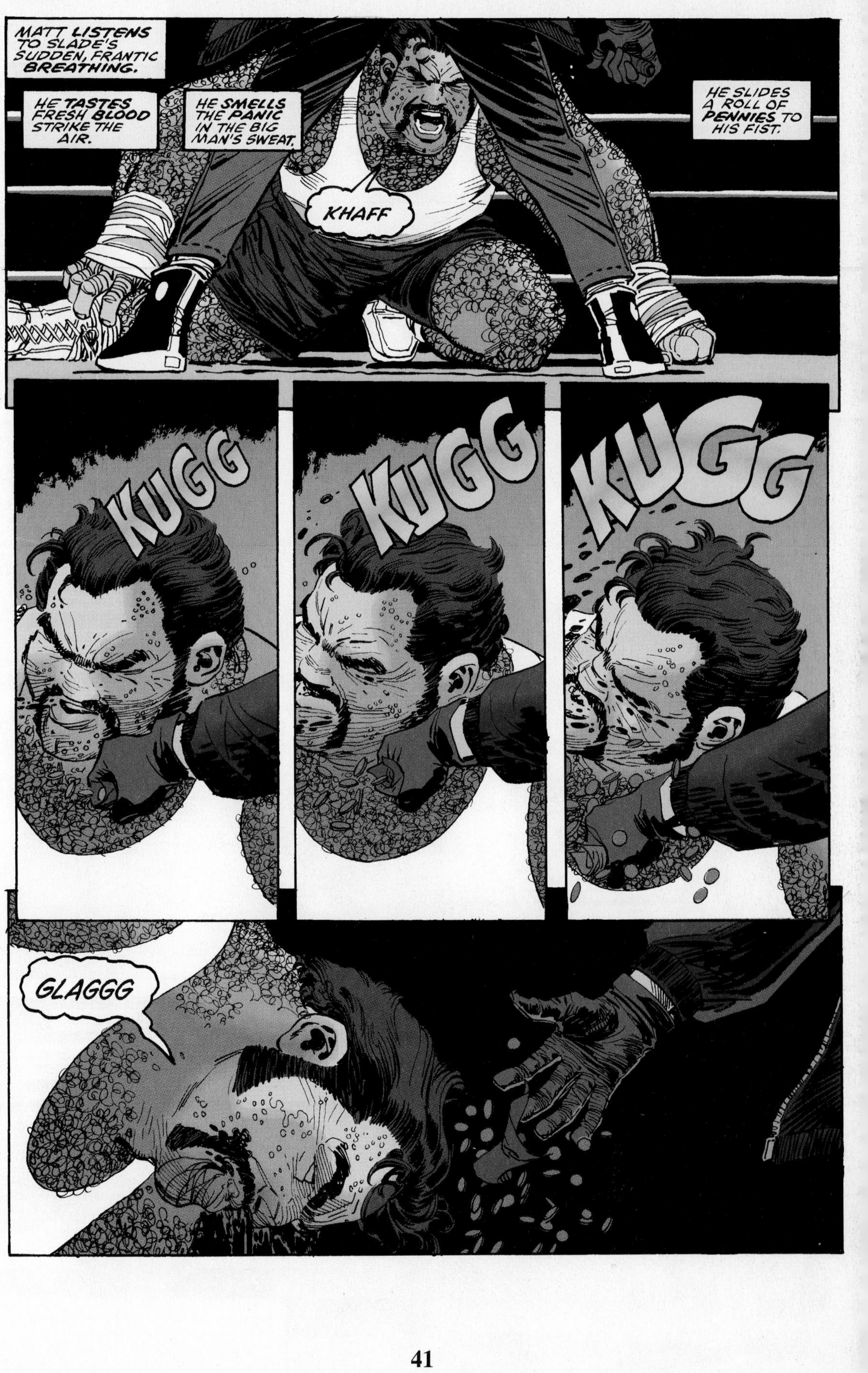
MATT LISTENS TO SLADE'S SUDDEN, FRANTIC BREATHING.
HE TASTES FRESH BLOOD STRIKE THE AIR.
HE SMELLS THE PANIC IN THE BIG MAN'S SWEAT.
HE SLIDES A ROLL OF PENNIES TO HIS FIST.
KHAFF
KUGG
KUGG
KUGG
GLAGGG

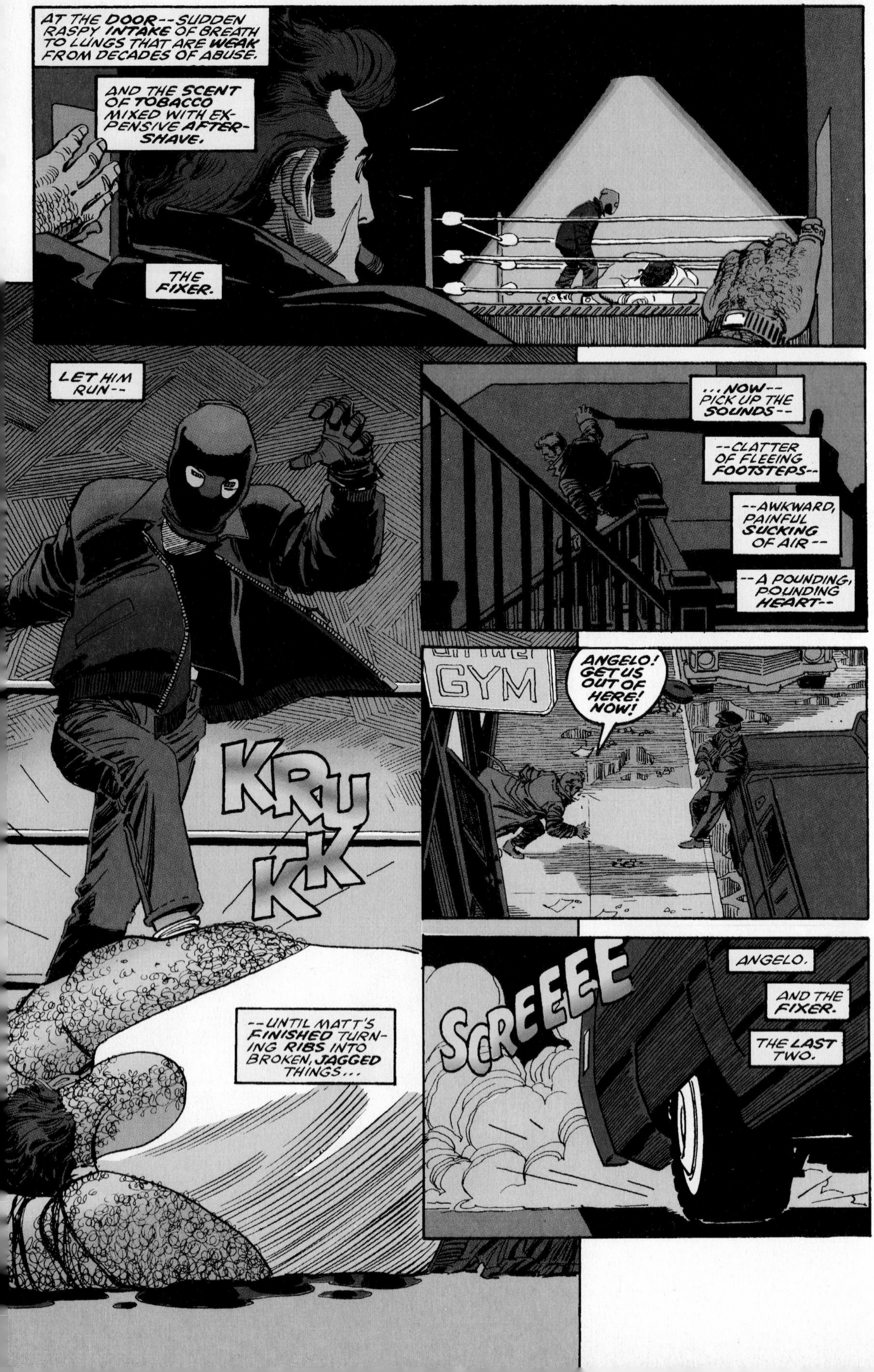
AT THE DOOR-- SUDDEN RASPY INTAKE OF BREATH TO LUNGS THAT ARE WEAK FROM DECADES OF ABUSE.
AND THE SCENT OF TOBACCO MIXED WITH EXPENSIVE AFTER-SHAVE.
THE FIXER.
LET HIM RUN--
KRUKKK
--UNTIL MATT'S FINISHED TURNING RIBS INTO BROKEN, JAGGED THINGS...
...NOW-- PICK UP THE SOUNDS--
--CLATTER OF FLEEING FOOTSTEPS--
--AWKWARD, PAINFUL SUCKING OF AIR--
--A POUNDING, POUNDING HEART--
GYM
ANGELO! GET US OUT OF HERE! NOW!
SCREEEE
ANGELO.
AND THE FIXER.
THE LAST TWO.

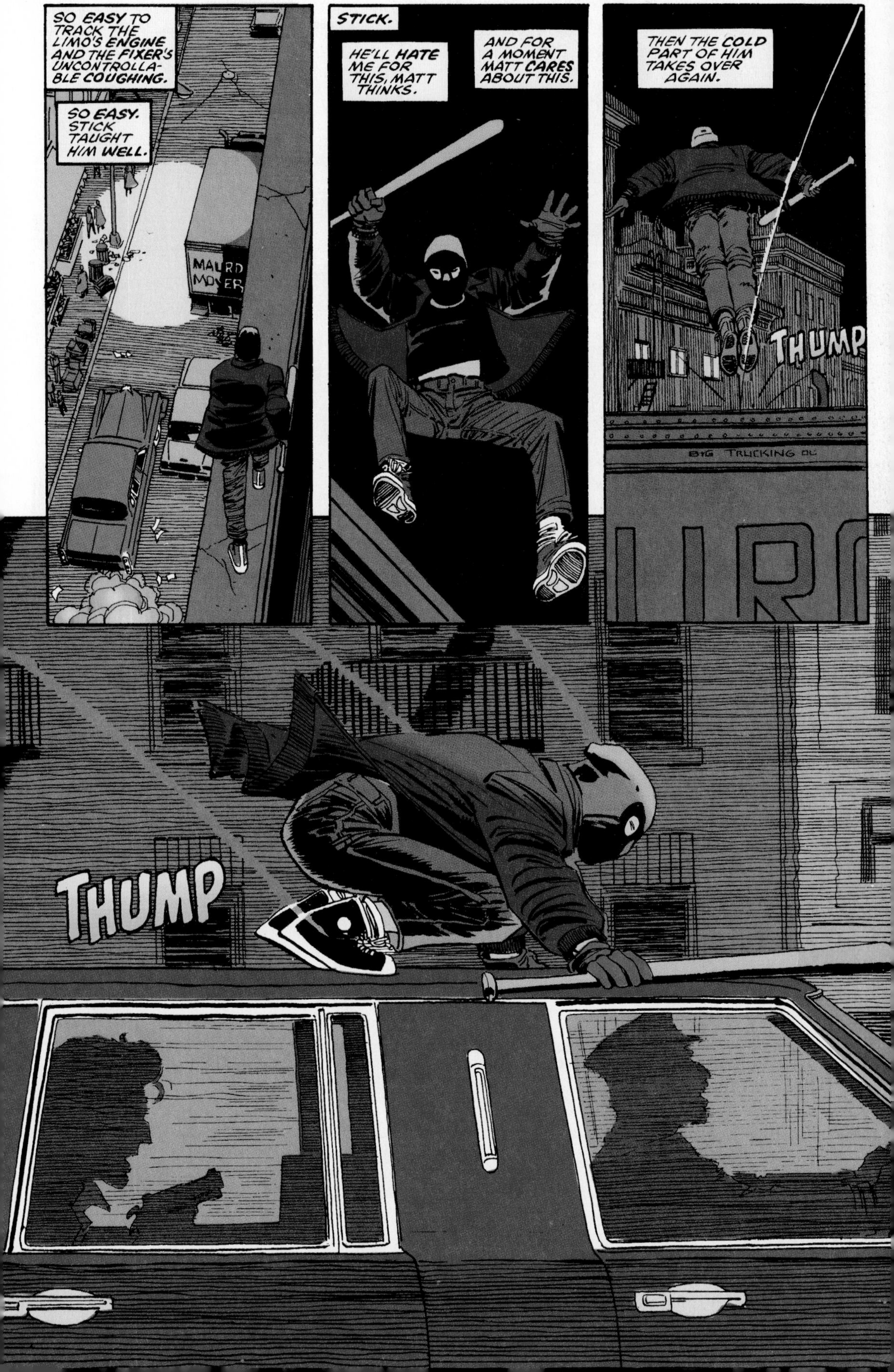
SO EASY TO TRACK THE LIMO'S ENGINE AND THE FIXER'S UNCONTROLLA-BLE COUGHING.
SO EASY. STICK TAUGHT HIM WELL.
MAURD MOVER
STICK.
HE'LL HATE ME FOR THIS, MATT THINKS.
AND FOR A MOMENT MATT CARES ABOUT THIS.
THEN THE COLD PART OF HIM TAKES OVER AGAIN.
THUMP
B&G TRUCKING CO.
THUMP

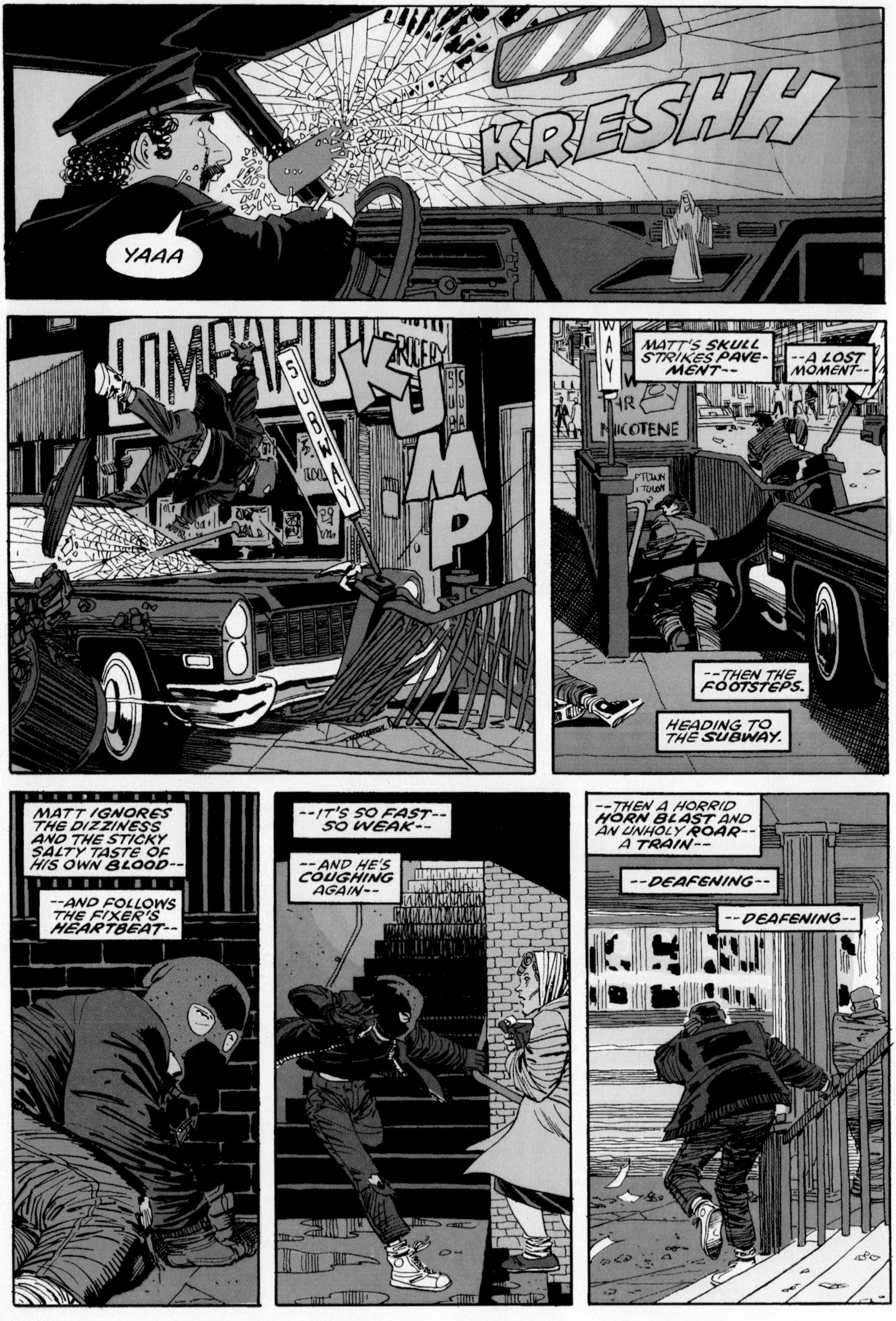
KRESHH
YAAA
KUMP
SUBWAY
MATT'S SKULL STRIKES PAVEMENT--
--A LOST MOMENT--
--THEN THE FOOTSTEPS.
HEADING TO THE SUBWAY.
MATT IGNORES THE DIZZINESS AND THE STICKY SALTY TASTE OF HIS OWN BLOOD--
--AND FOLLOWS THE FIXER'S HEARTBEAT--
--IT'S SO FAST--SO WEAK--
--AND HE'S COUGHING AGAIN--
--THEN A HORRID HORN BLAST AND AN UNHOLY ROAR--A TRAIN--
--DEAFENING--
--DEAFENING--

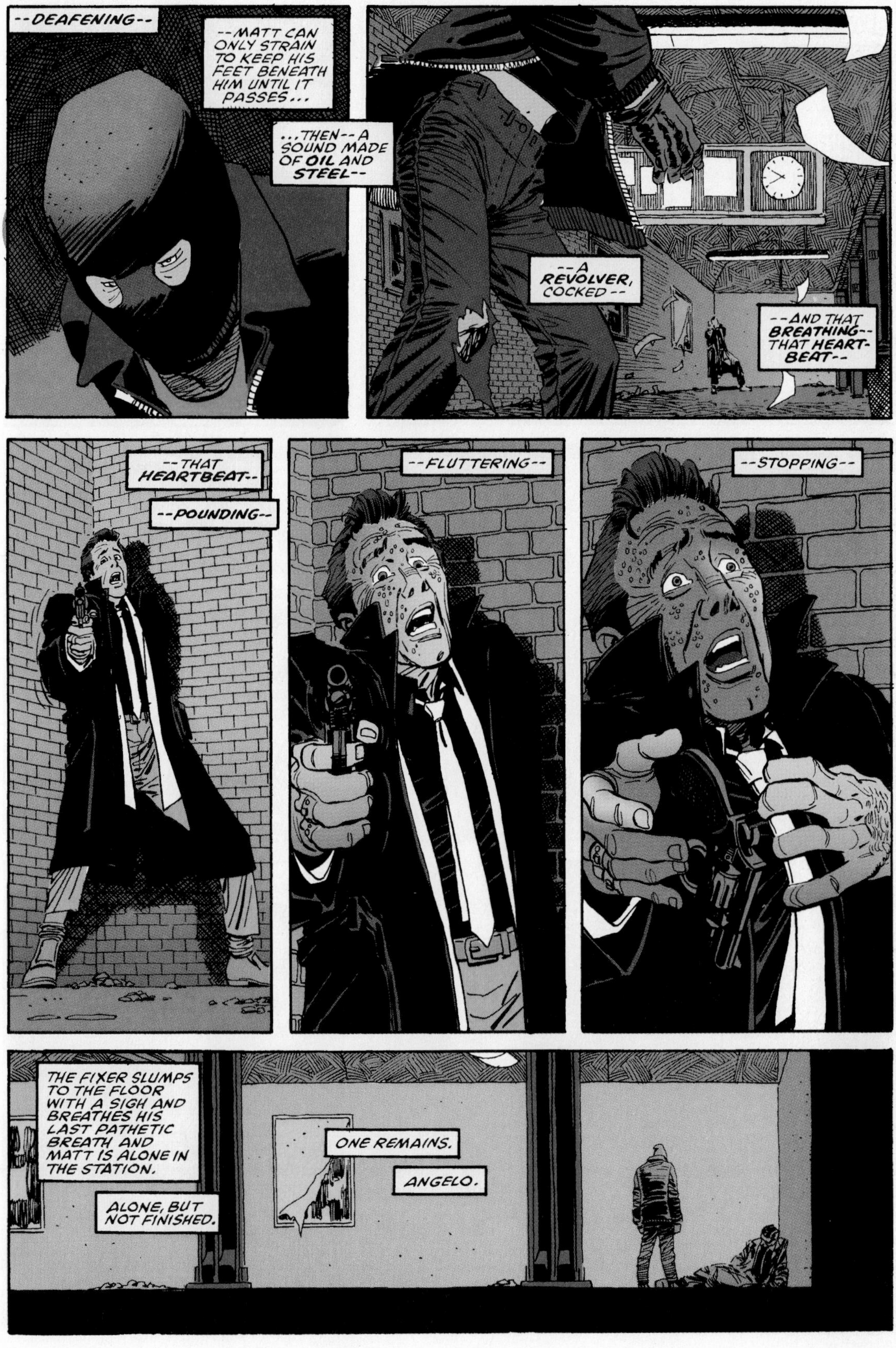
--DEAFENING--
--MATT CAN ONLY STRAIN TO KEEP HIS FEET BENEATH HIM UNTIL IT PASSES...
...THEN--A SOUND MADE OF OIL AND STEEL--
--A REVOLVER, COCKED--
--AND THAT BREATHING--THAT HEART-BEAT--
--THAT HEARTBEAT--
--POUNDING--
--FLUTTERING--
--STOPPING--
THE FIXER SLUMPS TO THE FLOOR WITH A SIGH AND BREATHES HIS LAST PATHETIC BREATH AND MATT IS ALONE IN THE STATION.
ALONE, BUT NOT FINISHED.
ONE REMAINS.
ANGELO.

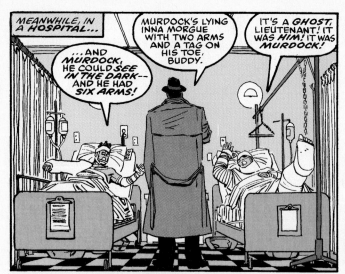

MEANWHILE, IN A *HOSPITAL*...

...AND *MURDOCK*, HE COULD *SEE* IN THE DARK-- AND HE HAD *SIX ARMS!*

MURDOCK'S LYING INNA MORGUE WITH *TWO ARMS* AND A TAG ON HIS TOE, BUDDY.

IT'S A *GHOST*, LIEUTENANT! IT WAS *HIM!* IT WAS *MURDOCK!*

SO EITHER WE GOT US A *GHOST* OR YOUSE GUYS BEEN HITTING THE *SAUCE* TOO HARD OR WE GOT US A *VIGILANTE*.

ME, I'M BETTING ON THE *SAUCE*.

ONE REMAINS.

ANGELO.

HE THINKS HE'S ES-CAPED.

ESCAPED TO A PLACE OF THICK *PERFUMES* AND PRACTICED *PASSION*.

THEY KNOW HIM HERE. HE THINKS HE'S *SAFE*.

JUST *RELAX*, ANGELO. *WE'LL* TAKE CARE OF YOU.

IT WAS SOME KIND OF *CRAZY MAN*--

--OUT OF *NOWHERE* HE--

AAAA

IT'S A *RAID!*

BUT WE'RE *PAID UP!*

THAT'S NO COP! KILL HIM!

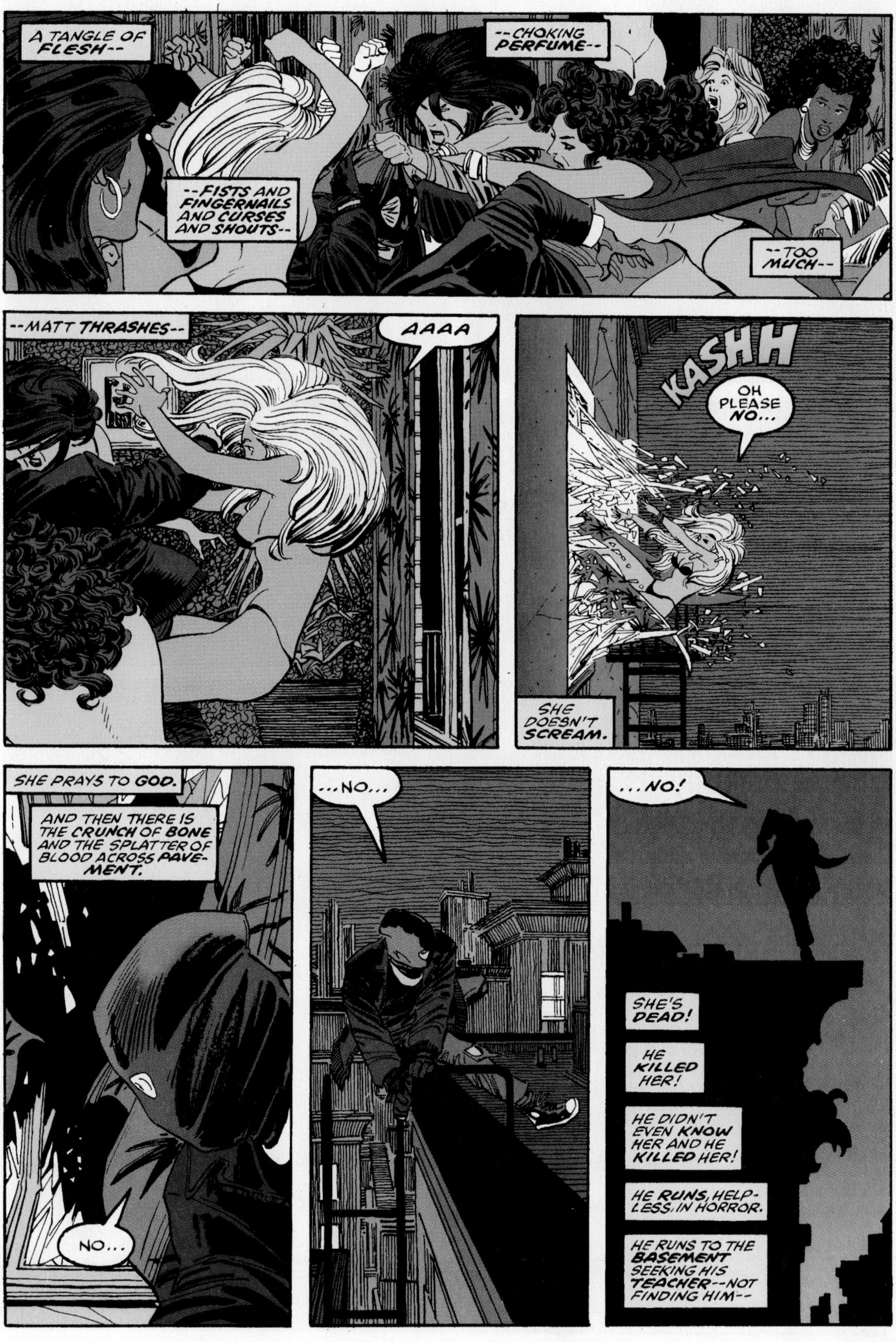
A TANGLE OF FLESH--
--FISTS AND FINGERNAILS AND CURSES AND SHOUTS--
--CHOKING PERFUME--
--TOO MUCH--
--MATT THRASHES--
AAAA
KASHH
OH PLEASE NO...
SHE DOESN'T SCREAM.
SHE PRAYS TO GOD.
AND THEN THERE IS THE CRUNCH OF BONE AND THE SPLATTER OF BLOOD ACROSS PAVE-MENT.
NO...
...NO...
...NO!
SHE'S DEAD!
HE KILLED HER!
HE DIDN'T EVEN KNOW HER AND HE KILLED HER!
HE RUNS, HELP-LESS, IN HORROR.
HE RUNS TO THE BASEMENT SEEKING HIS TEACHER--NOT FINDING HIM--

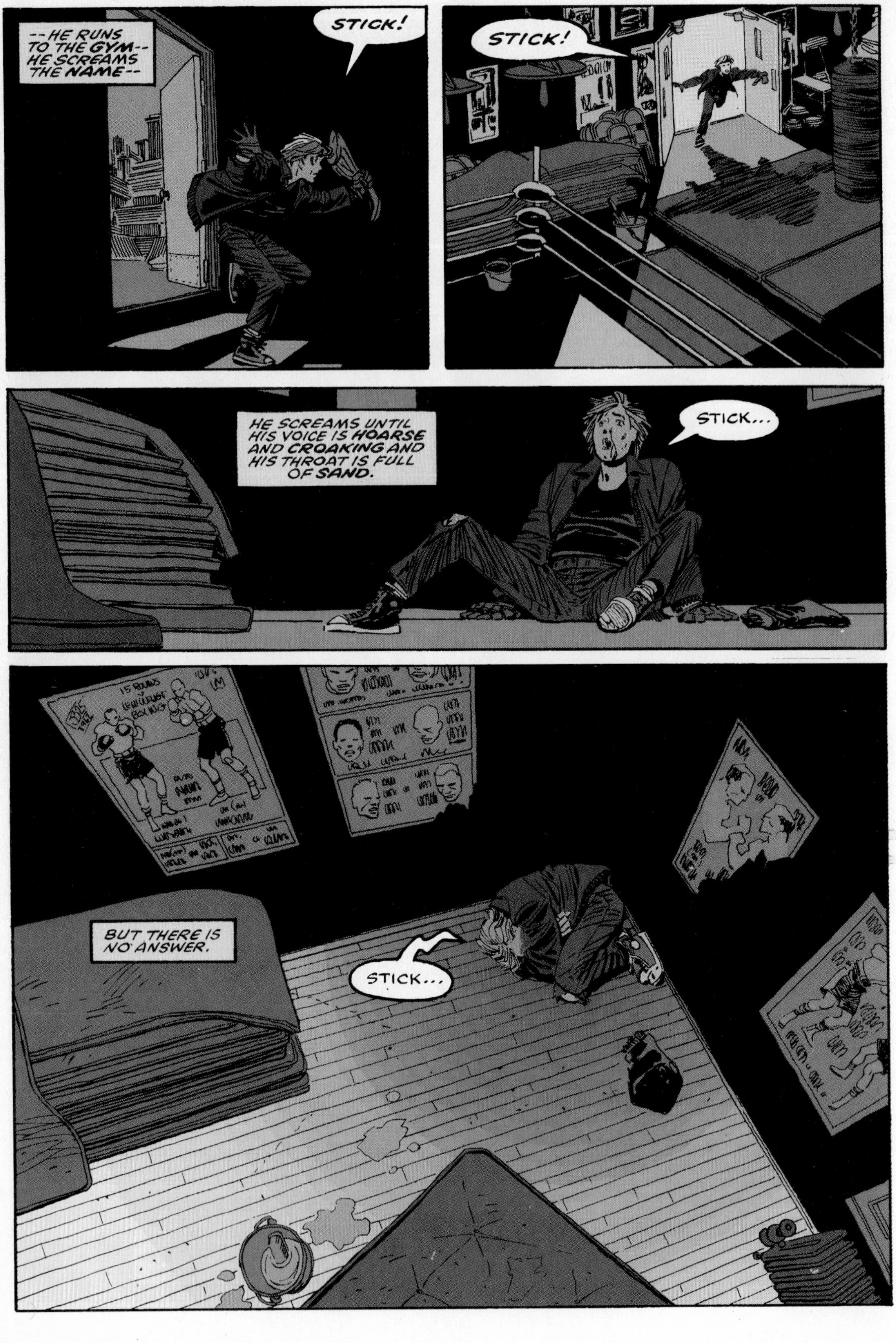
--HE RUNS TO THE GYM--
HE SCREAMS THE NAME--
STICK!
STICK!
HE SCREAMS UNTIL HIS VOICE IS HOARSE AND CROAKING AND HIS THROAT IS FULL OF SAND.
STICK...
BUT THERE IS NO ANSWER.
STICK...

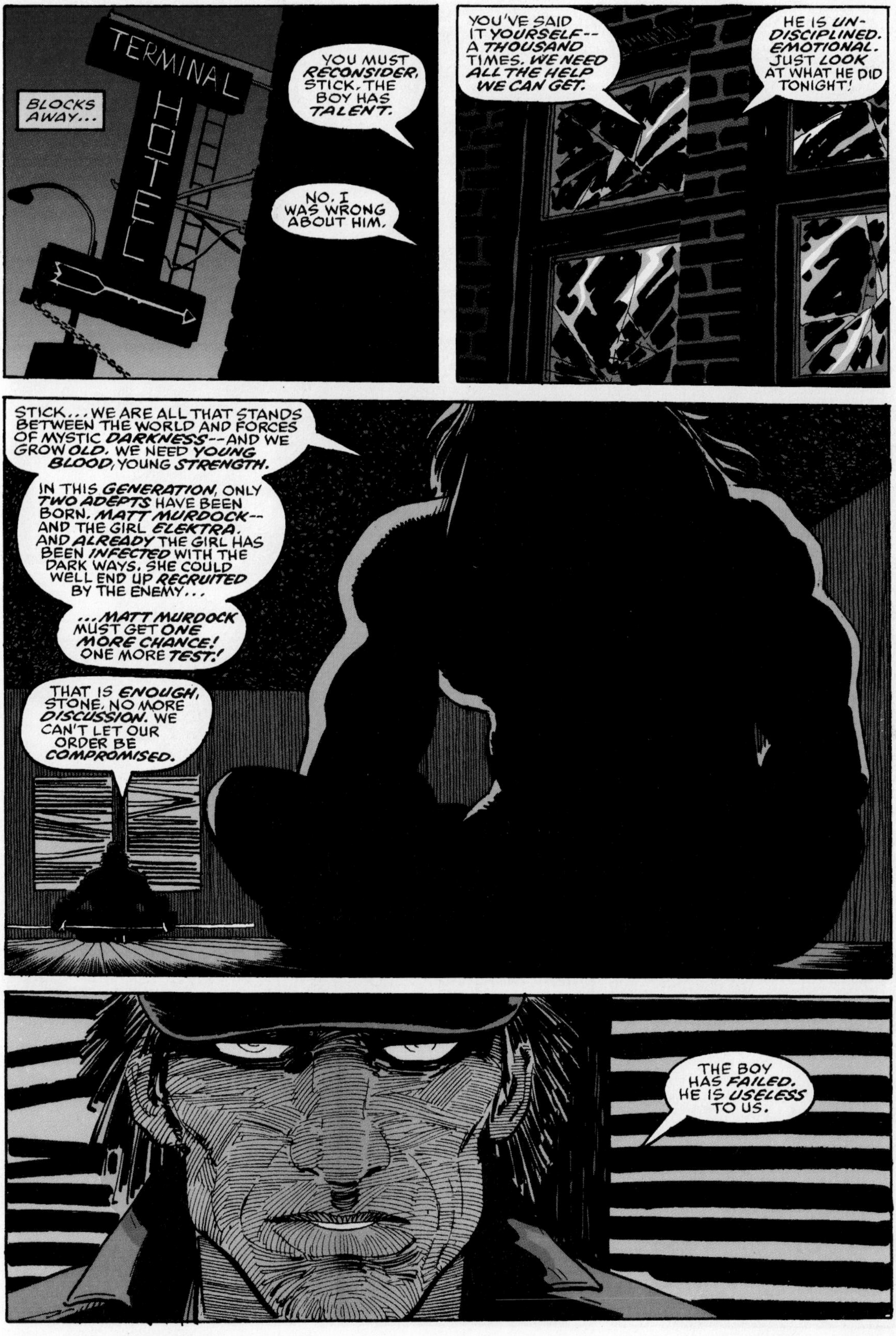
BLOCKS AWAY...
TERMINAL HOTEL
YOU MUST RECONSIDER, STICK. THE BOY HAS TALENT.
NO. I WAS WRONG ABOUT HIM.
YOU'VE SAID IT YOURSELF-- A THOUSAND TIMES. WE NEED ALL THE HELP WE CAN GET.
HE IS UN-DISCIPLINED. EMOTIONAL. JUST LOOK AT WHAT HE DID TONIGHT!
STICK... WE ARE ALL THAT STANDS BETWEEN THE WORLD AND FORCES OF MYSTIC DARKNESS--AND WE GROW OLD. WE NEED YOUNG BLOOD, YOUNG STRENGTH.
IN THIS GENERATION, ONLY TWO ADEPTS HAVE BEEN BORN. MATT MURDOCK-- AND THE GIRL ELEKTRA. AND ALREADY THE GIRL HAS BEEN INFECTED WITH THE DARK WAYS. SHE COULD WELL END UP RECRUITED BY THE ENEMY...
...MATT MURDOCK MUST GET ONE MORE CHANCE! ONE MORE TEST!
THAT IS ENOUGH, STONE. NO MORE DISCUSSION. WE CAN'T LET OUR ORDER BE COMPROMISED.
THE BOY HAS FAILED. HE IS USELESS TO US.

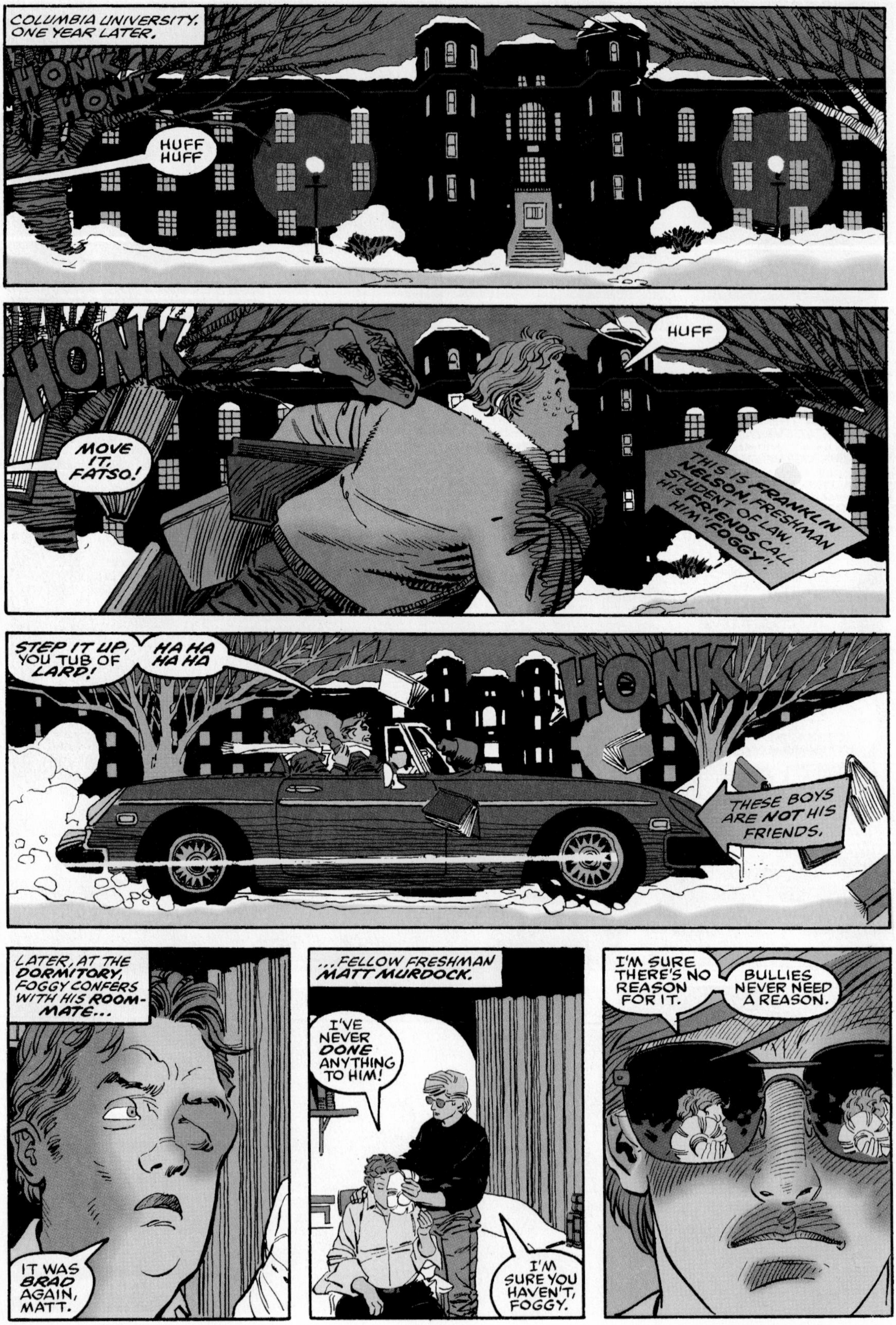
COLUMBIA UNIVERSITY. ONE YEAR LATER.
HONK HONK
HUFF HUFF
HONK
HUFF
MOVE IT, FATSO!
THIS IS FRANKLIN NELSON, FRESHMAN STUDENT OF LAW. HIS FRIENDS CALL HIM "FOGGY".
STEP IT UP, YOU TUB OF LARD!
HA HA HA HA
HONK
THESE BOYS ARE NOT HIS FRIENDS.
LATER, AT THE DORMITORY, FOGGY CONFERS WITH HIS ROOM-MATE...
IT WAS BRAD AGAIN, MATT.
...FELLOW FRESHMAN MATT MURDOCK.
I'VE NEVER DONE ANYTHING TO HIM!
I'M SURE YOU HAVEN'T, FOGGY.
I'M SURE THERE'S NO REASON FOR IT.
BULLIES NEVER NEED A REASON.

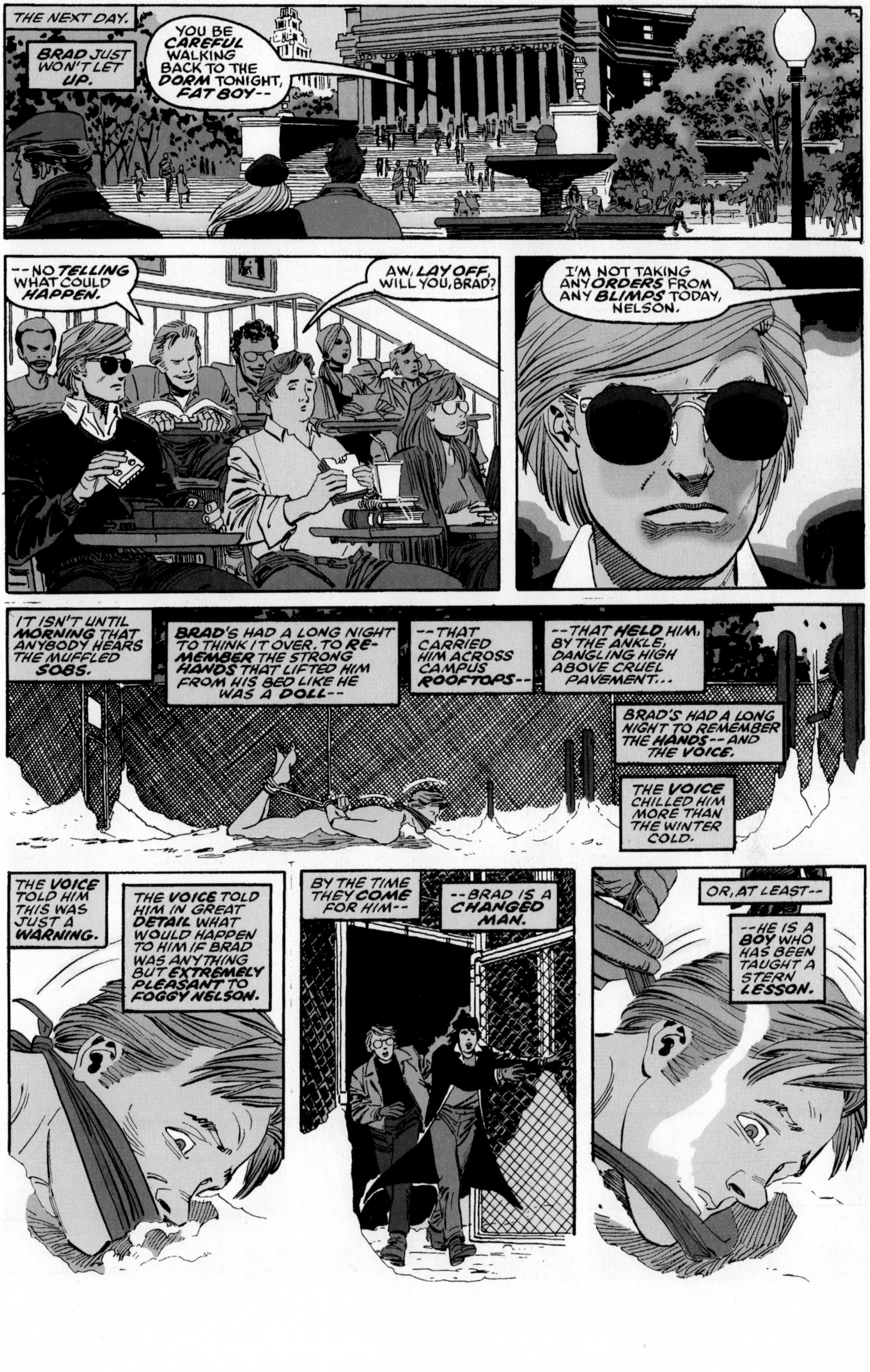
THE NEXT DAY.
BRAD JUST WON'T LET UP.
YOU BE CAREFUL WALKING BACK TO THE DORM TONIGHT, FAT BOY--
--NO TELLING WHAT COULD HAPPEN.
AW, LAY OFF, WILL YOU, BRAD?
I'M NOT TAKING ANY ORDERS FROM ANY BLIMPS TODAY, NELSON.
IT ISN'T UNTIL MORNING THAT ANYBODY HEARS THE MUFFLED SOBS.
BRAD'S HAD A LONG NIGHT TO THINK IT OVER. TO REMEMBER THE STRONG HANDS THAT LIFTED HIM FROM HIS BED LIKE HE WAS A DOLL--
--THAT CARRIED HIM ACROSS CAMPUS ROOFTOPS--
--THAT HELD HIM, BY THE ANKLE, DANGLING HIGH ABOVE CRUEL PAVEMENT...
BRAD'S HAD A LONG NIGHT TO REMEMBER THE HANDS-- AND THE VOICE.
THE VOICE CHILLED HIM MORE THAN THE WINTER COLD.
THE VOICE TOLD HIM THIS WAS JUST A WARNING.
THE VOICE TOLD HIM IN GREAT DETAIL WHAT WOULD HAPPEN TO HIM IF BRAD WAS ANYTHING BUT EXTREMELY PLEASANT TO FOGGY NELSON.
BY THE TIME THEY COME FOR HIM--
--BRAD IS A CHANGED MAN.
OR, AT LEAST--
--HE IS A BOY WHO HAS BEEN TAUGHT A STERN LESSON.

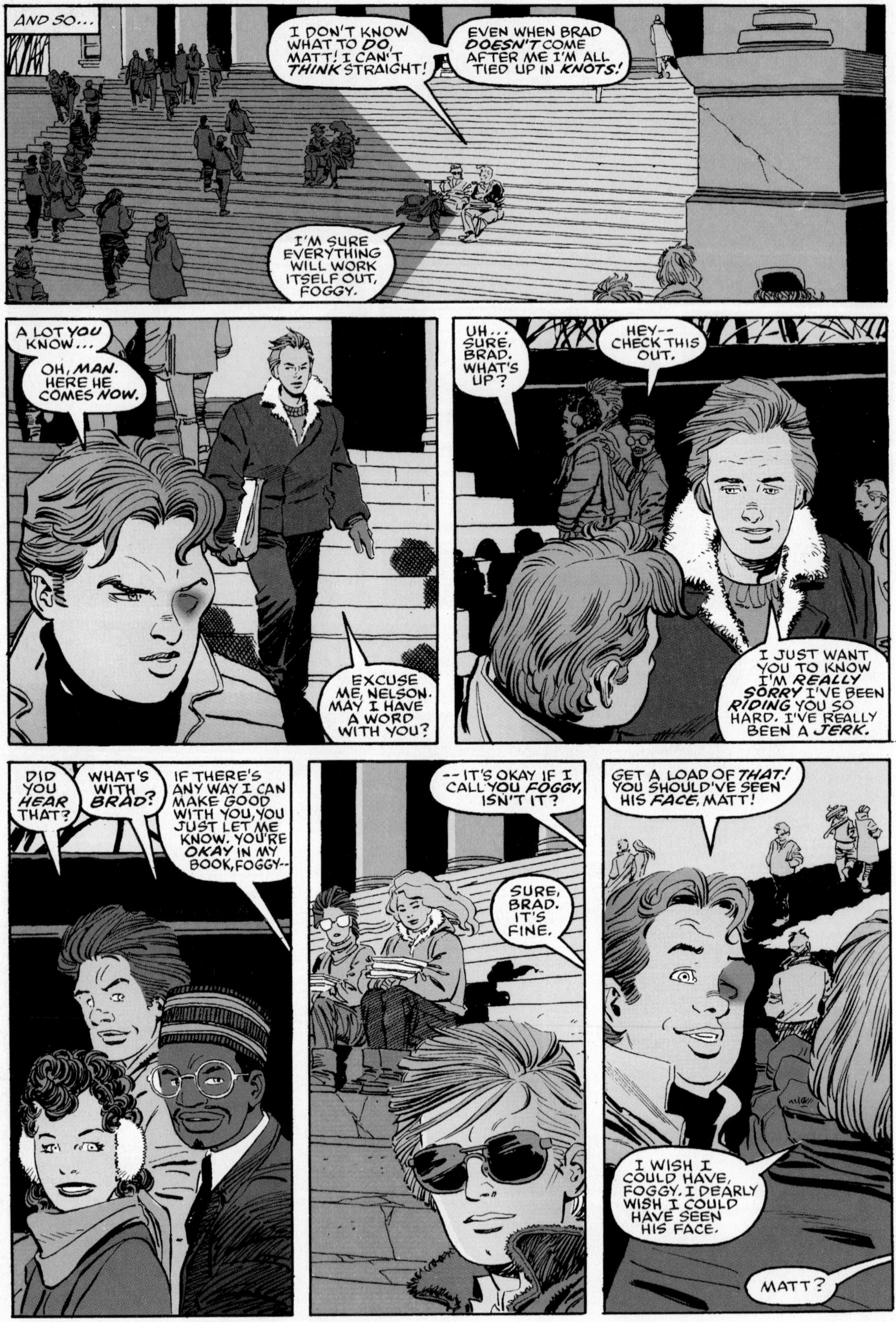
AND SO...
I DON'T KNOW WHAT TO DO, MATT! I CAN'T THINK STRAIGHT!
EVEN WHEN BRAD DOESN'T COME AFTER ME I'M ALL TIED UP IN KNOTS!
I'M SURE EVERYTHING WILL WORK ITSELF OUT, FOGGY.
A LOT YOU KNOW...
OH, MAN. HERE HE COMES NOW.
EXCUSE ME, NELSON. MAY I HAVE A WORD WITH YOU?
UH... SURE, BRAD. WHAT'S UP?
HEY-- CHECK THIS OUT.
I JUST WANT YOU TO KNOW I'M REALLY SORRY I'VE BEEN RIDING YOU SO HARD. I'VE REALLY BEEN A JERK.
DID YOU HEAR THAT?
WHAT'S WITH BRAD?
IF THERE'S ANY WAY I CAN MAKE GOOD WITH YOU, YOU JUST LET ME KNOW. YOU'RE OKAY IN MY BOOK, FOGGY--
--IT'S OKAY IF I CALL YOU FOGGY, ISN'T IT?
SURE, BRAD. IT'S FINE.
GET A LOAD OF THAT! YOU SHOULD'VE SEEN HIS FACE, MATT!
I WISH I COULD HAVE, FOGGY. I DEARLY WISH I COULD HAVE SEEN HIS FACE.
MATT?

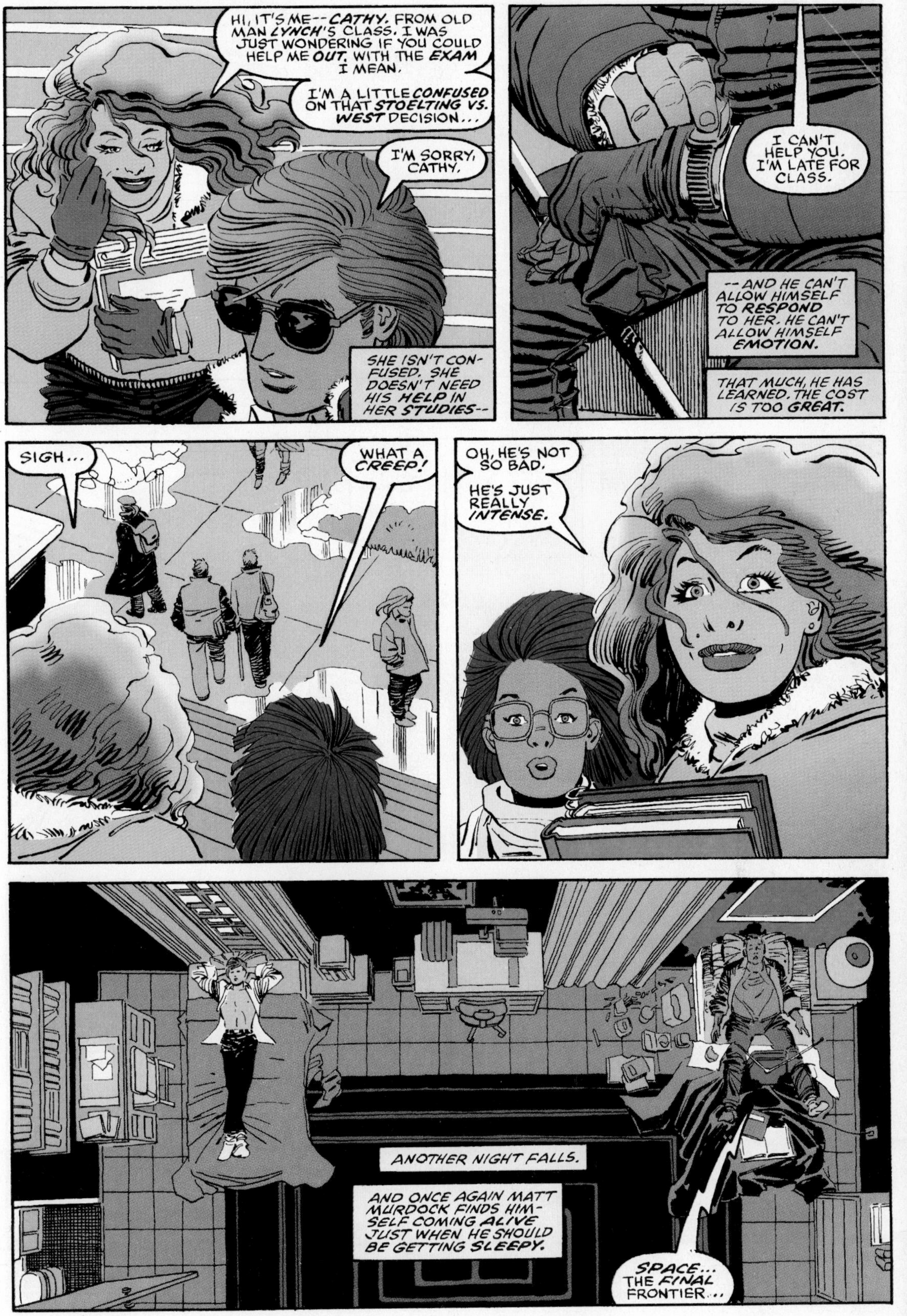
HI, IT'S ME-- CATHY. FROM OLD MAN LYNCH'S CLASS. I WAS JUST WONDERING IF YOU COULD HELP ME OUT. WITH THE EXAM I MEAN.
I'M A LITTLE CONFUSED ON THAT STOELTING VS. WEST DECISION...
I'M SORRY, CATHY.
SHE ISN'T CONFUSED. SHE DOESN'T NEED HIS HELP IN HER STUDIES--
I CAN'T HELP YOU. I'M LATE FOR CLASS.
--AND HE CAN'T ALLOW HIMSELF TO RESPOND TO HER. HE CAN'T ALLOW HIMSELF EMOTION.
THAT MUCH, HE HAS LEARNED. THE COST IS TOO GREAT.
SIGH...
WHAT A CREEP!
OH, HE'S NOT SO BAD.
HE'S JUST REALLY INTENSE.
ANOTHER NIGHT FALLS.
AND ONCE AGAIN MATT MURDOCK FINDS HIMSELF COMING ALIVE JUST WHEN HE SHOULD BE GETTING SLEEPY.
SPACE... THE FINAL FRONTIER...

...THESE ARE THE VOYAGES...

...IT'S FIVE YEAR MISSION...

...TO BOLDLY GO Klik

IT WASN'T JUST THE TELEVISION THAT KEPT MATT AWAKE.

ZZZZ NNKK

FOGGY'S SNORING COULD RAISE THE DEAD.

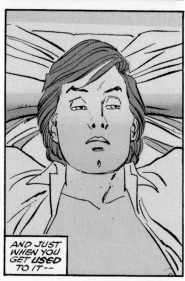

AND JUST WHEN YOU GET USED TO IT--

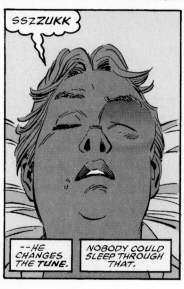

SSZZUKK

--HE CHANGES THE TUNE.

NOBODY COULD SLEEP THROUGH THAT.

NO. NO USE KIDDING HIMSELF.

ZERKK

IT'S NOT THE SNORING.

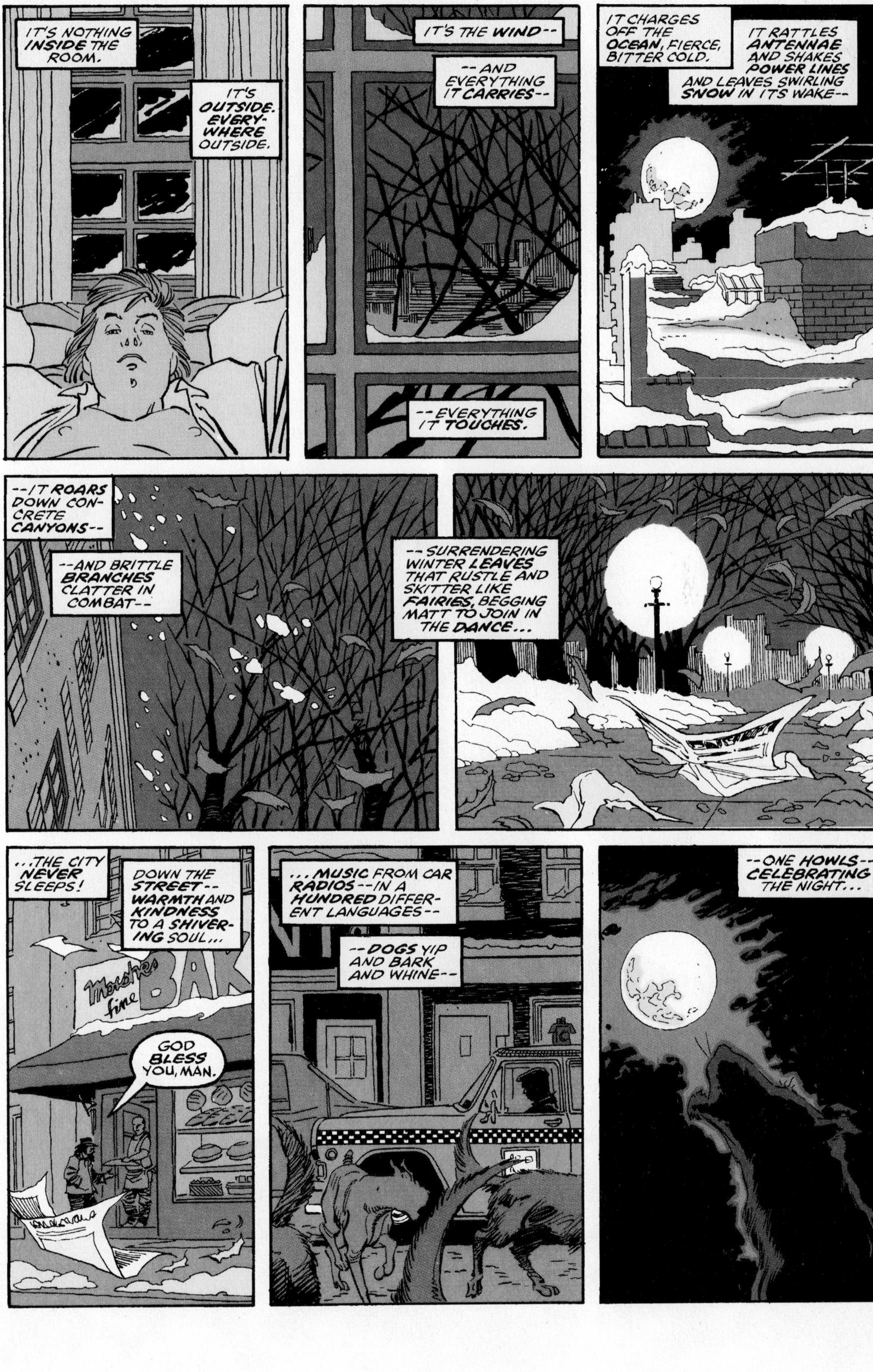
IT'S NOTHING INSIDE THE ROOM.
IT'S OUTSIDE. EVERYWHERE OUTSIDE.
IT'S THE WIND--
--AND EVERYTHING IT CARRIES--
--EVERYTHING IT TOUCHES.
IT CHARGES OFF THE OCEAN, FIERCE, BITTER COLD.
IT RATTLES ANTENNAE AND SHAKES POWER LINES AND LEAVES SWIRLING SNOW IN IT'S WAKE--
--IT ROARS DOWN CONCRETE CANYONS--
--AND BRITTLE BRANCHES CLATTER IN COMBAT--
--SURRENDERING WINTER LEAVES THAT RUSTLE AND SKITTER LIKE FAIRIES, BEGGING MATT TO JOIN IN THE DANCE...
...THE CITY NEVER SLEEPS!
DOWN THE STREET--WARMTH AND KINDNESS TO A SHIVERING SOUL...
GOD BLESS YOU, MAN.
...MUSIC FROM CAR RADIOS--IN A HUNDRED DIFFERENT LANGUAGES--
--DOGS YIP AND BARK AND WHINE--
--ONE HOWLS--CELEBRATING THE NIGHT...

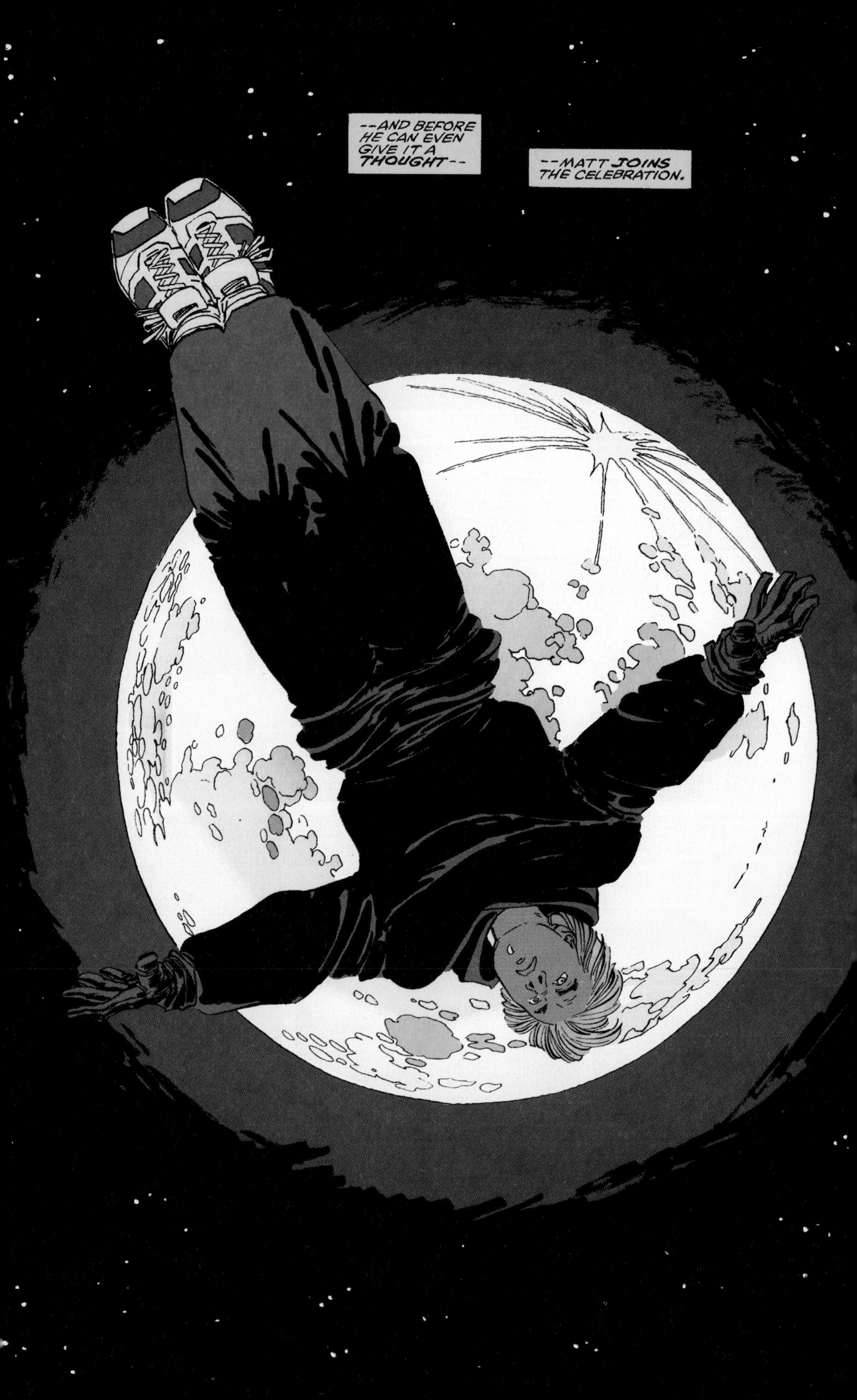
--AND BEFORE HE CAN EVEN GIVE IT A THOUGHT--
--MATT JOINS THE CELEBRATION.

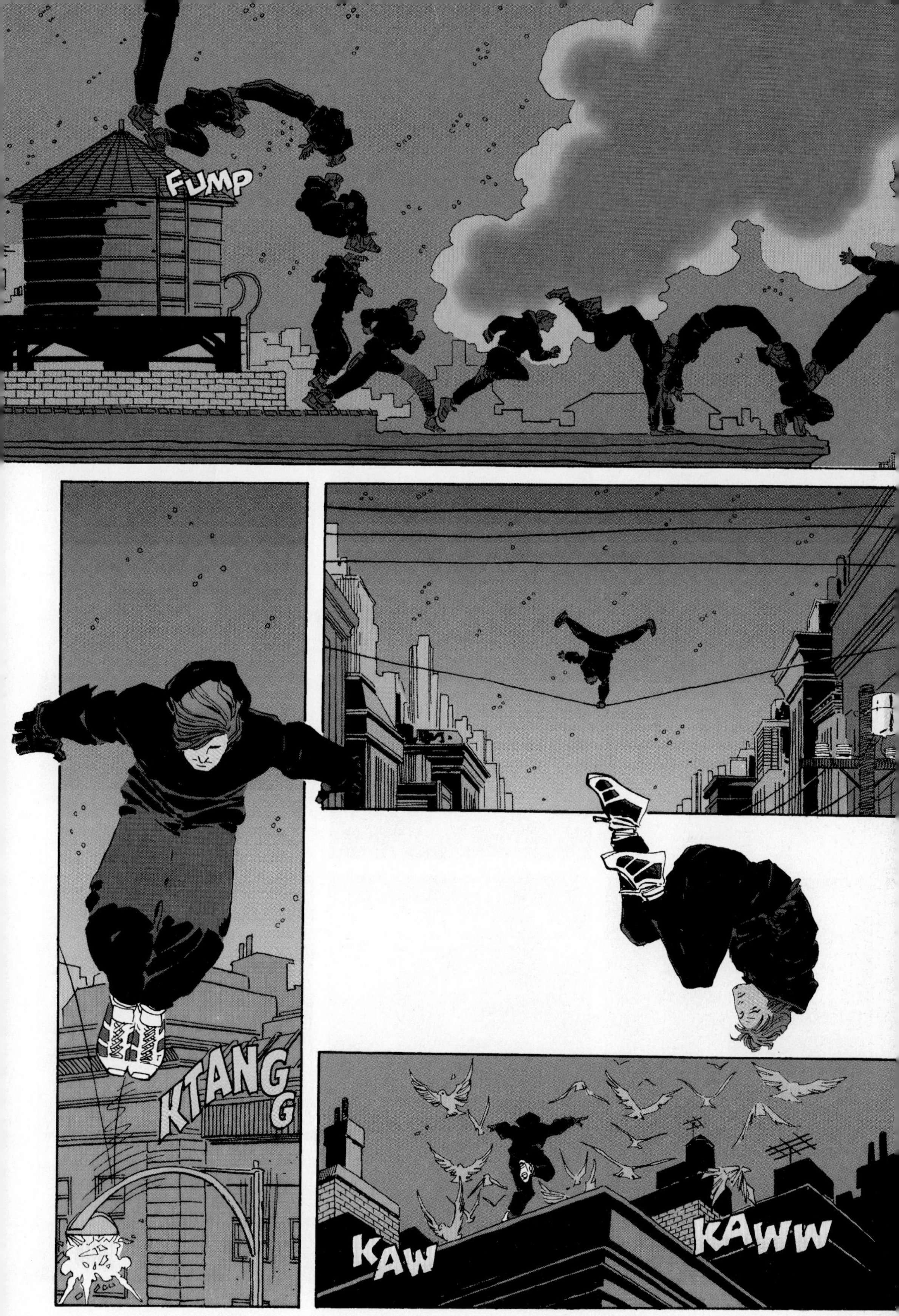
FUMP
KTANG
G
KAW
KAWW

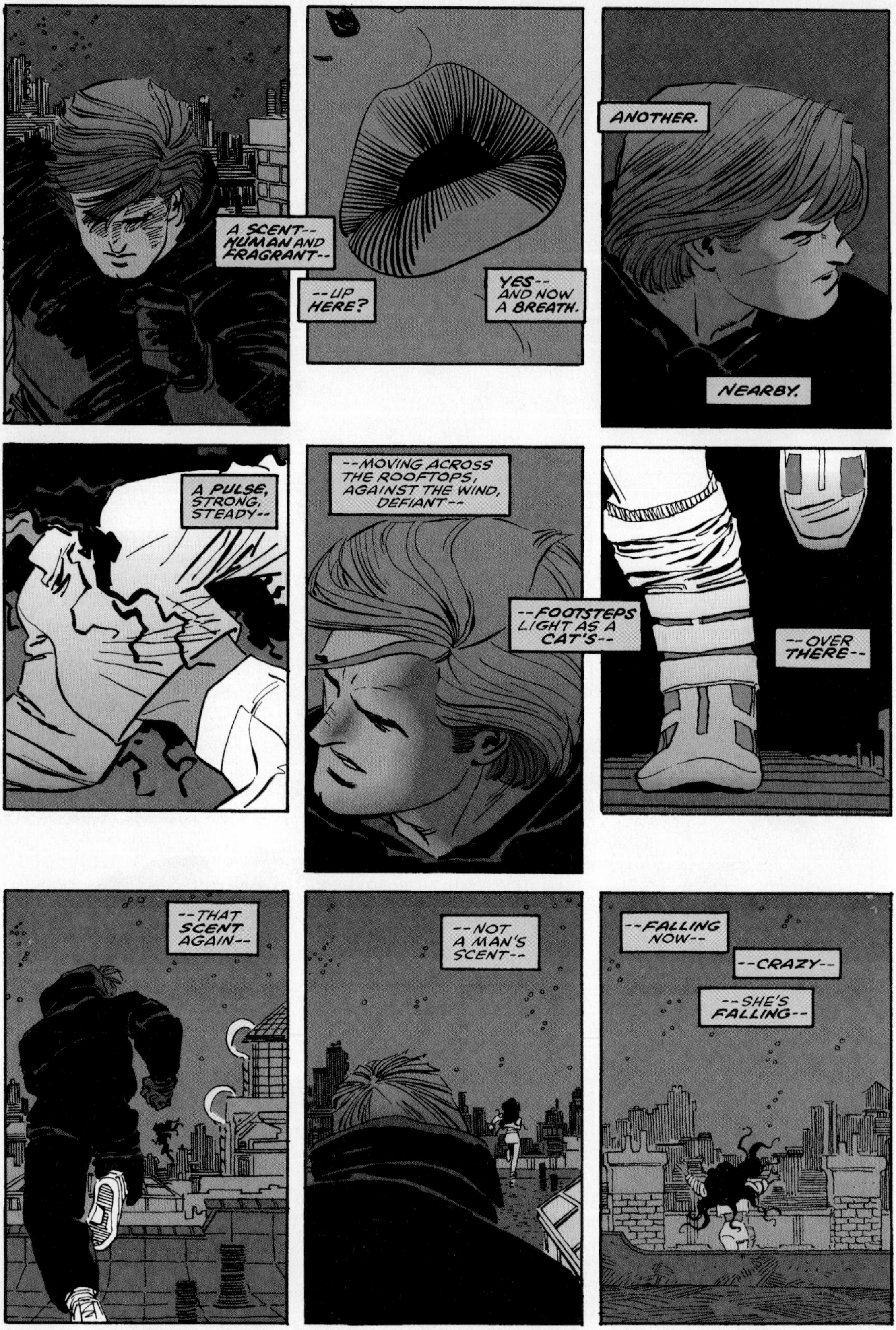
A SCENT--
HUMAN AND
FRAGRANT--
--UP
HERE?
YES--
AND NOW
A BREATH.
ANOTHER.
NEARBY.
A PULSE,
STRONG,
STEADY--
--MOVING ACROSS
THE ROOFTOPS,
AGAINST THE WIND,
DEFIANT--
--FOOTSTEPS
LIGHT AS A
CAT'S--
--OVER
THERE--
--THAT
SCENT
AGAIN--
--NOT
A MAN'S
SCENT--
--FALLING
NOW--
--CRAZY--
--SHE'S
FALLING--

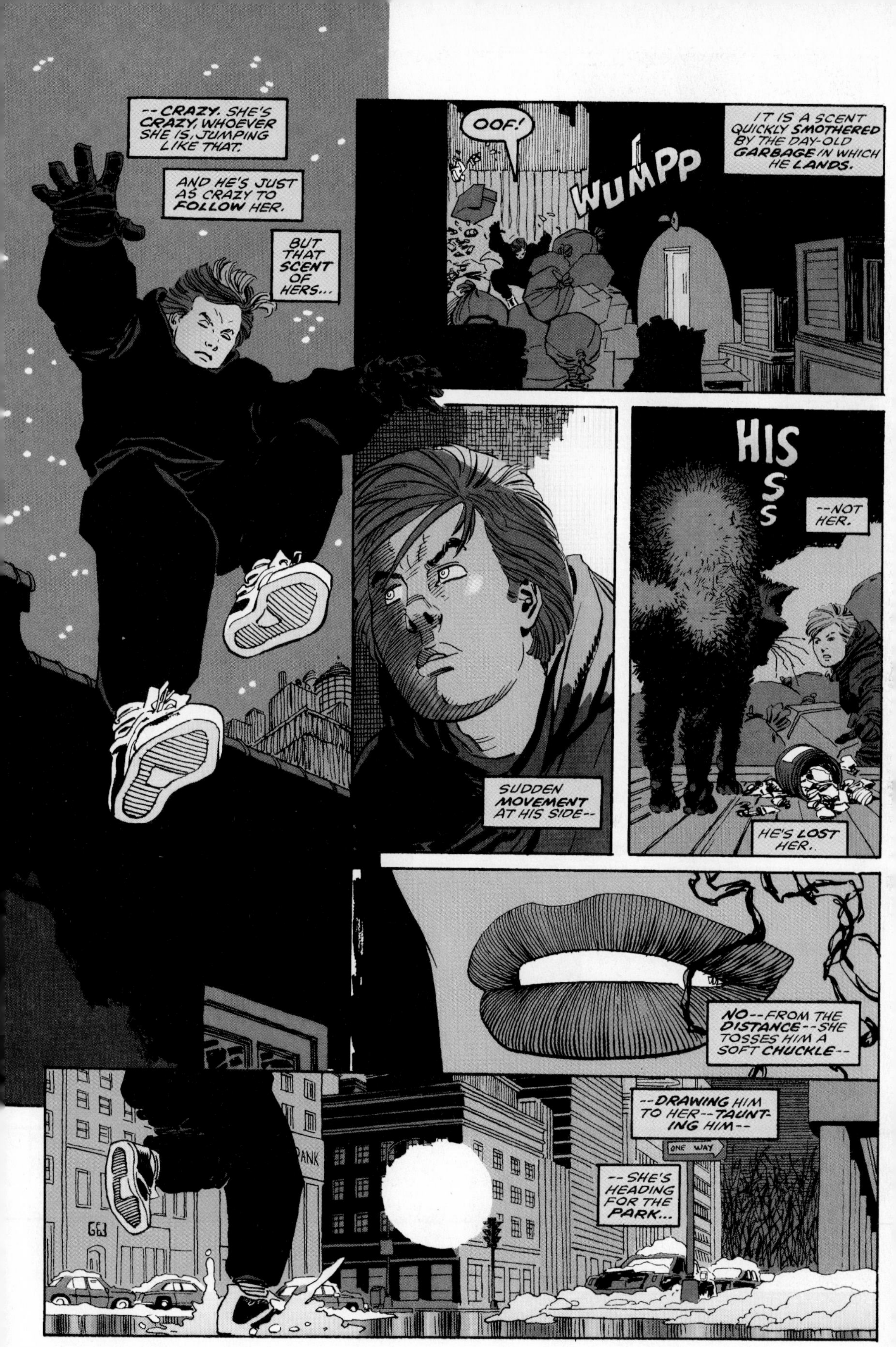
--CRAZY. SHE'S CRAZY, WHOEVER SHE IS, JUMPING LIKE THAT.
AND HE'S JUST AS CRAZY TO FOLLOW HER.
BUT THAT SCENT OF HERS...
OOF!
WUMPP
IT IS A SCENT QUICKLY SMOTHERED BY THE DAY-OLD GARBAGE IN WHICH HE LANDS.
SUDDEN MOVEMENT AT HIS SIDE--
HISSS
--NOT HER.
HE'S LOST HER.
NO--FROM THE DISTANCE--SHE TOSSES HIM A SOFT CHUCKLE--
--DRAWING HIM TO HER--TAUNTING HIM--
ONE WAY
--SHE'S HEADING FOR THE PARK...

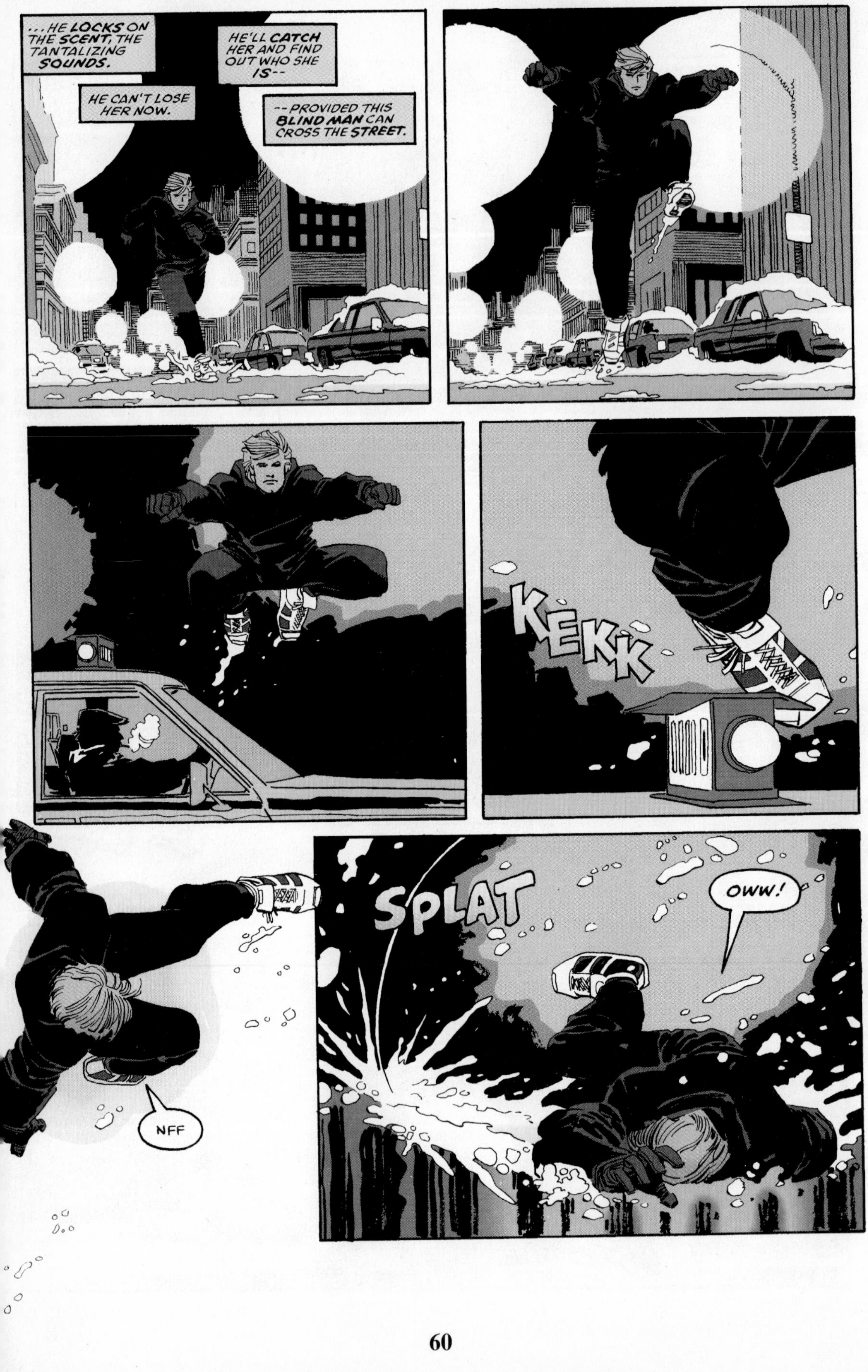
...HE LOCKS ON THE SCENT, THE TANTALIZING SOUNDS.
HE CAN'T LOSE HER NOW.
HE'LL CATCH HER AND FIND OUT WHO SHE IS--
--PROVIDED THIS BLIND MAN CAN CROSS THE STREET.
KEKK
SPLAT
OWW!
NFF

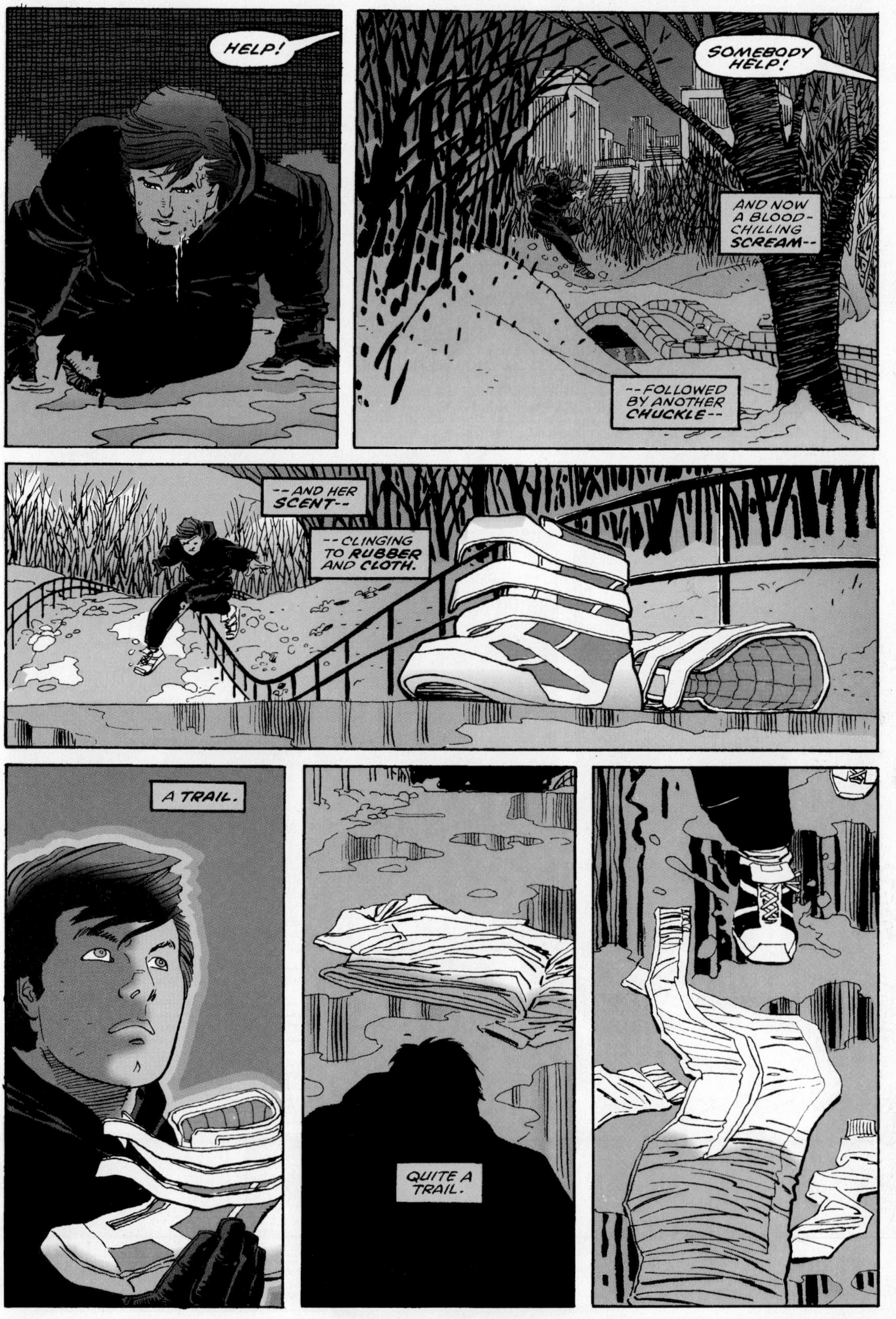
HELP!
SOMEBODY HELP!
AND NOW A BLOOD-CHILLING SCREAM--
--FOLLOWED BY ANOTHER CHUCKLE--
--AND HER SCENT--
--CLINGING TO RUBBER AND CLOTH.
A TRAIL.
QUITE A TRAIL.

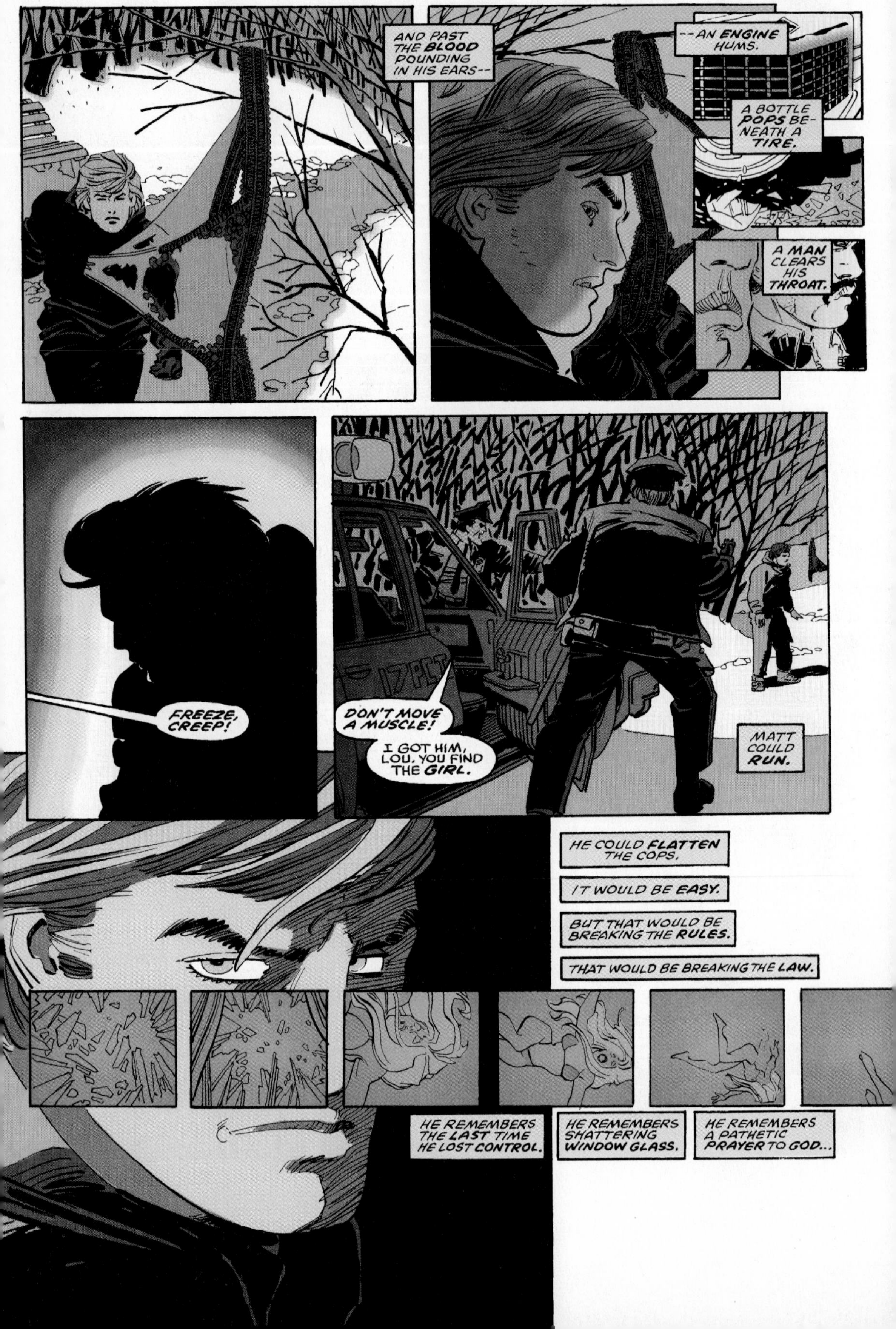
AND PAST THE BLOOD POUNDING IN HIS EARS--
--AN ENGINE HUMS.
A BOTTLE POPS BENEATH A TIRE.
A MAN CLEARS HIS THROAT.
FREEZE, CREEP!
DON'T MOVE A MUSCLE!
I GOT HIM, LOU. YOU FIND THE GIRL.
MATT COULD RUN.
HE COULD FLATTEN THE COPS.
IT WOULD BE EASY.
BUT THAT WOULD BE BREAKING THE RULES.
THAT WOULD BE BREAKING THE LAW.
HE REMEMBERS THE LAST TIME HE LOST CONTROL.
HE REMEMBERS SHATTERING WINDOW GLASS.
HE REMEMBERS A PATHETIC PRAYER TO GOD...

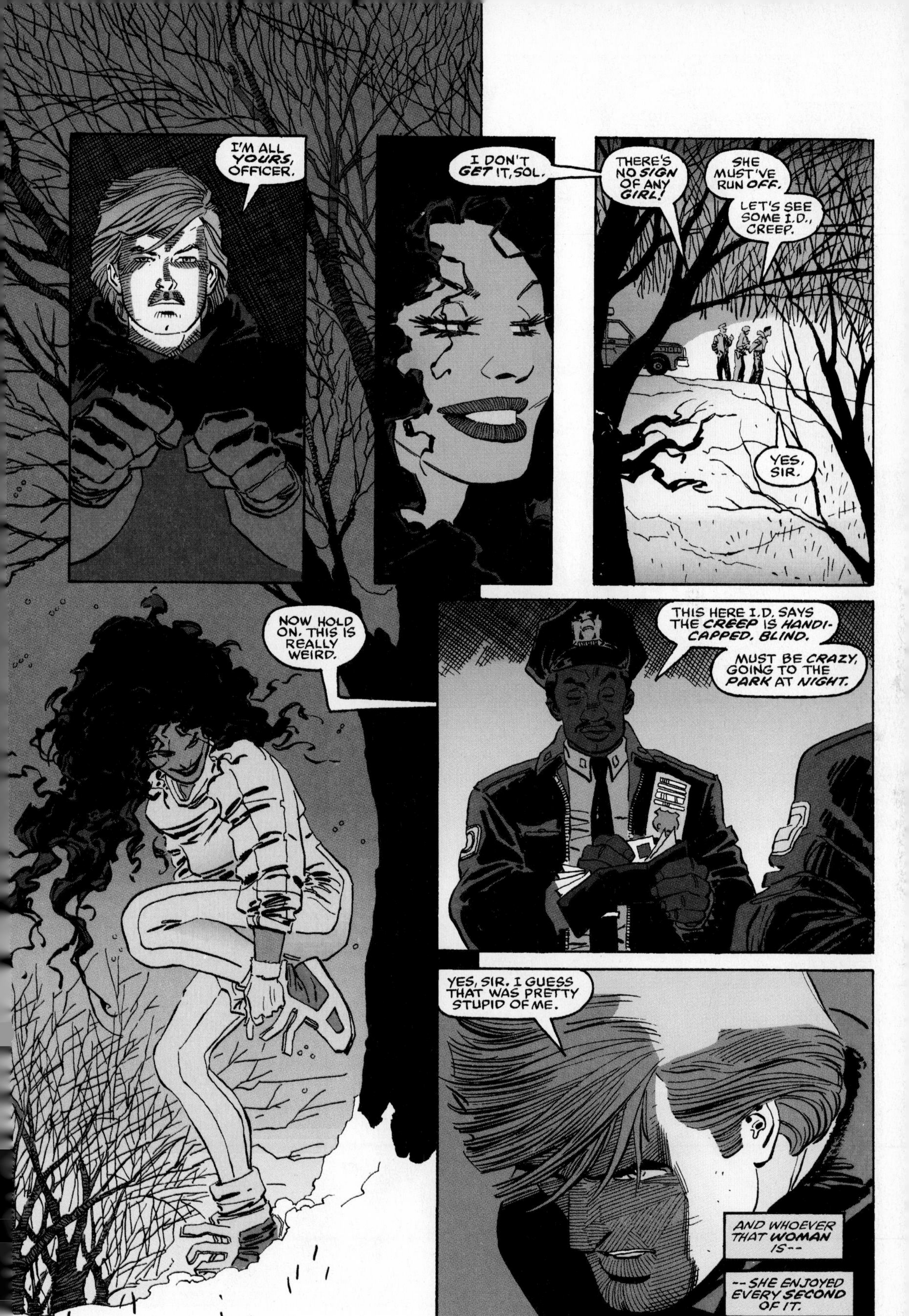
I'M ALL YOURS, OFFICER.
I DON'T GET IT, SOL.
THERE'S NO SIGN OF ANY GIRL!
SHE MUST'VE RUN OFF.
LET'S SEE SOME I.D., CREEP.
YES, SIR.
NOW HOLD ON. THIS IS REALLY WEIRD.
THIS HERE I.D. SAYS THE CREEP IS HANDI-CAPPED. BLIND.
MUST BE CRAZY, GOING TO THE PARK AT NIGHT.
YES, SIR. I GUESS THAT WAS PRETTY STUPID OF ME.
AND WHOEVER THAT WOMAN IS--
--SHE ENJOYED EVERY SECOND OF IT.

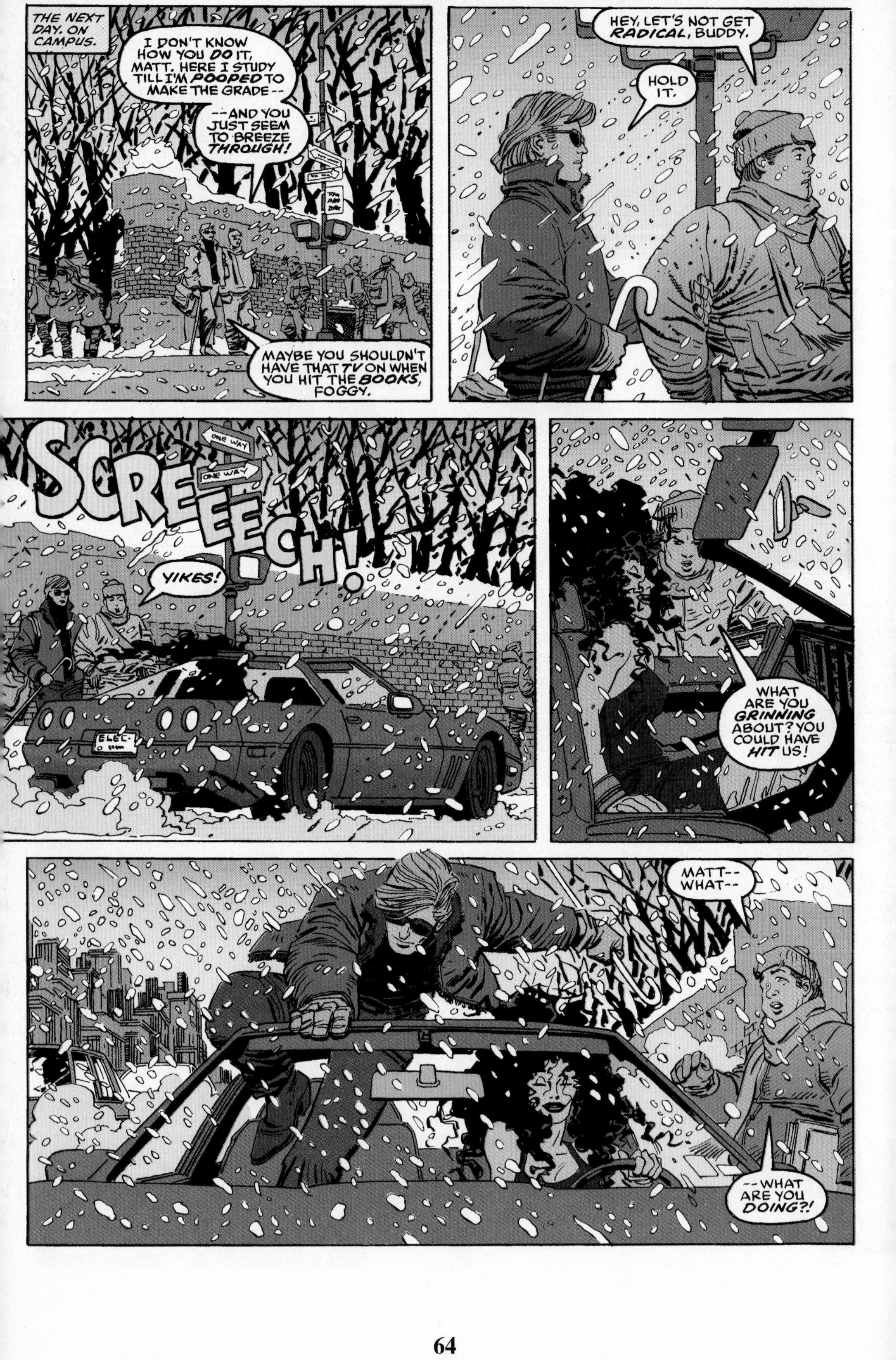
THE NEXT DAY. ON CAMPUS.
I DON'T KNOW HOW YOU DO IT, MATT. HERE I STUDY TILL I'M POOPED TO MAKE THE GRADE--
--AND YOU JUST SEEM TO BREEZE THROUGH!
MAYBE YOU SHOULDN'T HAVE THAT TV ON WHEN YOU HIT THE BOOKS, FOGGY.
HEY, LET'S NOT GET RADICAL, BUDDY.
HOLD IT.
ONE WAY
ONE WAY
SCREEEECH!
YIKES!
WHAT ARE YOU GRINNING ABOUT? YOU COULD HAVE HIT US!
MATT-- WHAT--
--WHAT ARE YOU DOING?!

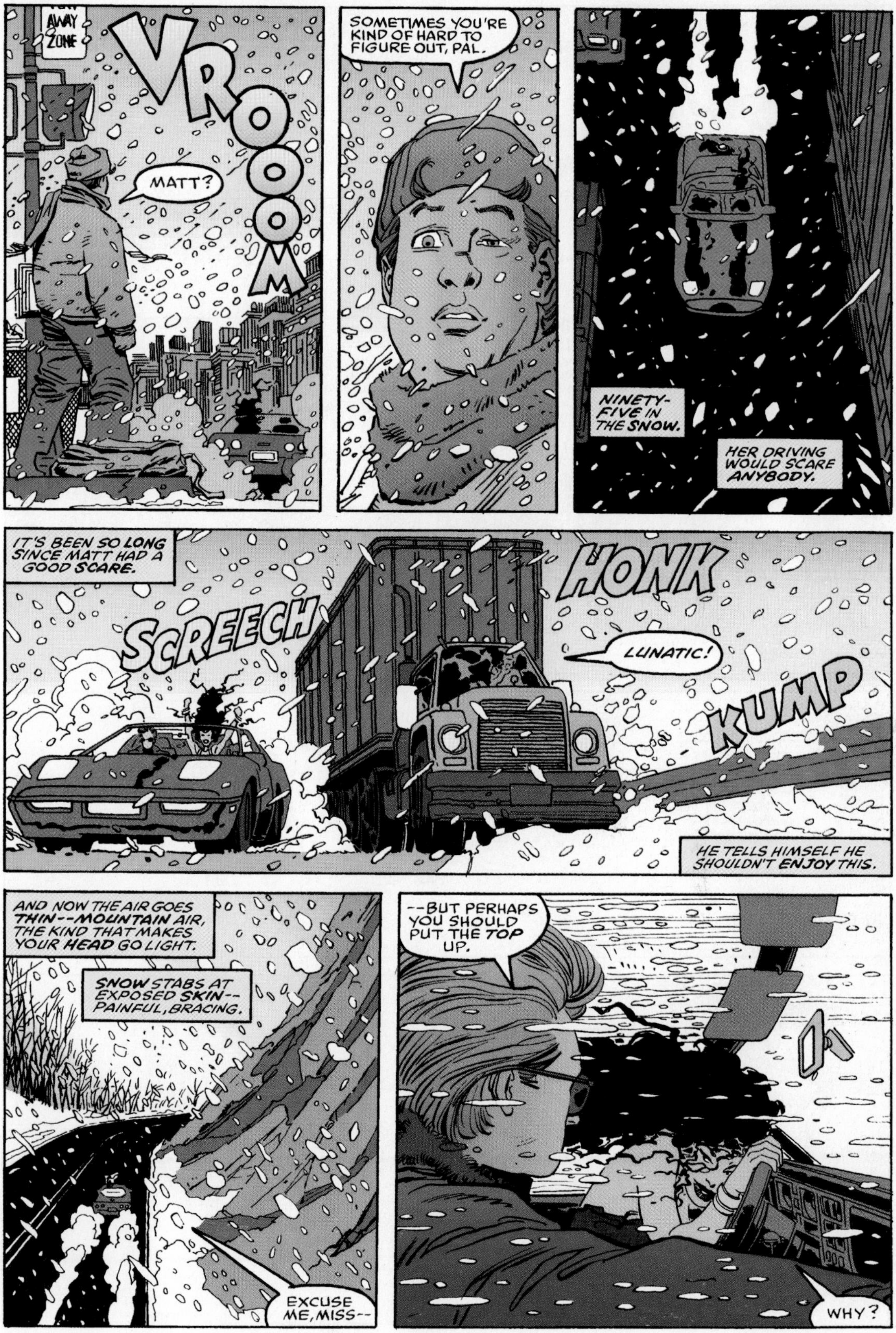
VROOOOM
MATT?
SOMETIMES YOU'RE KIND OF HARD TO FIGURE OUT, PAL.
NINETY-FIVE IN THE SNOW.
HER DRIVING WOULD SCARE ANYBODY.
IT'S BEEN SO LONG SINCE MATT HAD A GOOD SCARE.
SCREECH
HONK
LUNATIC!
KUMP
HE TELLS HIMSELF HE SHOULDN'T ENJOY THIS.
AND NOW THE AIR GOES THIN--MOUNTAIN AIR, THE KIND THAT MAKES YOUR HEAD GO LIGHT.
SNOW STABS AT EXPOSED SKIN--PAINFUL, BRACING.
EXCUSE ME, MISS--
--BUT PERHAPS YOU SHOULD PUT THE TOP UP.
WHY?

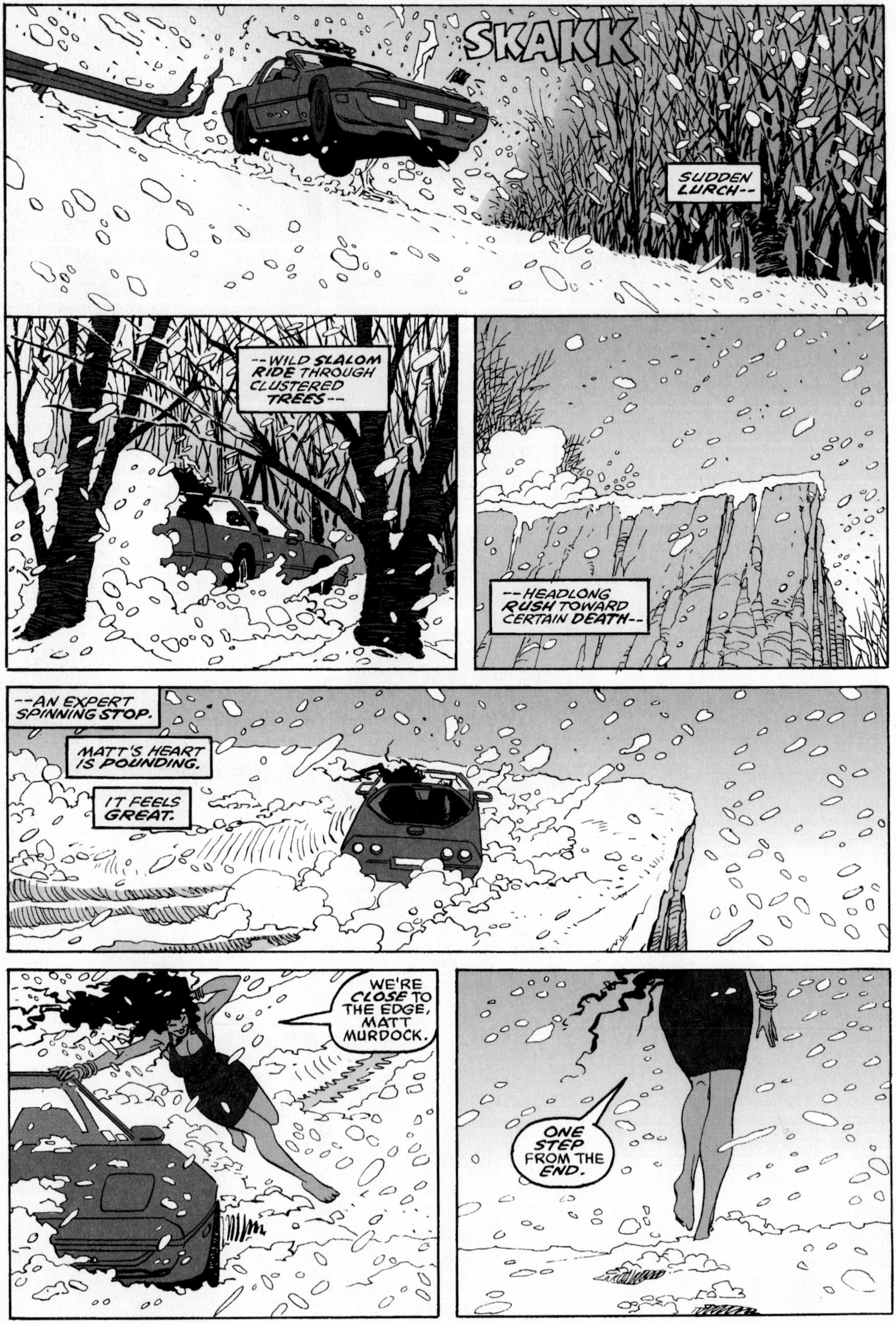
SKAKK
SUDDEN LURCH--
--WILD SLALOM RIDE THROUGH CLUSTERED TREES--
--HEADLONG RUSH TOWARD CERTAIN DEATH--
--AN EXPERT SPINNING STOP.
MATT'S HEART IS POUNDING.
IT FEELS GREAT.
WE'RE CLOSE TO THE EDGE, MATT MURDOCK.
ONE STEP FROM THE END.

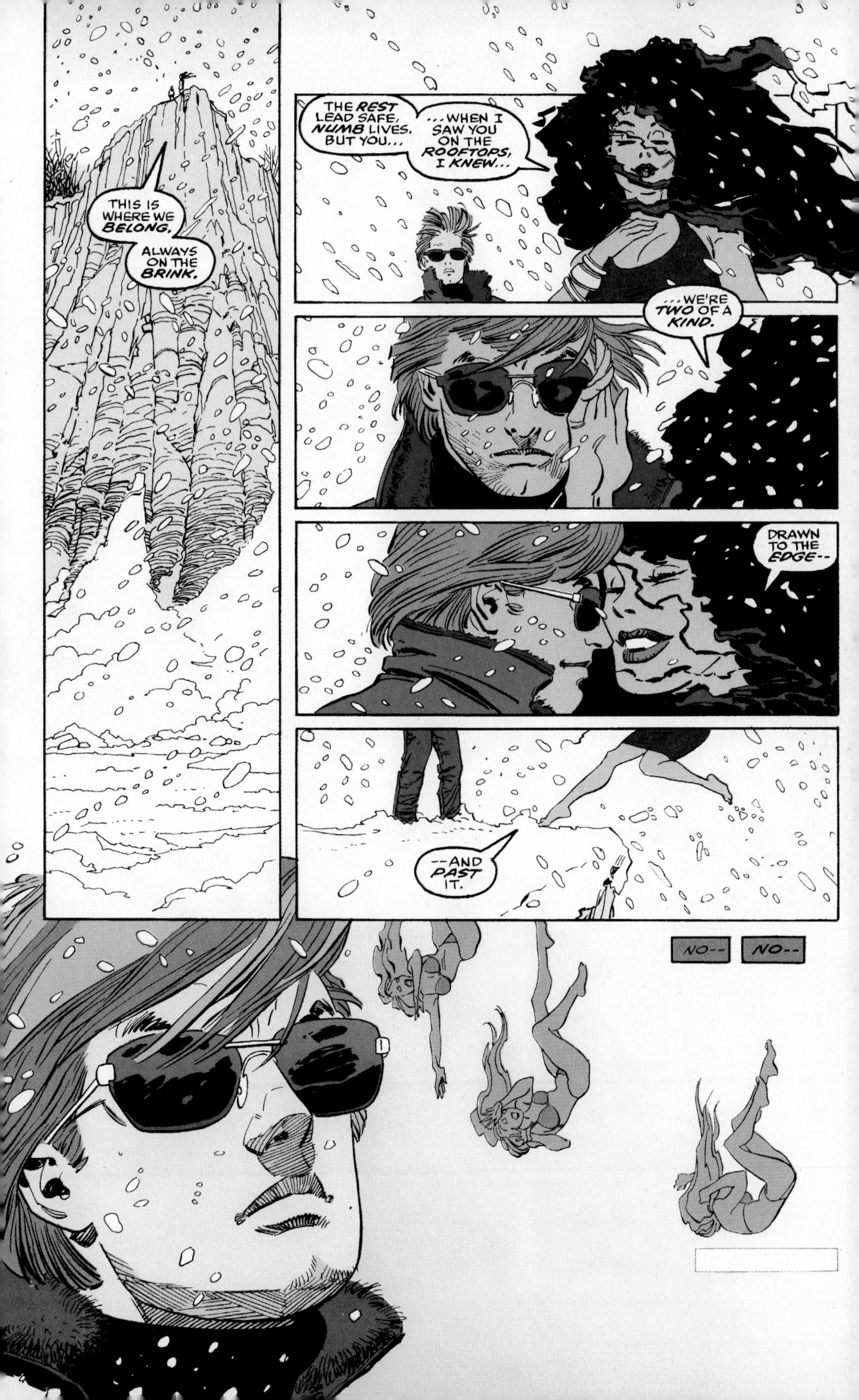
THIS IS WHERE WE BELONG.
ALWAYS ON THE BRINK.
THE REST LEAD SAFE, NUMB LIVES. BUT YOU...
...WHEN I SAW YOU ON THE ROOFTOPS, I KNEW...
...WE'RE TWO OF A KIND.
DRAWN TO THE EDGE--
--AND PAST IT.
NO--
NO--

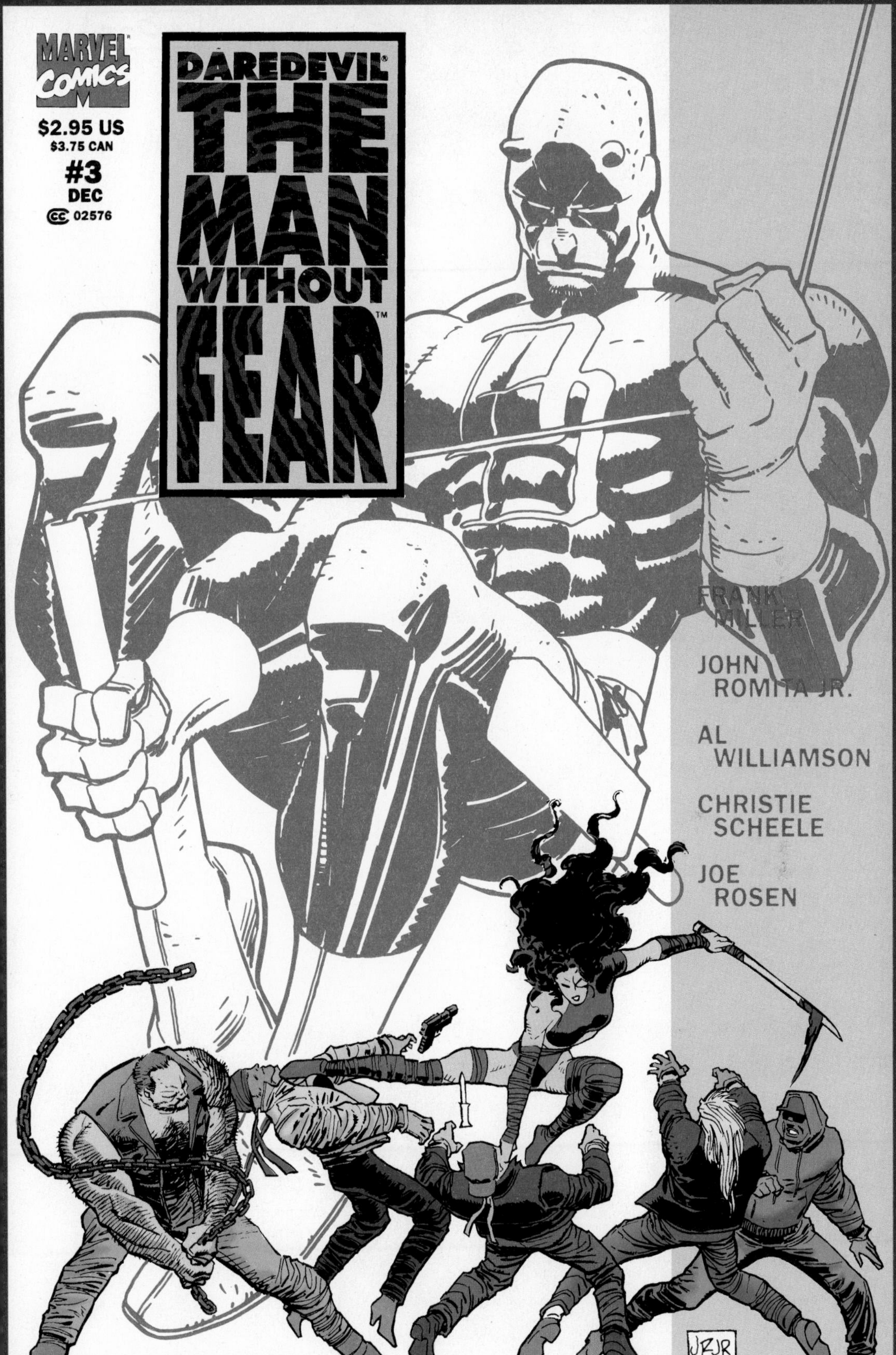
MARVEL COMICS
$2.95 US
$3.75 CAN
#3
DEC
02576
DAREDEVIL
THE MAN WITHOUT FEAR
FRANK MILLER
JOHN ROMITA JR.
AL WILLIAMSON
CHRISTIE SCHEELE
JOE ROSEN

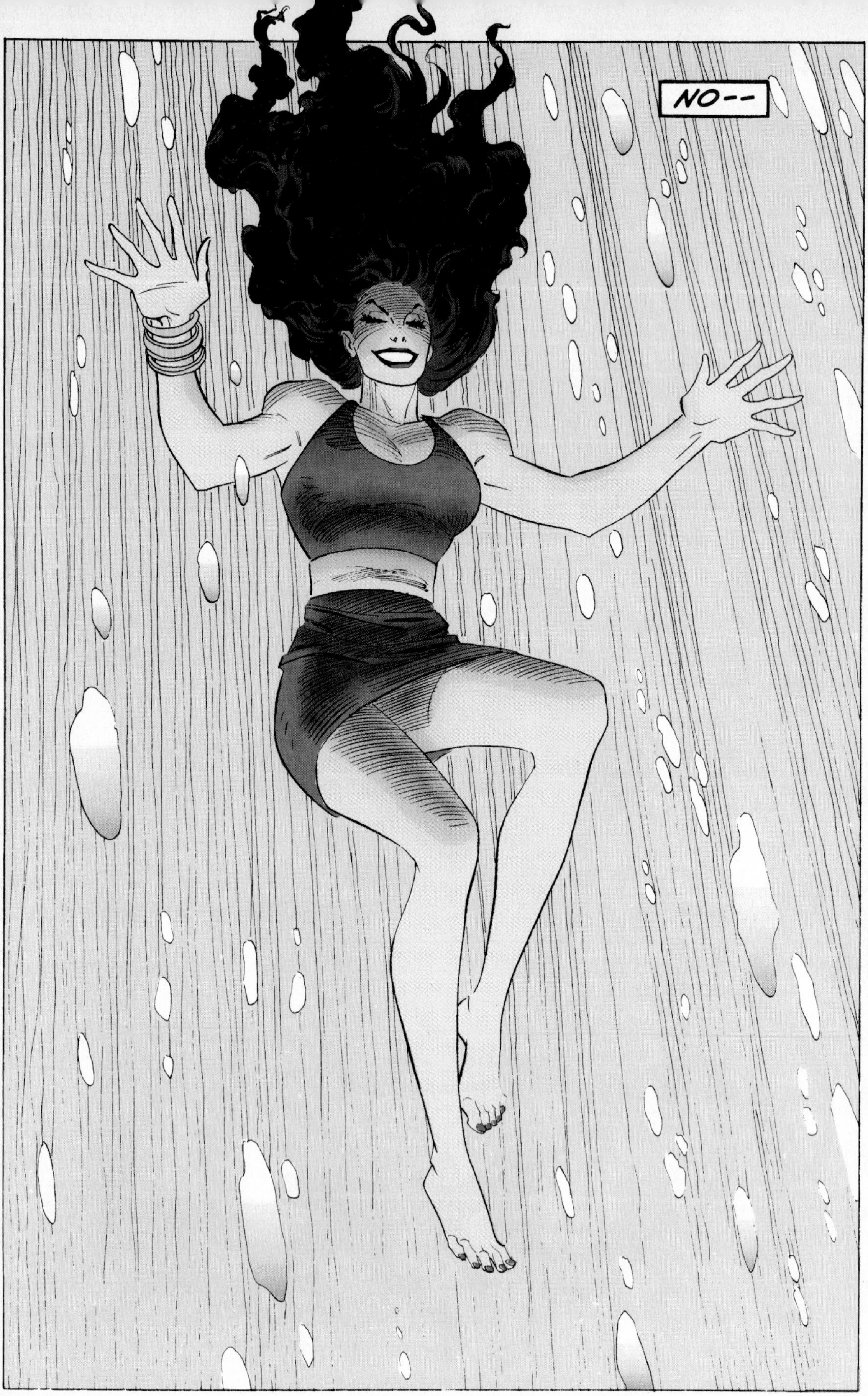
NO--

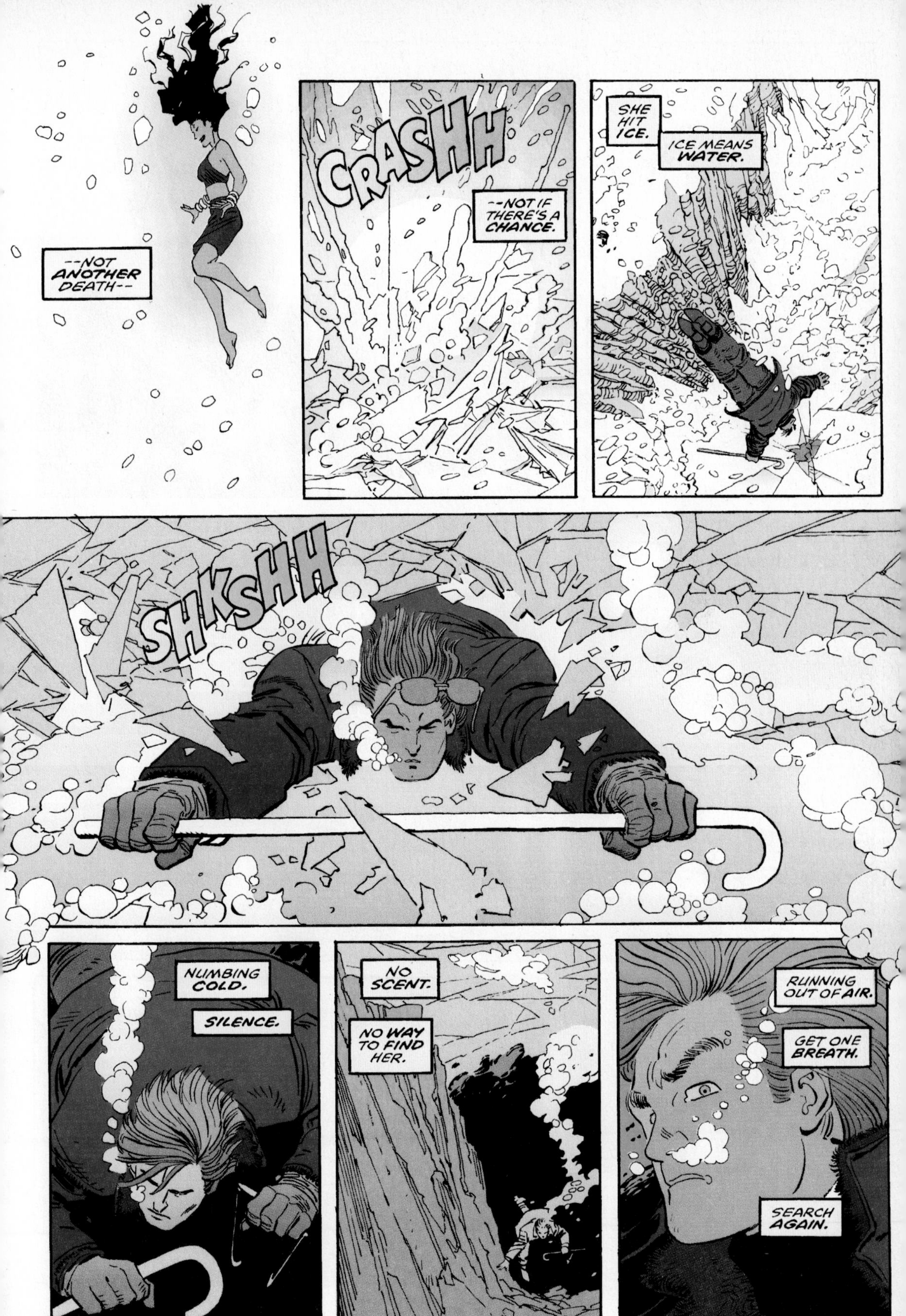
--NOT
ANOTHER
DEATH--
CRASHH
--NOT IF
THERE'S A
CHANCE.
SHE
HIT
ICE.
ICE MEANS
WATER.
SHKSHH
NUMBING
COLD.
SILENCE.
NO
SCENT.
NO WAY
TO FIND
HER.
RUNNING
OUT OF AIR.
GET ONE
BREATH.
SEARCH
AGAIN.

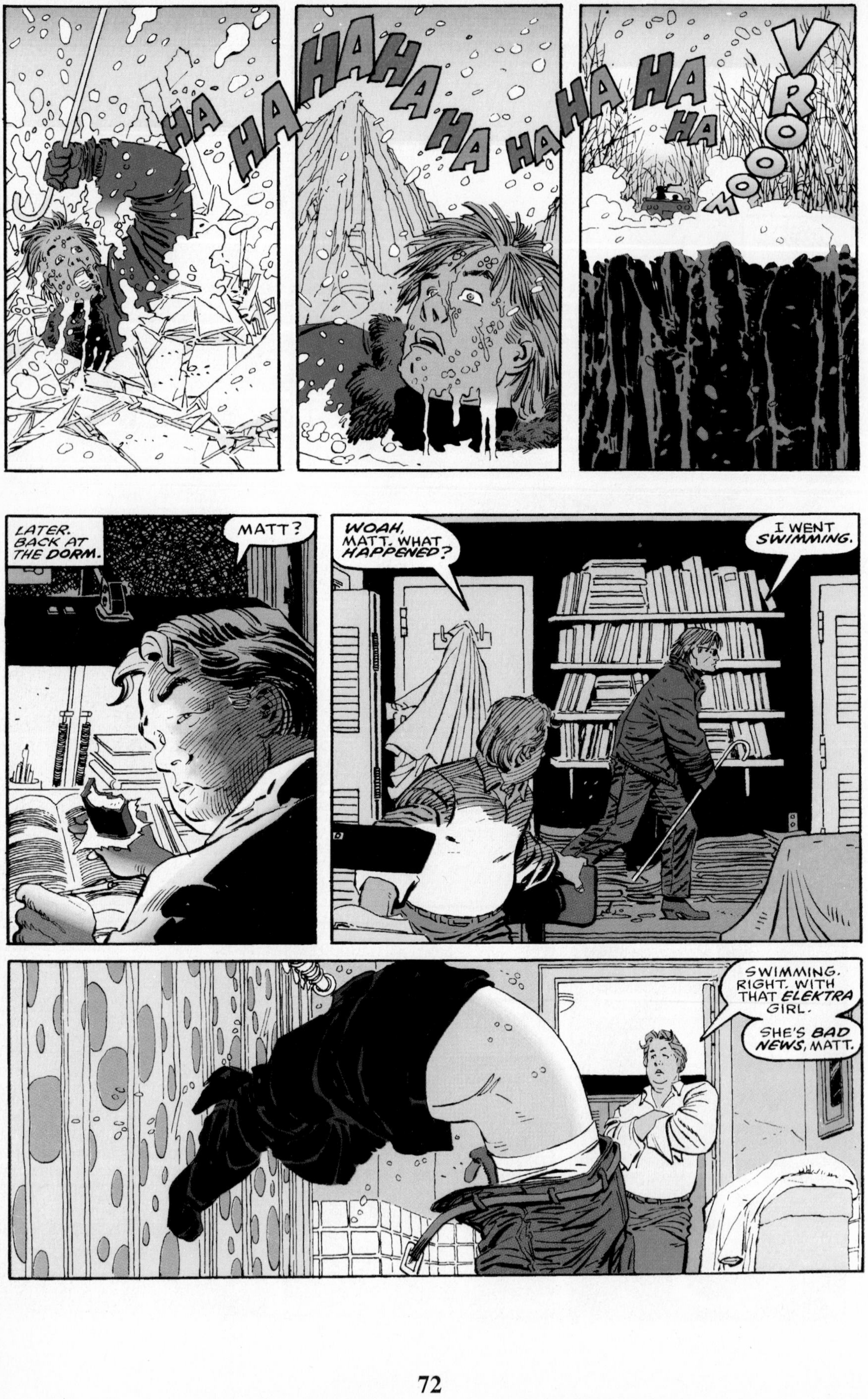

HA HA HA HA HA HA HA HA HA HA HA HA
VROOOOM
LATER. BACK AT THE DORM.
MATT?
WOAH, MATT. WHAT HAPPENED?
I WENT SWIMMING.
SWIMMING. RIGHT. WITH THAT ELEKTRA GIRL.
SHE'S BAD NEWS, MATT.

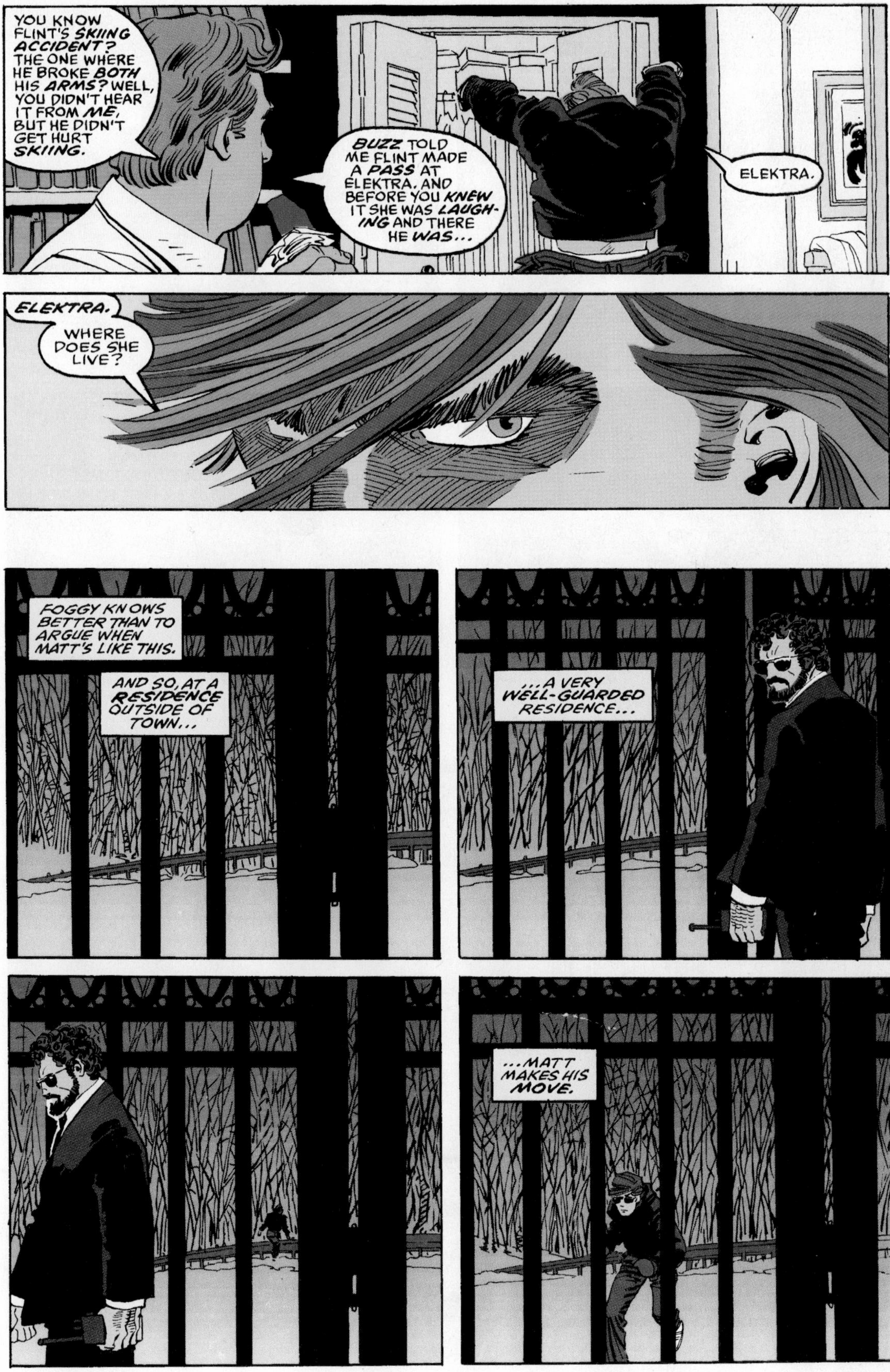
YOU KNOW FLINT'S SKIING ACCIDENT? THE ONE WHERE HE BROKE BOTH HIS ARMS? WELL, YOU DIDN'T HEAR IT FROM ME, BUT HE DIDN'T GET HURT SKIING.
BUZZ TOLD ME FLINT MADE A PASS AT ELEKTRA. AND BEFORE YOU KNEW IT SHE WAS LAUGHING AND THERE HE WAS...
ELEKTRA.
ELEKTRA.
WHERE DOES SHE LIVE?
FOGGY KNOWS BETTER THAN TO ARGUE WHEN MATT'S LIKE THIS.
AND SO, AT A RESIDENCE OUTSIDE OF TOWN...
...A VERY WELL-GUARDED RESIDENCE...
...MATT MAKES HIS MOVE.

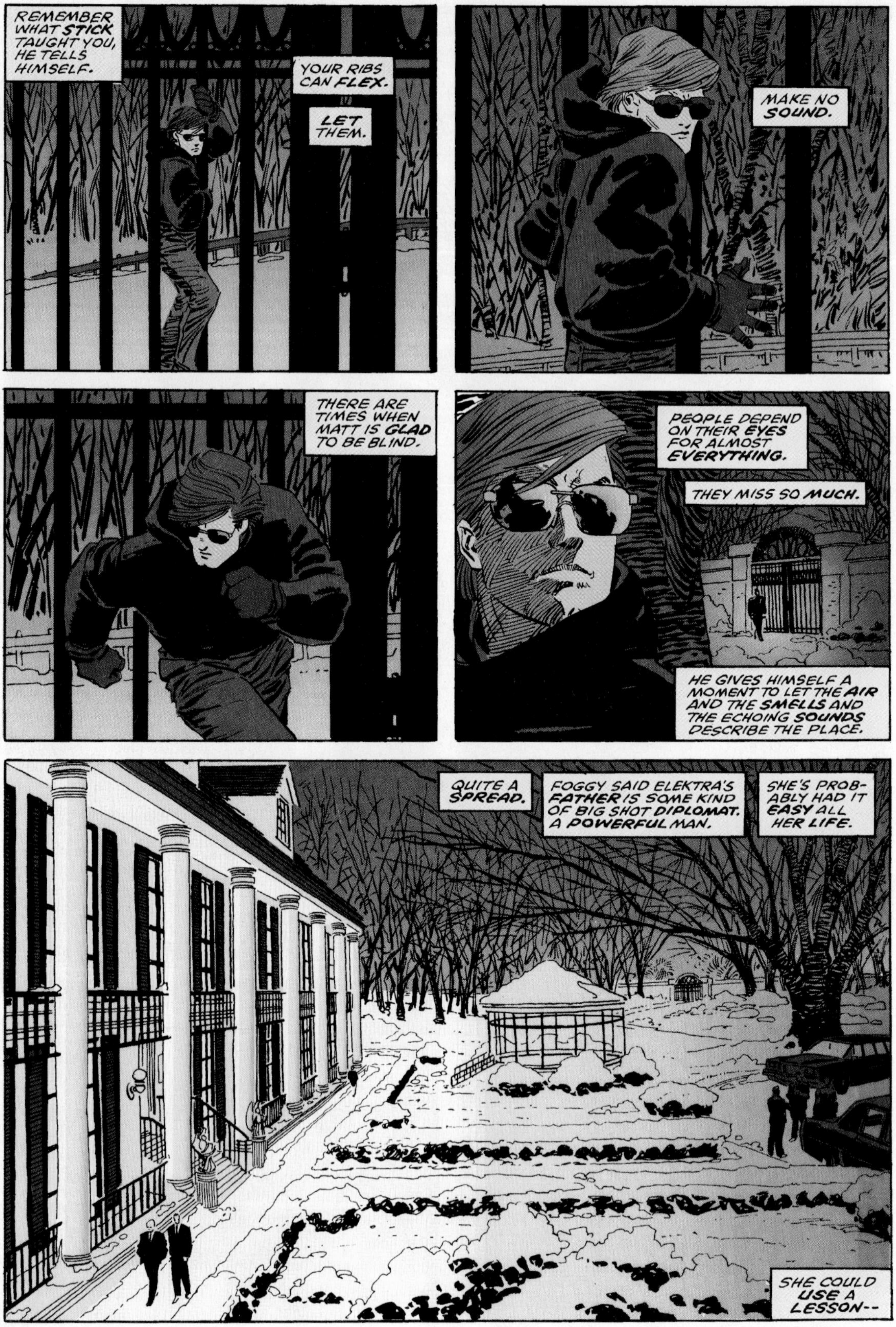
REMEMBER WHAT STICK TAUGHT YOU, HE TELLS HIMSELF.
YOUR RIBS CAN FLEX.
LET THEM.
MAKE NO SOUND.
THERE ARE TIMES WHEN MATT IS GLAD TO BE BLIND.
PEOPLE DEPEND ON THEIR EYES FOR ALMOST EVERYTHING.
THEY MISS SO MUCH.
HE GIVES HIMSELF A MOMENT TO LET THE AIR AND THE SMELLS AND THE ECHOING SOUNDS DESCRIBE THE PLACE.
QUITE A SPREAD.
FOGGY SAID ELEKTRA'S FATHER IS SOME KIND OF BIG SHOT DIPLOMAT. A POWERFUL MAN.
SHE'S PROBABLY HAD IT EASY ALL HER LIFE.
SHE COULD USE A LESSON--

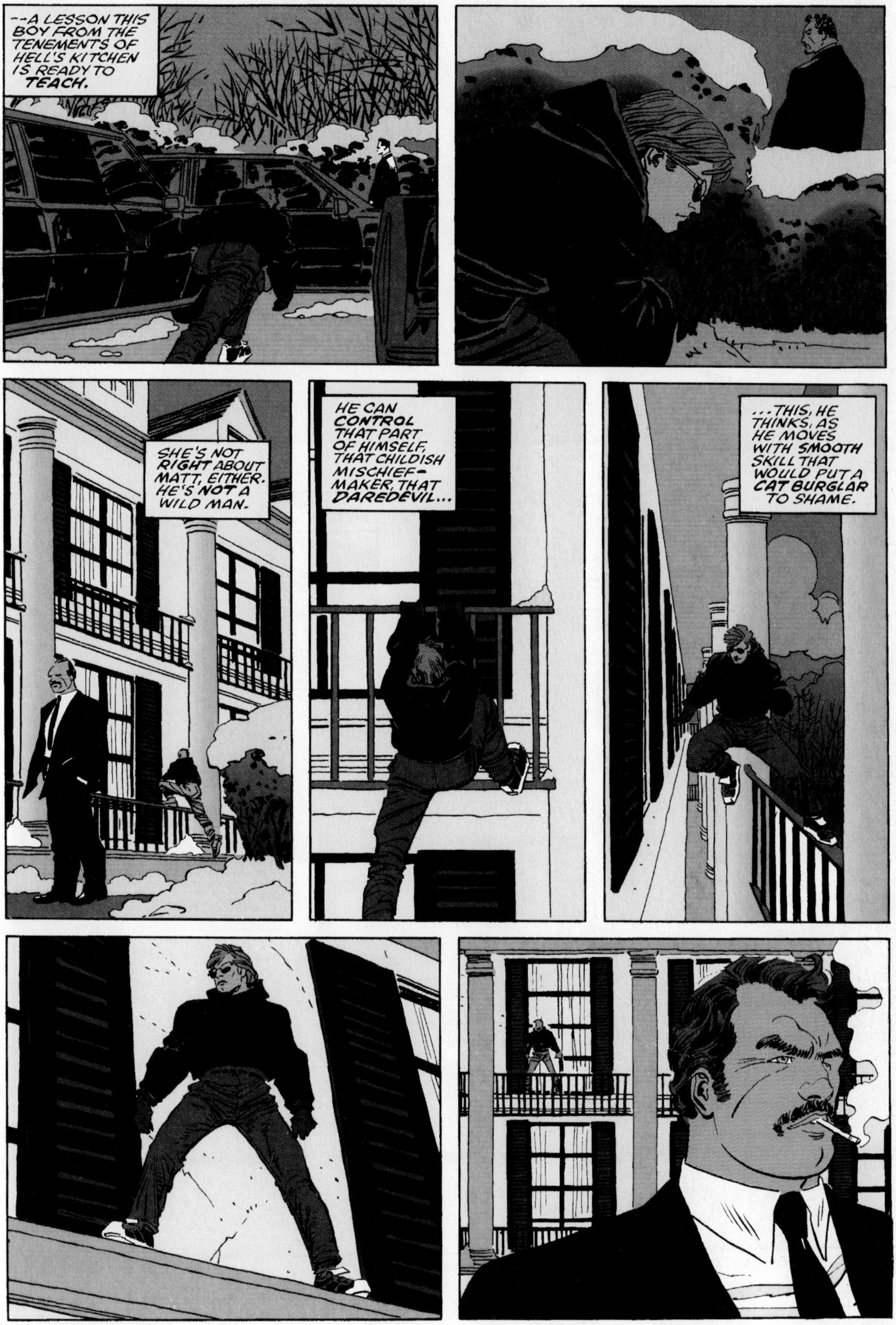
--A LESSON THIS BOY FROM THE TENEMENTS OF HELL'S KITCHEN IS READY TO TEACH.
SHE'S NOT RIGHT ABOUT MATT, EITHER. HE'S NOT A WILD MAN.
HE CAN CONTROL THAT PART OF HIMSELF, THAT CHILDISH MISCHIEF-MAKER, THAT DAREDEVIL...
...THIS, HE THINKS, AS HE MOVES WITH SMOOTH SKILL THAT WOULD PUT A CAT BURGLAR TO SHAME.

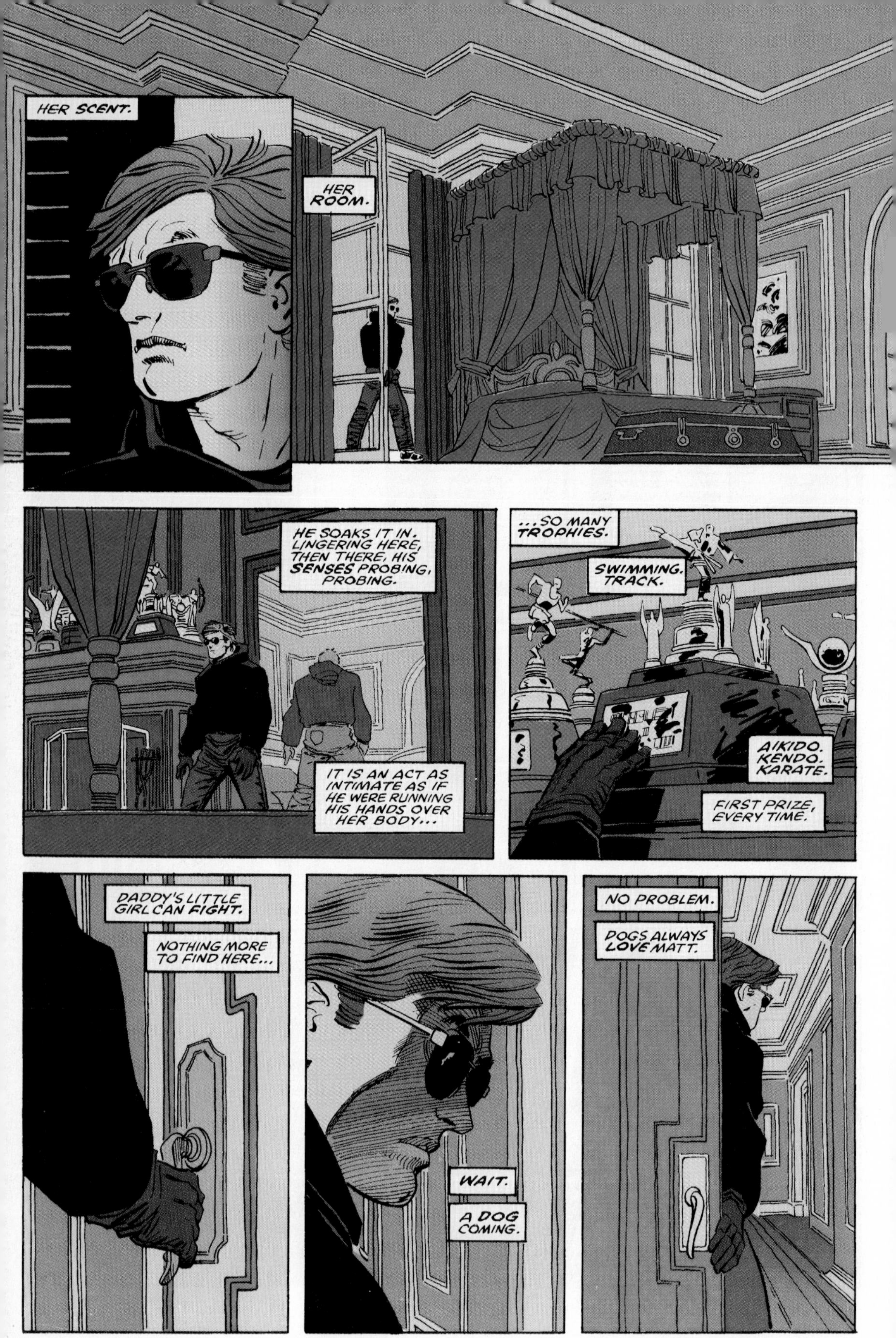
HER SCENT.
HER ROOM.
HE SOAKS IT IN. LINGERING HERE, THEN THERE, HIS SENSES PROBING, PROBING.
IT IS AN ACT AS INTIMATE AS IF HE WERE RUNNING HIS HANDS OVER HER BODY...
...SO MANY TROPHIES.
SWIMMING. TRACK.
AIKIDO. KENDO. KARATE.
FIRST PRIZE, EVERY TIME.
DADDY'S LITTLE GIRL CAN FIGHT.
NOTHING MORE TO FIND HERE...
WAIT.
A DOG COMING.
NO PROBLEM.
DOGS ALWAYS LOVE MATT.

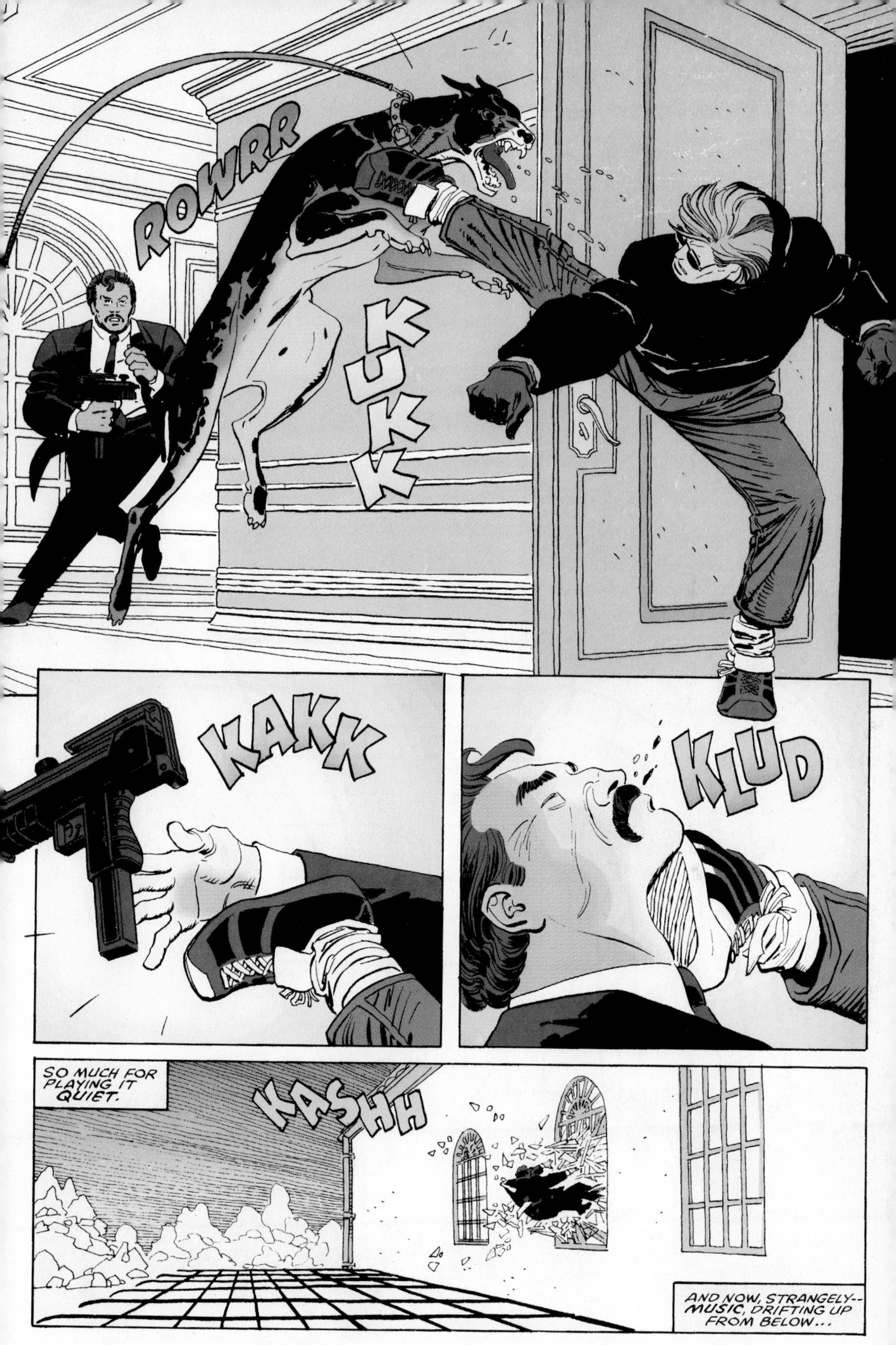
ROWRR
KKUK
KAKK
KLUD
SO MUCH FOR PLAYING IT QUIET.
KASHH
AND NOW, STRANGELY-- MUSIC, DRIFTING UP FROM BELOW...

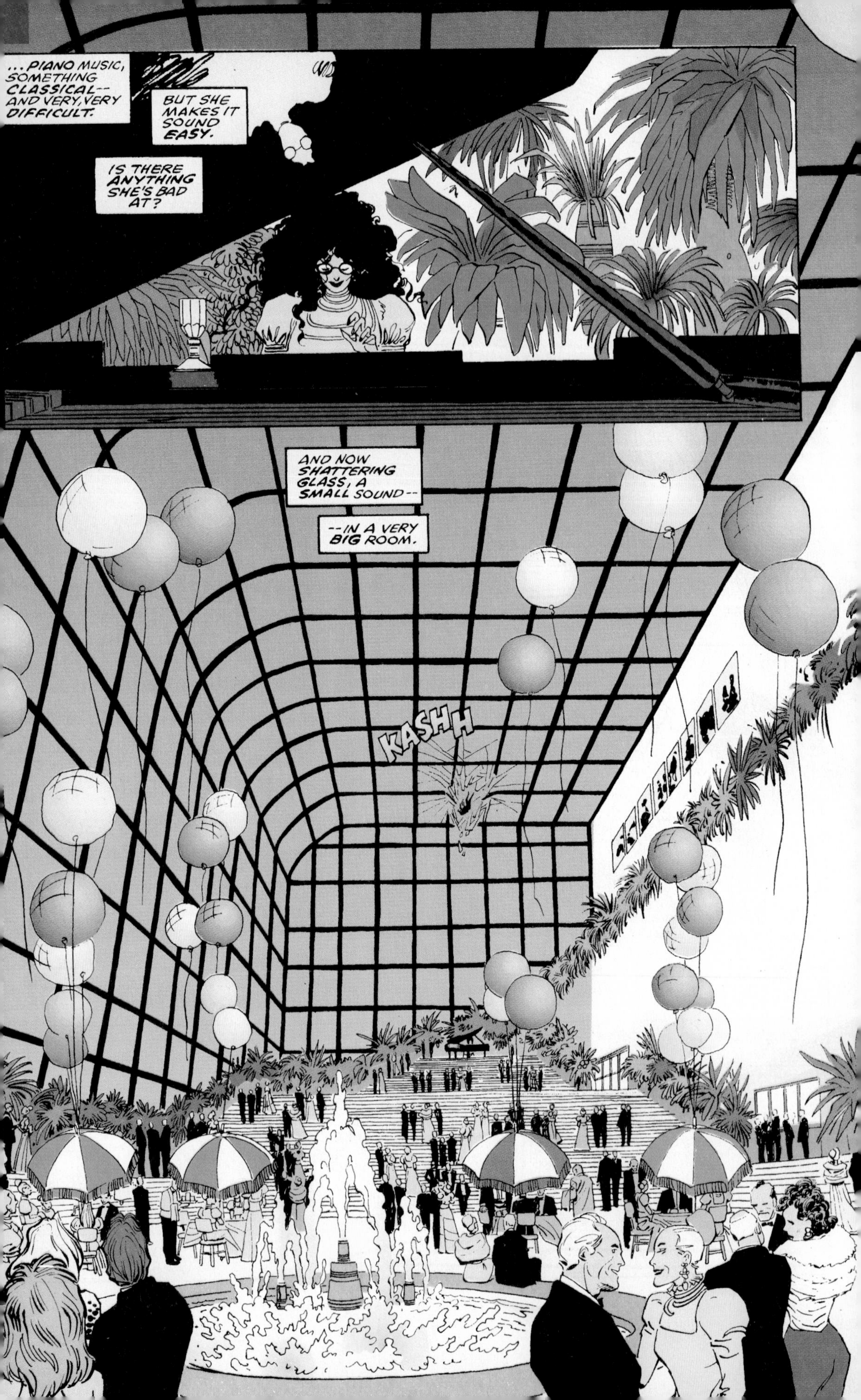
...PIANO MUSIC, SOMETHING CLASSICAL-- AND VERY, VERY DIFFICULT.
BUT SHE MAKES IT SOUND EASY.
IS THERE ANYTHING SHE'S BAD AT?
AND NOW SHATTERING GLASS, A SMALL SOUND--
--IN A VERY BIG ROOM.
KASHH

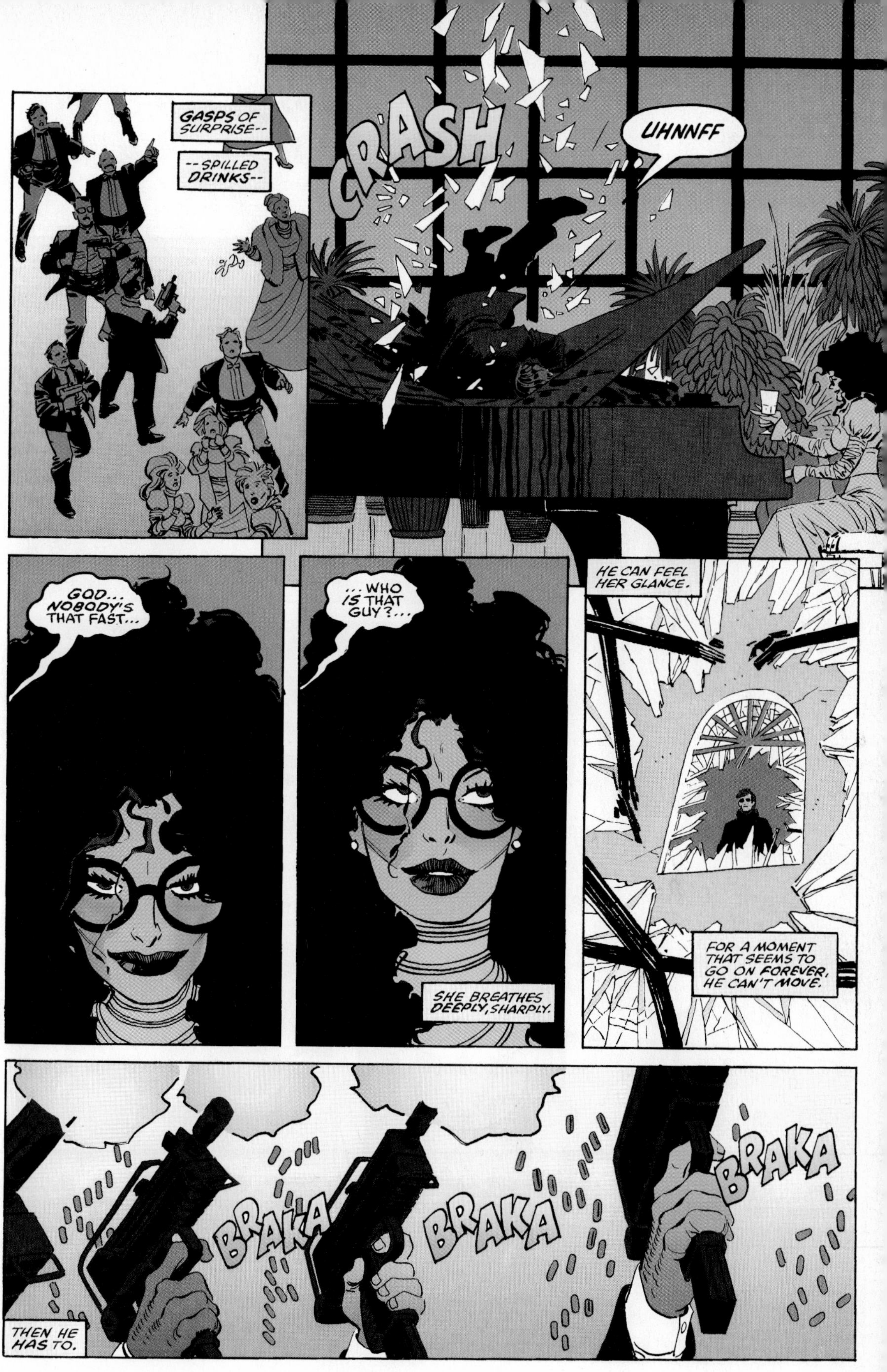
GASPS OF SURPRISE--
--SPILLED DRINKS--
CRASH
UHNNFF
GOD... NOBODY'S THAT FAST...
...WHO IS THAT GUY?...
SHE BREATHES DEEPLY, SHARPLY.
HE CAN FEEL HER GLANCE.
FOR A MOMENT THAT SEEMS TO GO ON FOREVER, HE CAN'T MOVE.
THEN HE HAS TO.
BRAKA
BRAKA
BRAKA

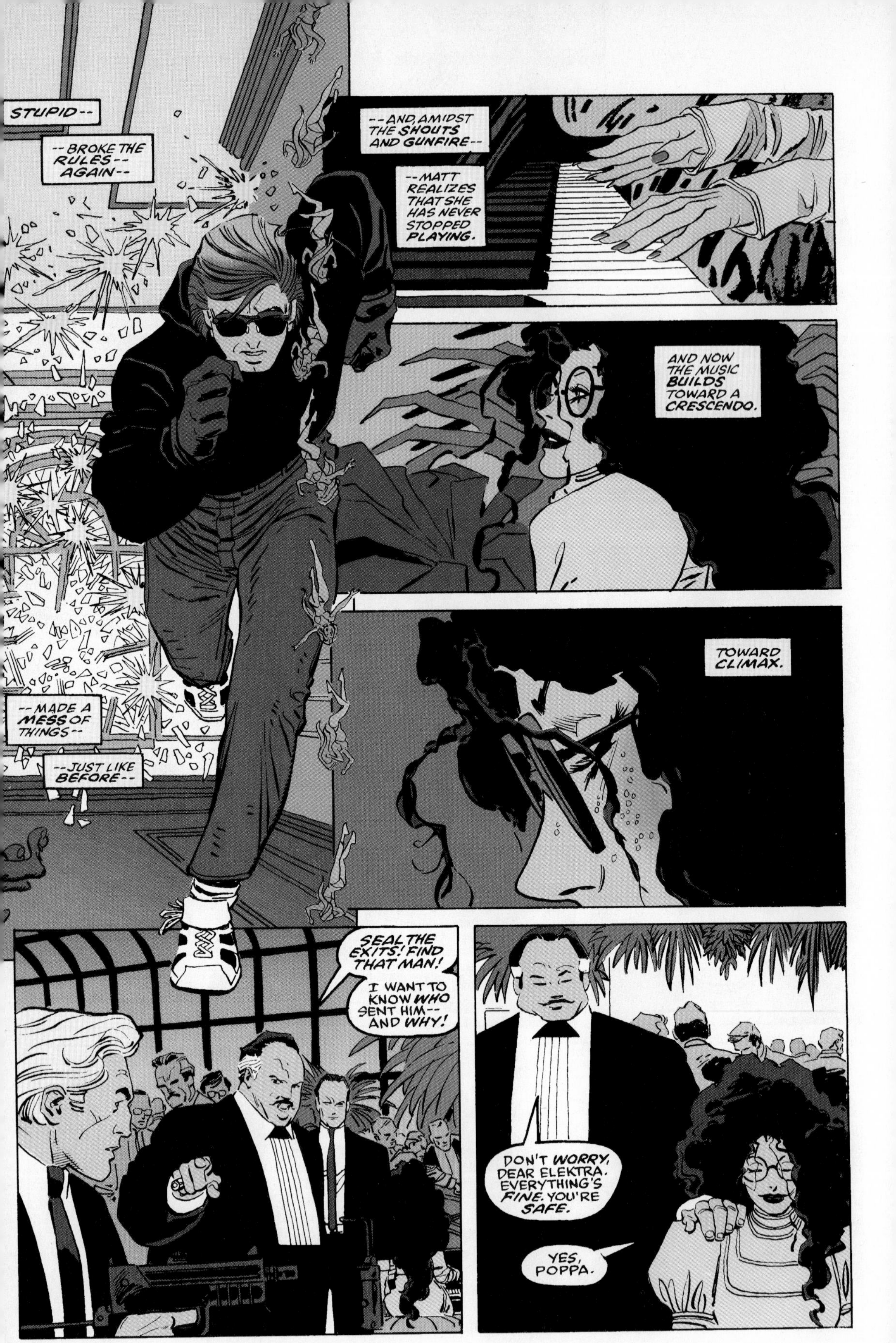
STUPID--
--BROKE THE RULES-- AGAIN--
--AND, AMIDST THE SHOUTS AND GUNFIRE--
--MATT REALIZES THAT SHE HAS NEVER STOPPED PLAYING.
AND NOW THE MUSIC BUILDS TOWARD A CRESCENDO.
TOWARD CLIMAX.
--MADE A MESS OF THINGS--
--JUST LIKE BEFORE--
SEAL THE EXITS! FIND THAT MAN!
I WANT TO KNOW WHO SENT HIM-- AND WHY!
DON'T WORRY, DEAR ELEKTRA. EVERYTHING'S FINE. YOU'RE SAFE.
YES, POPPA.

SIR, I'M *GETTING* SOMETHING, FROM THE *GATE*, THE *SUBJECT* HAS *ESCAPED*--

--HE USED SOME KIND OF *KARATE* MOVE ON *POULOS*-- BUT POULOS GOT A *SHOT* OFF, TAGGED HIM IN THE *ARM*.

HE MUST BE *BLEEDING*.

YES, MISS, HE'S *LOSING A LOT OF BLOOD*, HE *WON'T GET FAR*.

MATT *DOES GET FAR*.

MATT GETS *ALL THE WAY BACK* INTO *TOWN*.

HE *CAN'T RE-MEMBER HOW*.

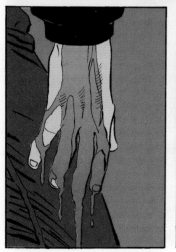

HIS *SENSES* COME AND GO.

HE HAS *NO IDEA* HOW MANY TIMES HE *FALLS*.

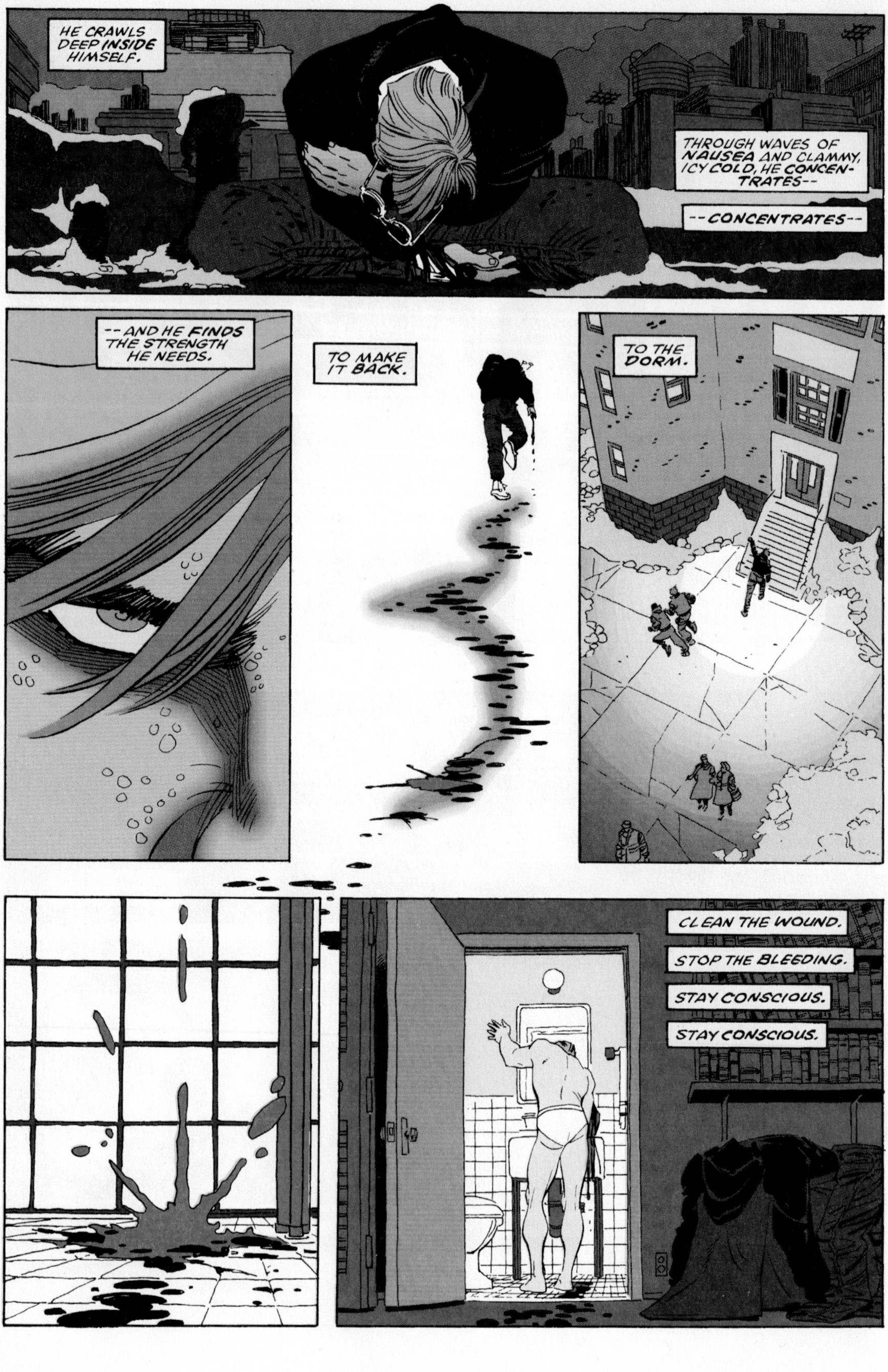
HE CRAWLS DEEP INSIDE HIMSELF.
THROUGH WAVES OF NAUSEA AND CLAMMY, ICY COLD, HE CONCENTRATES--
--CONCENTRATES--
--AND HE FINDS THE STRENGTH HE NEEDS.
TO MAKE IT BACK.
TO THE DORM.
CLEAN THE WOUND.
STOP THE BLEEDING.
STAY CONSCIOUS.
STAY CONSCIOUS.

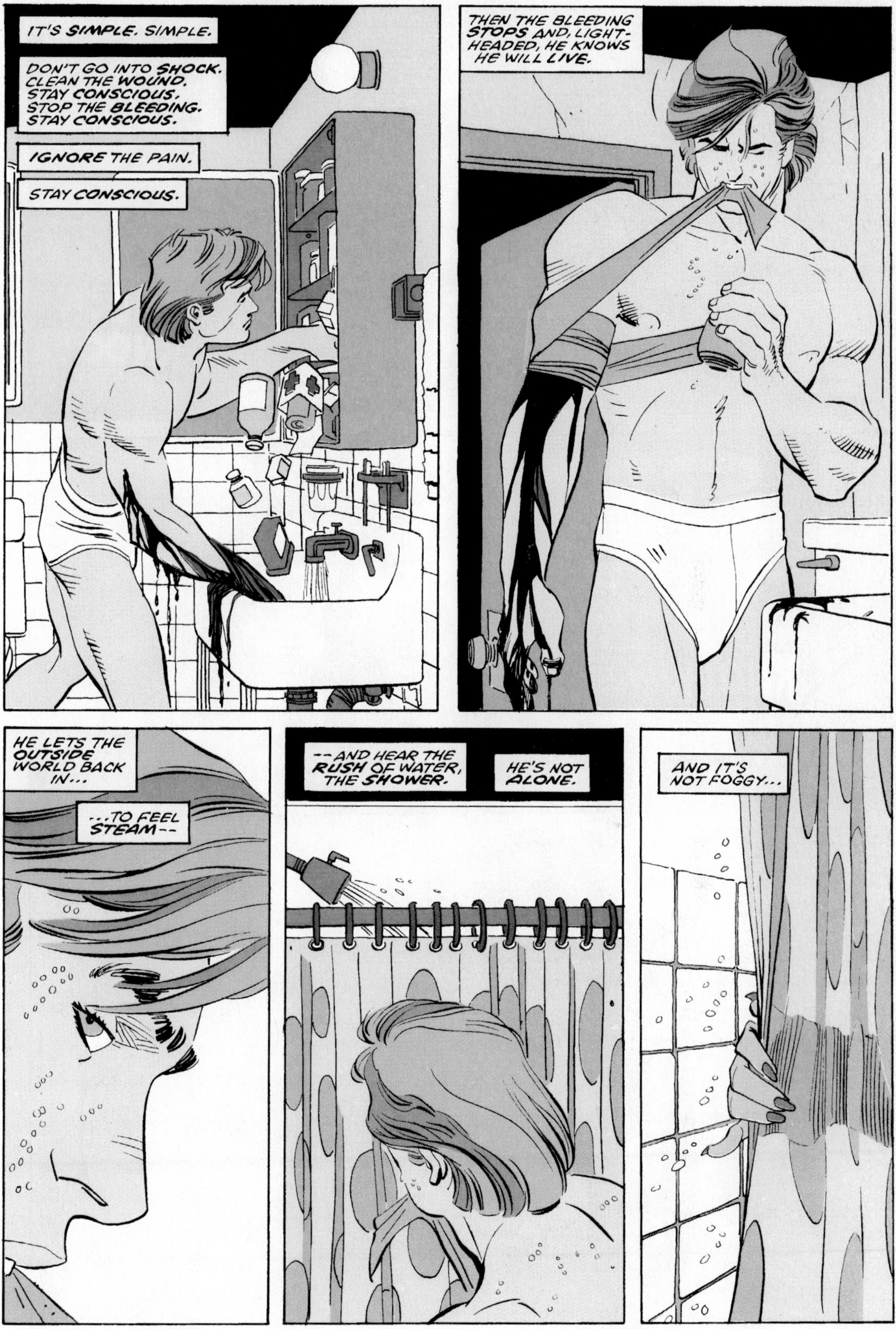
IT'S SIMPLE. SIMPLE.
DON'T GO INTO SHOCK. CLEAN THE WOUND. STAY CONSCIOUS. STOP THE BLEEDING. STAY CONSCIOUS.
IGNORE THE PAIN.
STAY CONSCIOUS.
THEN THE BLEEDING STOPS AND, LIGHT-HEADED, HE KNOWS HE WILL LIVE.
HE LETS THE OUTSIDE WORLD BACK IN...
...TO FEEL STEAM--
--AND HEAR THE RUSH OF WATER, THE SHOWER.
HE'S NOT ALONE.
AND IT'S NOT FOGGY...

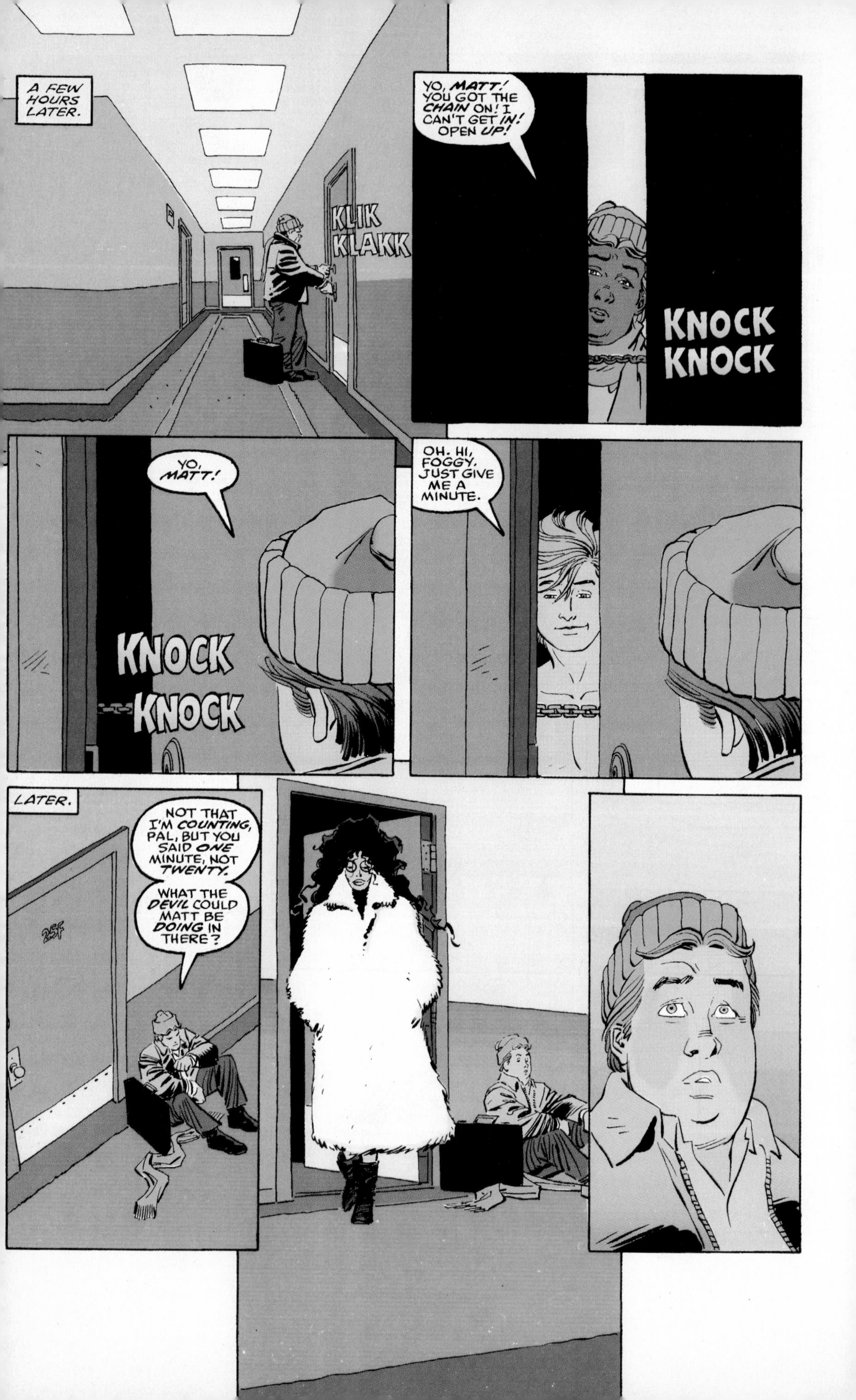

A FEW HOURS LATER.
KLIK KLAKK
YO, MATT! YOU GOT THE CHAIN ON! I CAN'T GET IN! OPEN UP!
KNOCK KNOCK
YO, MATT!
KNOCK KNOCK
OH. HI, FOGGY. JUST GIVE ME A MINUTE.
LATER.
NOT THAT I'M COUNTING, PAL, BUT YOU SAID ONE MINUTE, NOT TWENTY.
WHAT THE DEVIL COULD MATT BE DOING IN THERE?

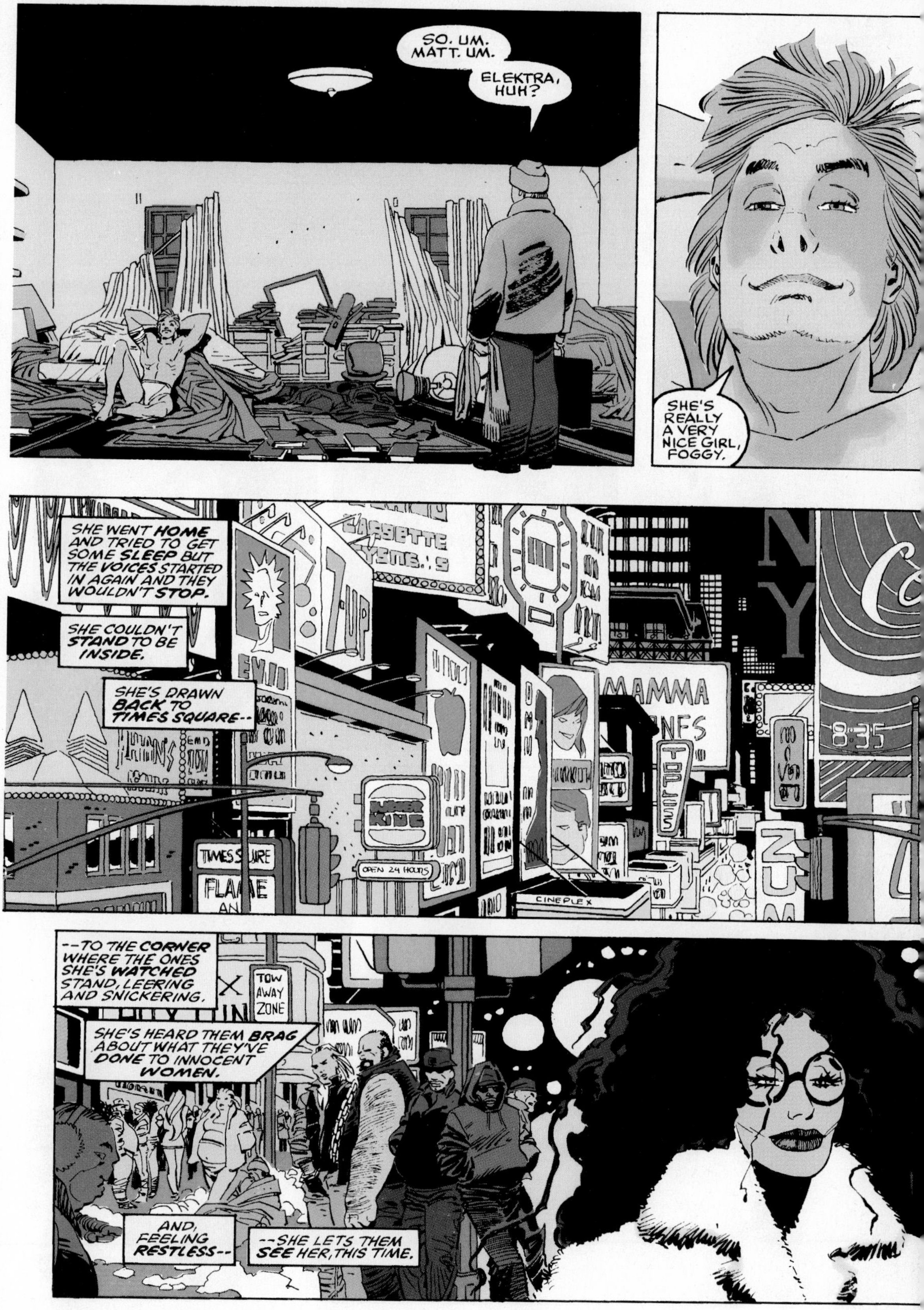
SO. UM. MATT. UM.
ELEKTRA, HUH?
SHE'S REALLY A VERY NICE GIRL, FOGGY.
SHE WENT HOME AND TRIED TO GET SOME SLEEP BUT THE VOICES STARTED IN AGAIN AND THEY WOULDN'T STOP.
SHE COULDN'T STAND TO BE INSIDE.
SHE'S DRAWN BACK TO TIMES SQUARE--
7UP
MAMMA
TOPLESS
OPEN 24 HOURS
CINEPLEX
8:35
--TO THE CORNER WHERE THE ONES SHE'S WATCHED STAND, LEERING AND SNICKERING.
TOW AWAY ZONE
SHE'S HEARD THEM BRAG ABOUT WHAT THEY'VE DONE TO INNOCENT WOMEN.
AND, FEELING RESTLESS--
--SHE LETS THEM SEE HER, THIS TIME.

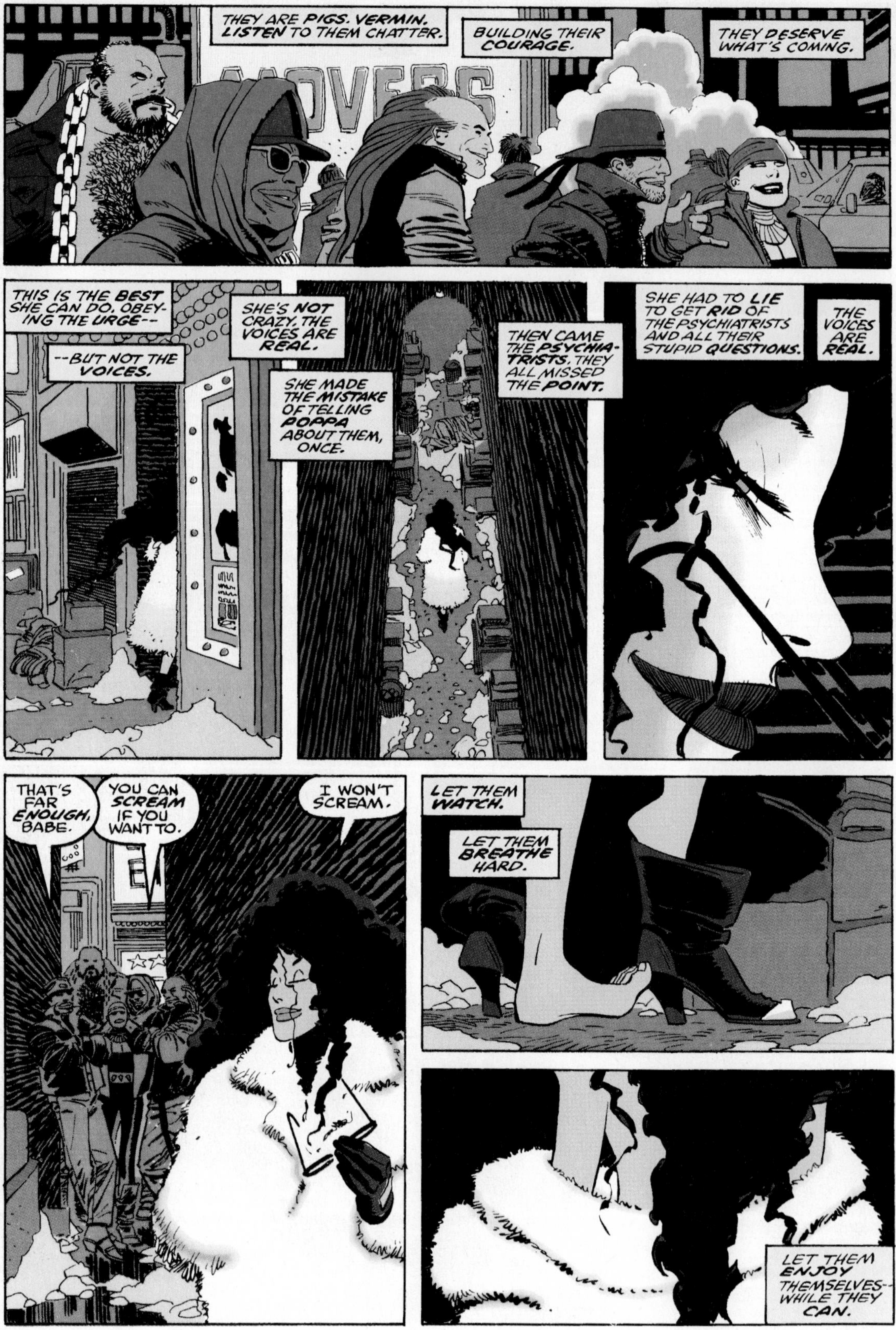

THEY ARE PIGS. VERMIN. LISTEN TO THEM CHATTER.
BUILDING THEIR COURAGE.
THEY DESERVE WHAT'S COMING.
MOVERS
THIS IS THE BEST SHE CAN DO. OBEYING THE URGE--
--BUT NOT THE VOICES.
SHE'S NOT CRAZY. THE VOICES ARE REAL.
SHE MADE THE MISTAKE OF TELLING POPPA ABOUT THEM, ONCE.
THEN CAME THE PSYCHIATRISTS. THEY ALL MISSED THE POINT.
SHE HAD TO LIE TO GET RID OF THE PSYCHIATRISTS AND ALL THEIR STUPID QUESTIONS.
THE VOICES ARE REAL.
THAT'S FAR ENOUGH, BABE.
YOU CAN SCREAM IF YOU WANT TO.
I WON'T SCREAM.
LET THEM WATCH.
LET THEM BREATHE HARD.
LET THEM ENJOY THEMSELVES-- WHILE THEY CAN.

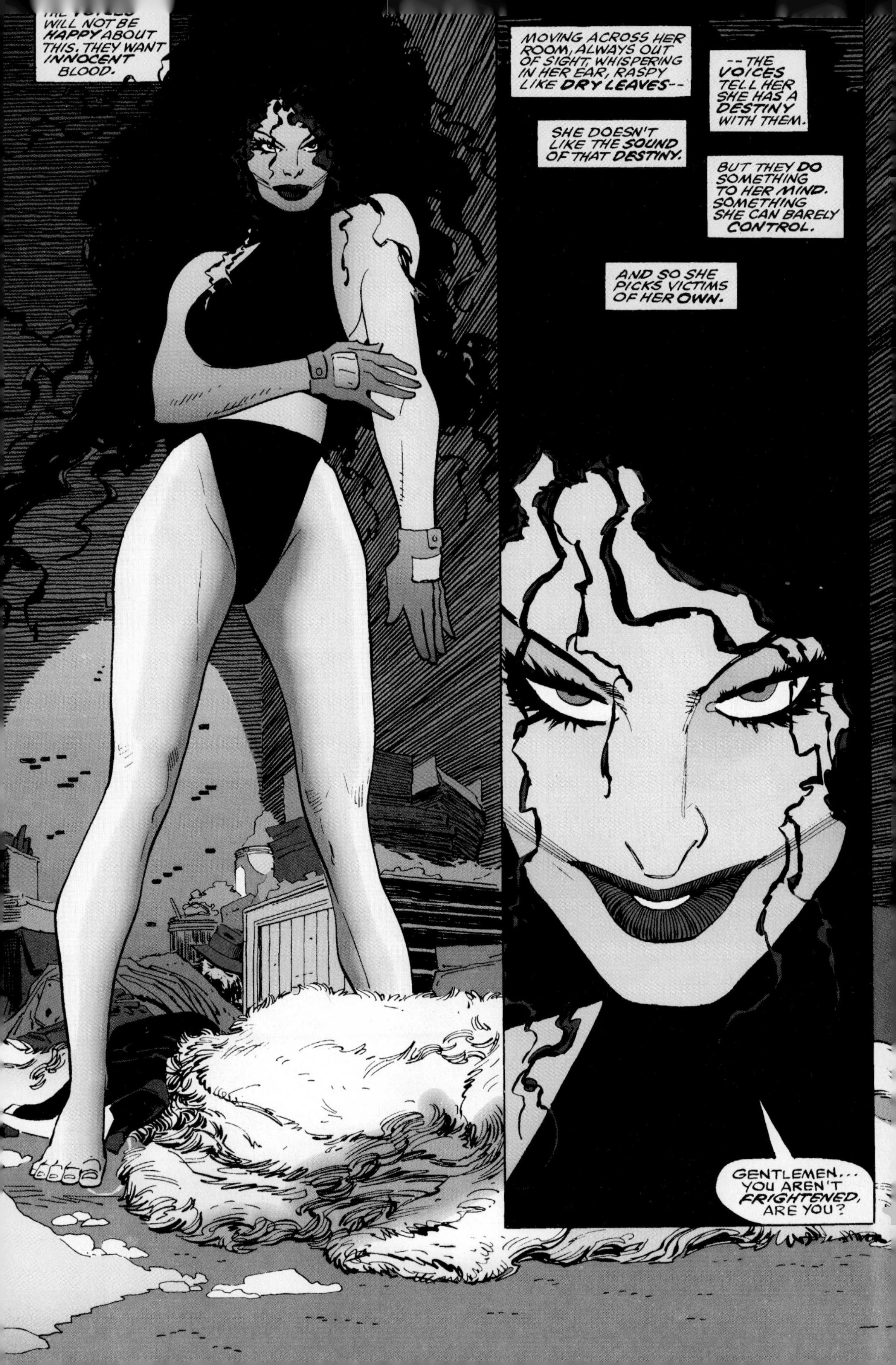

WILL NOT BE HAPPY ABOUT THIS. THEY WANT INNOCENT BLOOD.
MOVING ACROSS HER ROOM, ALWAYS OUT OF SIGHT, WHISPERING IN HER EAR, RASPY LIKE DRY LEAVES--
--THE VOICES TELL HER SHE HAS A DESTINY WITH THEM.
SHE DOESN'T LIKE THE SOUND OF THAT DESTINY.
BUT THEY DO SOMETHING TO HER MIND. SOMETHING SHE CAN BARELY CONTROL.
AND SO SHE PICKS VICTIMS OF HER OWN.
GENTLEMEN... YOU AREN'T FRIGHTENED, ARE YOU?

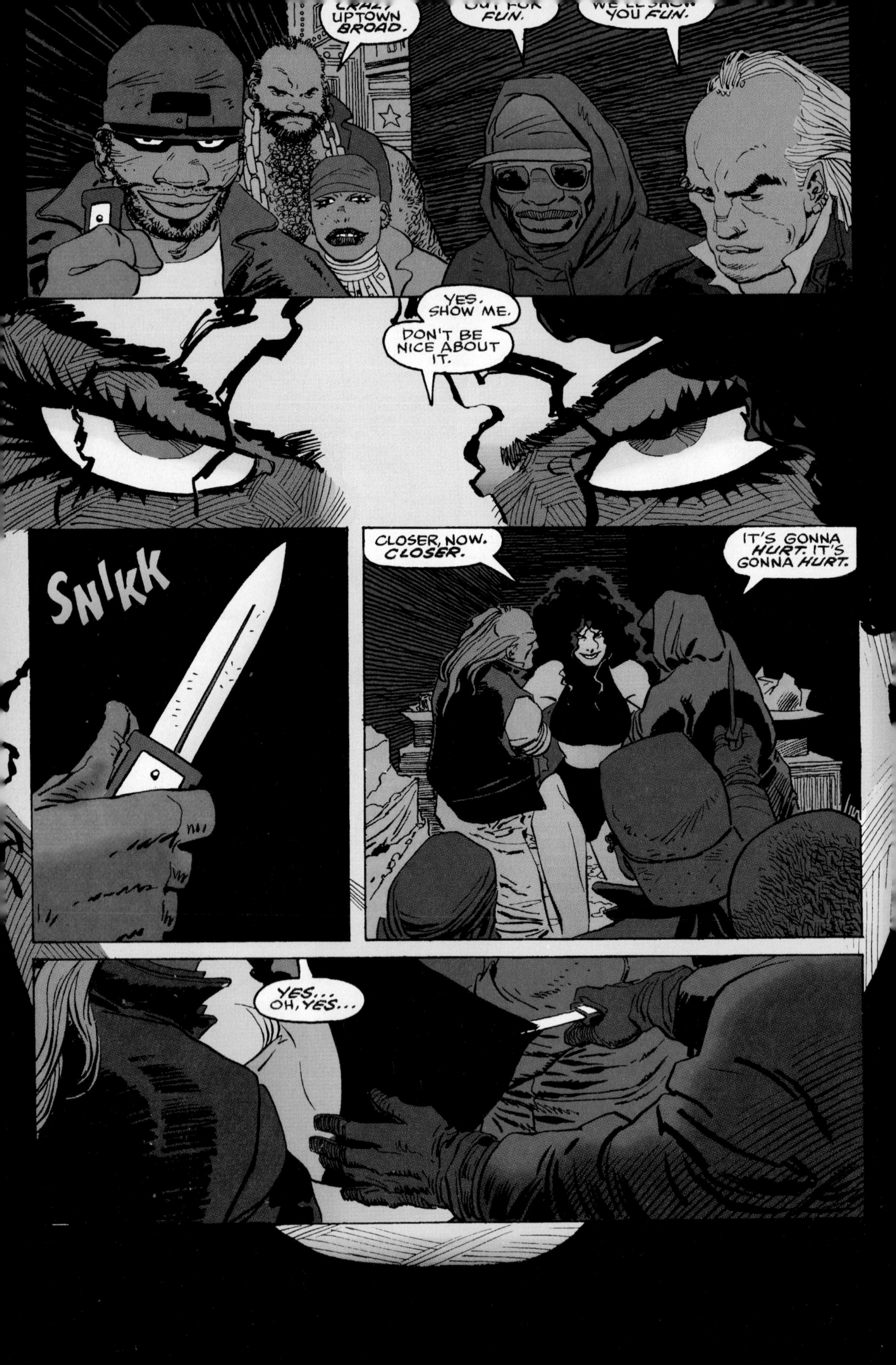
UPTOWN BROAD.
FUN.
YOU FUN.
YES. SHOW ME.
DON'T BE NICE ABOUT IT.
SNIKK
CLOSER, NOW. CLOSER.
IT'S GONNA HURT. IT'S GONNA HURT.
YES... OH, YES...

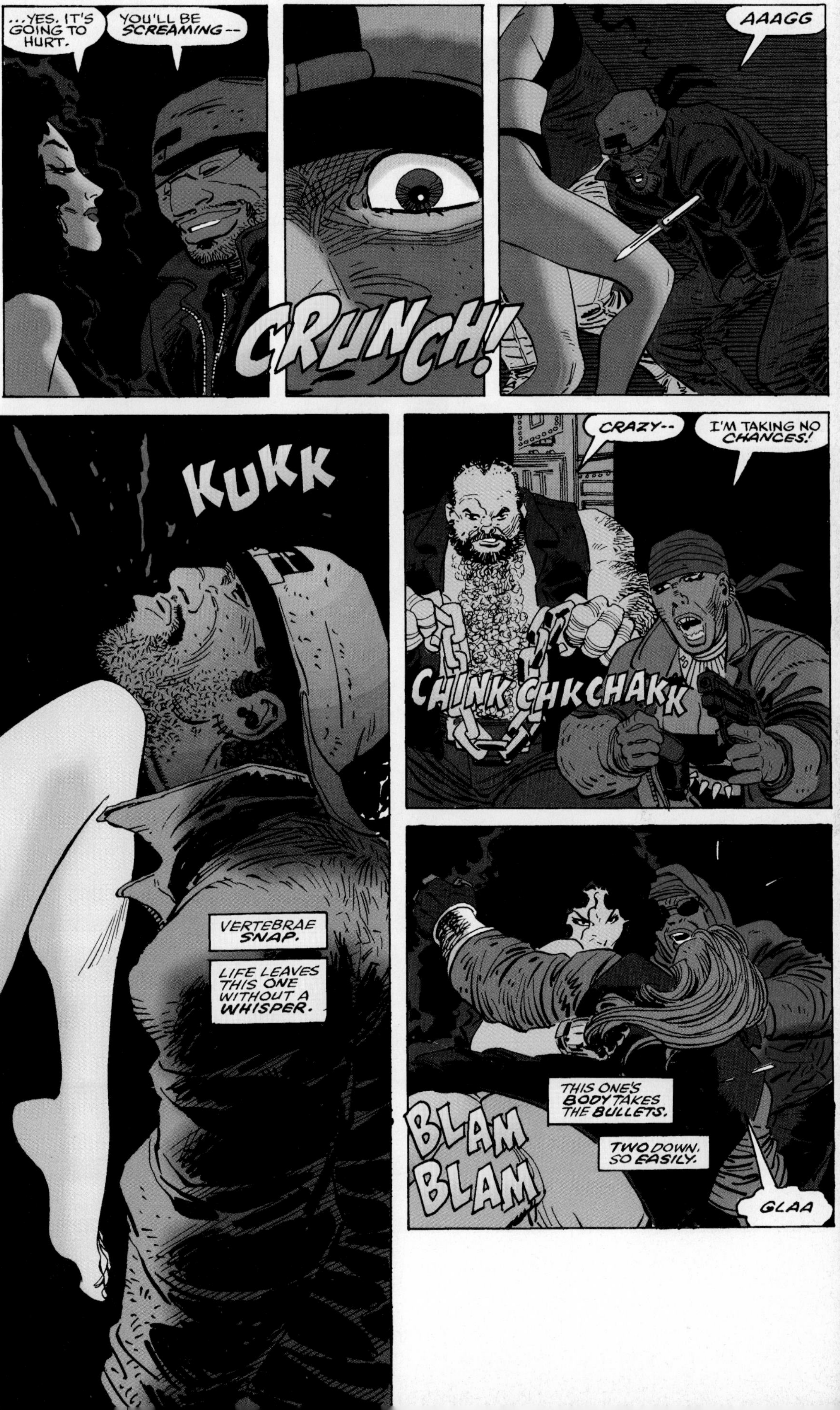
...YES. IT'S GOING TO HURT.
YOU'LL BE SCREAMING--
CRUNCH!
AAAGG
KUKK
VERTEBRAE SNAP.
LIFE LEAVES THIS ONE WITHOUT A WHISPER.
CRAZY--
I'M TAKING NO CHANCES!
CHINK CHKCHAKK
THIS ONE'S BODY TAKES THE BULLETS.
TWO DOWN. SO EASILY.
BLAM BLAM
GLAA

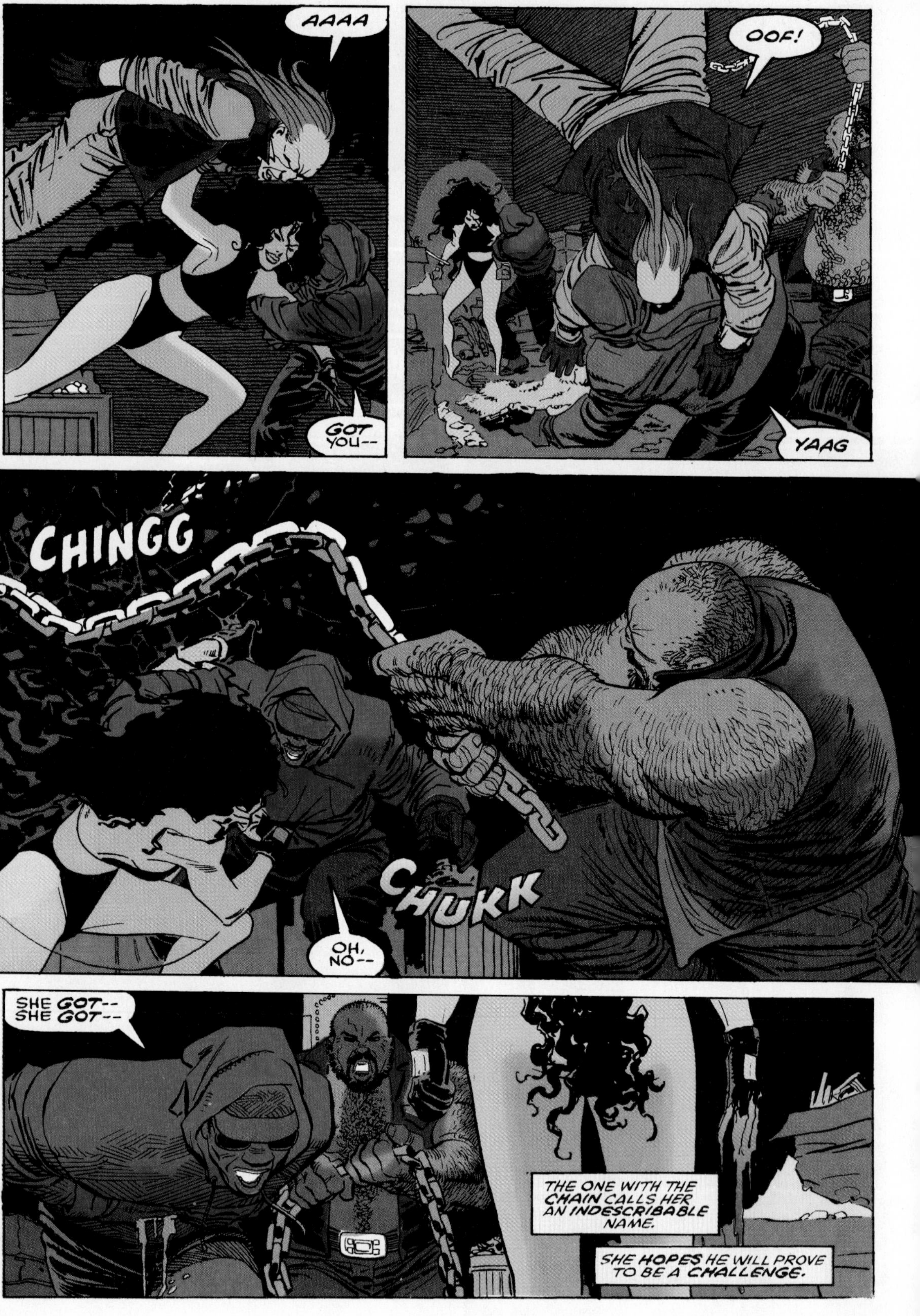
AAAA
GOT YOU--
OOF!
YAAG
CHINGG
CHUKK
OH, NO--
SHE GOT--
SHE GOT--
THE ONE WITH THE CHAIN CALLS HER AN INDESCRIBABLE NAME.
SHE HOPES HE WILL PROVE TO BE A CHALLENGE.

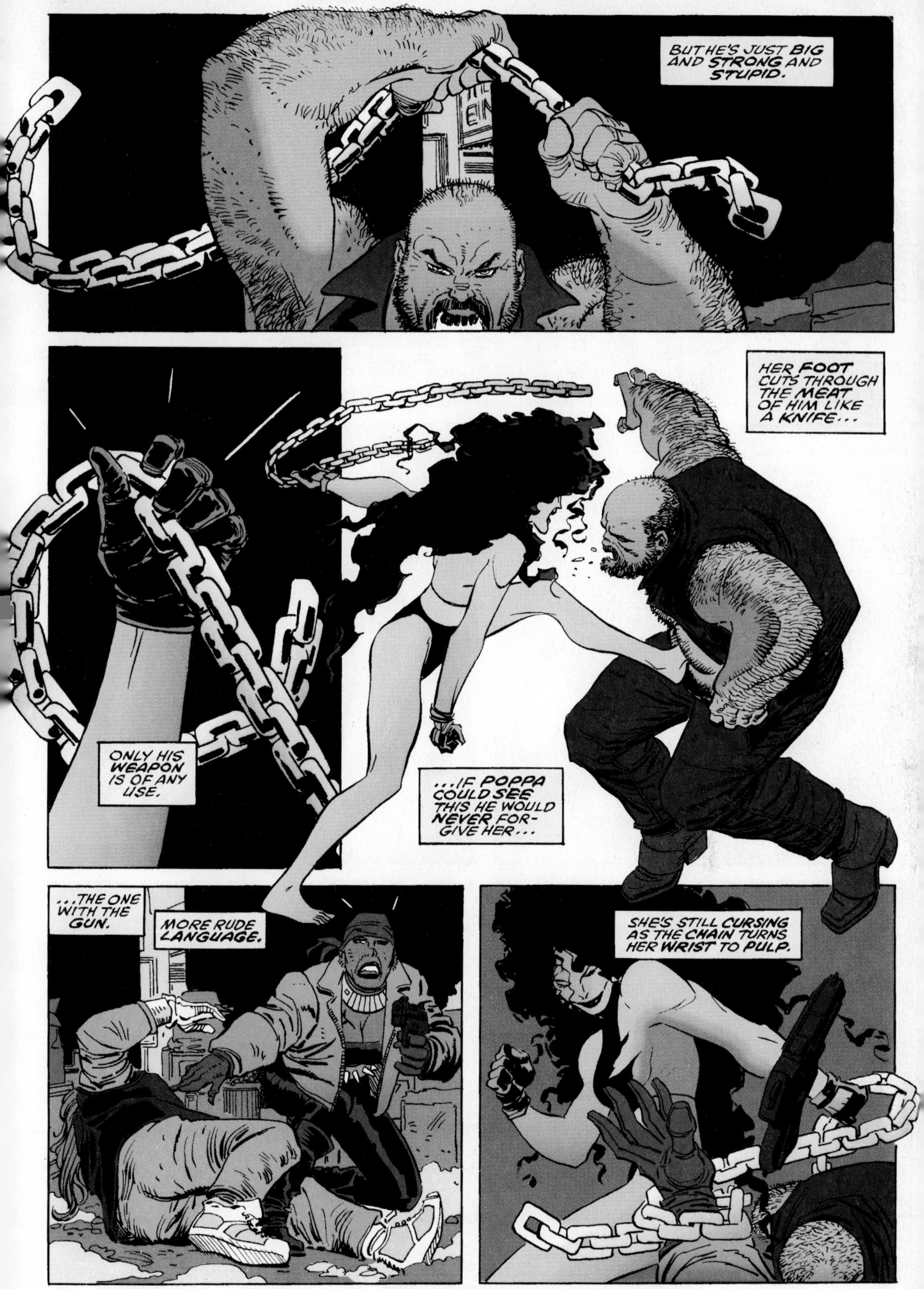
BUT HE'S JUST BIG AND STRONG AND STUPID.
ONLY HIS WEAPON IS OF ANY USE.
HER FOOT CUTS THROUGH THE MEAT OF HIM LIKE A KNIFE...
...IF POPPA COULD SEE THIS HE WOULD NEVER FORGIVE HER...
...THE ONE WITH THE GUN.
MORE RUDE LANGUAGE.
SHE'S STILL CURSING AS THE CHAIN TURNS HER WRIST TO PULP.

THEN IT'S A SIMPLE MATTER OF SHOVING SHARP BONE INTO SOFT BRAIN.

A NOVICE COULD DO IT.

ONLY THE BIG ONE REMAINS.

ELEKTRA HATES THE SMELL OF HIS SWEAT.

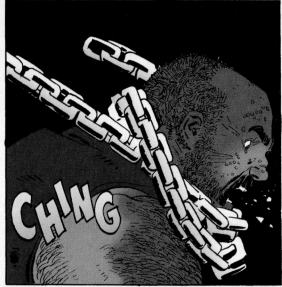

CHING

SNAP

A FEW LAST GURGLING SOUNDS AND THE ALLEY GOES QUIET.

IT TAKES THE POLICE A FULL TWENTY MINUTES TO ARRIVE.

ELEKTRA HAILS A CAB.

OH, BROTHER-- WHAT A MESS!

WHATTAYAMEAN YOU DIDN'T SEE NOTHING?

I WAS DRUNK!

MAN, WE GOT FIVE DEAD HERE!

I WAS DRUNK!

LOOK AT THIS. WHOEVER ACED THESE GUYS GOT ONE DAMN STRANGE SENSE OF HUMOR.

IT WAS A DIS- APPOINTING WORKOUT.

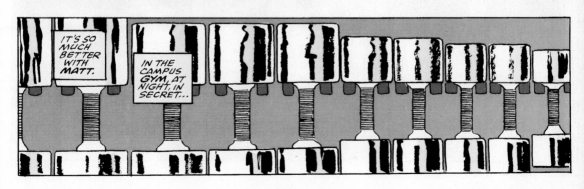

IT'S SO MUCH BETTER WITH MATT.

IN THE CAMPUS GYM, AT NIGHT, IN SECRET...

93

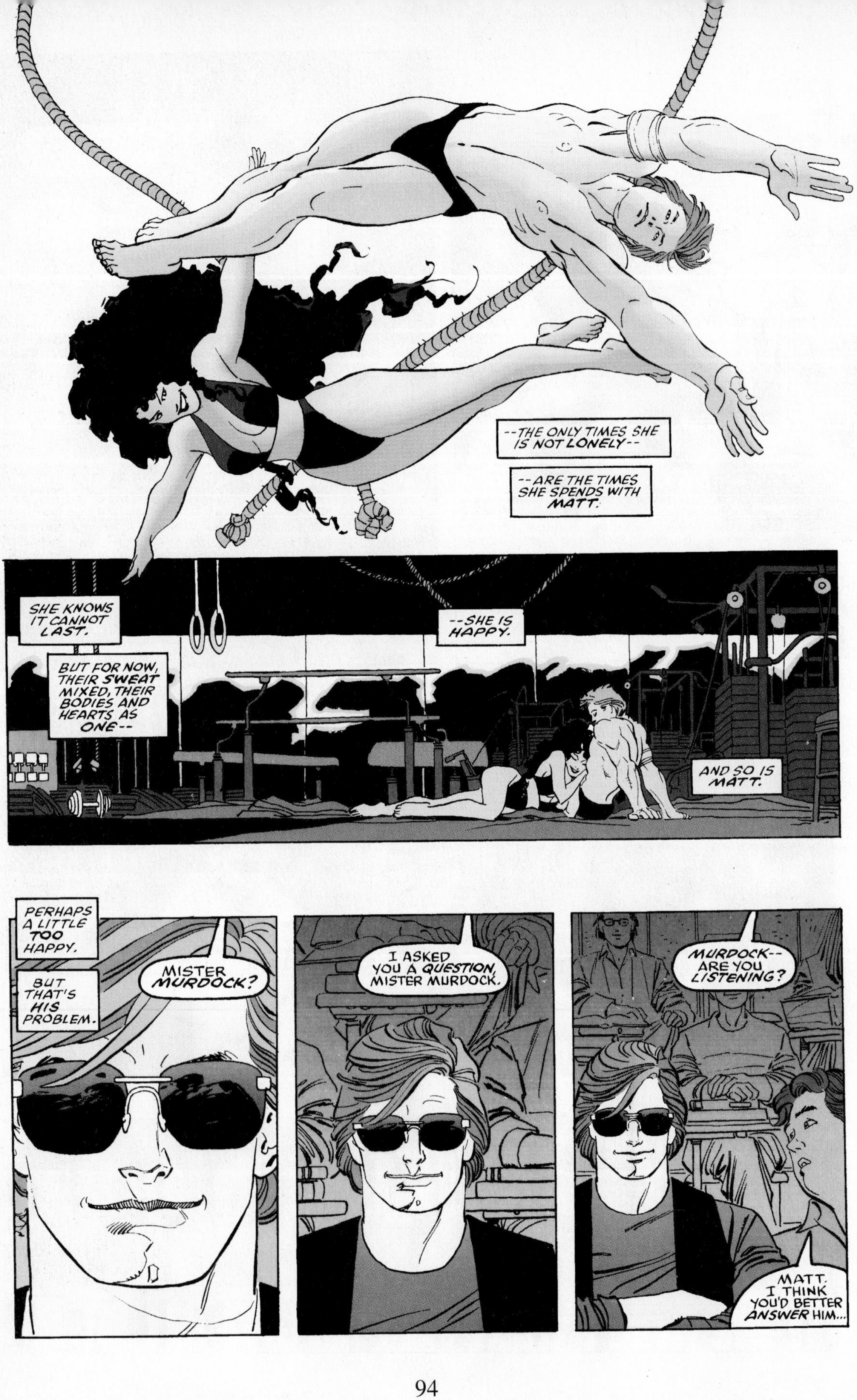

--THE ONLY TIMES SHE IS NOT LONELY--
--ARE THE TIMES SHE SPENDS WITH MATT.
SHE KNOWS IT CANNOT LAST.
BUT FOR NOW, THEIR SWEAT MIXED, THEIR BODIES AND HEARTS AS ONE--
--SHE IS HAPPY.
AND SO IS MATT.
PERHAPS A LITTLE TOO HAPPY.
BUT THAT'S HIS PROBLEM.
MISTER MURDOCK?
I ASKED YOU A QUESTION, MISTER MURDOCK.
MURDOCK-- ARE YOU LISTENING?
MATT. I THINK YOU'D BETTER ANSWER HIM...

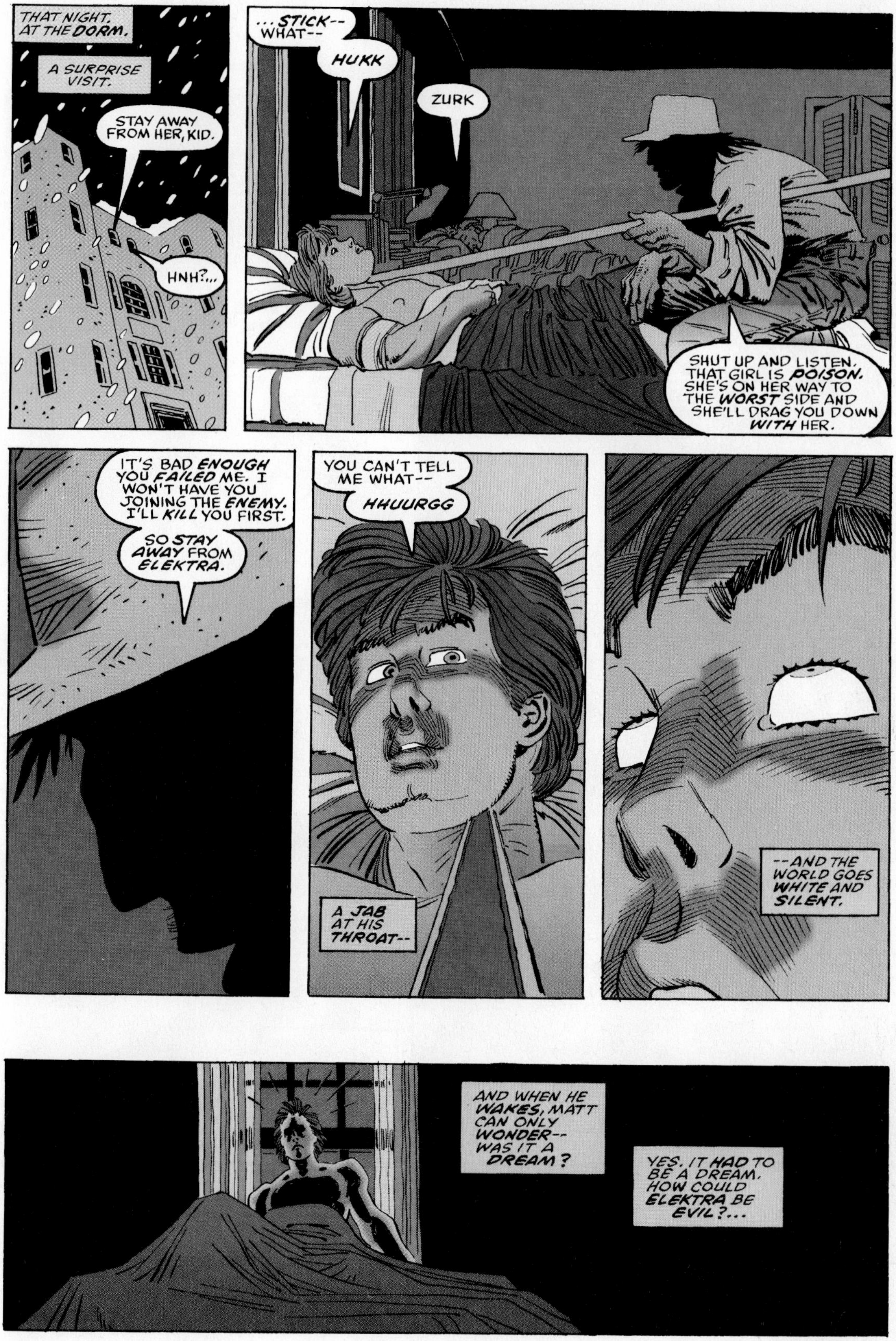
THAT NIGHT. AT THE DORM.
A SURPRISE VISIT.
STAY AWAY FROM HER, KID.
HNH?...
...STICK-- WHAT--
HUKK
ZURK
SHUT UP AND LISTEN. THAT GIRL IS POISON. SHE'S ON HER WAY TO THE WORST SIDE AND SHE'LL DRAG YOU DOWN WITH HER.
IT'S BAD ENOUGH YOU FAILED ME. I WON'T HAVE YOU JOINING THE ENEMY. I'LL KILL YOU FIRST.
SO STAY AWAY FROM ELEKTRA.
YOU CAN'T TELL ME WHAT--
HHUURGG
A JAB AT HIS THROAT--
--AND THE WORLD GOES WHITE AND SILENT.
AND WHEN HE WAKES, MATT CAN ONLY WONDER-- WAS IT A DREAM?
YES. IT HAD TO BE A DREAM. HOW COULD ELEKTRA BE EVIL?...

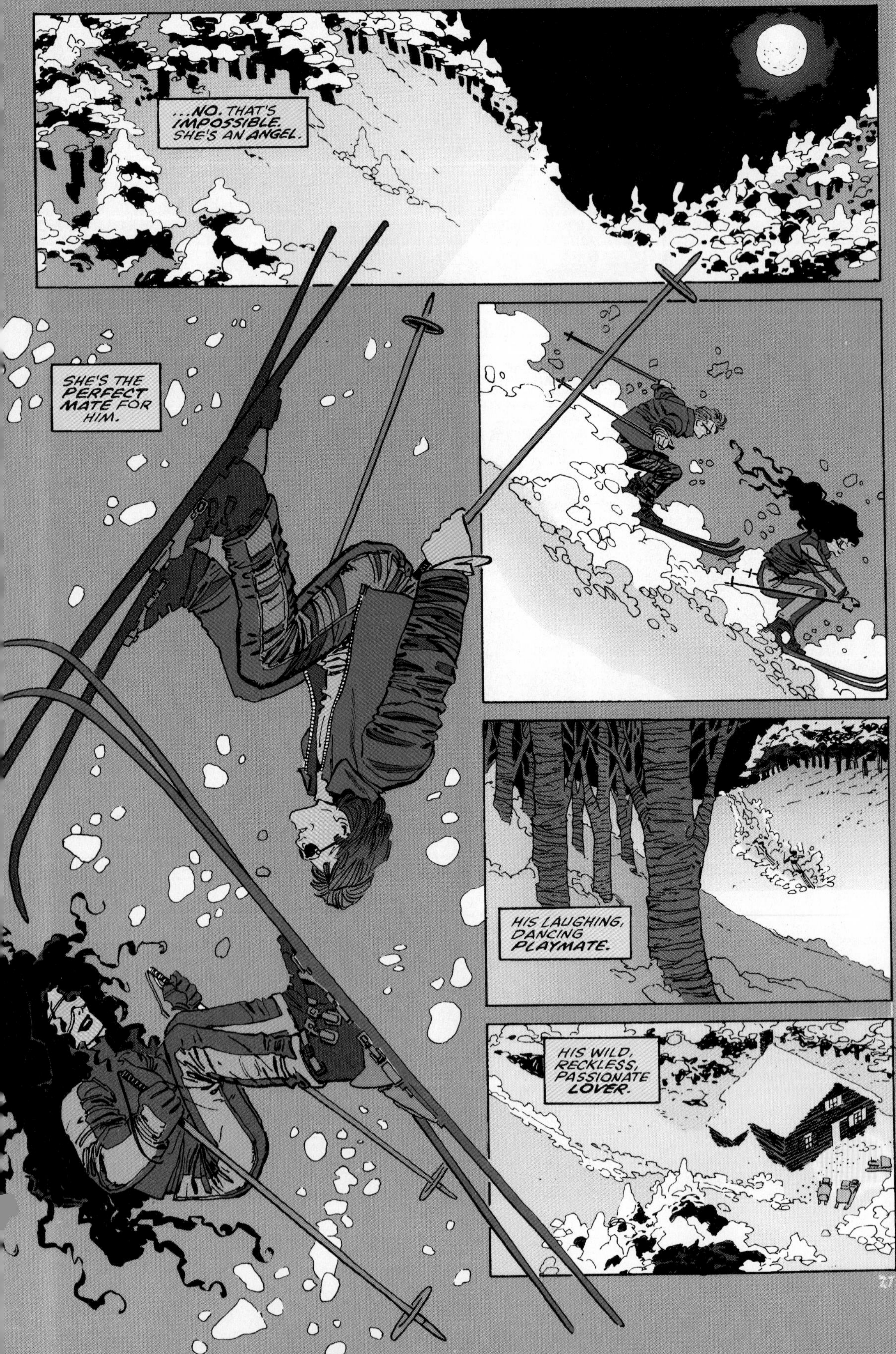
...NO. THAT'S IMPOSSIBLE. SHE'S AN ANGEL.
SHE'S THE PERFECT MATE FOR HIM.
HIS LAUGHING, DANCING PLAYMATE.
HIS WILD, RECKLESS, PASSIONATE LOVER.

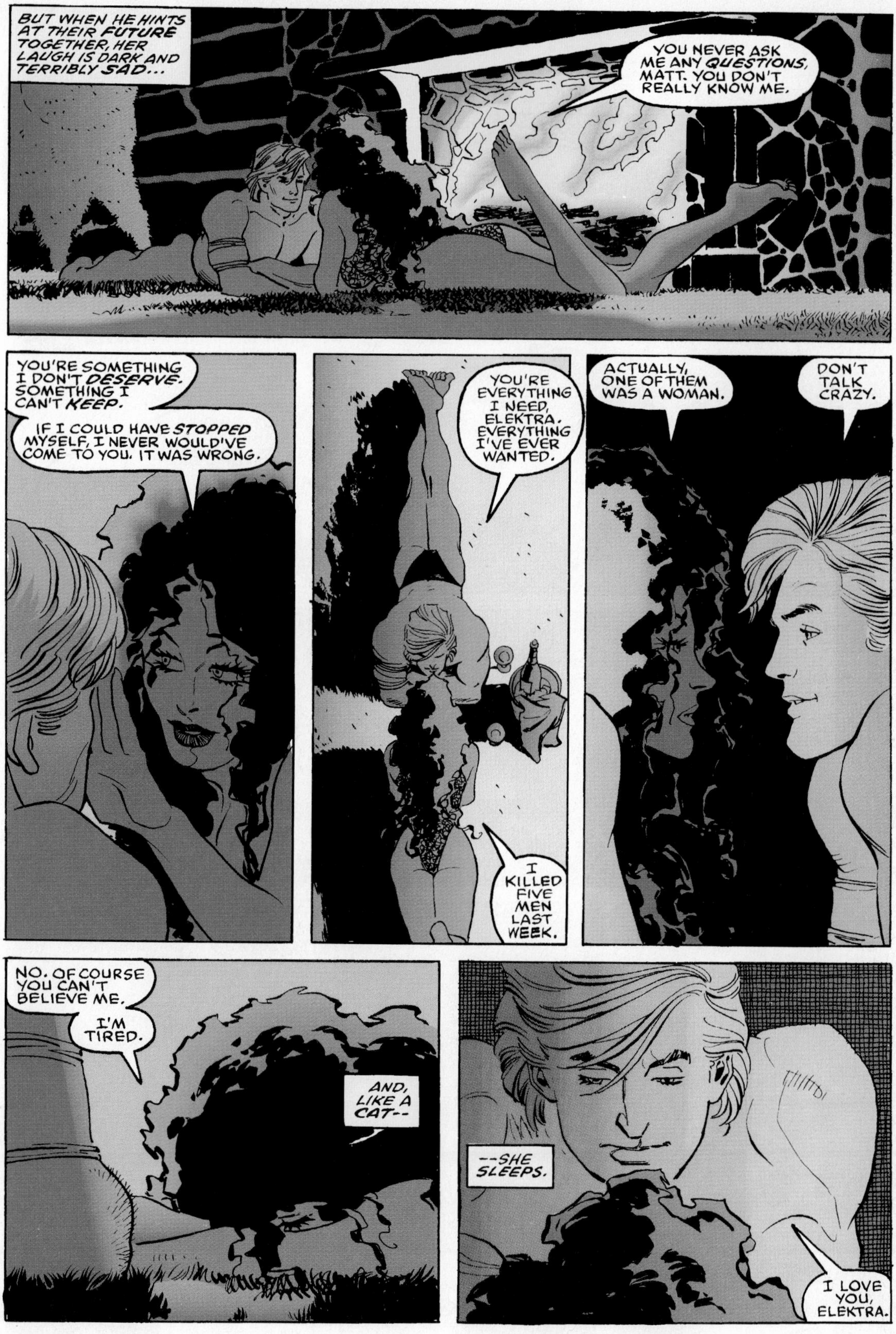
BUT WHEN HE HINTS AT THEIR FUTURE TOGETHER, HER LAUGH IS DARK AND TERRIBLY SAD...
YOU NEVER ASK ME ANY QUESTIONS, MATT. YOU DON'T REALLY KNOW ME.
YOU'RE SOMETHING I DON'T DESERVE. SOMETHING I CAN'T KEEP.
IF I COULD HAVE STOPPED MYSELF, I NEVER WOULD'VE COME TO YOU. IT WAS WRONG.
YOU'RE EVERYTHING I NEED, ELEKTRA. EVERYTHING I'VE EVER WANTED.
I KILLED FIVE MEN LAST WEEK.
ACTUALLY, ONE OF THEM WAS A WOMAN.
DON'T TALK CRAZY.
NO. OF COURSE YOU CAN'T BELIEVE ME.
I'M TIRED.
AND, LIKE A CAT--
--SHE SLEEPS.
I LOVE YOU, ELEKTRA.

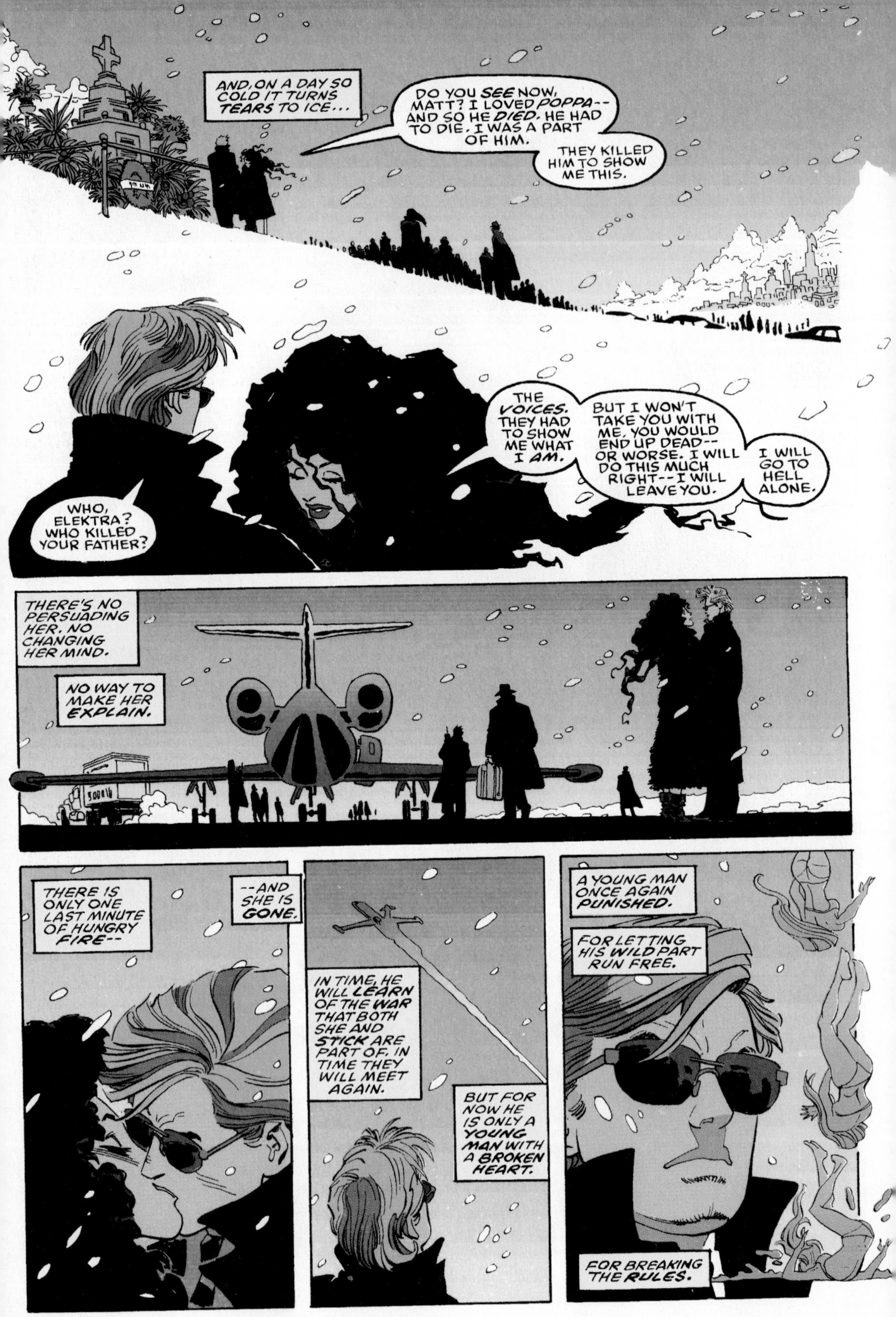
AND, ON A DAY SO COLD IT TURNS TEARS TO ICE...
DO YOU SEE NOW, MATT? I LOVED POPPA-- AND SO HE DIED. HE HAD TO DIE. I WAS A PART OF HIM.
THEY KILLED HIM TO SHOW ME THIS.
WHO, ELEKTRA? WHO KILLED YOUR FATHER?
THE VOICES. THEY HAD TO SHOW ME WHAT I AM.
BUT I WON'T TAKE YOU WITH ME. YOU WOULD END UP DEAD-- OR WORSE. I WILL DO THIS MUCH RIGHT-- I WILL LEAVE YOU.
I WILL GO TO HELL ALONE.
THERE'S NO PERSUADING HER. NO CHANGING HER MIND.
NO WAY TO MAKE HER EXPLAIN.
THERE IS ONLY ONE LAST MINUTE OF HUNGRY FIRE--
--AND SHE IS GONE.
IN TIME, HE WILL LEARN OF THE WAR THAT BOTH SHE AND STICK ARE PART OF. IN TIME THEY WILL MEET AGAIN.
BUT FOR NOW HE IS ONLY A YOUNG MAN WITH A BROKEN HEART.
A YOUNG MAN ONCE AGAIN PUNISHED.
FOR LETTING HIS WILD PART RUN FREE.
FOR BREAKING THE RULES.

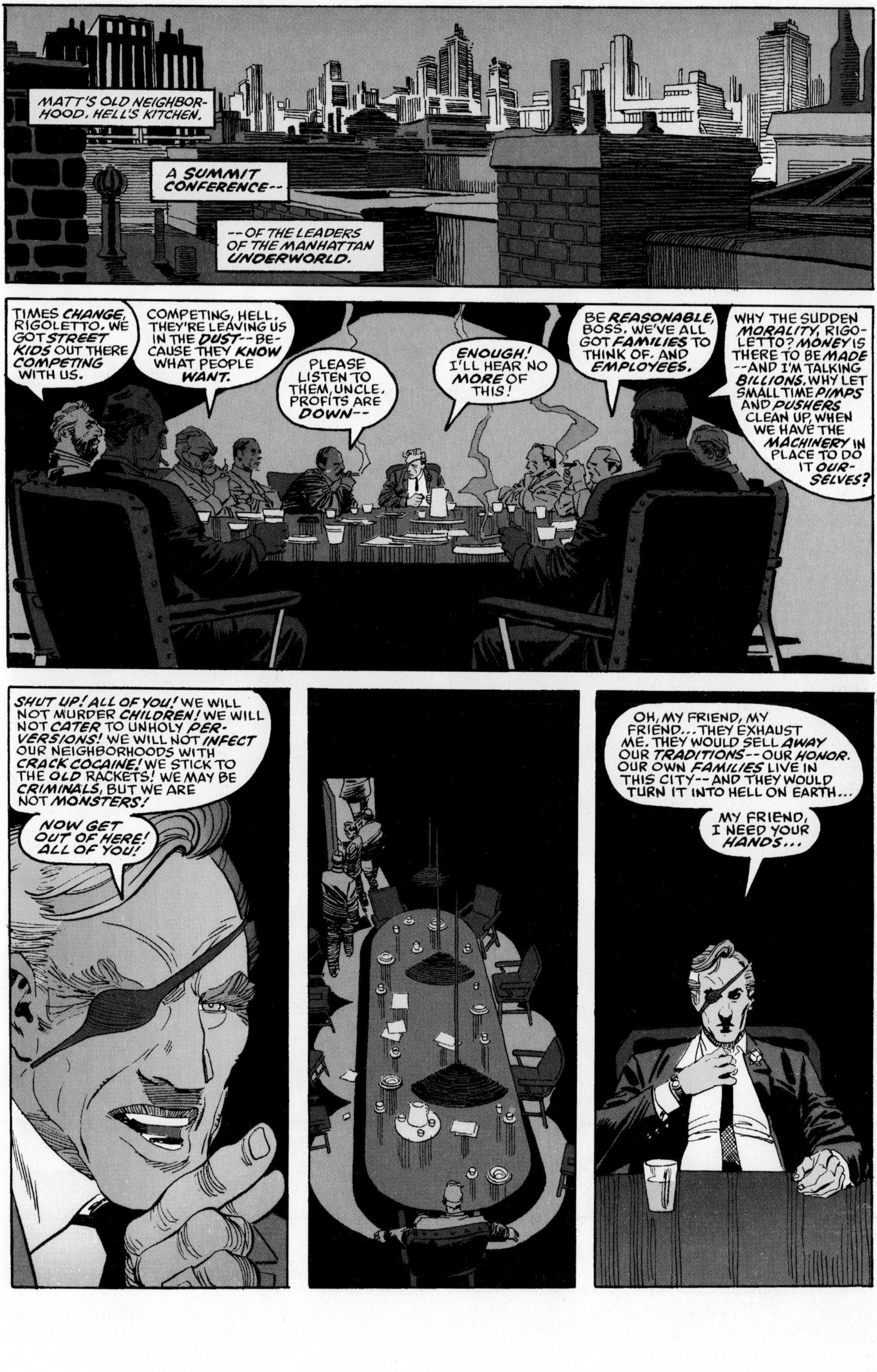
MATT'S OLD NEIGHBORHOOD, HELL'S KITCHEN.
A SUMMIT CONFERENCE--
--OF THE LEADERS OF THE MANHATTAN UNDERWORLD.
TIMES CHANGE, RIGOLETTO. WE GOT STREET KIDS OUT THERE COMPETING WITH US.
COMPETING, HELL. THEY'RE LEAVING US IN THE DUST--BECAUSE THEY KNOW WHAT PEOPLE WANT.
PLEASE LISTEN TO THEM, UNCLE. PROFITS ARE DOWN--
ENOUGH! I'LL HEAR NO MORE OF THIS!
BE REASONABLE, BOSS. WE'VE ALL GOT FAMILIES TO THINK OF. AND EMPLOYEES.
WHY THE SUDDEN MORALITY, RIGOLETTO? MONEY IS THERE TO BE MADE --AND I'M TALKING BILLIONS. WHY LET SMALL TIME PIMPS AND PUSHERS CLEAN UP, WHEN WE HAVE THE MACHINERY IN PLACE TO DO IT OURSELVES?
SHUT UP! ALL OF YOU! WE WILL NOT MURDER CHILDREN! WE WILL NOT CATER TO UNHOLY PERVERSIONS! WE WILL NOT INFECT OUR NEIGHBORHOODS WITH CRACK COCAINE! WE STICK TO THE OLD RACKETS! WE MAY BE CRIMINALS, BUT WE ARE NOT MONSTERS!
NOW GET OUT OF HERE! ALL OF YOU!
OH, MY FRIEND, MY FRIEND... THEY EXHAUST ME. THEY WOULD SELL AWAY OUR TRADITIONS--OUR HONOR. OUR OWN FAMILIES LIVE IN THIS CITY--AND THEY WOULD TURN IT INTO HELL ON EARTH...
MY FRIEND, I NEED YOUR HANDS...

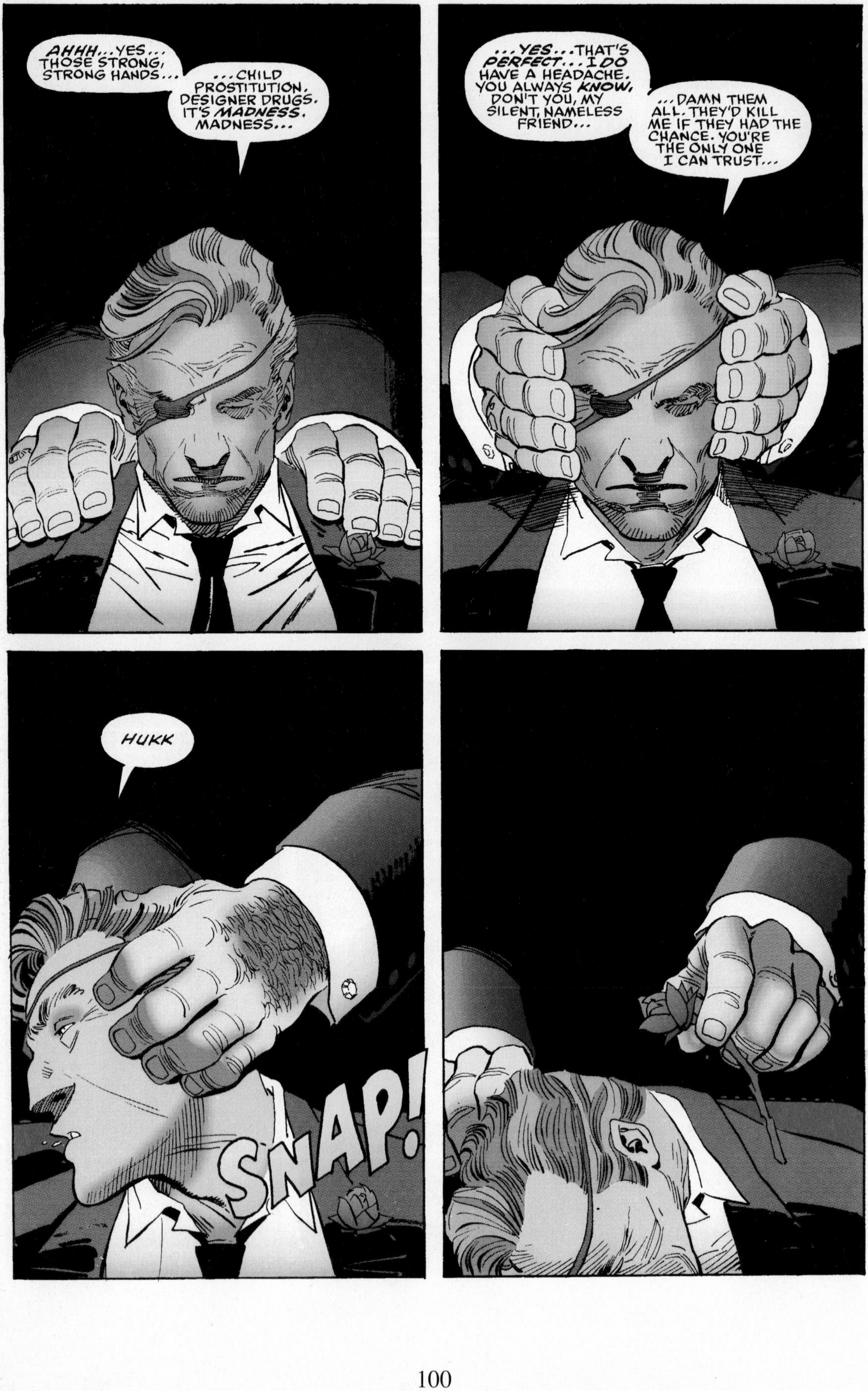
AHHH...YES... THOSE STRONG, STRONG HANDS...
...CHILD PROSTITUTION. DESIGNER DRUGS. IT'S MADNESS. MADNESS...
...YES...THAT'S PERFECT...I DO HAVE A HEADACHE. YOU ALWAYS KNOW, DON'T YOU, MY SILENT, NAMELESS FRIEND...
...DAMN THEM ALL. THEY'D KILL ME IF THEY HAD THE CHANCE. YOU'RE THE ONLY ONE I CAN TRUST...
HUKK
SNAP!

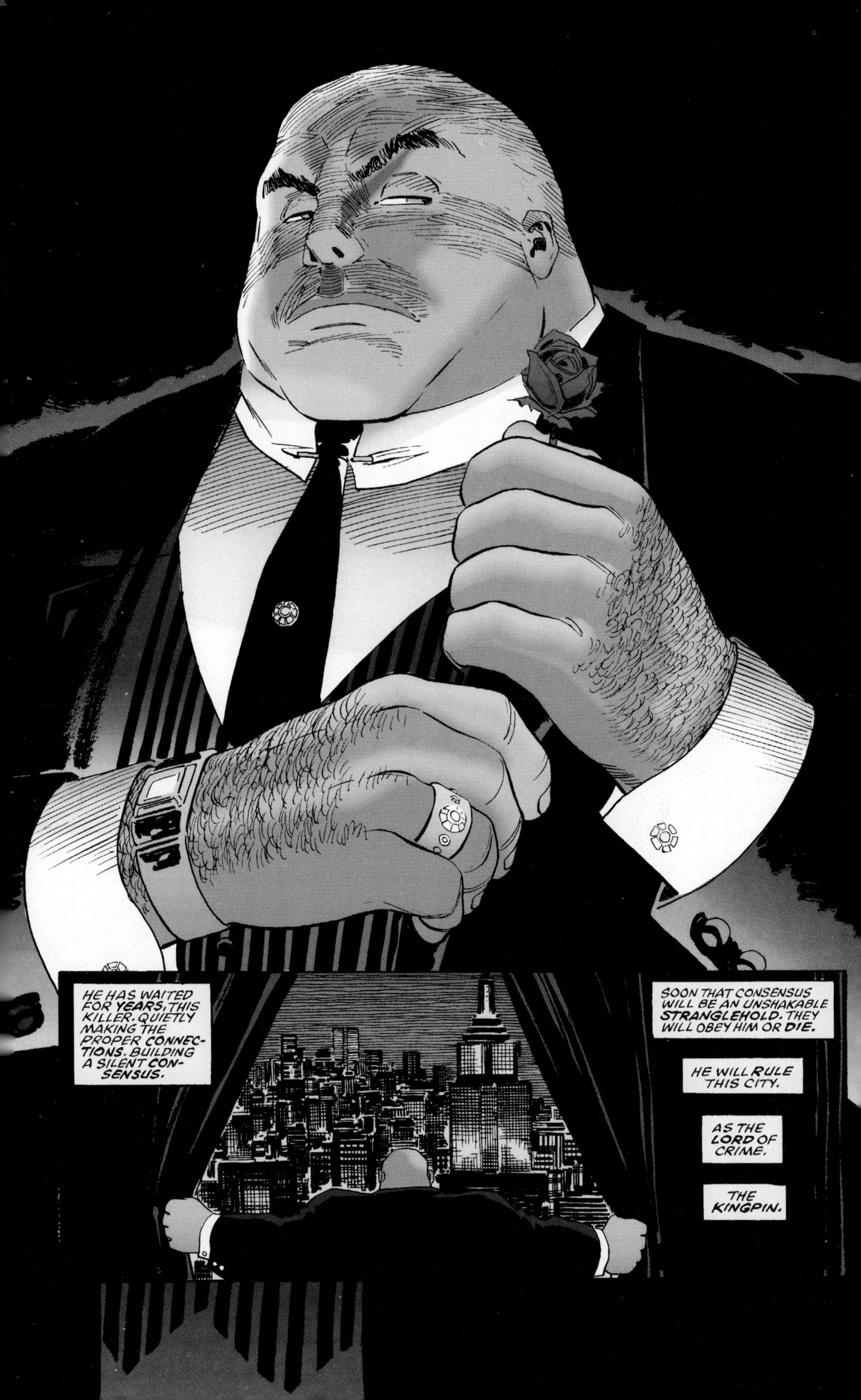
HE HAS WAITED FOR YEARS, THIS KILLER. QUIETLY MAKING THE PROPER CONNECTIONS. BUILDING A SILENT CONSENSUS.
SOON THAT CONSENSUS WILL BE AN UNSHAKABLE STRANGLEHOLD. THEY WILL OBEY HIM OR DIE.
HE WILL RULE THIS CITY.
AS THE LORD OF CRIME.
THE KINGPIN.

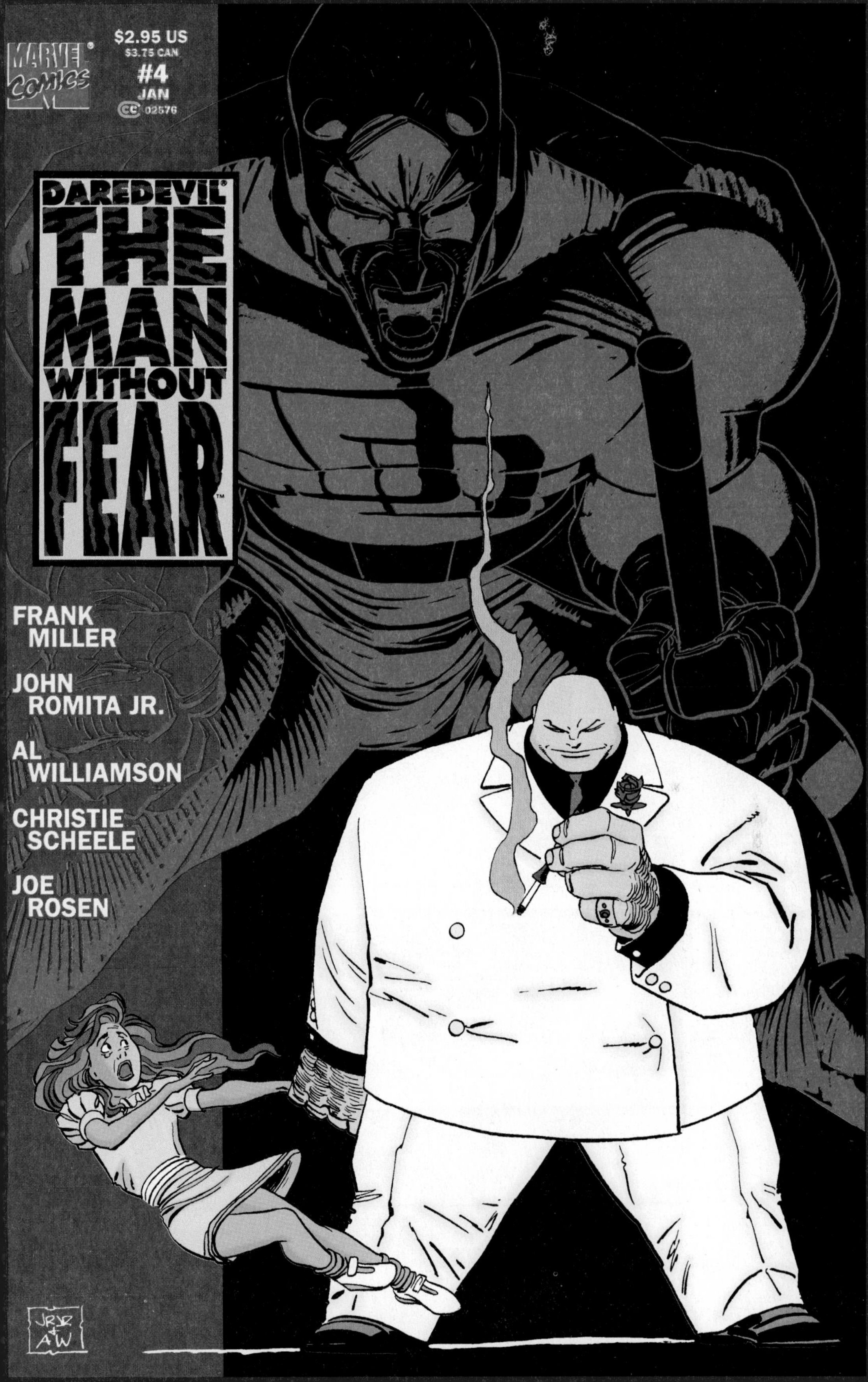
MARVEL COMICS
$2.95 US
$3.75 CAN
#4
JAN
02576
DAREDEVIL
THE MAN WITHOUT FEAR
FRANK MILLER
JOHN ROMITA JR.
AL WILLIAMSON
CHRISTIE SCHEELE
JOE ROSEN
JRJR + AW

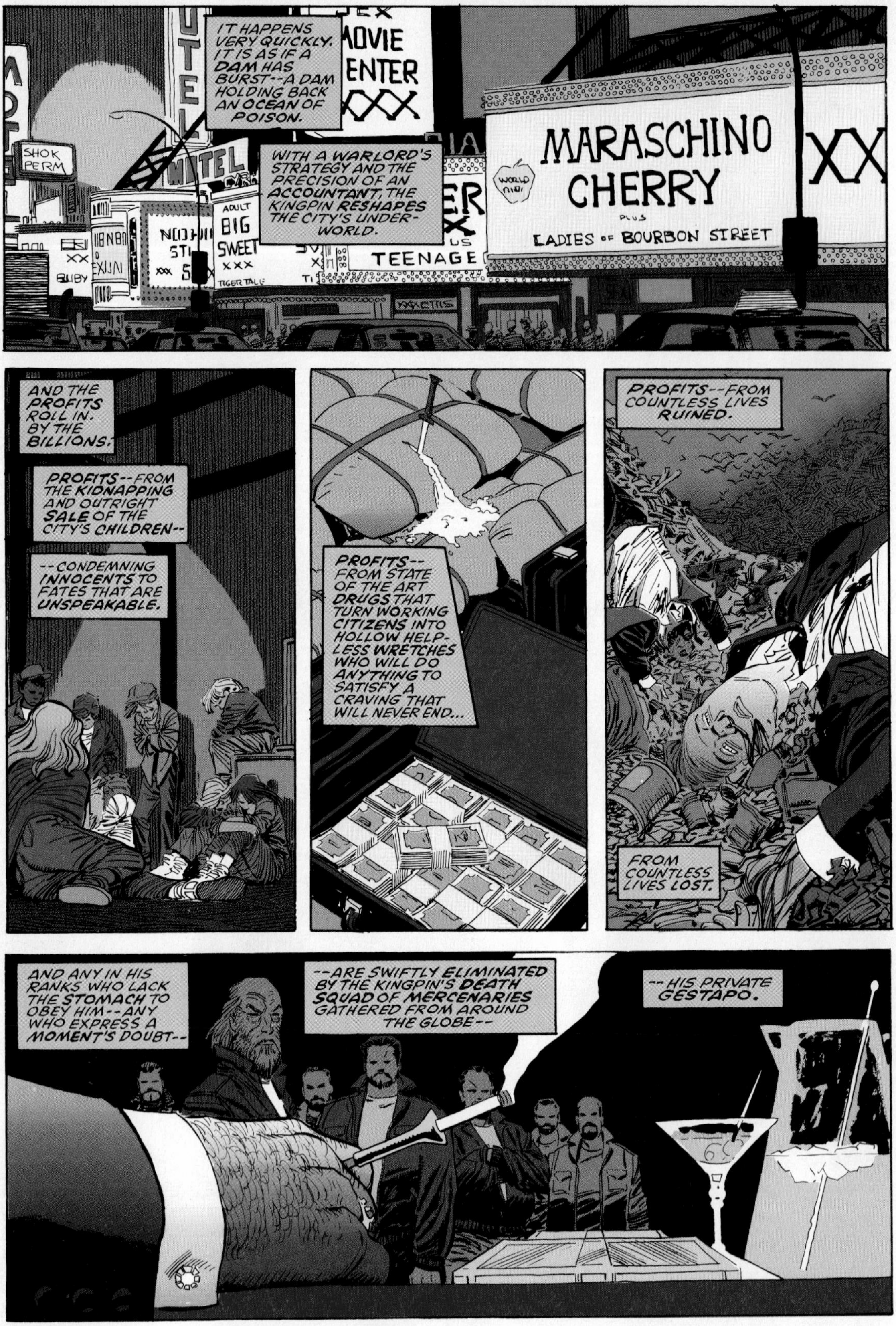
IT HAPPENS VERY QUICKLY. IT IS AS IF A DAM HAS BURST--A DAM HOLDING BACK AN OCEAN OF POISON.
WITH A WARLORD'S STRATEGY AND THE PRECISION OF AN ACCOUNTANT, THE KINGPIN RESHAPES THE CITY'S UNDER-WORLD.
MOVIE CENTER XXX
MARASCHINO CHERRY
PLUS
LADIES OF BOURBON STREET
TEENAGE
ADULT BIG SWEET XXX
SHOK PERM
AND THE PROFITS ROLL IN. BY THE BILLIONS.
PROFITS--FROM THE KIDNAPPING AND OUTRIGHT SALE OF THE CITY'S CHILDREN--
--CONDEMNING INNOCENTS TO FATES THAT ARE UNSPEAKABLE.
PROFITS--FROM STATE OF THE ART DRUGS THAT TURN WORKING CITIZENS INTO HOLLOW HELP-LESS WRETCHES WHO WILL DO ANYTHING TO SATISFY A CRAVING THAT WILL NEVER END...
PROFITS--FROM COUNTLESS LIVES RUINED.
FROM COUNTLESS LIVES LOST.
AND ANY IN HIS RANKS WHO LACK THE STOMACH TO OBEY HIM--ANY WHO EXPRESS A MOMENT'S DOUBT--
--ARE SWIFTLY ELIMINATED BY THE KINGPIN'S DEATH SQUAD OF MERCENARIES GATHERED FROM AROUND THE GLOBE--
--HIS PRIVATE GESTAPO.

BUT MOST FEARED OF ALL IS THE SILENT MAN AT THE KINGPIN'S SIDE. THE MAN CALLED *LARKS.*

THE KINGPIN *NURTURED* HIM, SINCE HE WAS A *BOY.* TRAINED HIM IN THE MANY WAYS OF *DEATH.*

DROVE HIS *SOUL* FROM HIM.

LEAVING A THING WITH AN *ICY MASK* FOR A FACE.

A THING TO WHOM *KILLING* IS AS NATURAL AS *BREATHING.*

A THING THAT FINDS PLEASURE ONLY IN COLD *CRUELTY.*

YEARS PASS.

MATT MURDOCK GRADUATES *SUMMA CUM LAUDE* FROM *HARVARD LAW SCHOOL* AND FINDS WORK AT THE BOSTON FIRM OF *SUSSMAN* AND *CASTRO.*

HE IS NOT HAPPY, BUT HE IS *BUSY.* AND THAT'S *CLOSE* ENOUGH.

UNTIL THE *PAST* COMES CALLING.

EXCUSE ME, MURDOCK, BUT I'M *NOT* ASKING. YOU SHOULD BE *GRATEFUL* FOR THIS OPPORTUNITY.

YES, SIR.

YOU'VE DONE *GOOD WORK* FOR US, MATT. KEEP IT UP AND YOU'RE ON YOUR WAY TO BE- COMING THE YOUNGEST *JUNIOR PARTNER* WE'VE EVER HAD.

NOW GET YOUR BRIEF ON THAT PLANE TO *NEW YORK* AND NO MORE *ARGU- MENTS!*

YES, SIR.

NEW YORK. IT STILL *SOUNDS* THE SAME. IT STILL *FEELS* THE SAME.

AND ALL THE MEMORIES SURGE UP, LAUGHING AT HIM LIKE SCHOOLYARD *BULLIES.*

YOU CAN'T ESCAPE ME, THE CITY ROARS.

YOU CAN'T ESCAPE YOURSELF.

AND SO MATT COMES *BACK.*

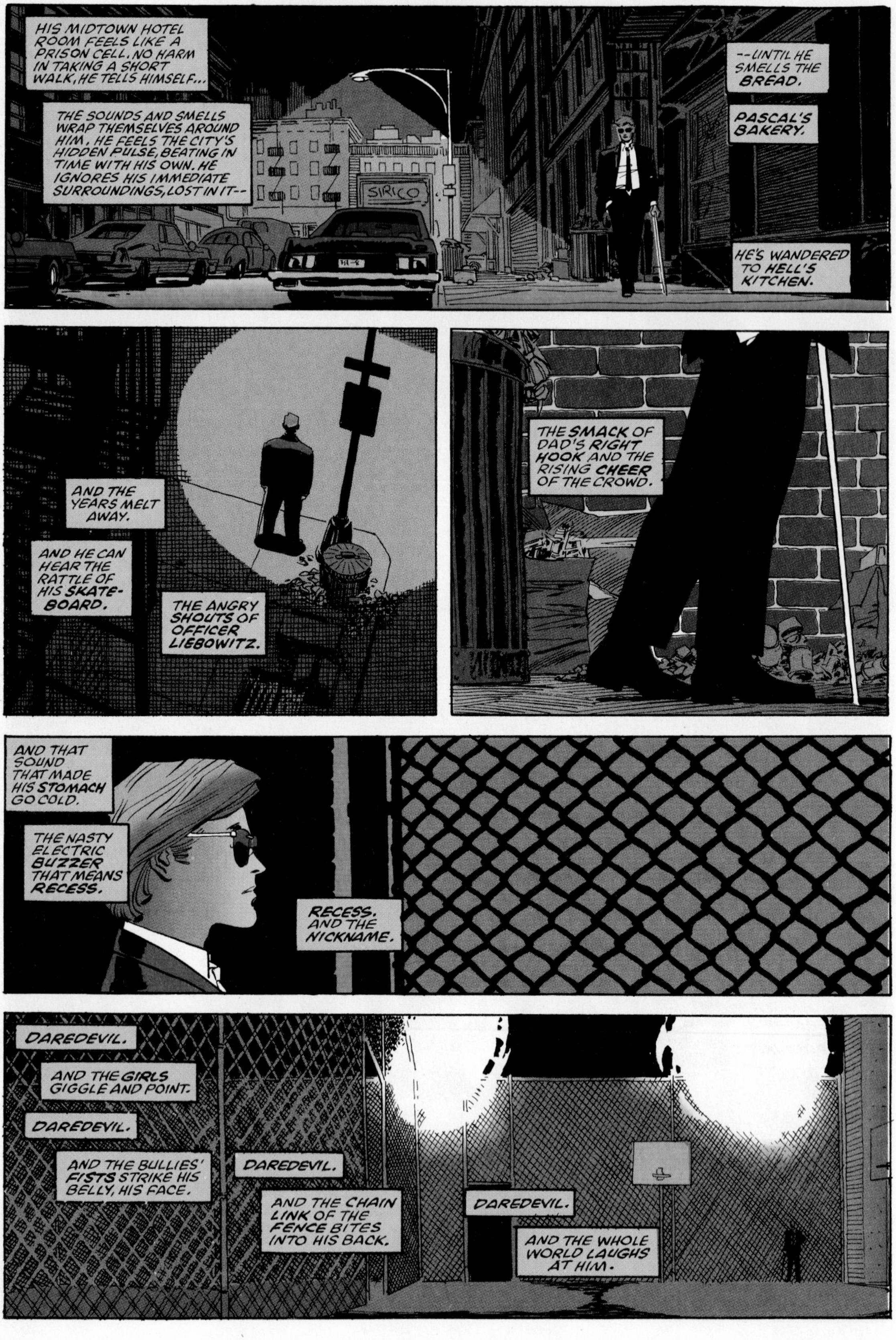
HIS MIDTOWN HOTEL ROOM FEELS LIKE A PRISON CELL. NO HARM IN TAKING A SHORT WALK, HE TELLS HIMSELF...
THE SOUNDS AND SMELLS WRAP THEMSELVES AROUND HIM. HE FEELS THE CITY'S HIDDEN PULSE, BEATING IN TIME WITH HIS OWN. HE IGNORES HIS IMMEDIATE SURROUNDINGS, LOST IN IT--
--UNTIL HE SMELLS THE BREAD.
PASCAL'S BAKERY.
HE'S WANDERED TO HELL'S KITCHEN.
AND THE YEARS MELT AWAY.
AND HE CAN HEAR THE RATTLE OF HIS SKATE-BOARD.
THE ANGRY SHOUTS OF OFFICER LIEBOWITZ.
THE SMACK OF DAD'S RIGHT HOOK AND THE RISING CHEER OF THE CROWD.
AND THAT SOUND THAT MADE HIS STOMACH GO COLD.
THE NASTY ELECTRIC BUZZER THAT MEANS RECESS.
RECESS. AND THE NICKNAME.
DAREDEVIL.
AND THE GIRLS GIGGLE AND POINT.
DAREDEVIL.
AND THE BULLIES' FISTS STRIKE HIS BELLY, HIS FACE.
DAREDEVIL.
AND THE CHAIN LINK OF THE FENCE BITES INTO HIS BACK.
DAREDEVIL.
AND THE WHOLE WORLD LAUGHS AT HIM.

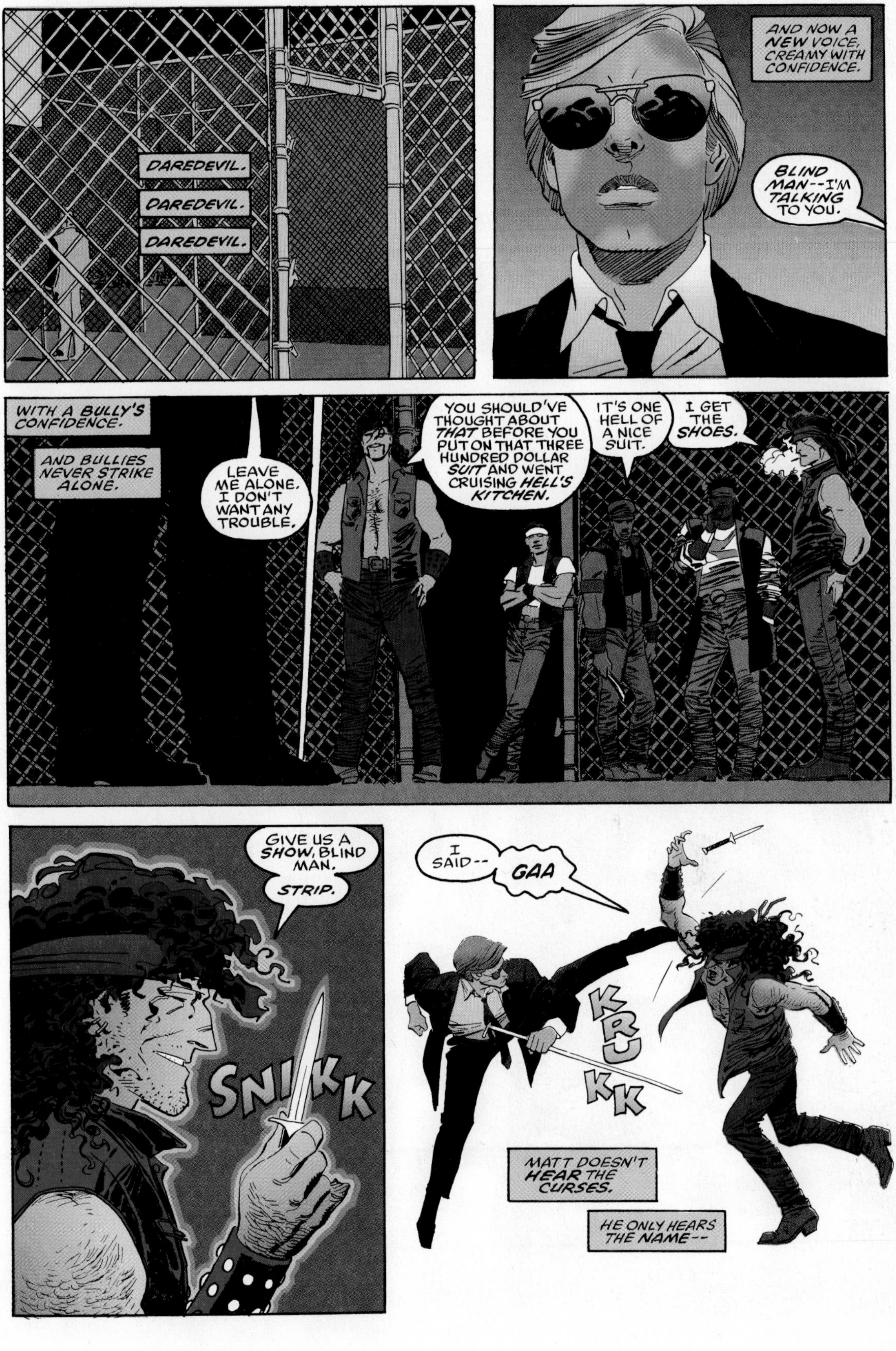
DAREDEVIL.
DAREDEVIL.
DAREDEVIL.
AND NOW A NEW VOICE, CREAMY WITH CONFIDENCE.
BLIND MAN--I'M TALKING TO YOU.
WITH A BULLY'S CONFIDENCE.
AND BULLIES NEVER STRIKE ALONE.
LEAVE ME ALONE. I DON'T WANT ANY TROUBLE.
YOU SHOULD'VE THOUGHT ABOUT THAT BEFORE YOU PUT ON THAT THREE HUNDRED DOLLAR SUIT AND WENT CRUISING HELL'S KITCHEN.
IT'S ONE HELL OF A NICE SUIT.
I GET THE SHOES.
GIVE US A SHOW, BLIND MAN.
STRIP.
SNIKKK
I SAID--
GAA
KRUKK
MATT DOESN'T HEAR THE CURSES.
HE ONLY HEARS THE NAME--

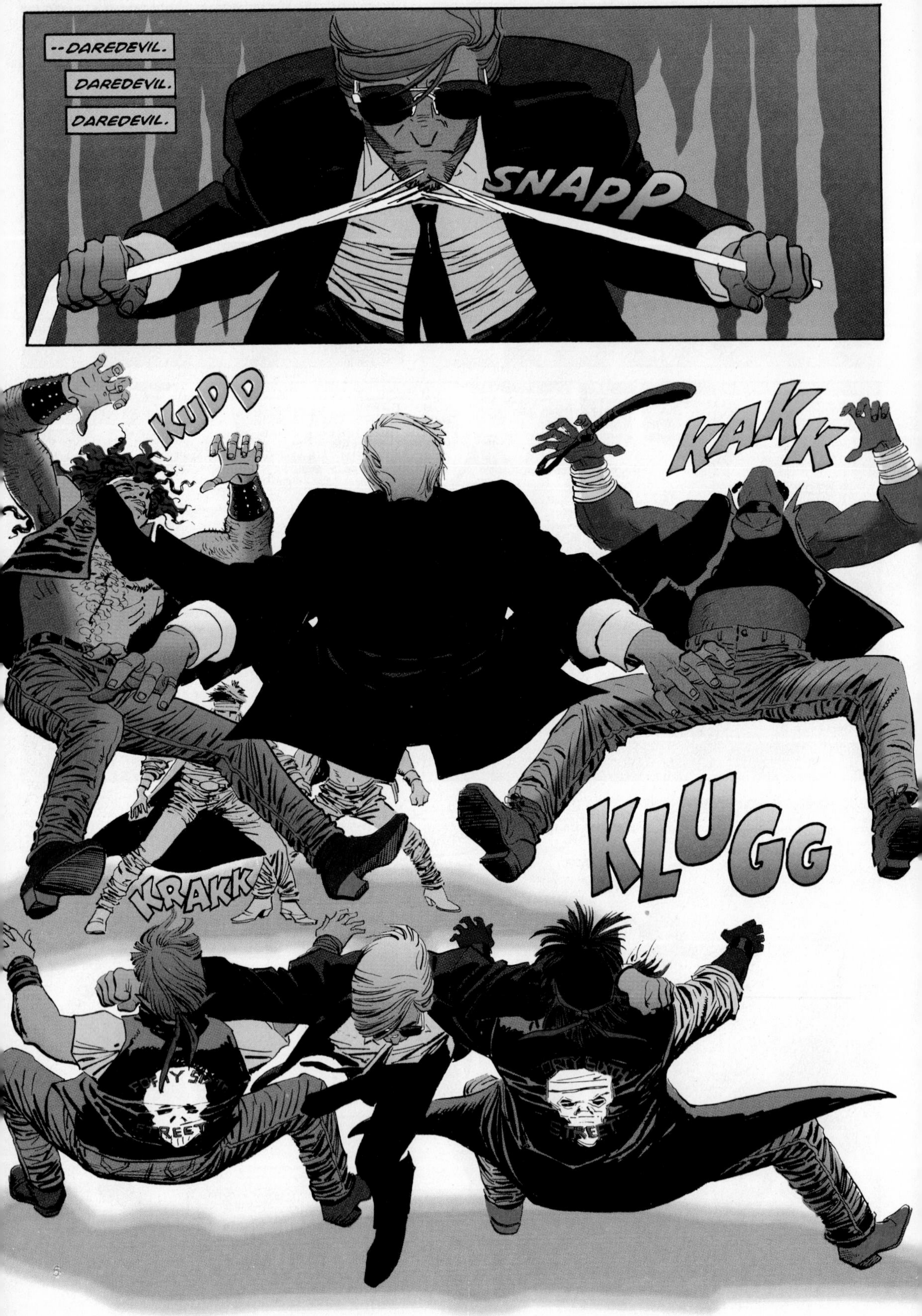
--DAREDEVIL.
DAREDEVIL.
DAREDEVIL.
SNAPP
KUDD
KAKK
KLUGG
KRAKK

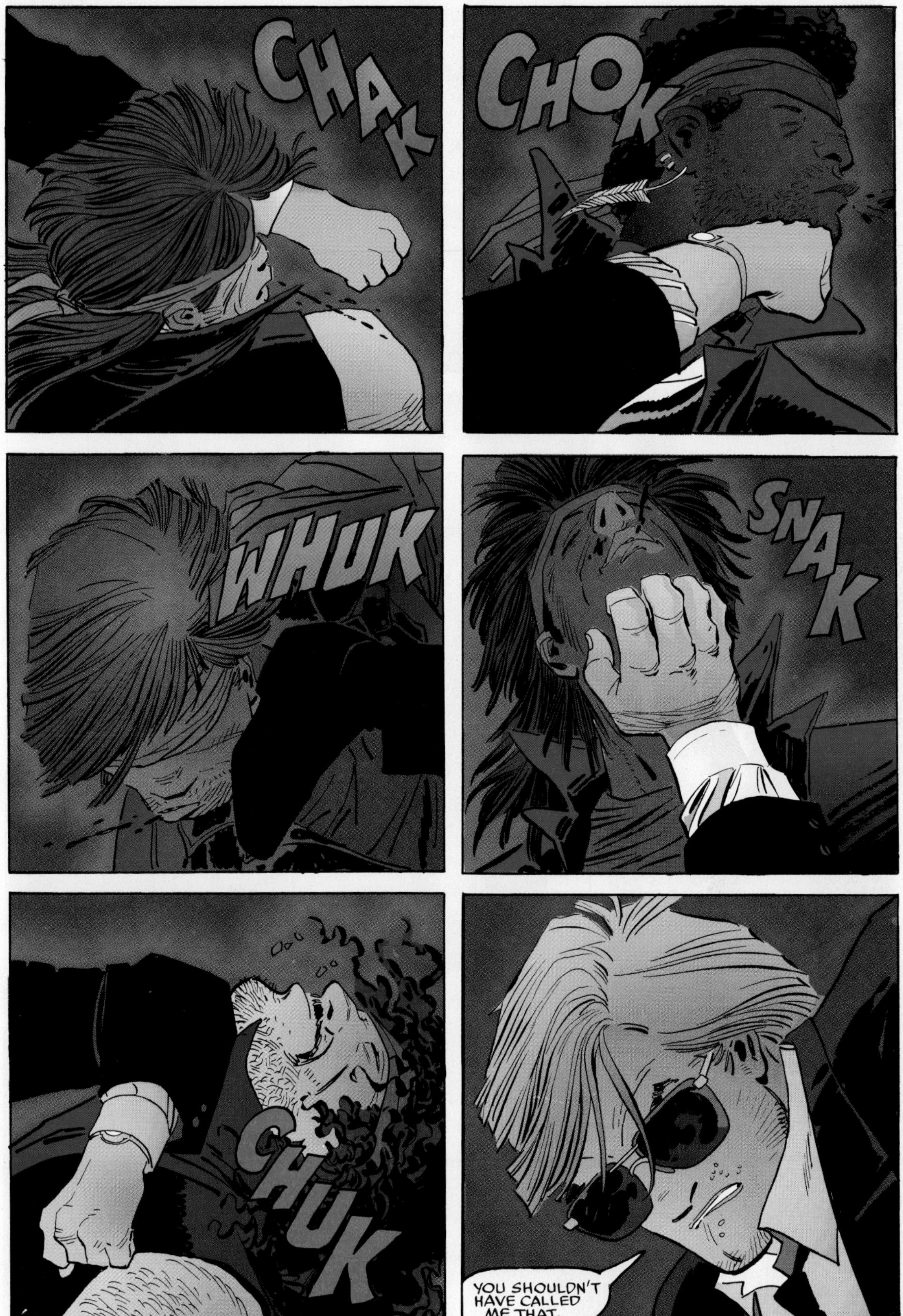
CHAK
CHOK
WHUK
SNAK
CHUK
YOU SHOULDN'T HAVE CALLED ME THAT.

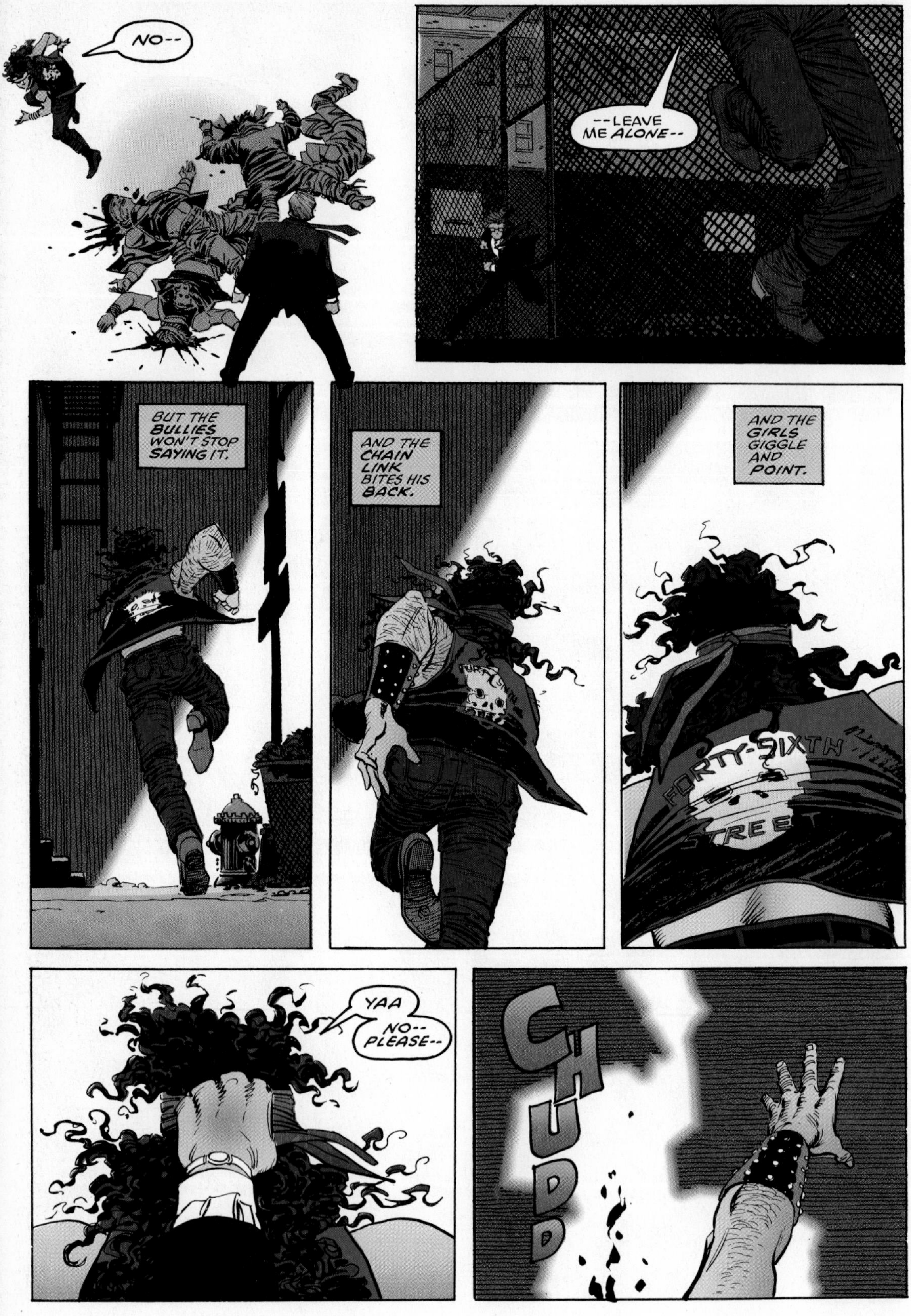
NO--
--LEAVE ME ALONE--
BUT THE BULLIES WON'T STOP SAYING IT.
AND THE CHAIN LINK BITES HIS BACK.
AND THE GIRLS GIGGLE AND POINT.
FORTY-SIXTH STREET
YAA NO-- PLEASE--
CHUDD

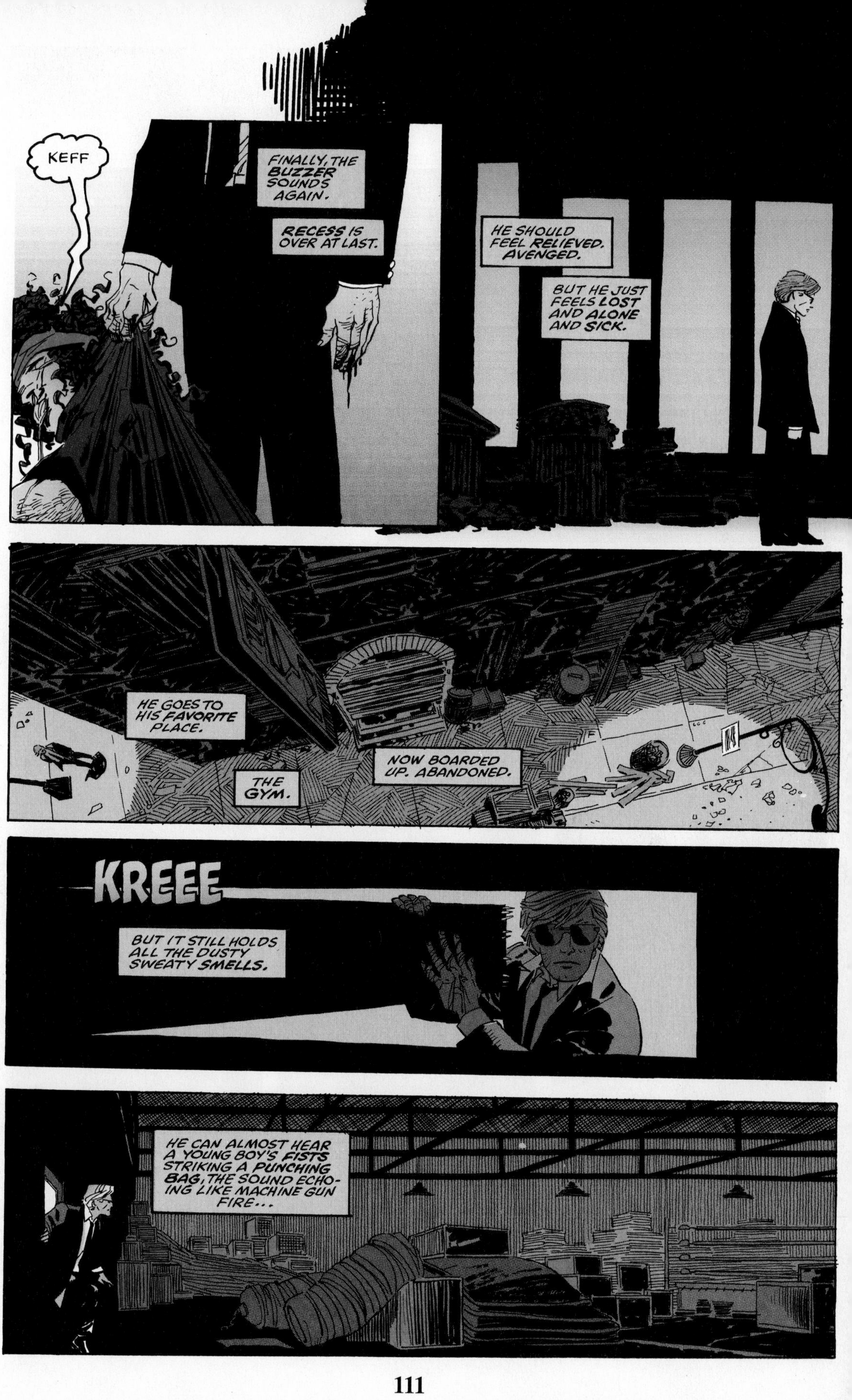
KEFF
FINALLY, THE BUZZER SOUNDS AGAIN.
RECESS IS OVER AT LAST.
HE SHOULD FEEL RELIEVED. AVENGED.
BUT HE JUST FEELS LOST AND ALONE AND SICK.
HE GOES TO HIS FAVORITE PLACE.
THE GYM.
NOW BOARDED UP. ABANDONED.
KREEE
BUT IT STILL HOLDS ALL THE DUSTY SWEATY SMELLS.
HE CAN ALMOST HEAR A YOUNG BOY'S FISTS STRIKING A PUNCHING BAG, THE SOUND ECHOING LIKE MACHINE GUN FIRE...

BUT THAT'S ALL GONE NOW. DEAD AND BURIED. IN THE PAST.

MURDOCK vs RIGGER

BURIED WITH DAD.

BURIED WITH MATT'S SKATE-BOARD AND SKI MASK AND ALL HIS MISCHIEF.

BICO RUIZ VS

TONY little boy BOYARDO VS

HIS FEVER BREAKS. HE'S IN CONTROL AGAIN. HE CALMS HIS HEART...

...AND HEARS ANOTHER'S BEAT.

HE GETS HER SCENT.

FEMALE. YOUNG. STRONG. SCARED.

SHE'S HOLDING HER BREATH.

NOW-- SHE'S MOVING--

--RUBBER GIVES OUT A GROAN--

--THEN SIGHS, IN RELIEF.

I MEAN YOU NO HARM, YOUNG LADY.

THPP

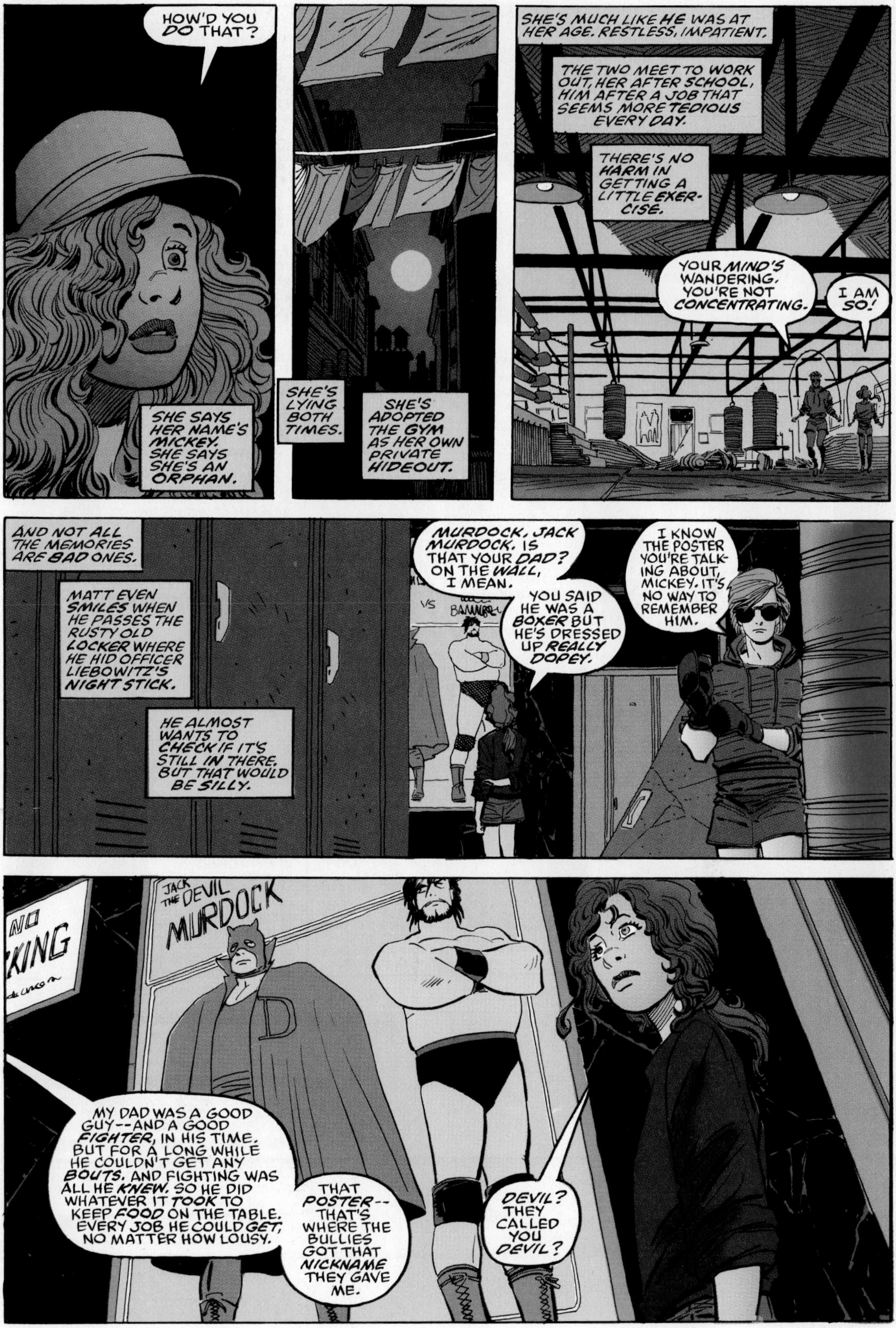
HOW'D YOU DO THAT?
SHE SAYS HER NAME'S MICKEY. SHE SAYS SHE'S AN ORPHAN.
SHE'S LYING BOTH TIMES.
SHE'S ADOPTED THE GYM AS HER OWN PRIVATE HIDEOUT.
SHE'S MUCH LIKE HE WAS AT HER AGE. RESTLESS, IMPATIENT.
THE TWO MEET TO WORK OUT, HER AFTER SCHOOL, HIM AFTER A JOB THAT SEEMS MORE TEDIOUS EVERY DAY.
THERE'S NO HARM IN GETTING A LITTLE EXER-CISE.
YOUR MIND'S WANDERING. YOU'RE NOT CONCENTRATING.
I AM SO!
AND NOT ALL THE MEMORIES ARE BAD ONES.
MATT EVEN SMILES WHEN HE PASSES THE RUSTY OLD LOCKER WHERE HE HID OFFICER LIEBOWITZ'S NIGHT STICK.
HE ALMOST WANTS TO CHECK IF IT'S STILL IN THERE. BUT THAT WOULD BE SILLY.
MURDOCK. JACK MURDOCK. IS THAT YOUR DAD? ON THE WALL, I MEAN.
YOU SAID HE WAS A BOXER BUT HE'S DRESSED UP REALLY DOPEY.
I KNOW THE POSTER YOU'RE TALK-ING ABOUT, MICKEY. IT'S NO WAY TO REMEMBER HIM.
JACK THE DEVIL MURDOCK
MY DAD WAS A GOOD GUY--AND A GOOD FIGHTER, IN HIS TIME. BUT FOR A LONG WHILE HE COULDN'T GET ANY BOUTS. AND FIGHTING WAS ALL HE KNEW. SO HE DID WHATEVER IT TOOK TO KEEP FOOD ON THE TABLE. EVERY JOB HE COULD GET, NO MATTER HOW LOUSY.
THAT POSTER--THAT'S WHERE THE BULLIES GOT THAT NICKNAME THEY GAVE ME.
DEVIL? THEY CALLED YOU DEVIL?

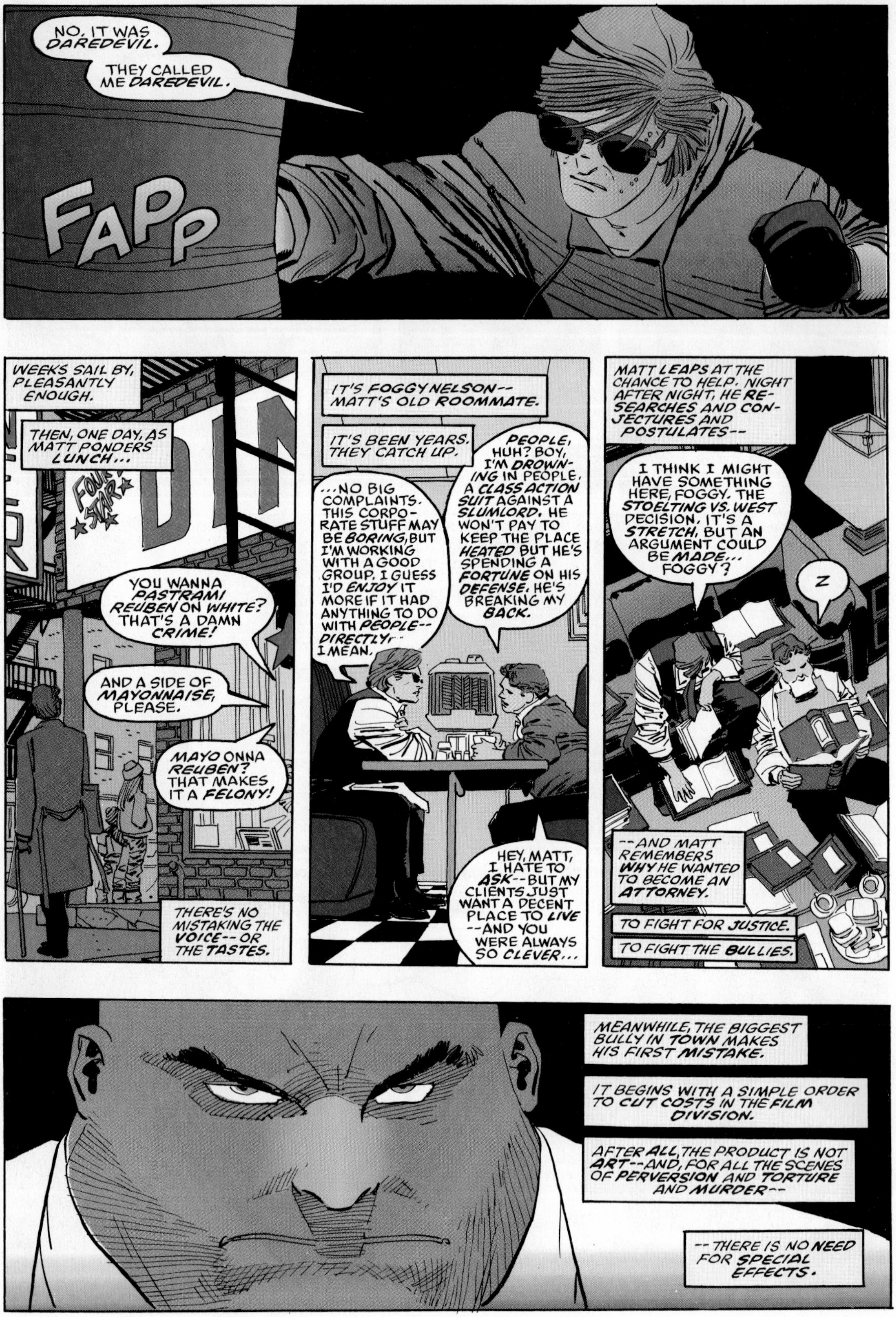
NO, IT WAS DAREDEVIL.
THEY CALLED ME DAREDEVIL.
FAPP
WEEKS SAIL BY, PLEASANTLY ENOUGH.
THEN, ONE DAY, AS MATT PONDERS LUNCH...
YOU WANNA PASTRAMI REUBEN ON WHITE? THAT'S A DAMN CRIME!
AND A SIDE OF MAYONNAISE, PLEASE.
MAYO ONNA REUBEN? THAT MAKES IT A FELONY!
THERE'S NO MISTAKING THE VOICE-- OR THE TASTES.
IT'S FOGGY NELSON-- MATT'S OLD ROOMMATE.
IT'S BEEN YEARS. THEY CATCH UP.
...NO BIG COMPLAINTS. THIS CORPORATE STUFF MAY BE BORING, BUT I'M WORKING WITH A GOOD GROUP. I GUESS I'D ENJOY IT MORE IF IT HAD ANYTHING TO DO WITH PEOPLE-- DIRECTLY, I MEAN.
PEOPLE, HUH? BOY, I'M DROWNING IN PEOPLE. A CLASS ACTION SUIT AGAINST A SLUMLORD. HE WON'T PAY TO KEEP THE PLACE HEATED BUT HE'S SPENDING A FORTUNE ON HIS DEFENSE. HE'S BREAKING MY BACK.
HEY, MATT, I HATE TO ASK-- BUT MY CLIENTS JUST WANT A DECENT PLACE TO LIVE --AND YOU WERE ALWAYS SO CLEVER...
MATT LEAPS AT THE CHANCE TO HELP. NIGHT AFTER NIGHT, HE RESEARCHES AND CONJECTURES AND POSTULATES--
I THINK I MIGHT HAVE SOMETHING HERE, FOGGY. THE STOELTING VS. WEST DECISION. IT'S A STRETCH, BUT AN ARGUMENT COULD BE MADE... FOGGY?
Z
--AND MATT REMEMBERS WHY HE WANTED TO BECOME AN ATTORNEY.
TO FIGHT FOR JUSTICE.
TO FIGHT THE BULLIES.
MEANWHILE, THE BIGGEST BULLY IN TOWN MAKES HIS FIRST MISTAKE.
IT BEGINS WITH A SIMPLE ORDER TO CUT COSTS IN THE FILM DIVISION.
AFTER ALL, THE PRODUCT IS NOT ART--AND, FOR ALL THE SCENES OF PERVERSION AND TORTURE AND MURDER--
--THERE IS NO NEED FOR SPECIAL EFFECTS.

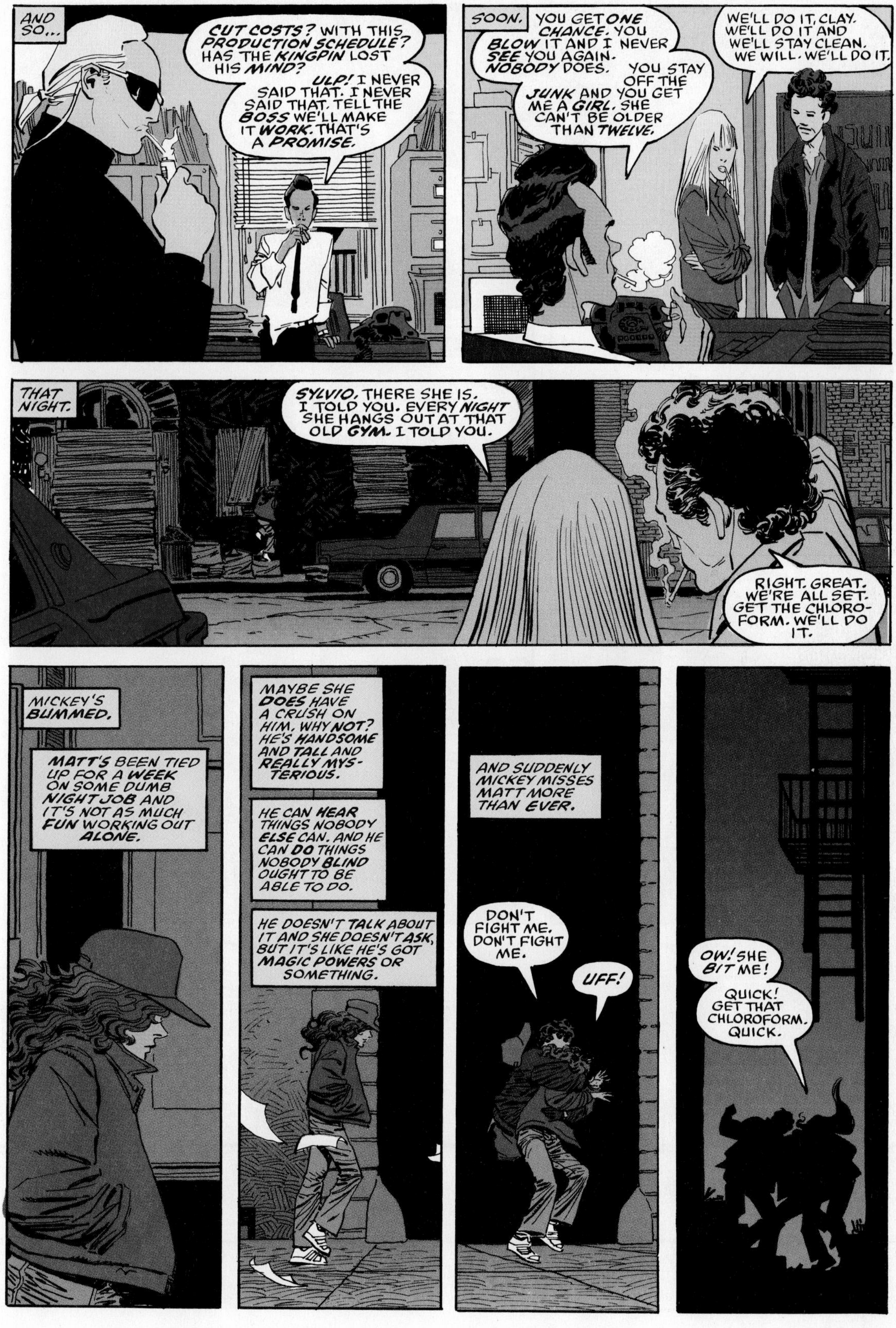
AND SO...
CUT COSTS? WITH THIS PRODUCTION SCHEDULE? HAS THE KINGPIN LOST HIS MIND?
ULP! I NEVER SAID THAT. I NEVER SAID THAT. TELL THE BOSS WE'LL MAKE IT WORK. THAT'S A PROMISE.
SOON.
YOU GET ONE CHANCE. YOU BLOW IT AND I NEVER SEE YOU AGAIN. NOBODY DOES.
YOU STAY OFF THE JUNK AND YOU GET ME A GIRL. SHE CAN'T BE OLDER THAN TWELVE.
WE'LL DO IT, CLAY. WE'LL DO IT AND WE'LL STAY CLEAN. WE WILL. WE'LL DO IT.
THAT NIGHT.
SYLVIO. THERE SHE IS. I TOLD YOU. EVERY NIGHT SHE HANGS OUT AT THAT OLD GYM. I TOLD YOU.
RIGHT. GREAT. WE'RE ALL SET. GET THE CHLOROFORM. WE'LL DO IT.
MICKEY'S BUMMED.
MATT'S BEEN TIED UP FOR A WEEK ON SOME DUMB NIGHT JOB AND IT'S NOT AS MUCH FUN WORKING OUT ALONE.
MAYBE SHE DOES HAVE A CRUSH ON HIM. WHY NOT? HE'S HANDSOME AND TALL AND REALLY MYSTERIOUS.
HE CAN HEAR THINGS NOBODY ELSE CAN. AND HE CAN DO THINGS NOBODY BLIND OUGHT TO BE ABLE TO DO.
HE DOESN'T TALK ABOUT IT AND SHE DOESN'T ASK, BUT IT'S LIKE HE'S GOT MAGIC POWERS OR SOMETHING.
AND SUDDENLY MICKEY MISSES MATT MORE THAN EVER.
DON'T FIGHT ME. DON'T FIGHT ME.
UFF!
OW! SHE BIT ME!
QUICK! GET THAT CHLOROFORM. QUICK.

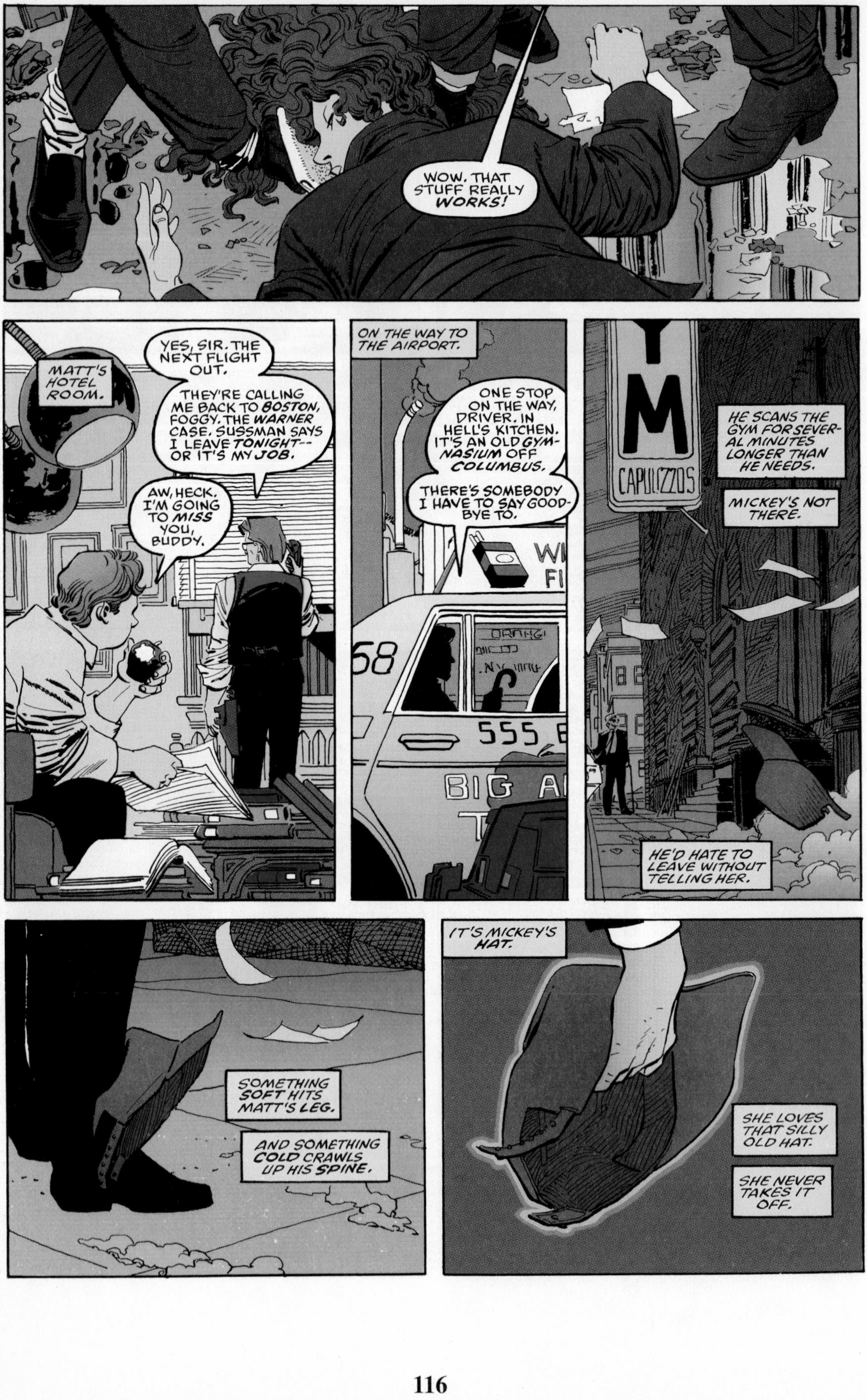
WOW. THAT STUFF REALLY WORKS!
MATT'S HOTEL ROOM.
YES, SIR. THE NEXT FLIGHT OUT.
THEY'RE CALLING ME BACK TO BOSTON, FOGGY. THE WARNER CASE. SUSSMAN SAYS I LEAVE TONIGHT-- OR IT'S MY JOB.
AW, HECK. I'M GOING TO MISS YOU, BUDDY.
ON THE WAY TO THE AIRPORT.
ONE STOP ON THE WAY, DRIVER. IN HELL'S KITCHEN. IT'S AN OLD GYMNASIUM OFF COLUMBUS.
THERE'S SOMEBODY I HAVE TO SAY GOOD-BYE TO.
HE SCANS THE GYM FOR SEVERAL MINUTES LONGER THAN HE NEEDS.
MICKEY'S NOT THERE.
HE'D HATE TO LEAVE WITHOUT TELLING HER.
SOMETHING SOFT HITS MATT'S LEG.
AND SOMETHING COLD CRAWLS UP HIS SPINE.
IT'S MICKEY'S HAT.
SHE LOVES THAT SILLY OLD HAT.
SHE NEVER TAKES IT OFF.

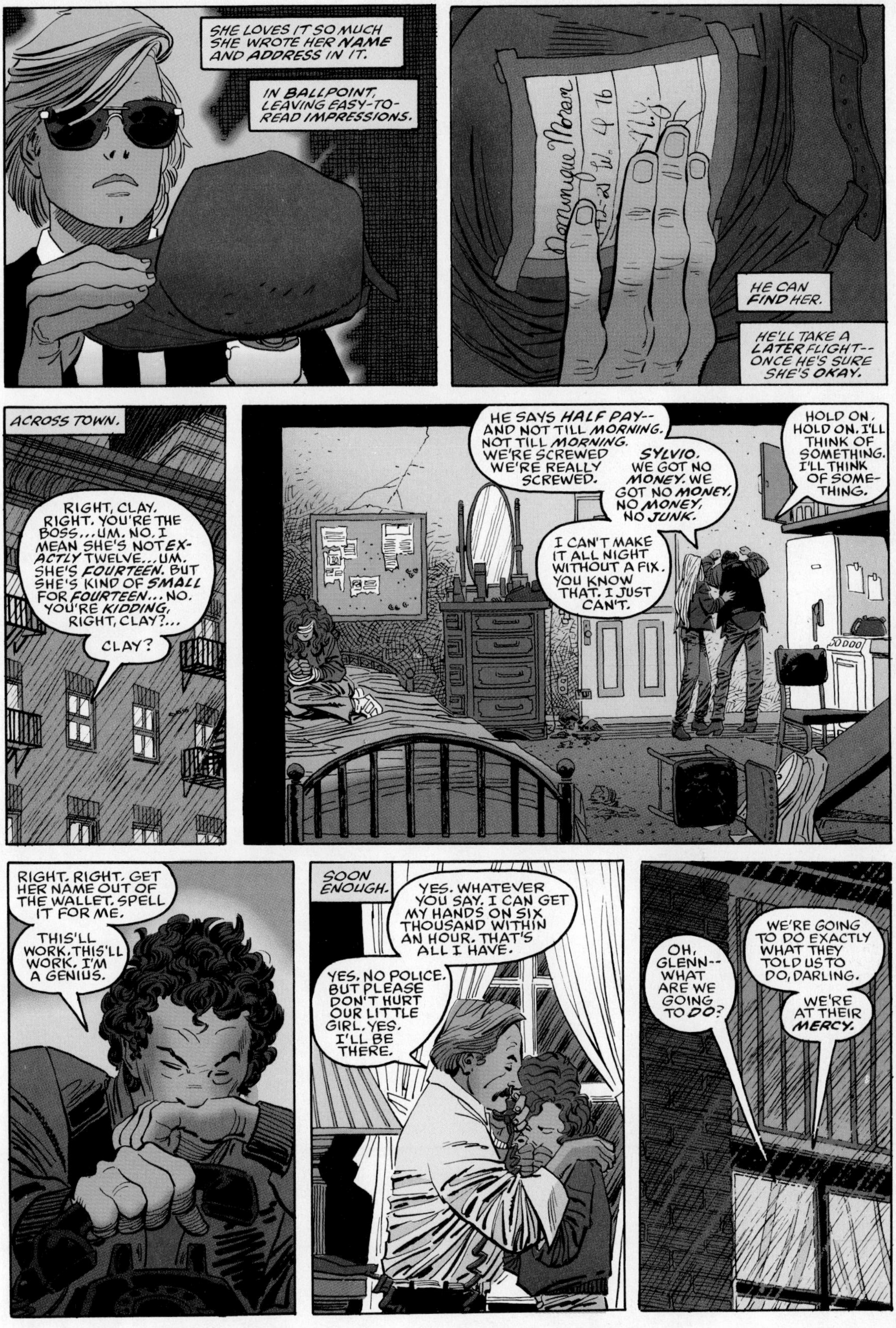
SHE LOVES IT SO MUCH SHE WROTE HER NAME AND ADDRESS IN IT.
IN BALLPOINT, LEAVING EASY-TO-READ IMPRESSIONS.
HE CAN FIND HER.
HE'LL TAKE A LATER FLIGHT-- ONCE HE'S SURE SHE'S OKAY.
ACROSS TOWN.
RIGHT, CLAY. RIGHT. YOU'RE THE BOSS... UM. NO, I MEAN SHE'S NOT EXACTLY TWELVE... UM. SHE'S FOURTEEN. BUT SHE'S KIND OF SMALL FOR FOURTEEN... NO. YOU'RE KIDDING, RIGHT, CLAY?...
CLAY?
HE SAYS HALF PAY-- AND NOT TILL MORNING. NOT TILL MORNING. WE'RE SCREWED WE'RE REALLY SCREWED.
SYLVIO. WE GOT NO MONEY. WE GOT NO MONEY. NO MONEY, NO JUNK.
I CAN'T MAKE IT ALL NIGHT WITHOUT A FIX. YOU KNOW THAT. I JUST CAN'T.
HOLD ON. HOLD ON. I'LL THINK OF SOMETHING. I'LL THINK OF SOMETHING.
RIGHT. RIGHT. GET HER NAME OUT OF THE WALLET. SPELL IT FOR ME.
THIS'LL WORK, THIS'LL WORK. I'M A GENIUS.
SOON ENOUGH.
YES. WHATEVER YOU SAY. I CAN GET MY HANDS ON SIX THOUSAND WITHIN AN HOUR. THAT'S ALL I HAVE.
YES. NO POLICE. BUT PLEASE DON'T HURT OUR LITTLE GIRL. YES. I'LL BE THERE.
OH, GLENN-- WHAT ARE WE GOING TO DO?
WE'RE GOING TO DO EXACTLY WHAT THEY TOLD US TO DO, DARLING.
WE'RE AT THEIR MERCY.

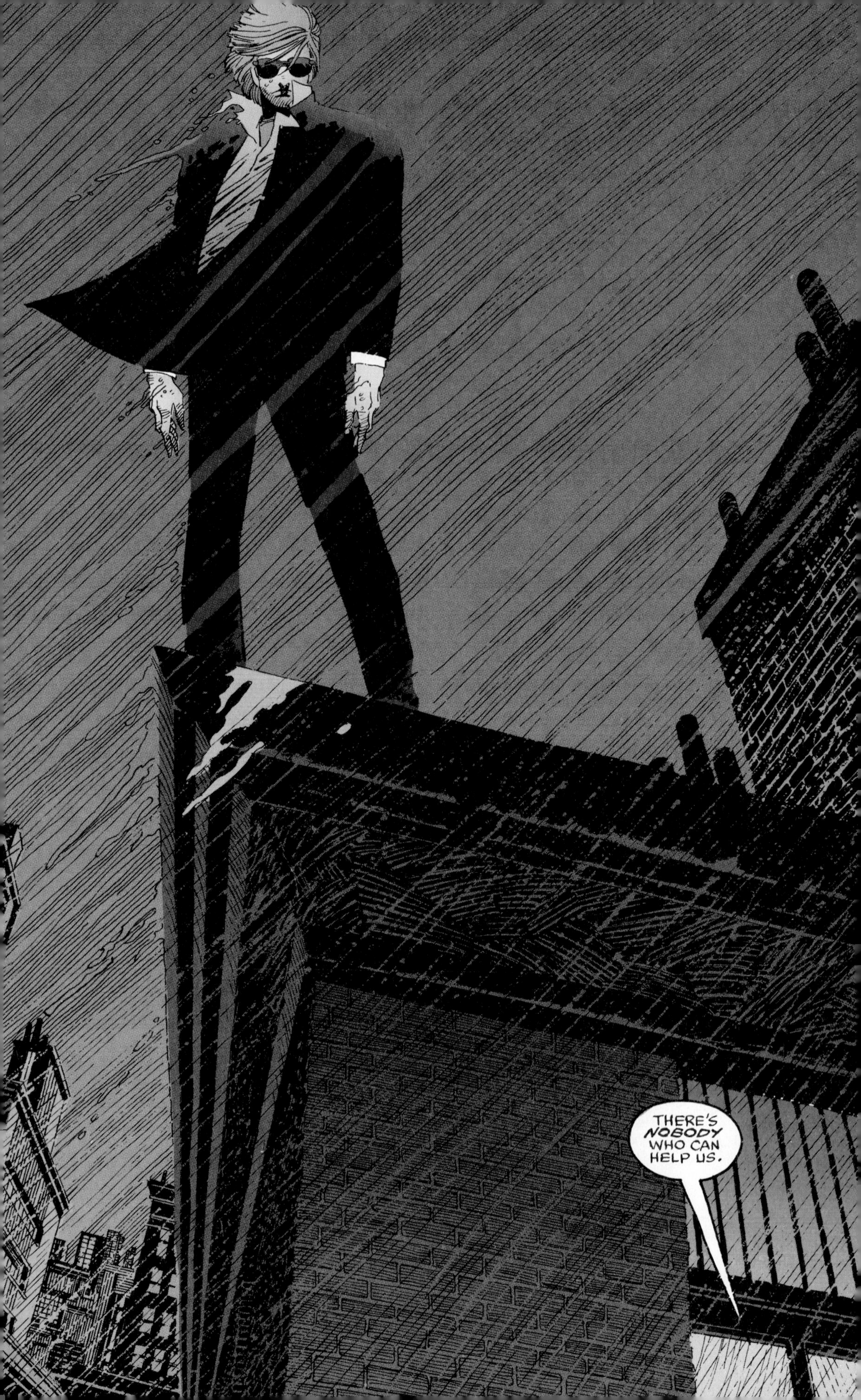
THERE'S NOBODY WHO CAN HELP US.

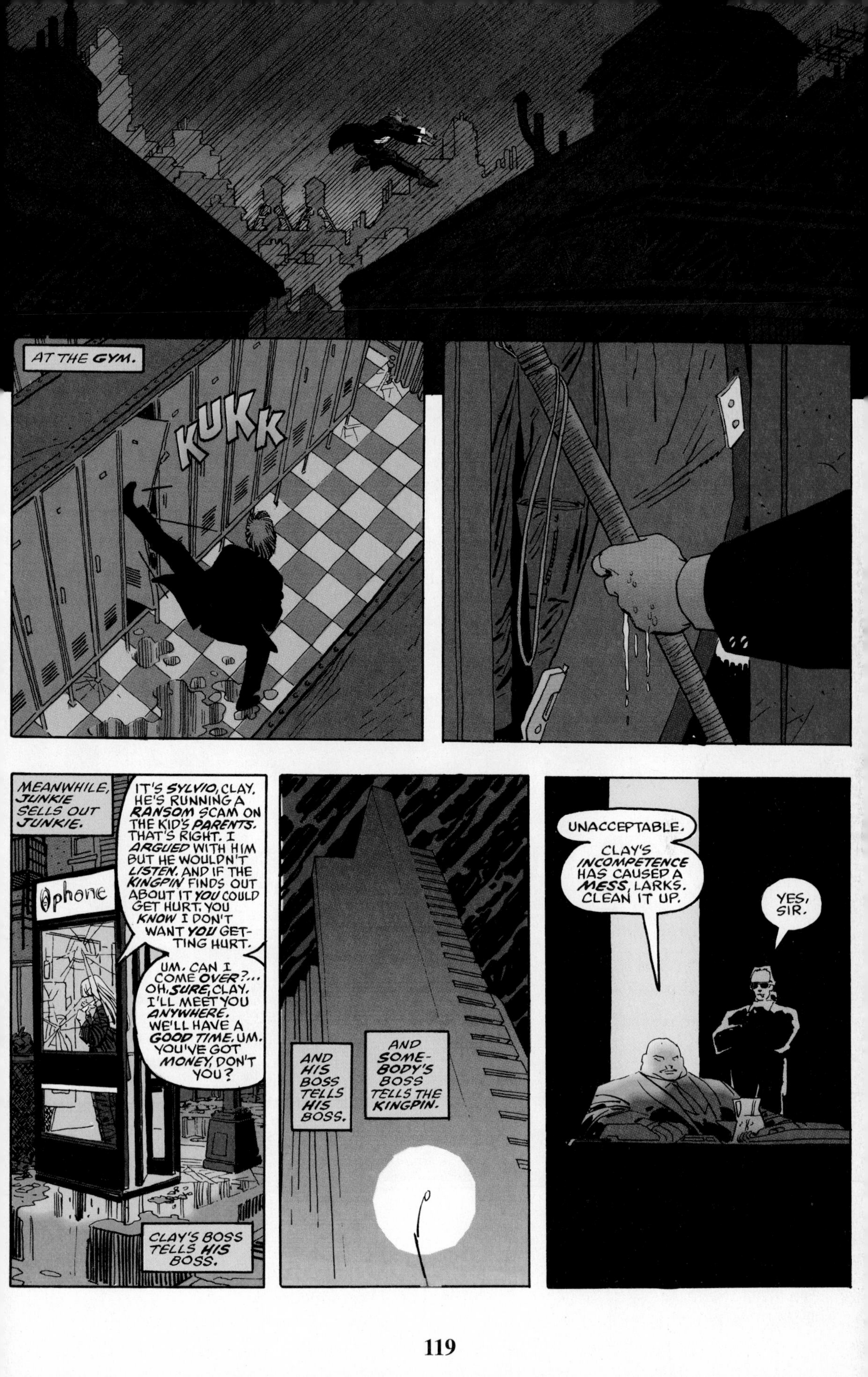
AT THE GYM.
KUKK
MEANWHILE, JUNKIE SELLS OUT JUNKIE.
IT'S SYLVIO, CLAY. HE'S RUNNING A RANSOM SCAM ON THE KID'S PARENTS. THAT'S RIGHT. I ARGUED WITH HIM BUT HE WOULDN'T LISTEN. AND IF THE KINGPIN FINDS OUT ABOUT IT YOU COULD GET HURT. YOU KNOW I DON'T WANT YOU GETTING HURT.
UM. CAN I COME OVER?... OH, SURE, CLAY, I'LL MEET YOU ANYWHERE. WE'LL HAVE A GOOD TIME. UM. YOU'VE GOT MONEY, DON'T YOU?
phone
CLAY'S BOSS TELLS HIS BOSS.
AND HIS BOSS TELLS HIS BOSS.
AND SOMEBODY'S BOSS TELLS THE KINGPIN.
UNACCEPTABLE.
CLAY'S INCOMPETENCE HAS CAUSED A MESS, LARKS. CLEAN IT UP.
YES, SIR.

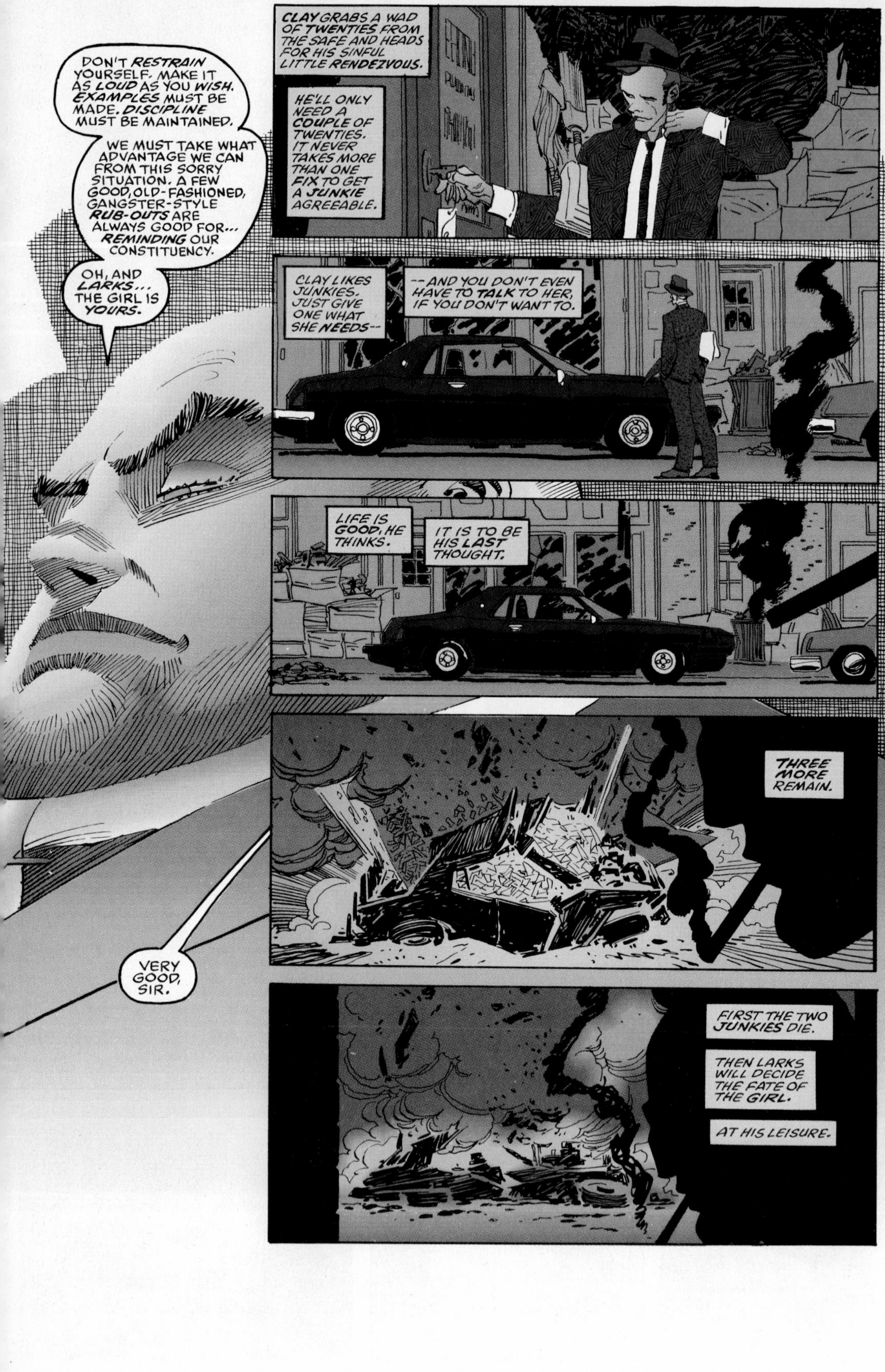
DON'T RESTRAIN YOURSELF. MAKE IT AS LOUD AS YOU WISH. EXAMPLES MUST BE MADE. DISCIPLINE MUST BE MAINTAINED.
WE MUST TAKE WHAT ADVANTAGE WE CAN FROM THIS SORRY SITUATION. A FEW GOOD, OLD-FASHIONED, GANGSTER-STYLE RUB-OUTS ARE ALWAYS GOOD FOR... REMINDING OUR CONSTITUENCY.
OH, AND LARKS... THE GIRL IS YOURS.
CLAY GRABS A WAD OF TWENTIES FROM THE SAFE AND HEADS FOR HIS SINFUL LITTLE RENDEZVOUS.
HE'LL ONLY NEED A COUPLE OF TWENTIES. IT NEVER TAKES MORE THAN ONE FIX TO GET A JUNKIE AGREEABLE.
CLAY LIKES JUNKIES. JUST GIVE ONE WHAT SHE NEEDS--
--AND YOU DON'T EVEN HAVE TO TALK TO HER, IF YOU DON'T WANT TO.
LIFE IS GOOD, HE THINKS.
IT IS TO BE HIS LAST THOUGHT.
THREE MORE REMAIN.
VERY GOOD, SIR.
FIRST THE TWO JUNKIES DIE.
THEN LARKS WILL DECIDE THE FATE OF THE GIRL.
AT HIS LEISURE.

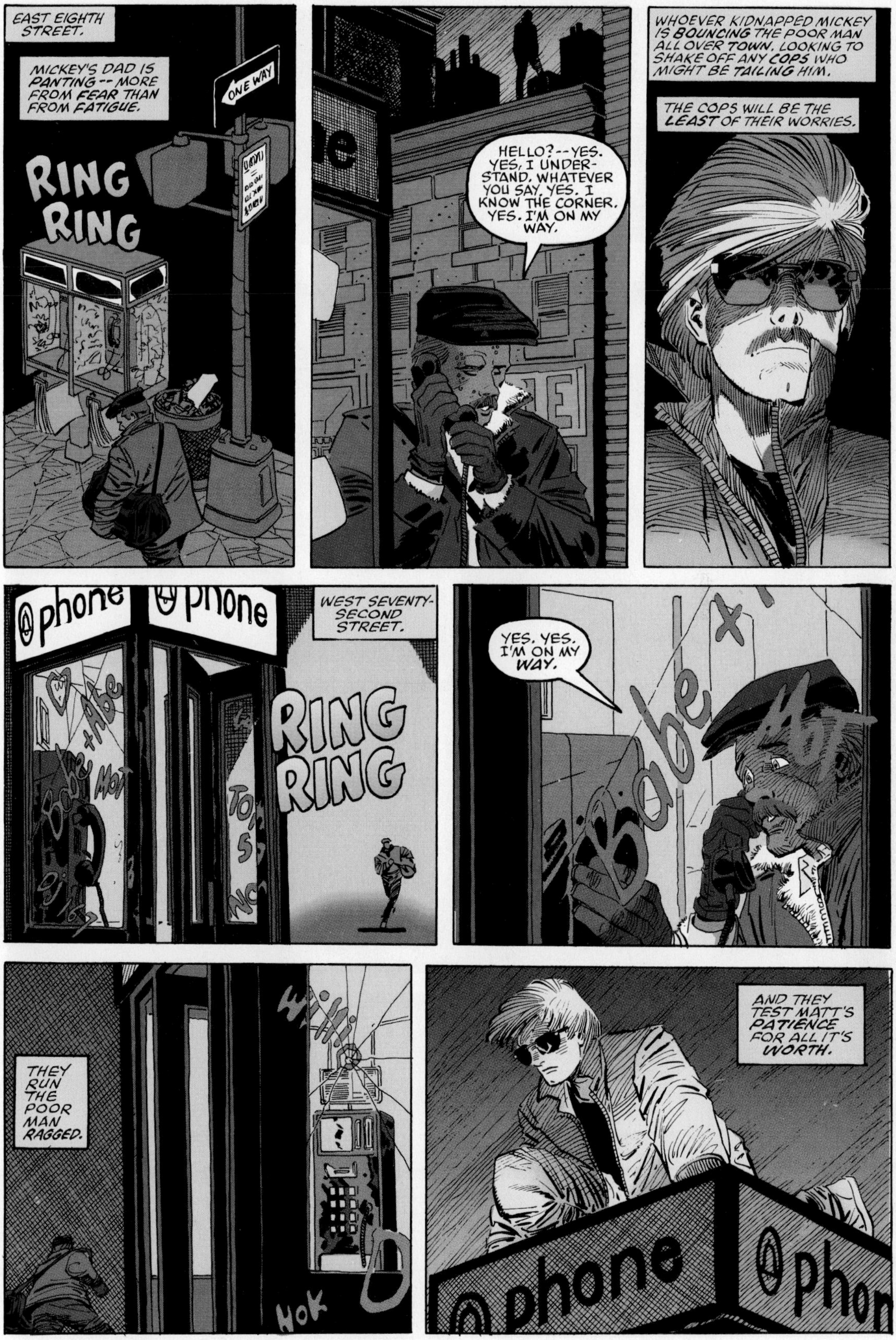
EAST EIGHTH STREET.
MICKEY'S DAD IS PANTING -- MORE FROM FEAR THAN FROM FATIGUE.
ONE WAY
RING RING
HELLO?--YES. YES, I UNDERSTAND. WHATEVER YOU SAY. YES. I KNOW THE CORNER. YES. I'M ON MY WAY.
WHOEVER KIDNAPPED MICKEY IS BOUNCING THE POOR MAN ALL OVER TOWN. LOOKING TO SHAKE OFF ANY COPS WHO MIGHT BE TAILING HIM.
THE COPS WILL BE THE LEAST OF THEIR WORRIES.
phone
phone
WEST SEVENTY-SECOND STREET.
RING RING
YES. YES. I'M ON MY WAY.
THEY RUN THE POOR MAN RAGGED.
AND THEY TEST MATT'S PATIENCE FOR ALL IT'S WORTH.
phone
Phon

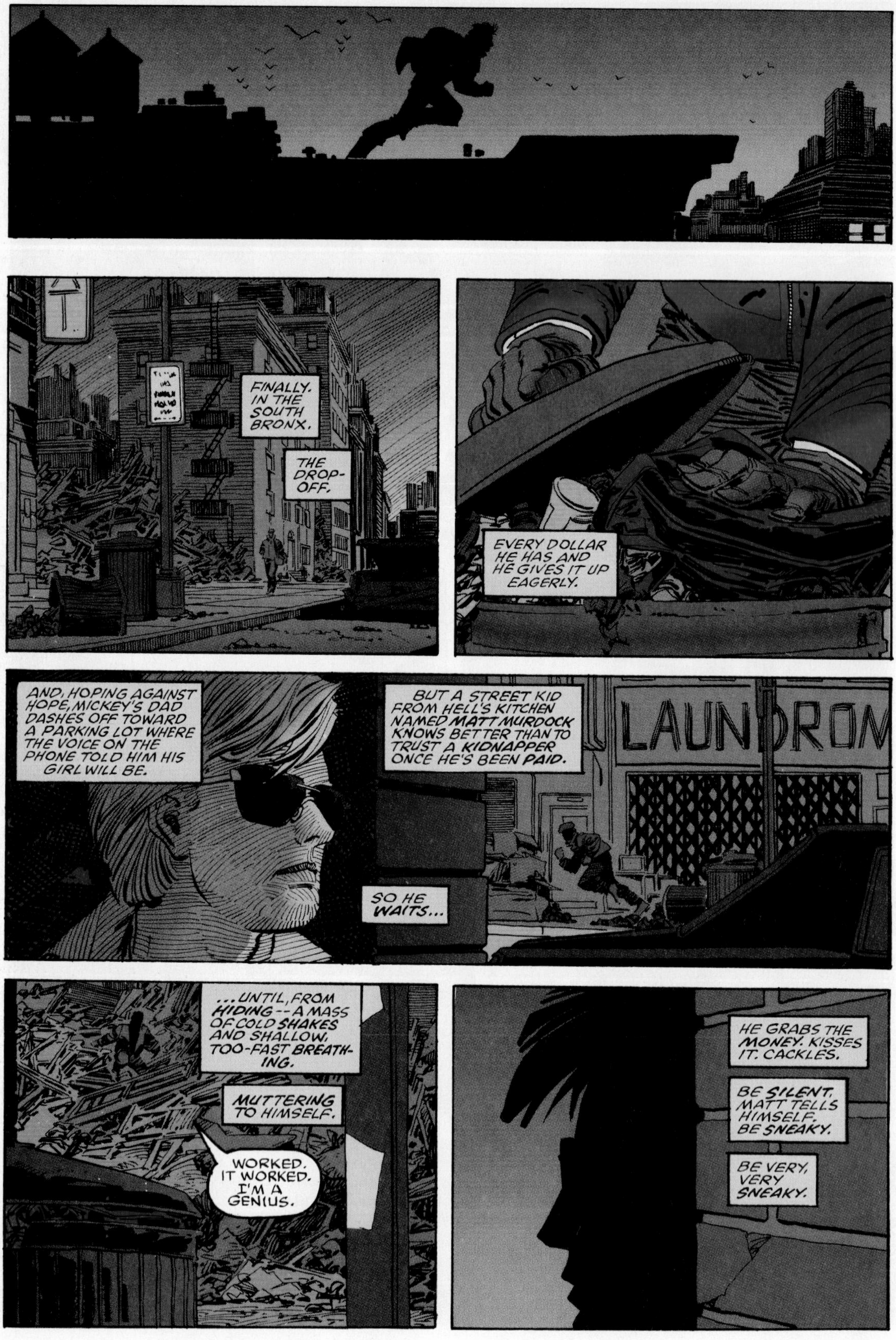

FINALLY. IN THE SOUTH BRONX.
THE DROP-OFF.
EVERY DOLLAR HE HAS AND HE GIVES IT UP EAGERLY.
AND, HOPING AGAINST HOPE, MICKEY'S DAD DASHES OFF TOWARD A PARKING LOT WHERE THE VOICE ON THE PHONE TOLD HIM HIS GIRL WILL BE.
BUT A STREET KID FROM HELL'S KITCHEN NAMED MATT MURDOCK KNOWS BETTER THAN TO TRUST A KIDNAPPER ONCE HE'S BEEN PAID.
LAUNDROM
SO HE WAITS...
...UNTIL, FROM HIDING -- A MASS OF COLD SHAKES AND SHALLOW, TOO-FAST BREATHING.
MUTTERING TO HIMSELF.
WORKED. IT WORKED. I'M A GENIUS.
HE GRABS THE MONEY. KISSES IT. CACKLES.
BE SILENT, MATT TELLS HIMSELF. BE SNEAKY.
BE VERY, VERY SNEAKY.

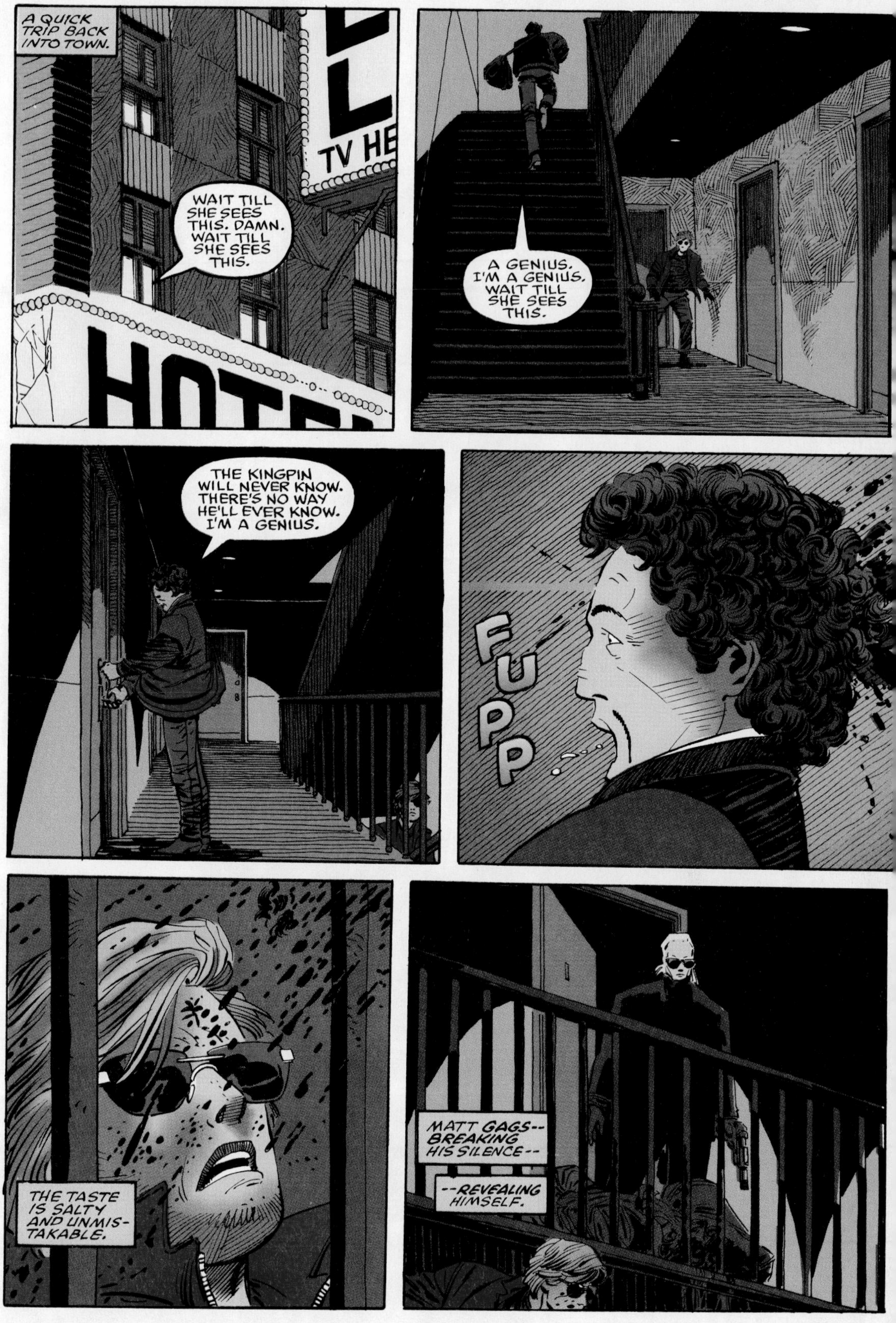
A QUICK TRIP BACK INTO TOWN.
TV HE
WAIT TILL SHE SEES THIS. DAMN. WAIT TILL SHE SEES THIS.
HOTE
A GENIUS. I'M A GENIUS. WAIT TILL SHE SEES THIS.
THE KINGPIN WILL NEVER KNOW. THERE'S NO WAY HE'LL EVER KNOW. I'M A GENIUS.
FUPP
THE TASTE IS SALTY AND UNMISTAKABLE.
MATT GAGS-- BREAKING HIS SILENCE--
--REVEALING HIMSELF.

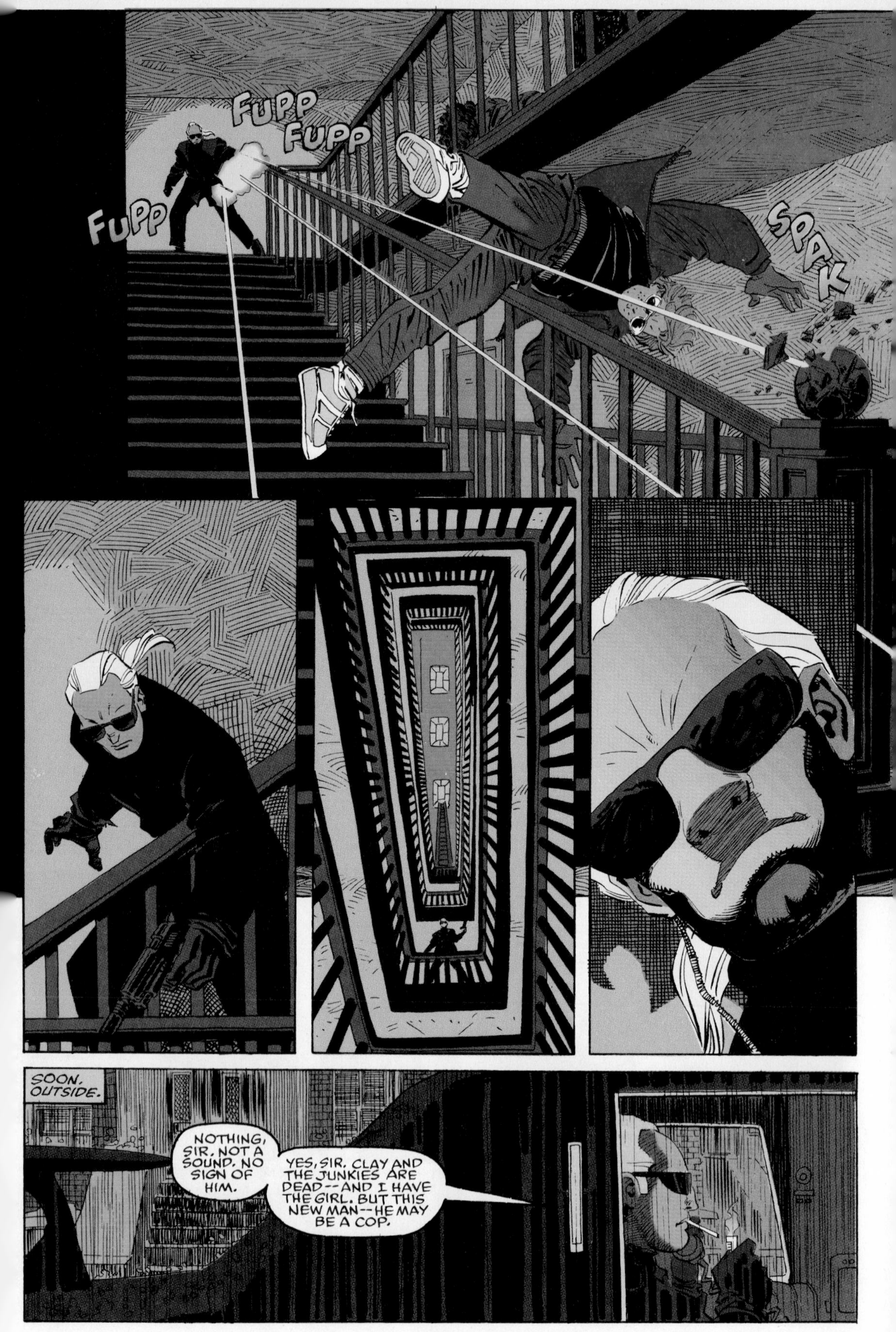
FUPP
FUPP
FUPP
SPAK
SOON. OUTSIDE.
NOTHING, SIR. NOT A SOUND. NO SIGN OF HIM.
YES, SIR. CLAY AND THE JUNKIES ARE DEAD--AND I HAVE THE GIRL. BUT THIS NEW MAN--HE MAY BE A COP.

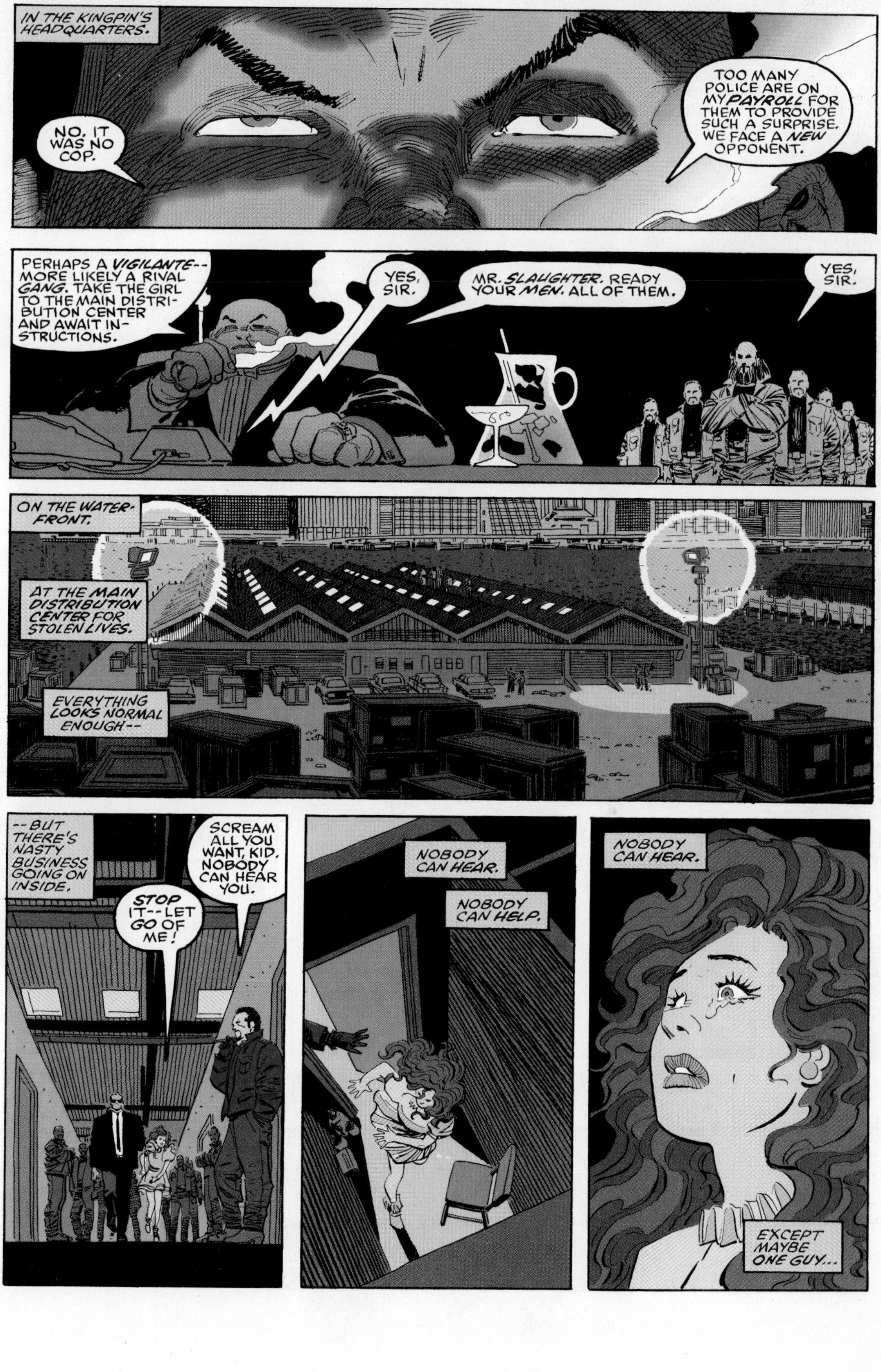
IN THE KINGPIN'S HEADQUARTERS.
NO, IT WAS NO COP.
TOO MANY POLICE ARE ON MY PAYROLL FOR THEM TO PROVIDE SUCH A SURPRISE. WE FACE A NEW OPPONENT.
PERHAPS A VIGILANTE-- MORE LIKELY A RIVAL GANG. TAKE THE GIRL TO THE MAIN DISTRIBUTION CENTER AND AWAIT INSTRUCTIONS.
YES, SIR.
MR. SLAUGHTER. READY YOUR MEN. ALL OF THEM.
YES, SIR.
ON THE WATERFRONT.
AT THE MAIN DISTRIBUTION CENTER FOR STOLEN LIVES.
EVERYTHING LOOKS NORMAL ENOUGH--
--BUT THERE'S NASTY BUSINESS GOING ON INSIDE.
SCREAM ALL YOU WANT, KID. NOBODY CAN HEAR YOU.
STOP IT--LET GO OF ME!
NOBODY CAN HEAR.
NOBODY CAN HELP.
NOBODY CAN HEAR.
EXCEPT MAYBE ONE GUY...

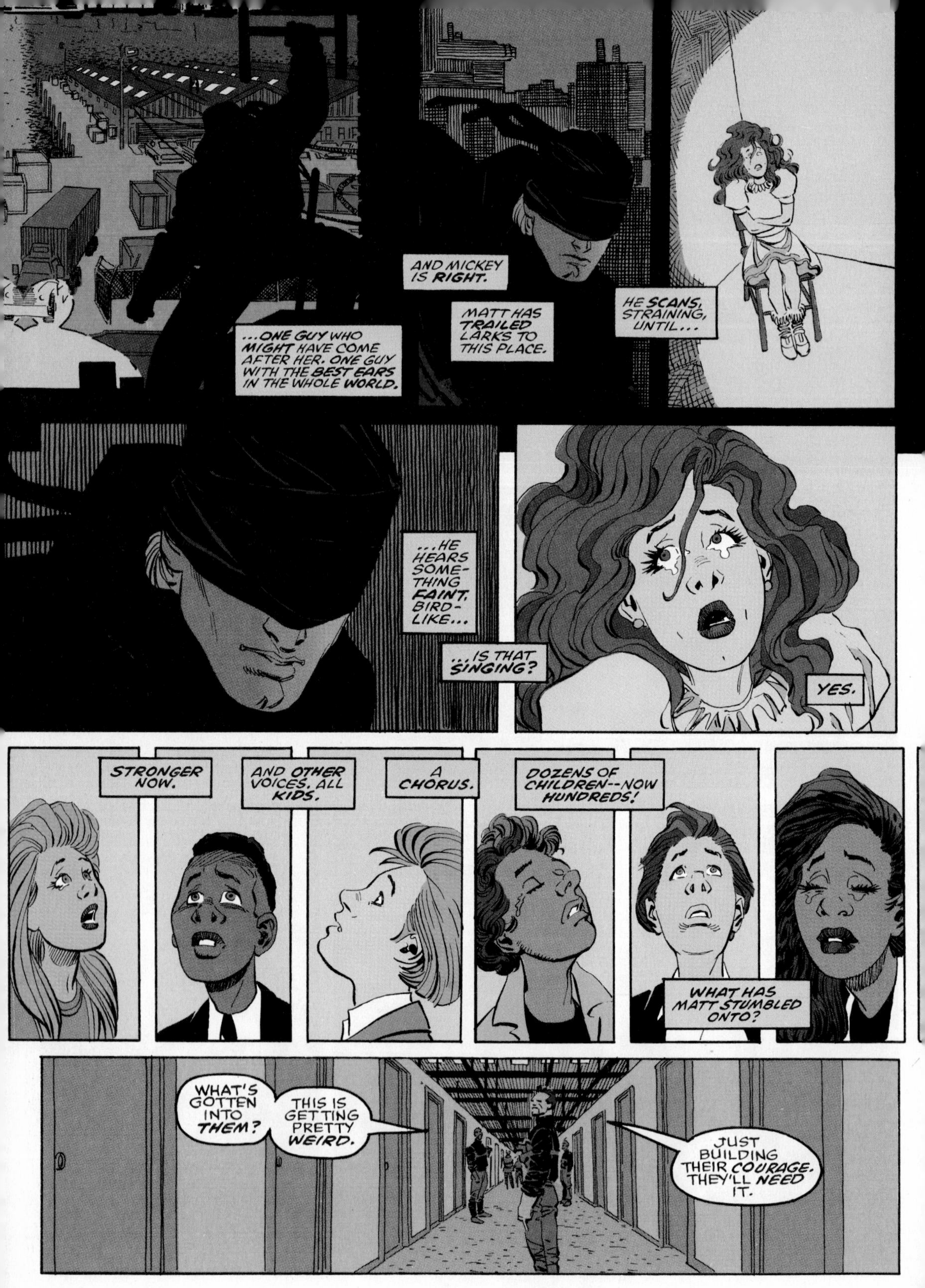
...ONE GUY WHO MIGHT HAVE COME AFTER HER. ONE GUY WITH THE BEST EARS IN THE WHOLE WORLD.
AND MICKEY IS RIGHT.
MATT HAS TRAILED LARKS TO THIS PLACE.
HE SCANS, STRAINING, UNTIL...
...HE HEARS SOMETHING FAINT, BIRD-LIKE...
...IS THAT SINGING?
YES.
STRONGER NOW.
AND OTHER VOICES, ALL KIDS.
A CHORUS.
DOZENS OF CHILDREN--NOW HUNDREDS!
WHAT HAS MATT STUMBLED ONTO?
WHAT'S GOTTEN INTO THEM?
THIS IS GETTING PRETTY WEIRD.
JUST BUILDING THEIR COURAGE. THEY'LL NEED IT.

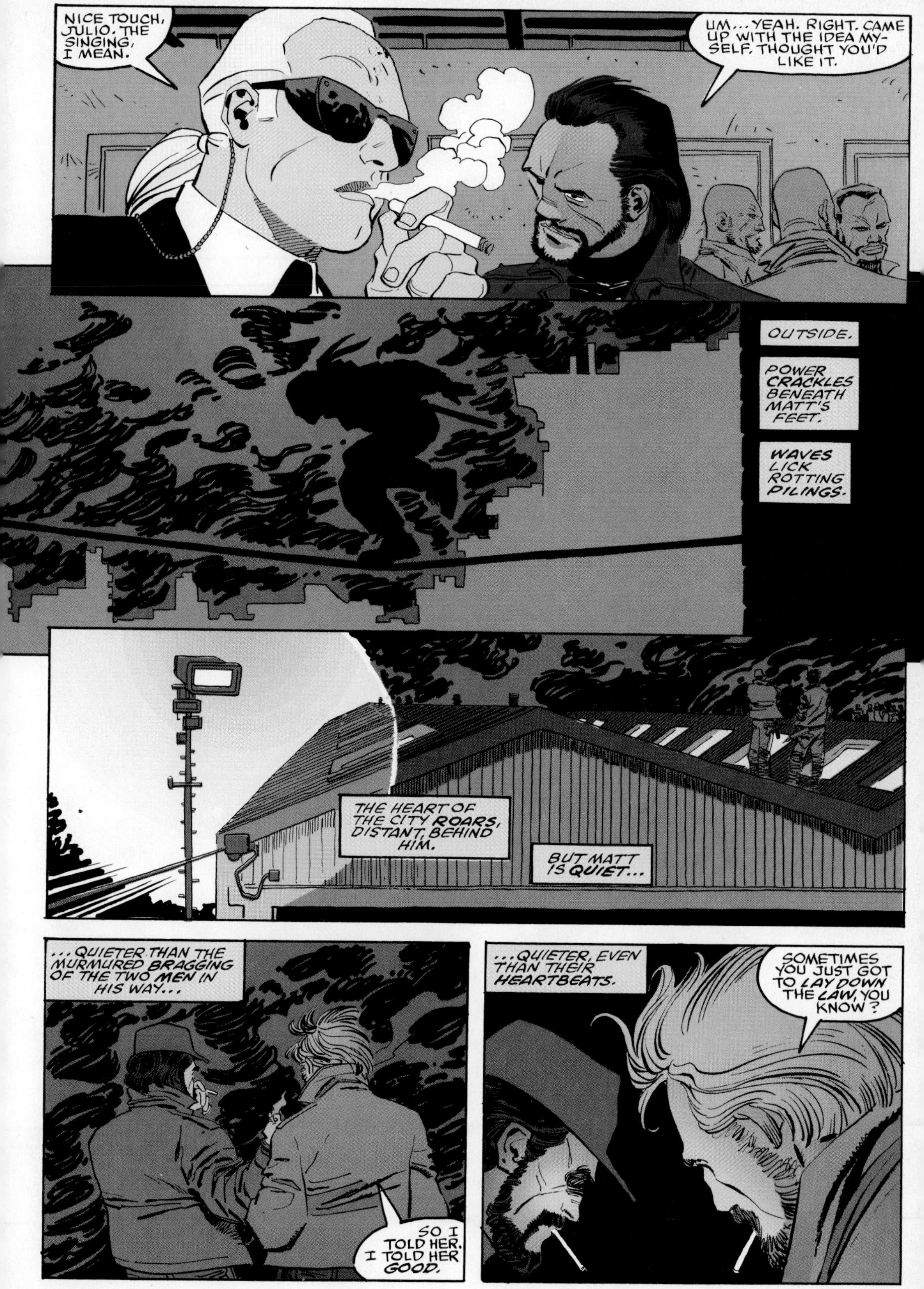

NICE TOUCH, JULIO. THE SINGING, I MEAN.
UM... YEAH. RIGHT. CAME UP WITH THE IDEA MYSELF. THOUGHT YOU'D LIKE IT.
OUTSIDE.
POWER CRACKLES BENEATH MATT'S FEET.
WAVES LICK ROTTING PILINGS.
THE HEART OF THE CITY ROARS, DISTANT, BEHIND HIM.
BUT MATT IS QUIET...
...QUIETER THAN THE MURMURED BRAGGING OF THE TWO MEN IN HIS WAY...
SO I TOLD HER. I TOLD HER GOOD.
...QUIETER, EVEN THAN THEIR HEARTBEATS.
SOMETIMES YOU JUST GOT TO LAY DOWN THE LAW, YOU KNOW?

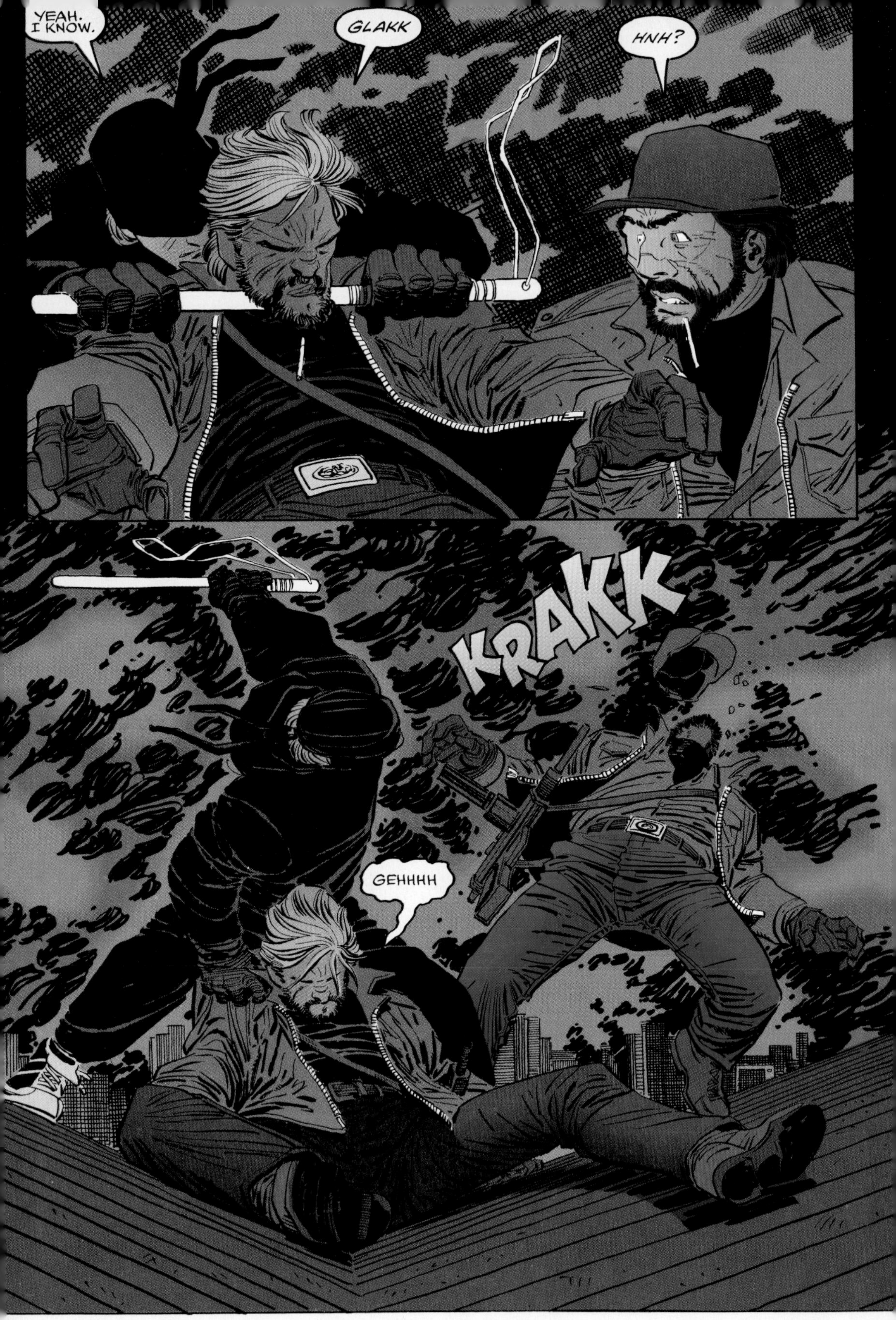
YEAH. I KNOW.
GLAKK
HNH?
KRAKK
GEHHHH

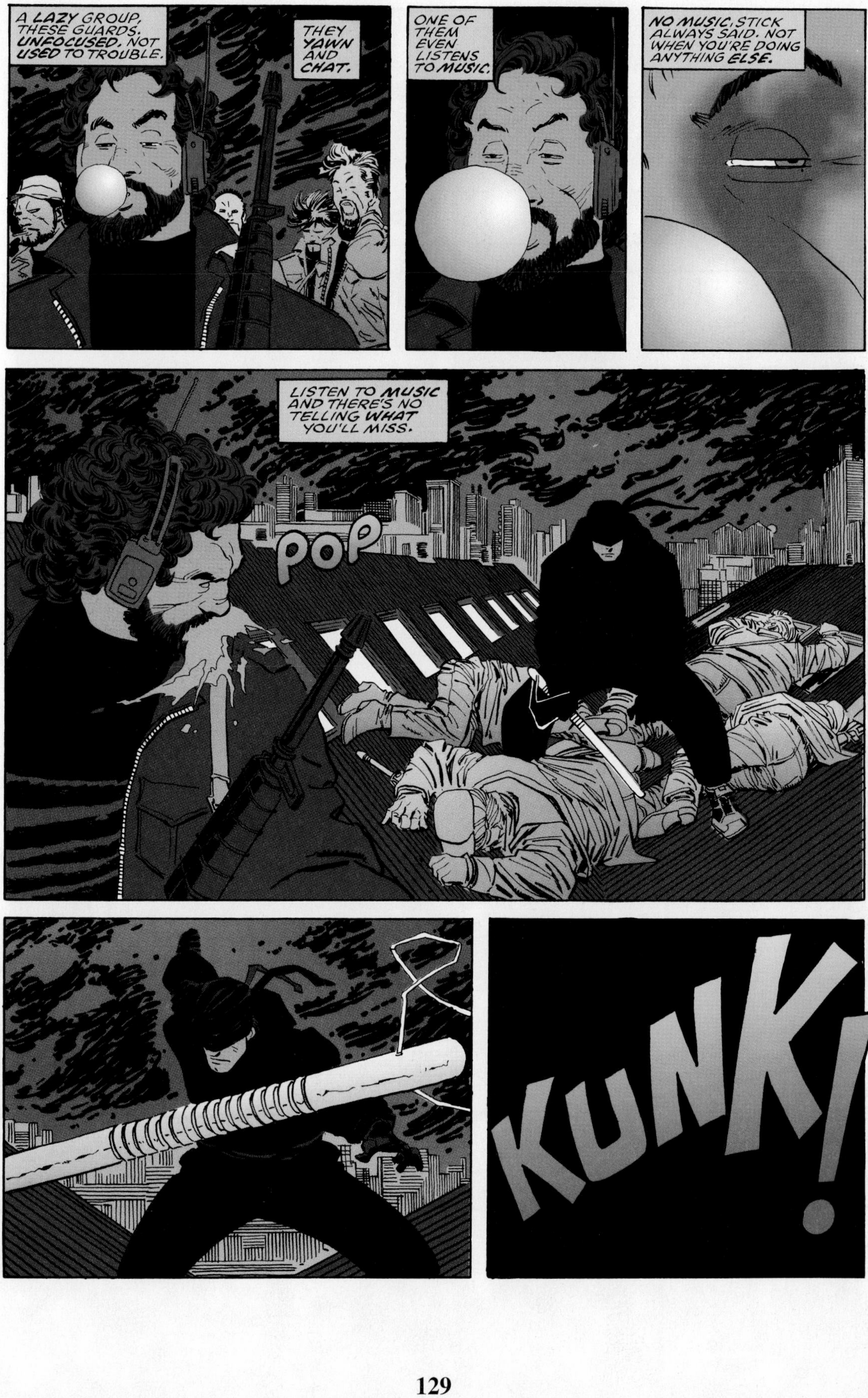
A LAZY GROUP, THESE GUARDS. UNFOCUSED. NOT USED TO TROUBLE.
THEY YAWN AND CHAT.
ONE OF THEM EVEN LISTENS TO MUSIC.
NO MUSIC, STICK ALWAYS SAID. NOT WHEN YOU'RE DOING ANYTHING ELSE.
LISTEN TO MUSIC AND THERE'S NO TELLING WHAT YOU'LL MISS.
POP
KUNK!

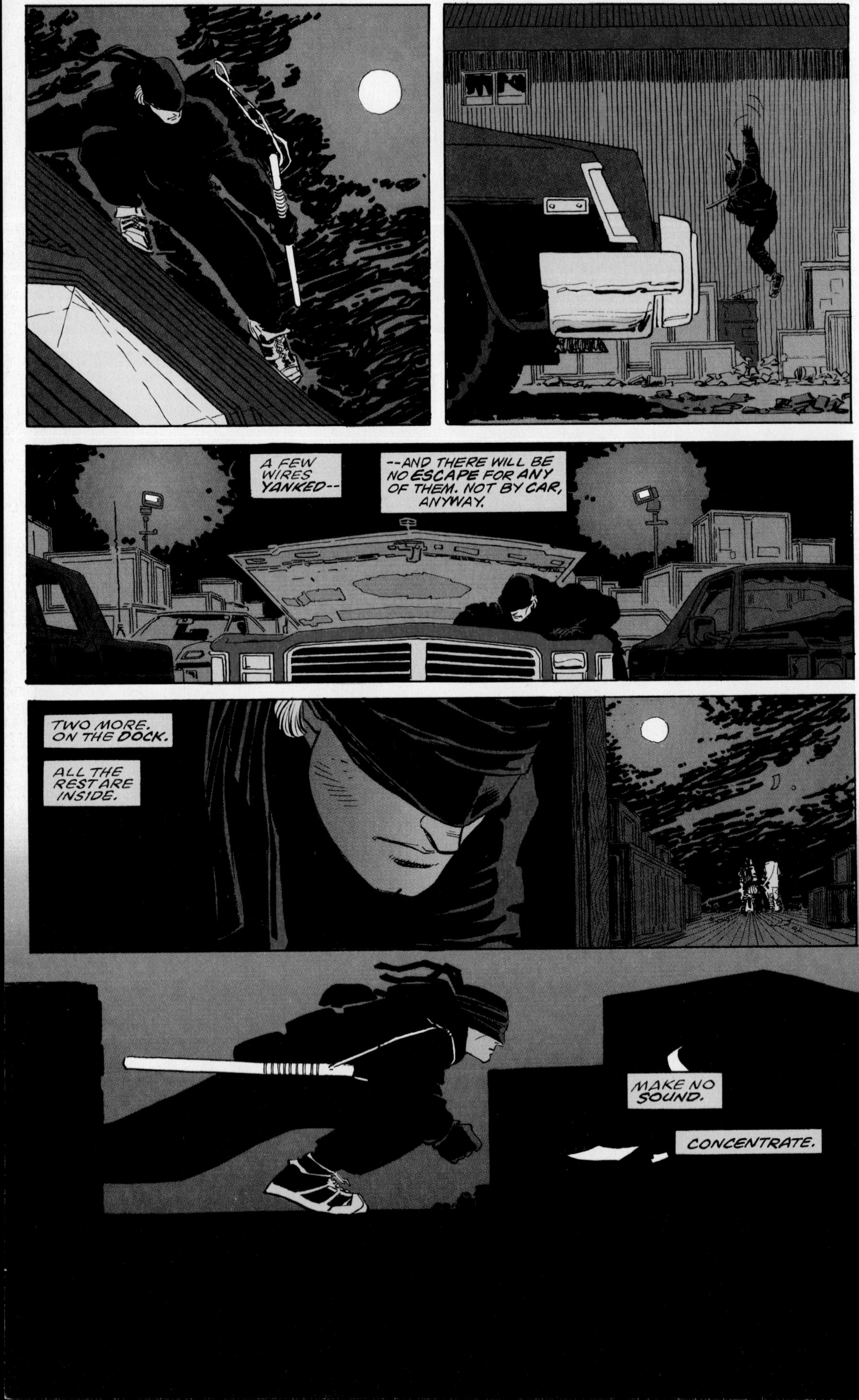
A FEW WIRES YANKED--
--AND THERE WILL BE NO ESCAPE FOR ANY OF THEM. NOT BY CAR, ANYWAY.
TWO MORE. ON THE DOCK.
ALL THE REST ARE INSIDE.
MAKE NO SOUND.
CONCENTRATE.

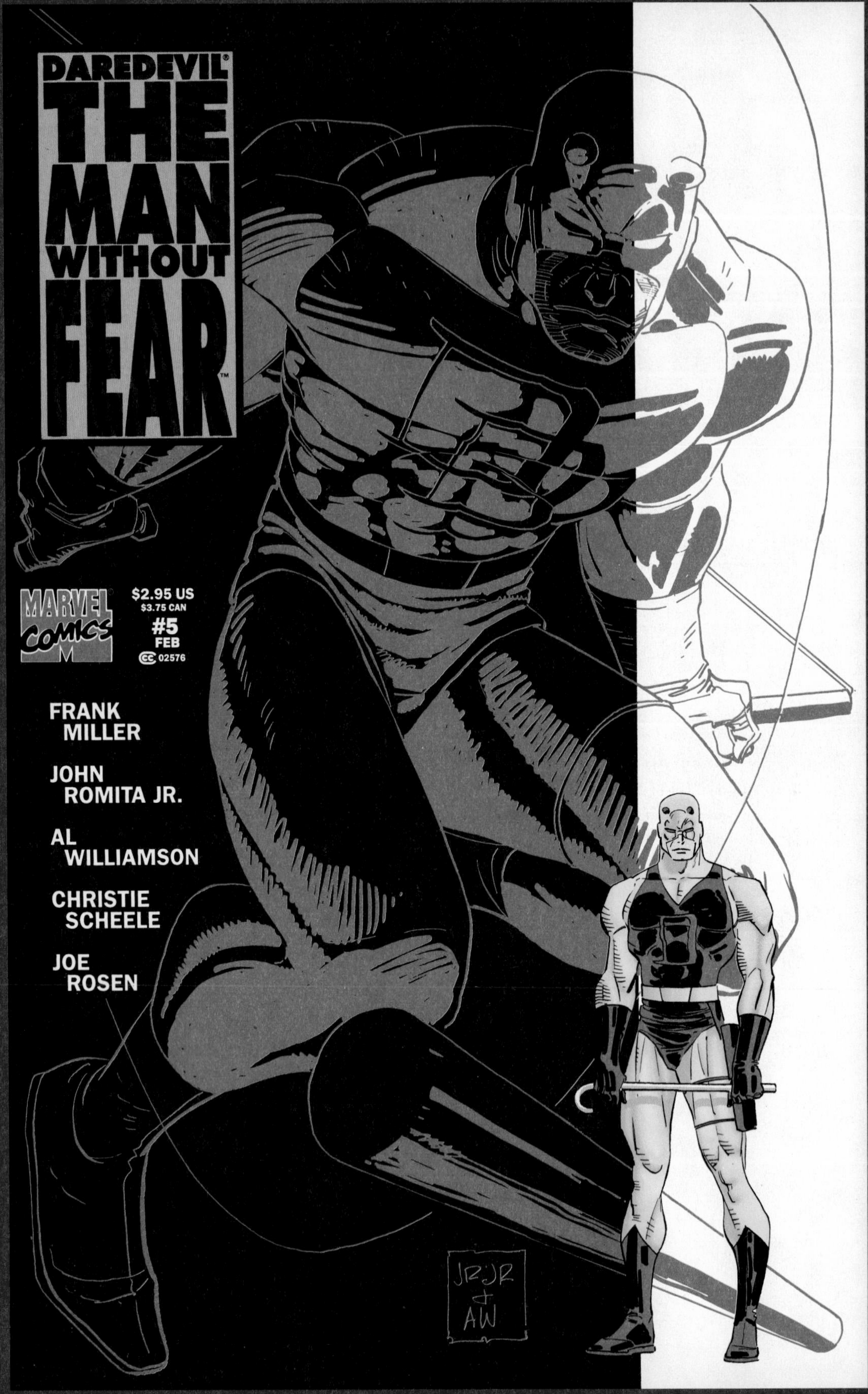
DAREDEVIL®
THE MAN WITHOUT FEAR™
MARVEL COMICS
$2.95 US
$3.75 CAN
#5
FEB
02576
FRANK MILLER
JOHN ROMITA JR.
AL WILLIAMSON
CHRISTIE SCHEELE
JOE ROSEN
JRJR & AW

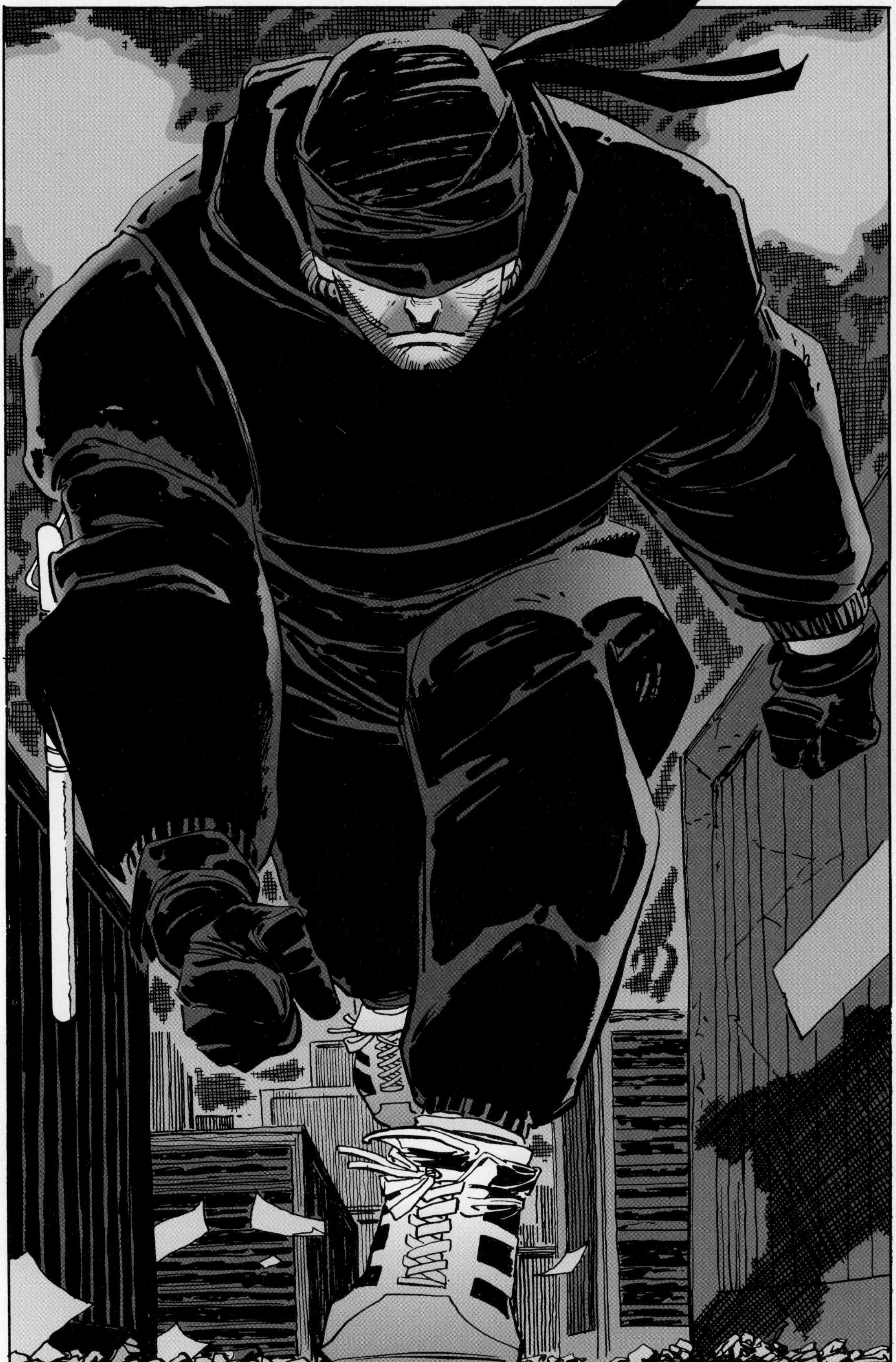

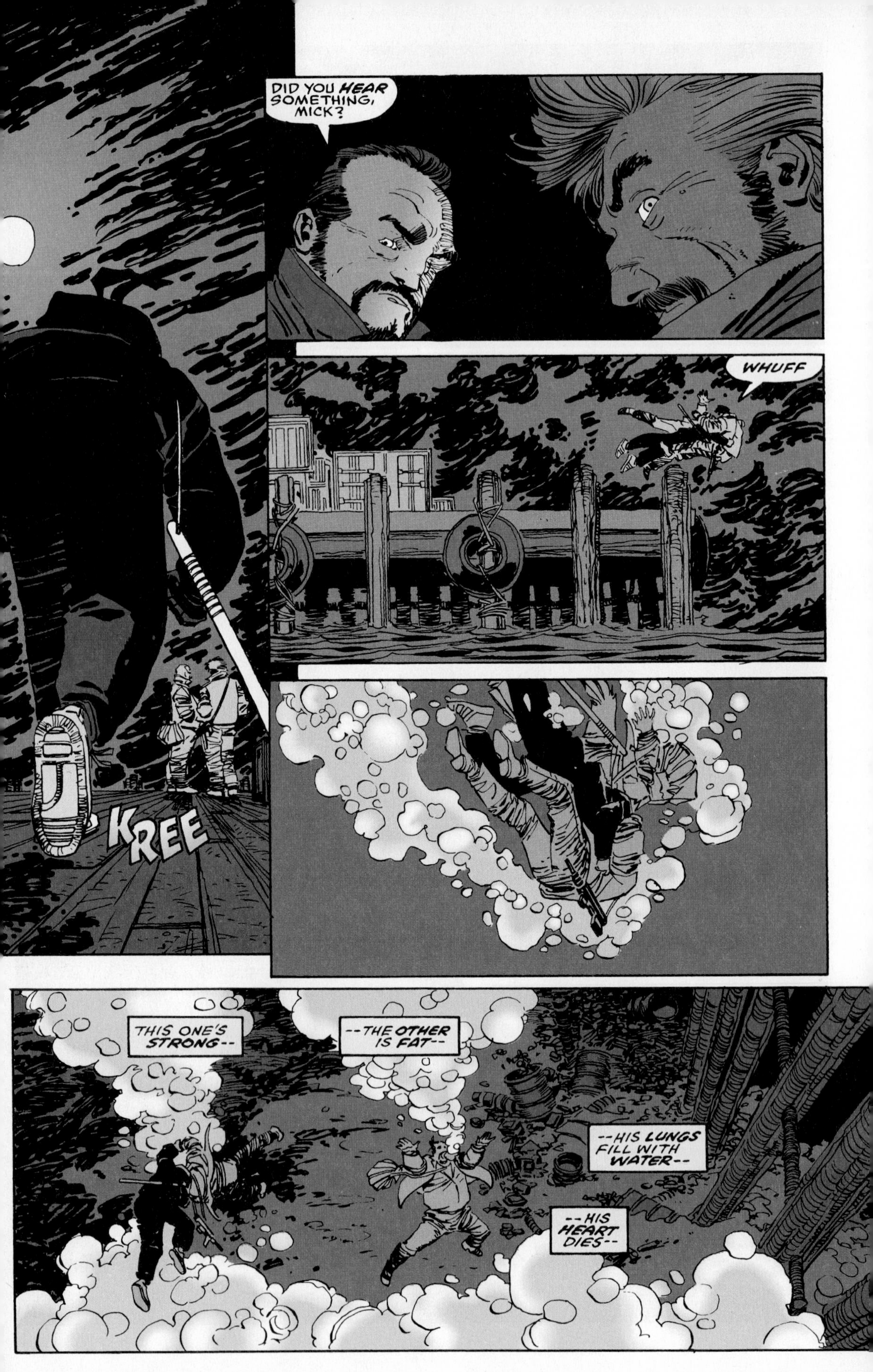
DID YOU HEAR SOMETHING, MICK?
WHUFF
KREE
THIS ONE'S STRONG--
--THE OTHER IS FAT--
--HIS LUNGS FILL WITH WATER--
--HIS HEART DIES--

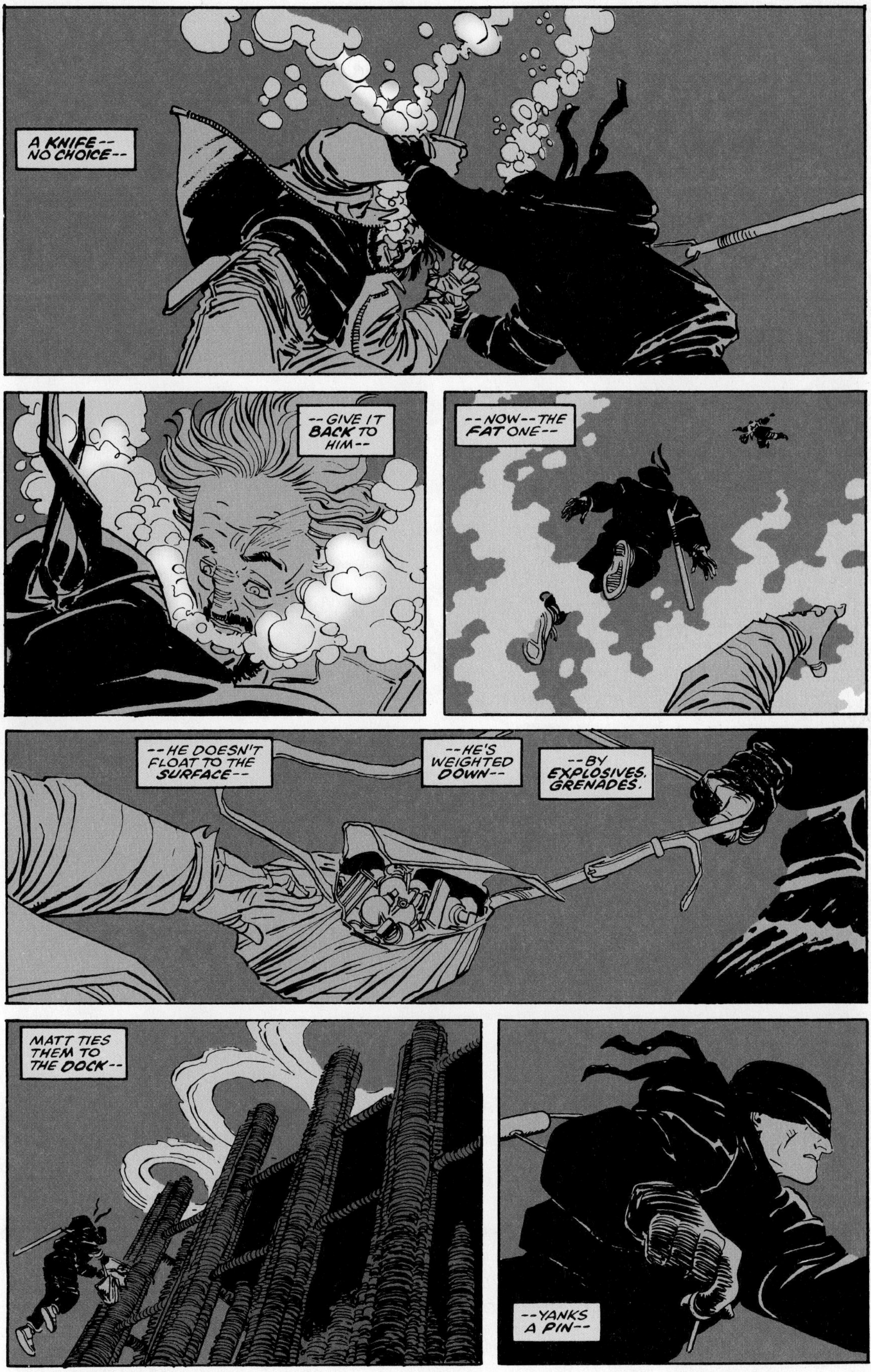
A KNIFE--
NO CHOICE--
--GIVE IT BACK TO HIM--
--NOW--THE FAT ONE--
--HE DOESN'T FLOAT TO THE SURFACE--
--HE'S WEIGHTED DOWN--
--BY EXPLOSIVES. GRENADES.
MATT TIES THEM TO THE DOCK--
--YANKS A PIN--

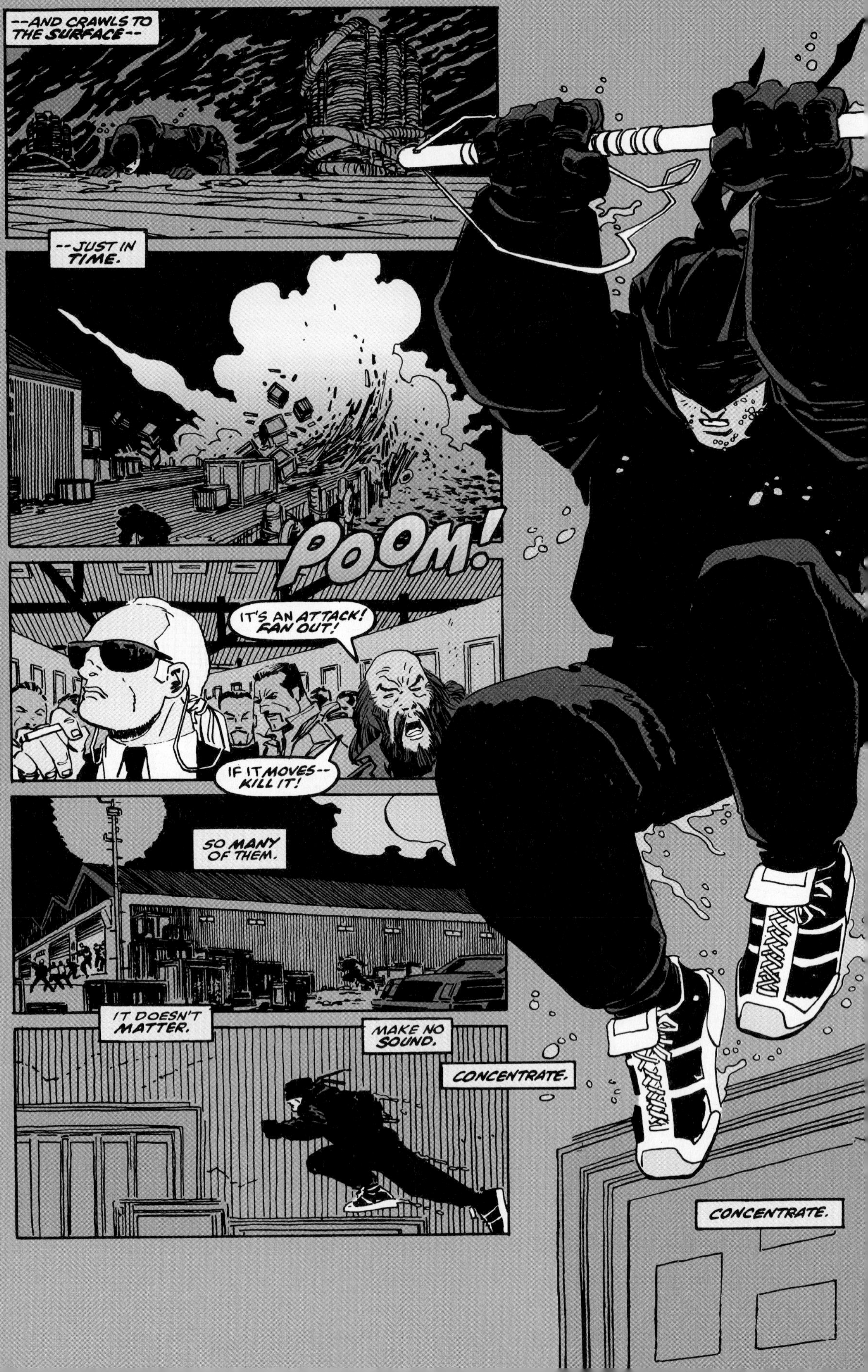
--AND CRAWLS TO THE SURFACE--
--JUST IN TIME.
POOM!
IT'S AN ATTACK! FAN OUT!
IF IT MOVES-- KILL IT!
SO MANY OF THEM.
IT DOESN'T MATTER.
MAKE NO SOUND.
CONCENTRATE.
CONCENTRATE.

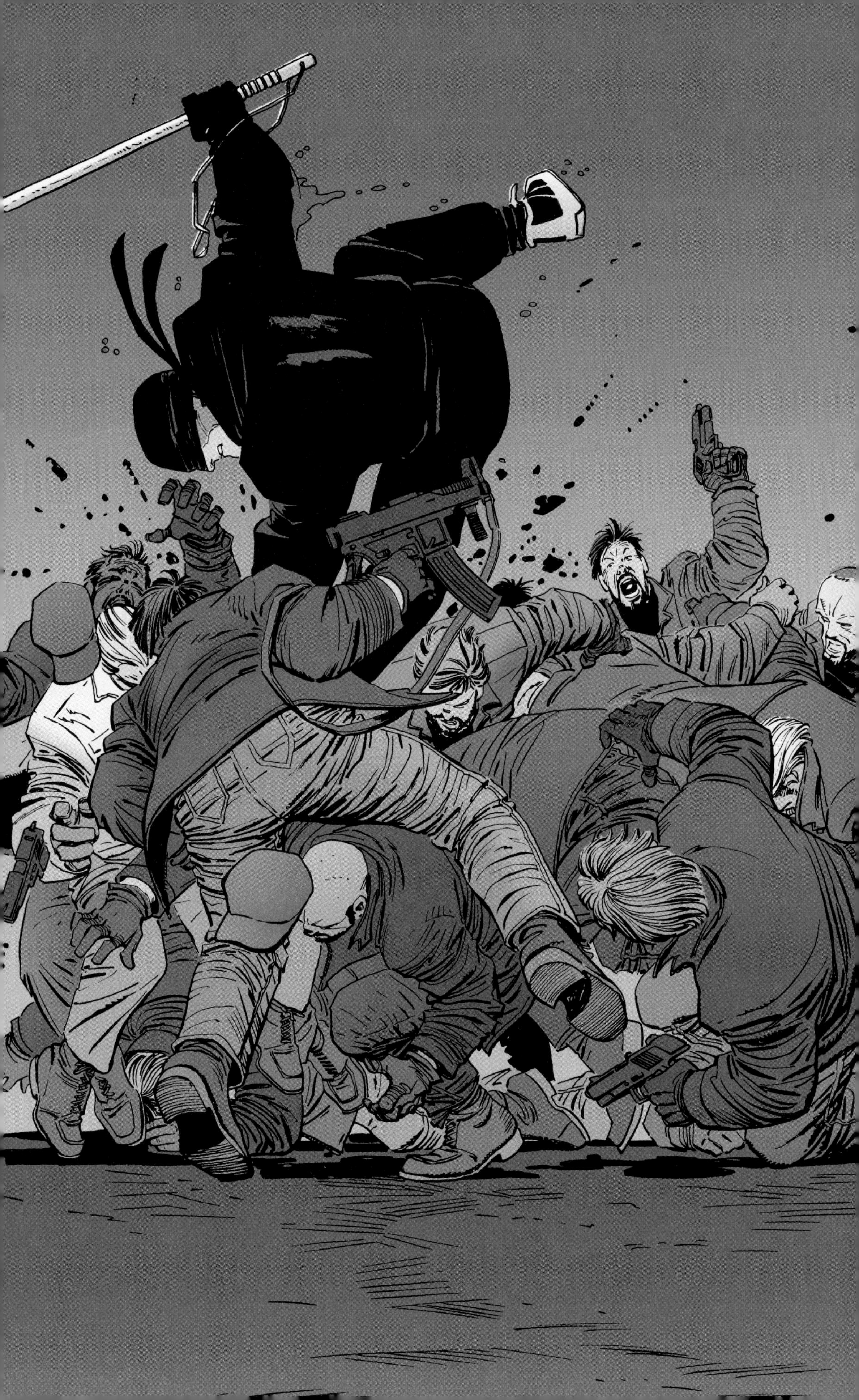

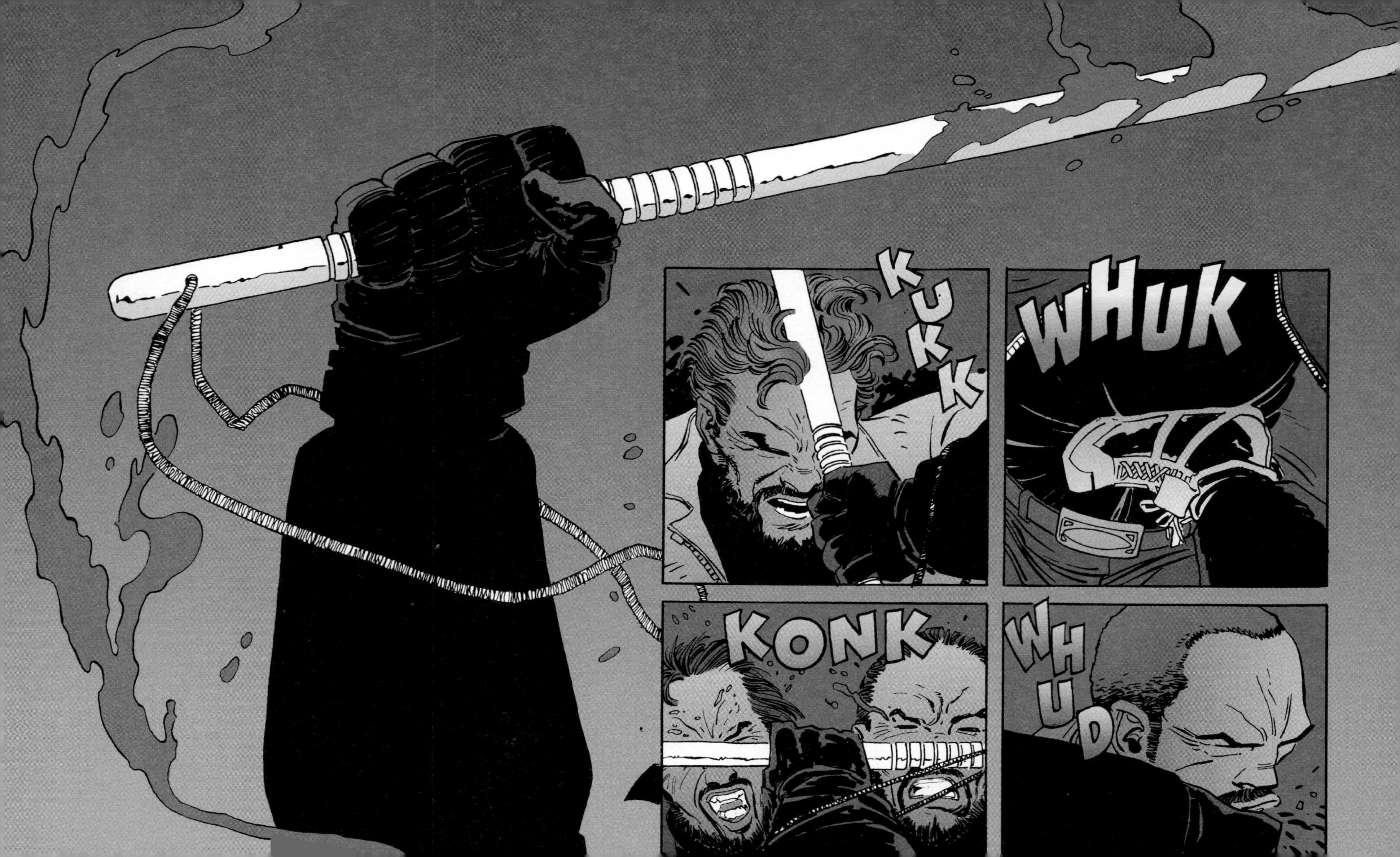
KUKK
WHUK
KONK
WHUD

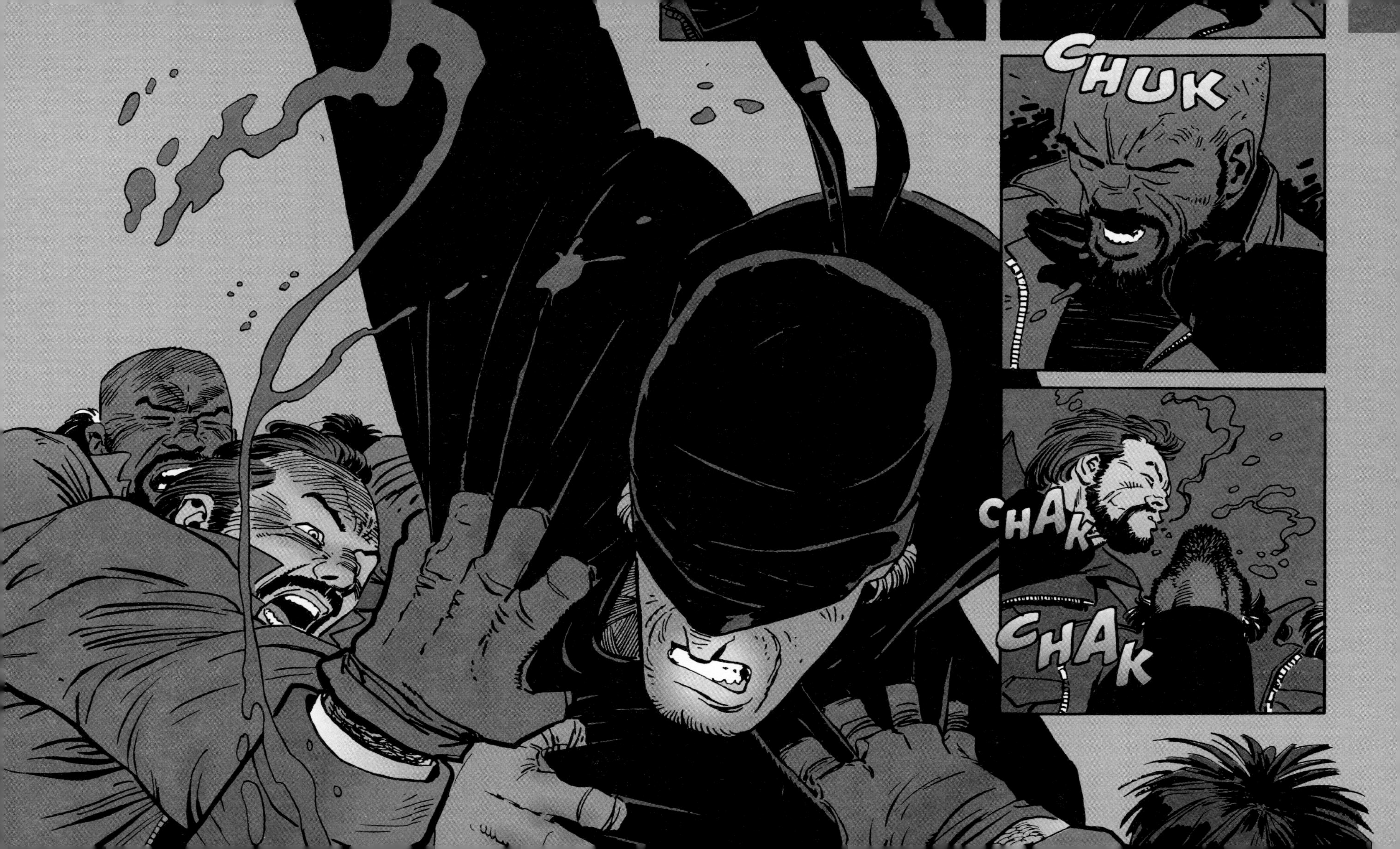
CHUK
CHAK
CHAK

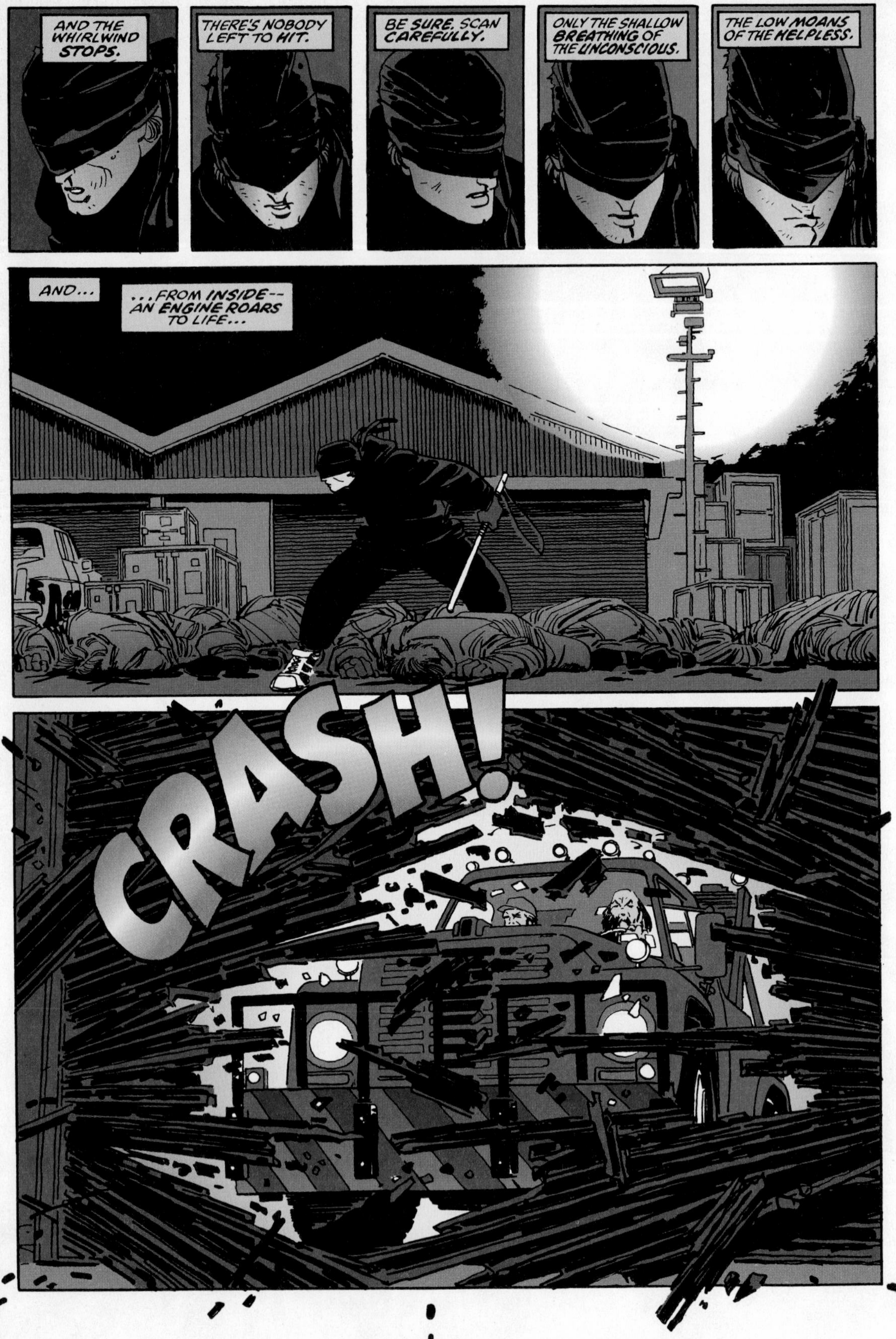
AND THE WHIRLWIND STOPS.
THERE'S NOBODY LEFT TO HIT.
BE SURE. SCAN CAREFULLY.
ONLY THE SHALLOW BREATHING OF THE UNCONSCIOUS.
THE LOW MOANS OF THE HELPLESS.
AND...
...FROM INSIDE-- AN ENGINE ROARS TO LIFE...
CRASH!

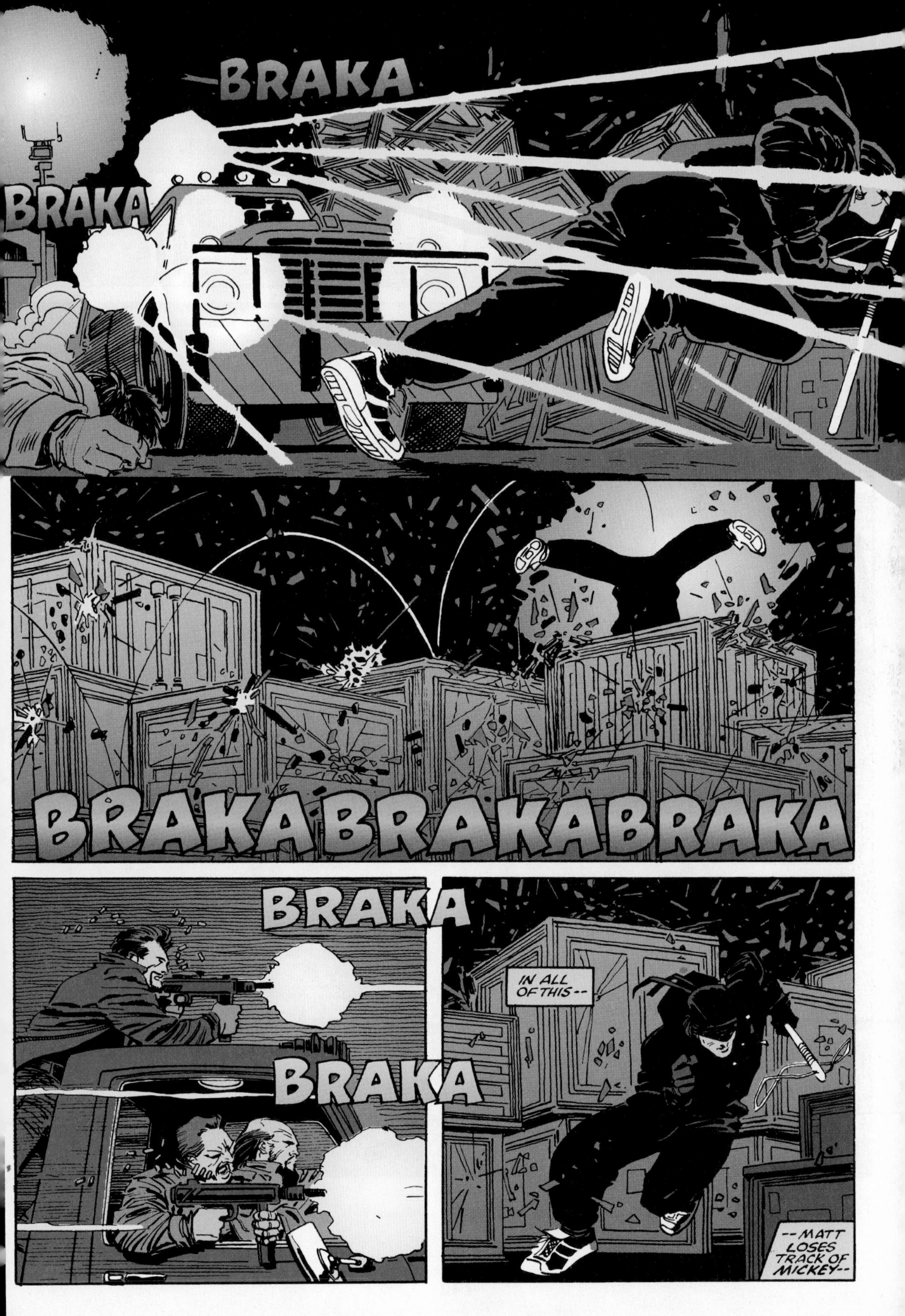
BRAKA
BRAKA
BRAKABRAKABRAKA
BRAKA
BRAKA
IN ALL OF THIS--
--MATT LOSES TRACK OF MICKEY--

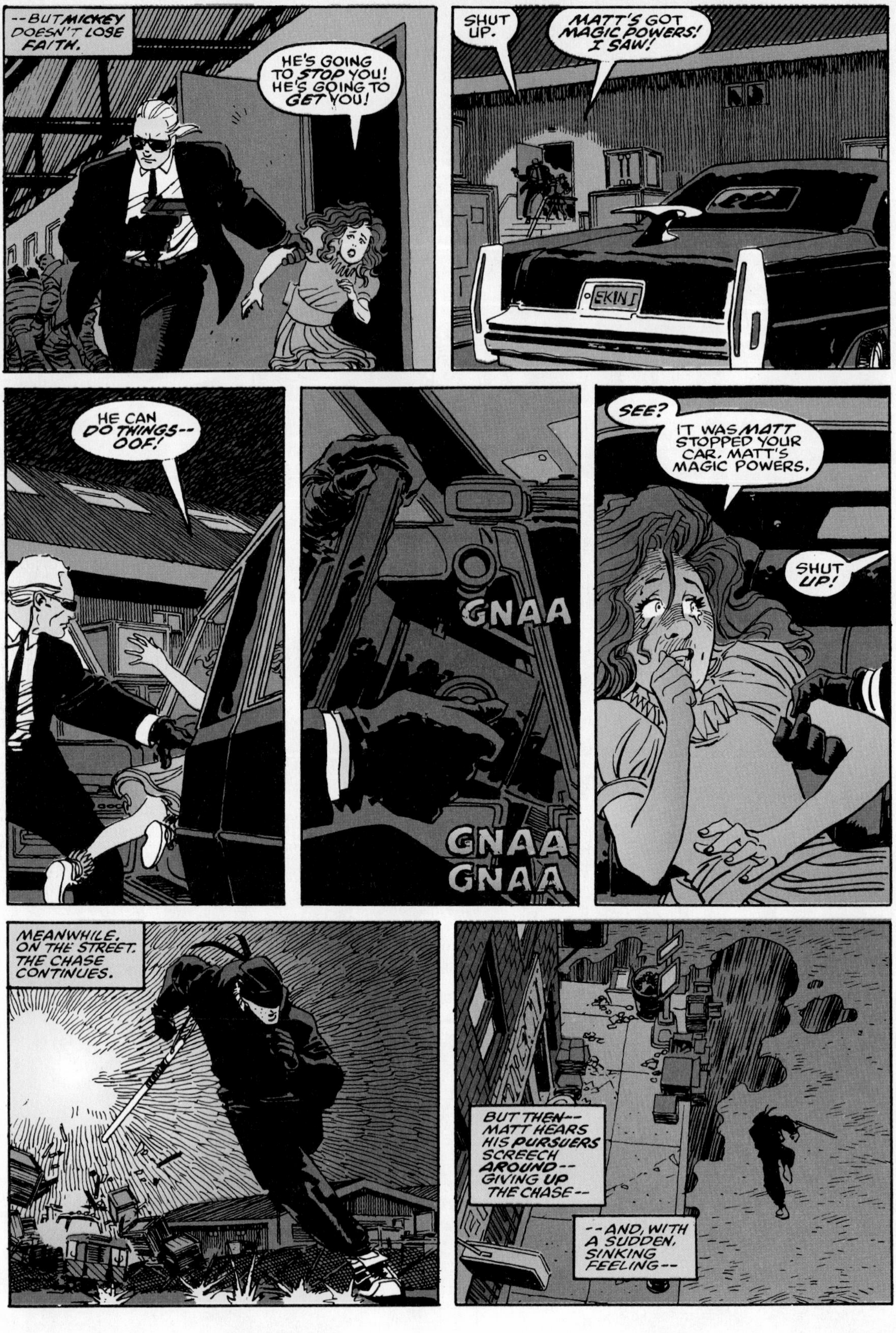
--BUT MICKEY DOESN'T LOSE FAITH.
HE'S GOING TO STOP YOU! HE'S GOING TO GET YOU!
SHUT UP.
MATT'S GOT MAGIC POWERS! I SAW!
HE CAN DO THINGS-- OOF!
GNAA
GNAA
GNAA
SEE?
IT WAS MATT STOPPED YOUR CAR. MATT'S MAGIC POWERS.
SHUT UP!
MEANWHILE. ON THE STREET. THE CHASE CONTINUES.
BUT THEN-- MATT HEARS HIS PURSUERS SCREECH AROUND-- GIVING UP THE CHASE--
--AND, WITH A SUDDEN, SINKING FEELING--

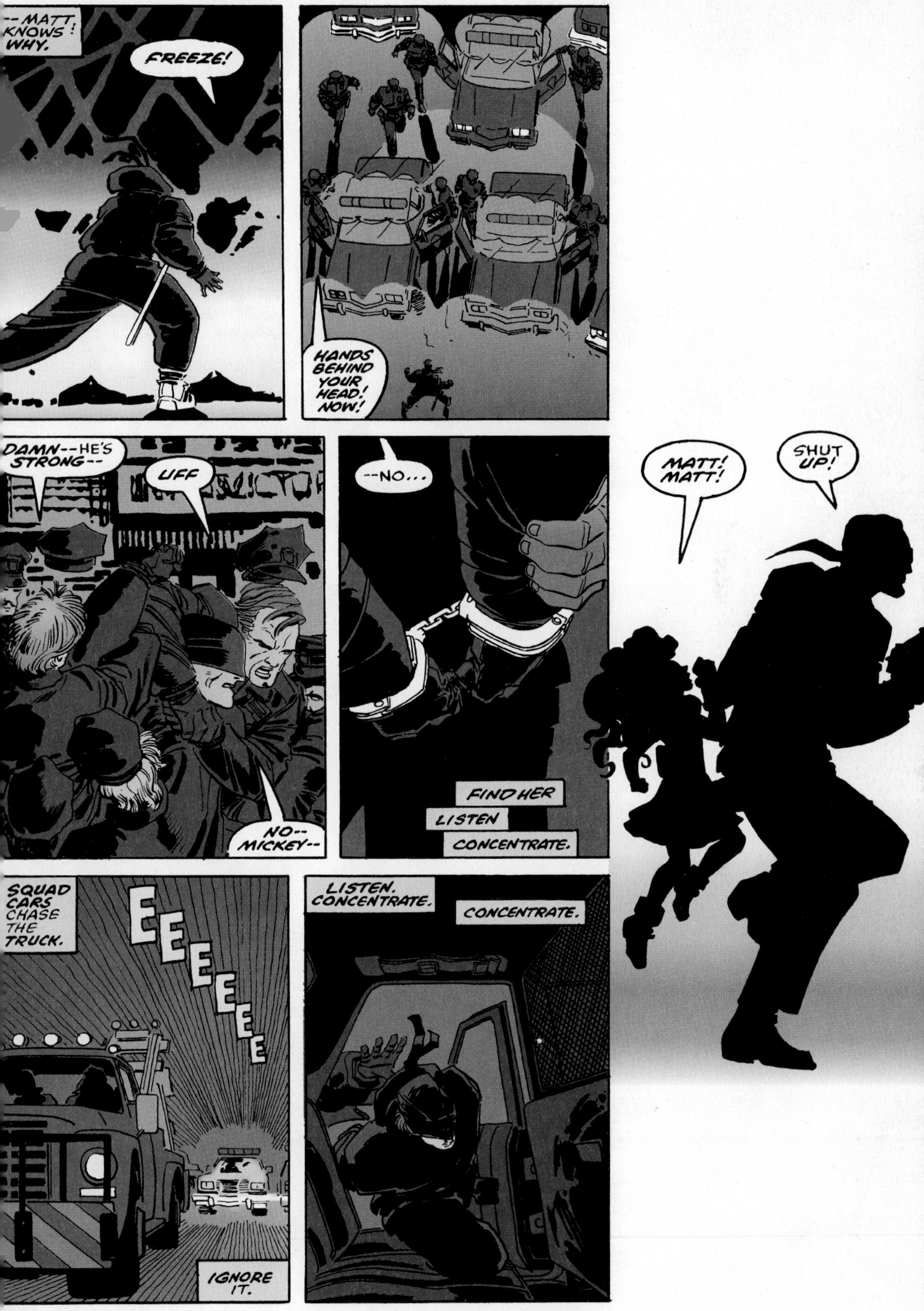
--MATT KNOWS! WHY.
FREEZE!
HANDS BEHIND YOUR HEAD! NOW!
DAMN--HE'S STRONG--
UFF
NO-- MICKEY--
--NO...
FIND HER
LISTEN
CONCENTRATE.
MATT! MATT!
SHUT UP!
SQUAD CARS CHASE THE TRUCK.
EEEEEEE
IGNORE IT.
LISTEN. CONCENTRATE.
CONCENTRATE.

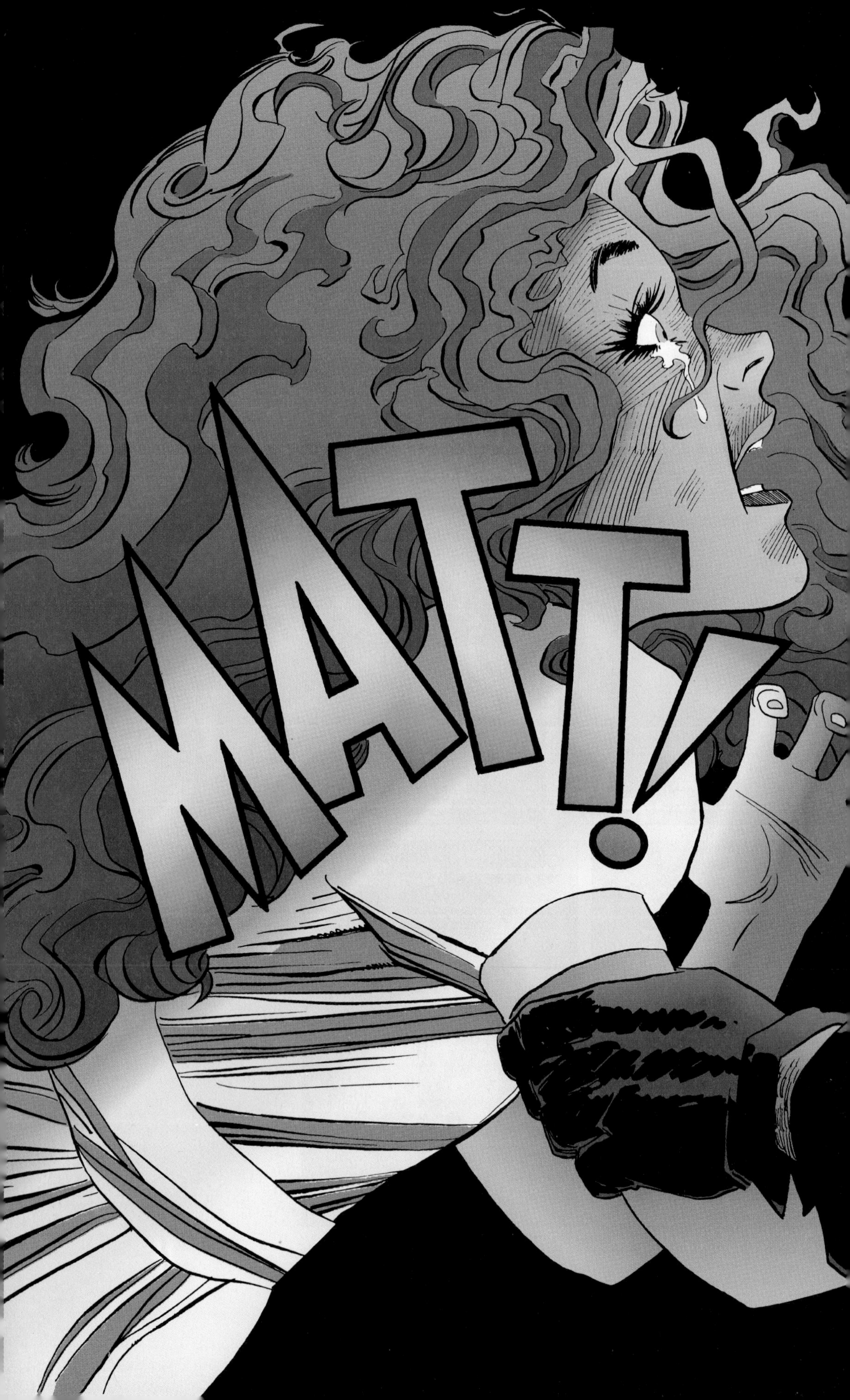
MATT!

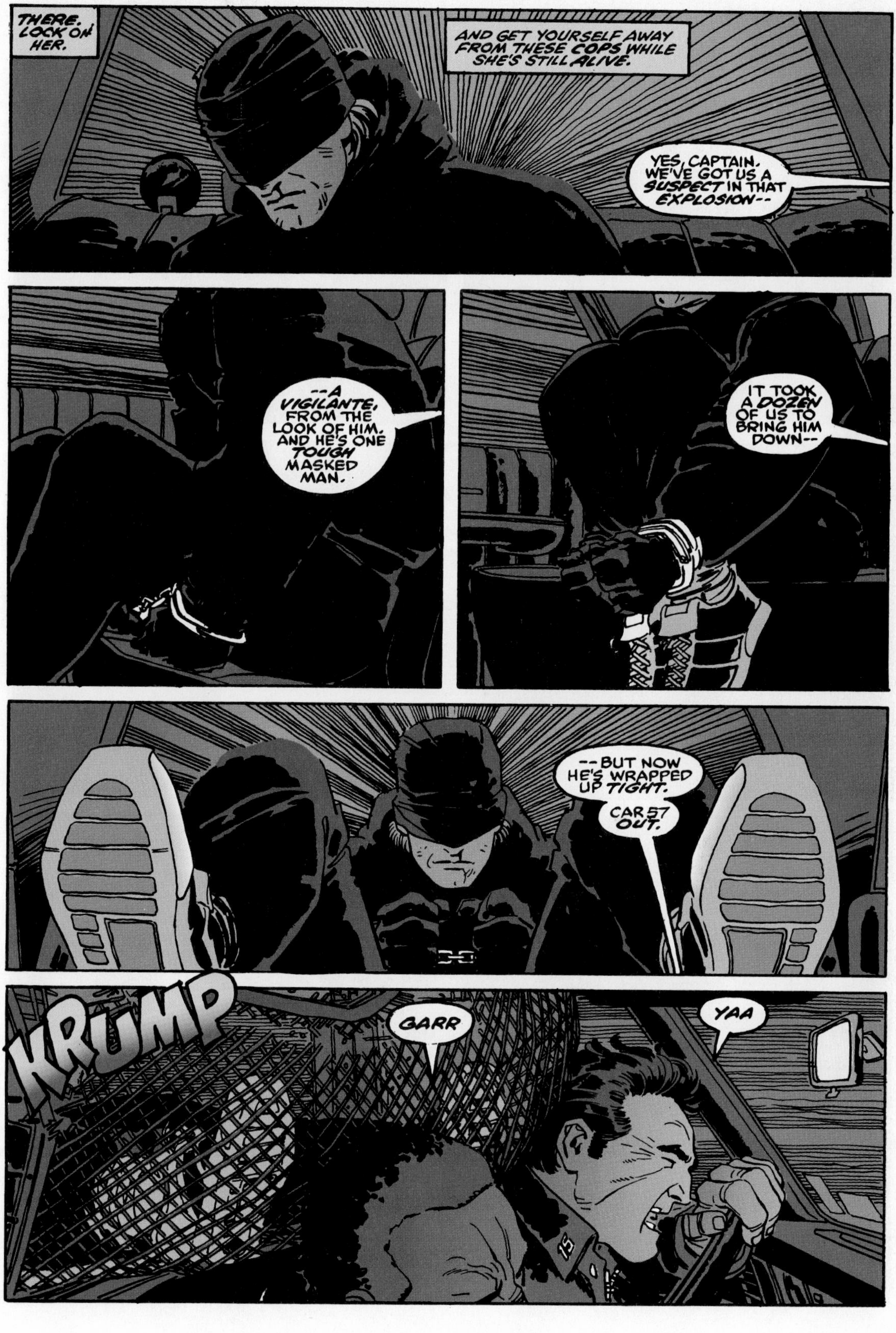
THERE. LOCK ON HER.
AND GET YOURSELF AWAY FROM THESE COPS WHILE SHE'S STILL ALIVE.
YES, CAPTAIN. WE'VE GOT US A SUSPECT IN THAT EXPLOSION--
--A VIGILANTE, FROM THE LOOK OF HIM. AND HE'S ONE TOUGH MASKED MAN.
IT TOOK A DOZEN OF US TO BRING HIM DOWN--
--BUT NOW HE'S WRAPPED UP TIGHT.
CAR 57 OUT.
KRUMP
GARR
YAA

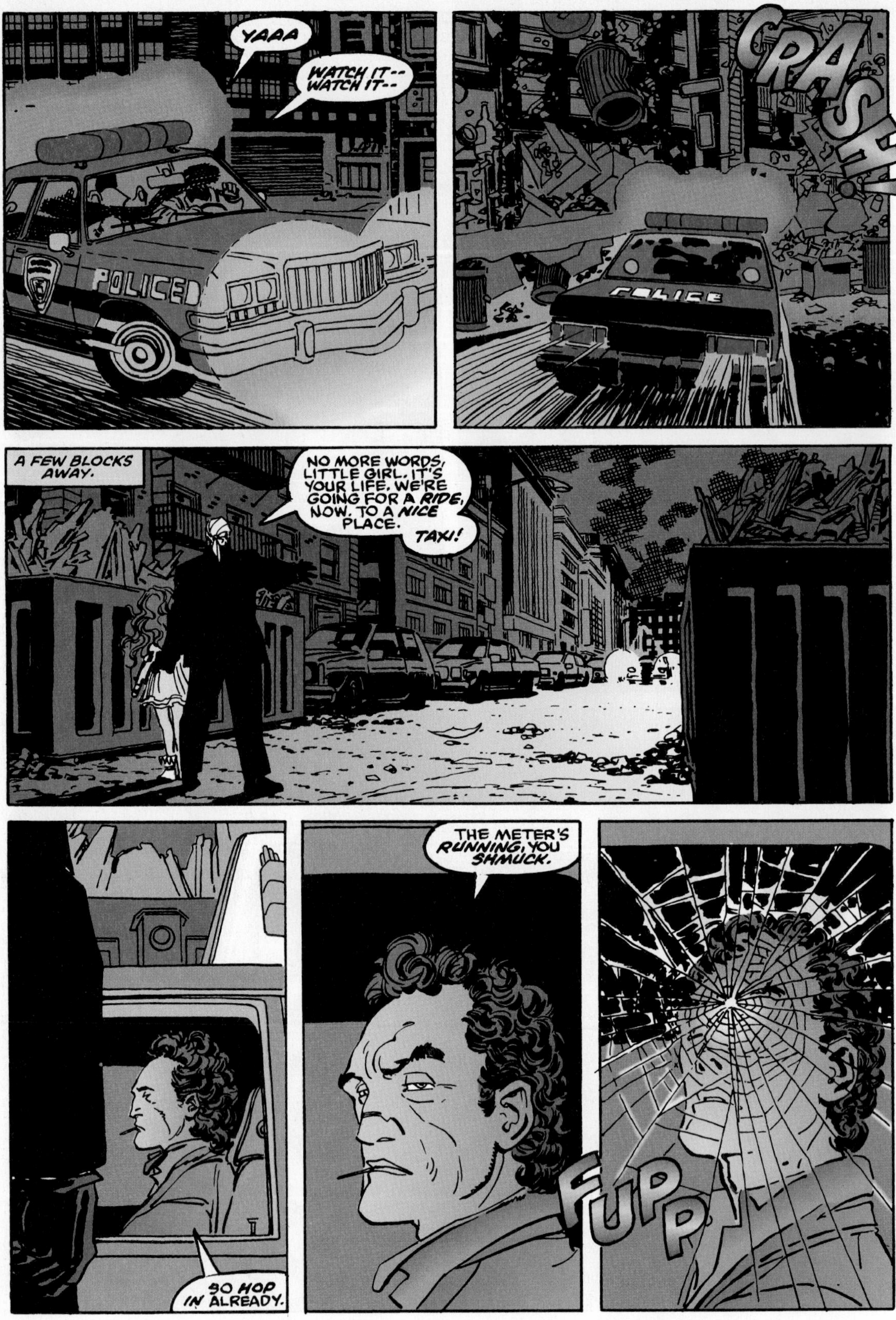
YAAA
WATCH IT-- WATCH IT--
CRASH!
A FEW BLOCKS AWAY.
NO MORE WORDS, LITTLE GIRL. IT'S YOUR LIFE. WE'RE GOING FOR A RIDE, NOW. TO A NICE PLACE.
TAXI!
SO HOP IN ALREADY.
THE METER'S RUNNING, YOU SHMUCK.
FUPP

ONE MORE MURDER.

THEY'RE IN A CAB NOW. MOVING SOUTH.

STAY LOCKED ON THEM.

AND USE THE COP'S KEYS AND GET THE CUFFS OFF.

IN NO CONDITION TO CHASE THEM. NOT ON FOOT.

DIZZY...

SCREEECH

KLUMP.

...DIZZY BLIND MAN.

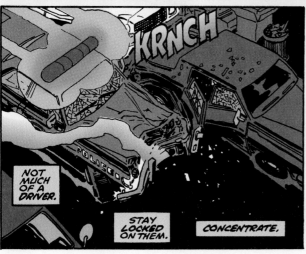

KRNCH

NOT MUCH OF A DRIVER.

STAY LOCKED ON THEM.

CONCENTRATE.

NEARBY.

TAXI

YOU JUST KILLED THAT GUY. LIKE IT WAS NOTHING.

IT WAS NOTHING.

STAY LOCKED.

STAY LOCKED,

THERE. NOW.

CRASHH

A DEAD MOMENT-- FIGHT IT--

--LET THE RAIN DE- SCRIBE THEM--

--CATCH THEIR SCENT--

--STAY LOCKED--

--FOLLOW THEM--AS BEST YOU CAN...

KRAK

SILENCE NOW, SWEETHEART. EVERYTHING'S GOING TO BE FINE...

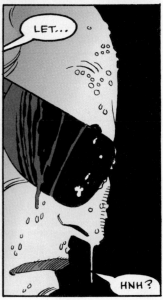

LET...

HNH?

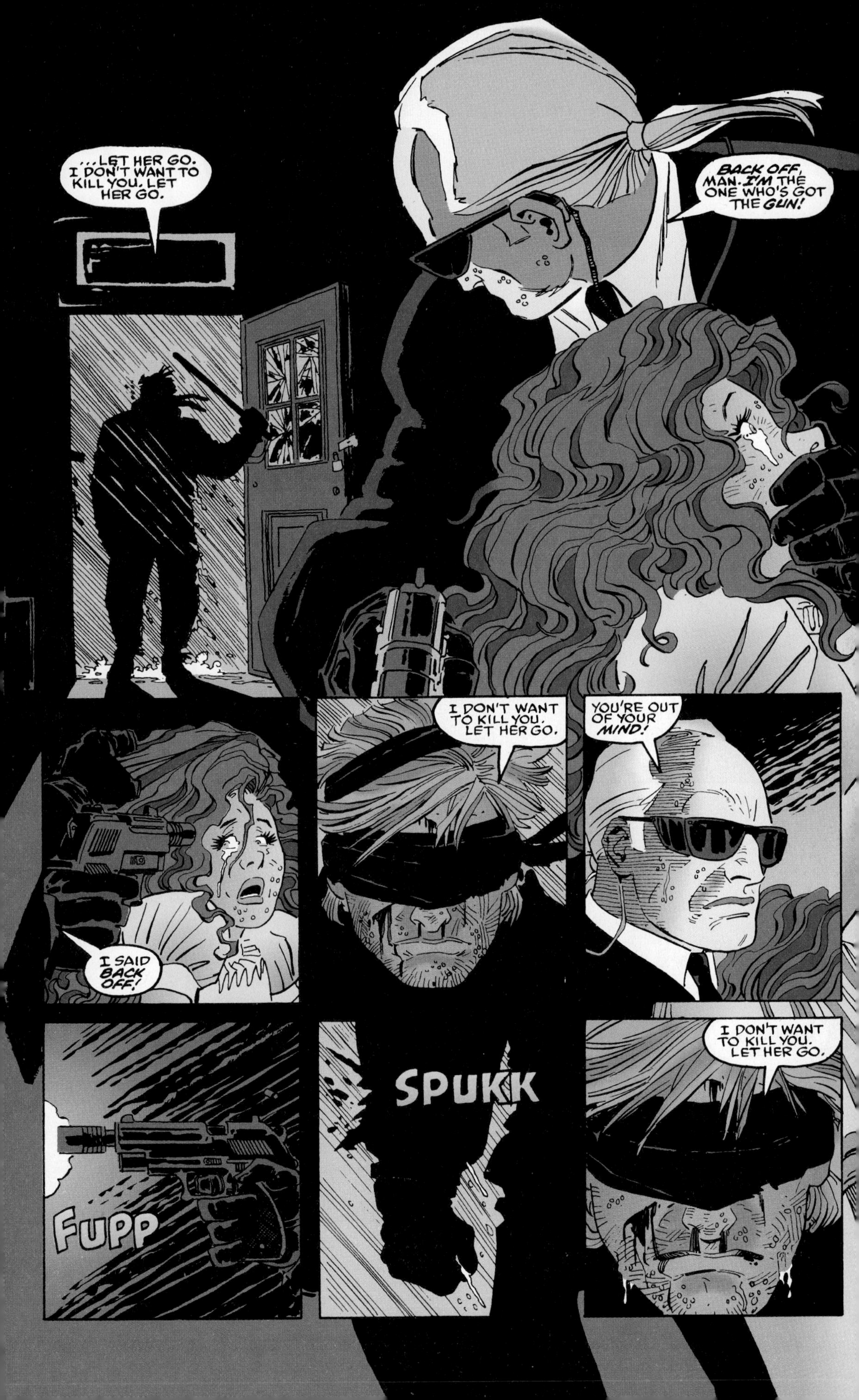
...LET HER GO. I DON'T WANT TO KILL YOU. LET HER GO.
BACK OFF, MAN. I'M THE ONE WHO'S GOT THE GUN!
I SAID BACK OFF!
I DON'T WANT TO KILL YOU. LET HER GO.
YOU'RE OUT OF YOUR MIND!
FUPP
SPUKK
I DON'T WANT TO KILL YOU. LET HER GO.

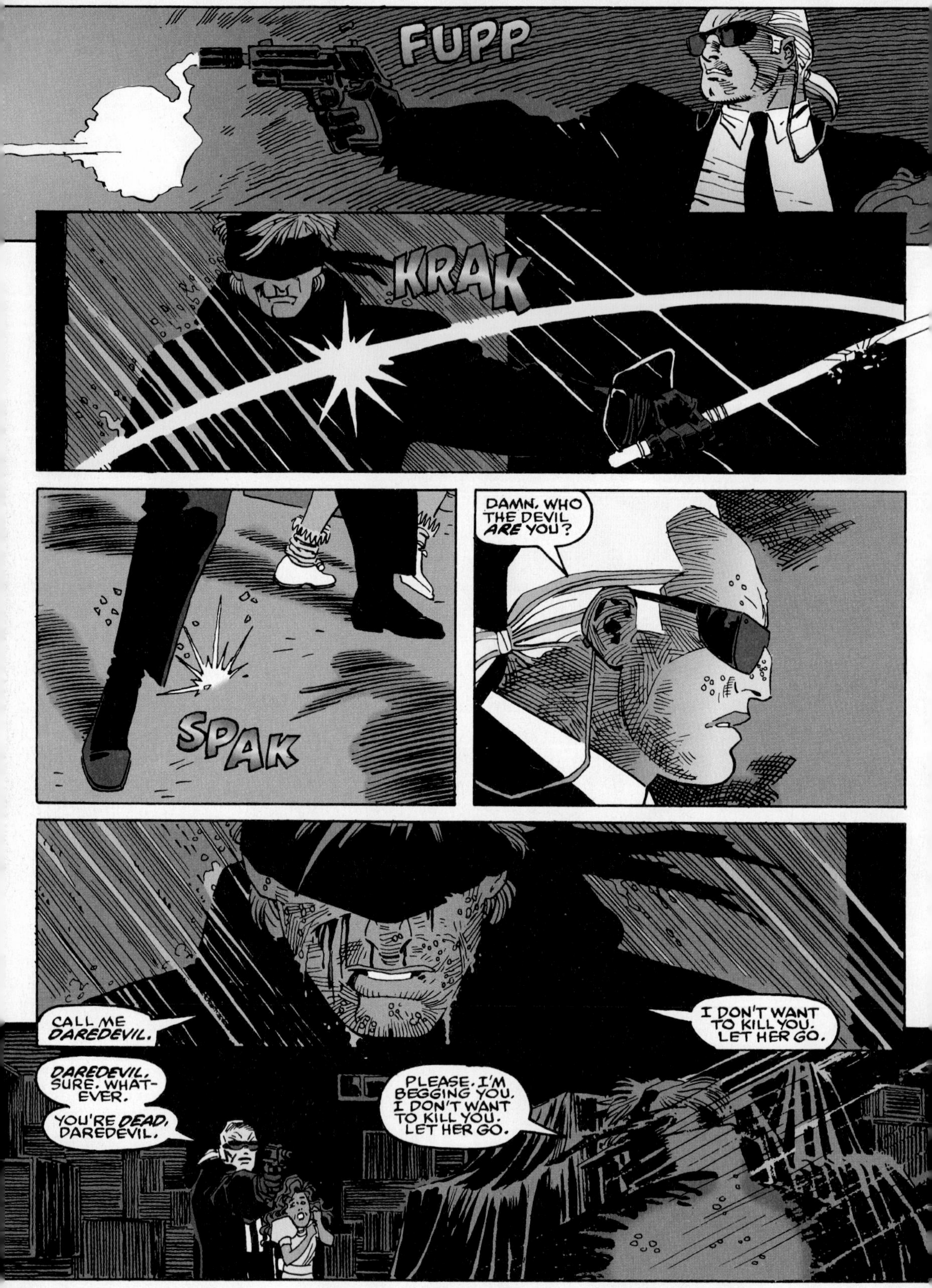
FUPP
KRAK
SPAK
DAMN. WHO THE DEVIL ARE YOU?
CALL ME DAREDEVIL.
I DON'T WANT TO KILL YOU. LET HER GO.
DAREDEVIL. SURE. WHAT-EVER.
YOU'RE DEAD, DAREDEVIL.
PLEASE. I'M BEGGING YOU. I DON'T WANT TO KILL YOU. LET HER GO.

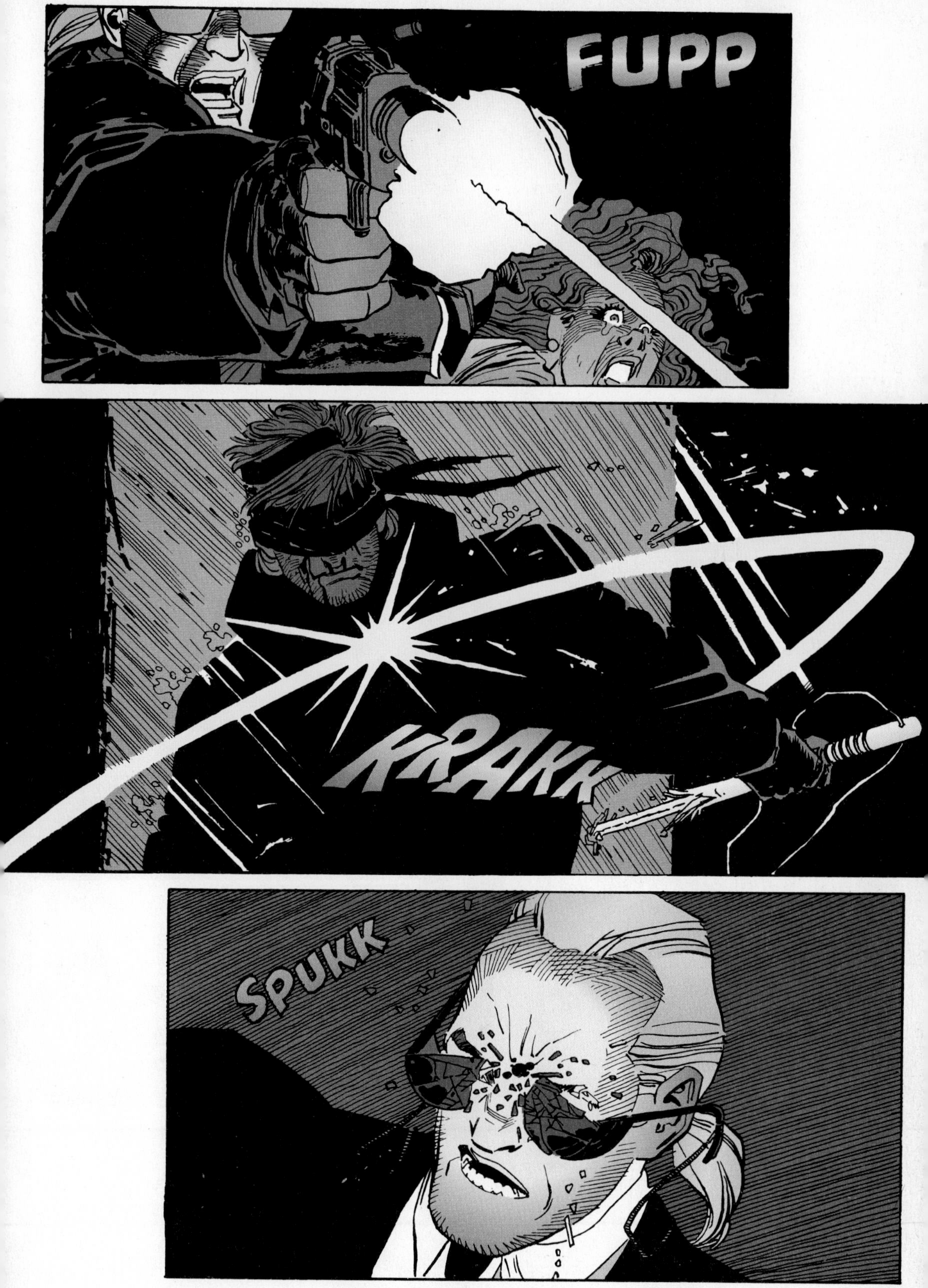
FUPP
KRAKK
SPUKK

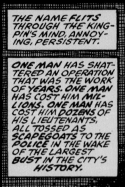

THE NAME FLITS THROUGH THE KINGPIN'S MIND, ANNOYING, PERSISTENT.

ONE MAN HAS SHATTERED AN OPERATION THAT WAS THE WORK OF YEARS. ONE MAN HAS COST HIM MILLIONS. ONE MAN HAS COST HIM DOZENS OF HIS LIEUTENANTS, ALL TOSSED AS SCAPEGOATS TO THE POLICE IN THE WAKE OF THE LARGEST BUST IN THE CITY'S HISTORY.

BUT SOON THE COPS WILL HAVE THEIR HEADLINES AND EVERYTHING WILL BE BACK IN ORDER. THE KINGPIN WILL NOT BE TOUCHED-- AND HIS EMPIRE WILL GROW AGAIN, RAPACIOUS, AS IMMORTAL AS HUMAN SIN.

AND IT WILL NOT BE TOO VERY OFTEN THAT THIS PARTICULAR BULLY WONDERS...

BY THE TIME THE COPS ARRIVE, MATT IS GONE-- LEAVING A MYSTERY AND THE FIRST RUMBLINGS OF A LEGEND.

DAREDEVIL.

THE NAME IS TO BE HEARD AGAIN-- FROM QUIVERING THUGS AND FROM GRATEFUL VICTIMS.

DAREDEVIL.

IT IS THE NAME OF A SHADOWED DEMON-- AN UNSEEN AVENGER-- A SILENT, INVISIBLE SAVIOR OF THE INNOCENT.

DAREDEVIL.

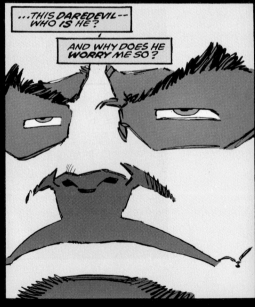

...THIS DAREDEVIL-- WHO IS HE?

AND WHY DOES HE WORRY ME SO?

MATT MURDOCK SITS IN THE RAIN AND *LAUGHS.*

HIS DAY BEGAN WITH A RINGING *PHONE* AND AN ANGRY *VOICE.*

IT WAS HIS *BOSS.* FROM *BOSTON.* TELLING HIM HE'S *FIRED.*

THAT WAS WHEN MATT STARTED LAUGHING. IT MADE HIS *BOSS* SO FURIOUS HE *HUNG UP* ON MATT. BUT STILL MATT COULDN'T STOP *LAUGHING.*

BOSTON.

MATT COULDN'T LEAVE NEW YORK NOW IF HE *WANTED* TO.

THE BOY FROM HELL'S KITCHEN HAS COME *HOME.*

HOME--TO A *NEW LIFE.*

THEN IT'S A *DEAL,* MATT! MY *DAD* WILL LEND US THE MONEY FOR AN *OFFICE,* PROVIDED IT'S NOT TOO *FANCY.*

WE WON'T NEED ANYTHING FANCY, FOGGY. NOT FOR THE KIND OF WORK WE'VE GOT IN FRONT OF US. ALL THAT STUFF WE TALKED ABOUT IN *COLLEGE*-- ALL THOSE *IDEALS*-- WE CAN *DO* IT, FOGGY.

THEN WE'RE ALL *SET*--ONCE WE FIGURE OUT WHOSE NAME COMES *FIRST* ON THE *DOOR.* IS IT *MURDOCK* AND *NELSON* OR *NELSON* AND *MURDOCK?*

I SAY, WE *FLIP,* A *COIN,* I MEAN.

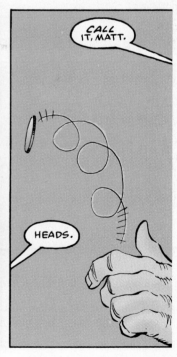

CALL IT, MATT.

HEADS.

153

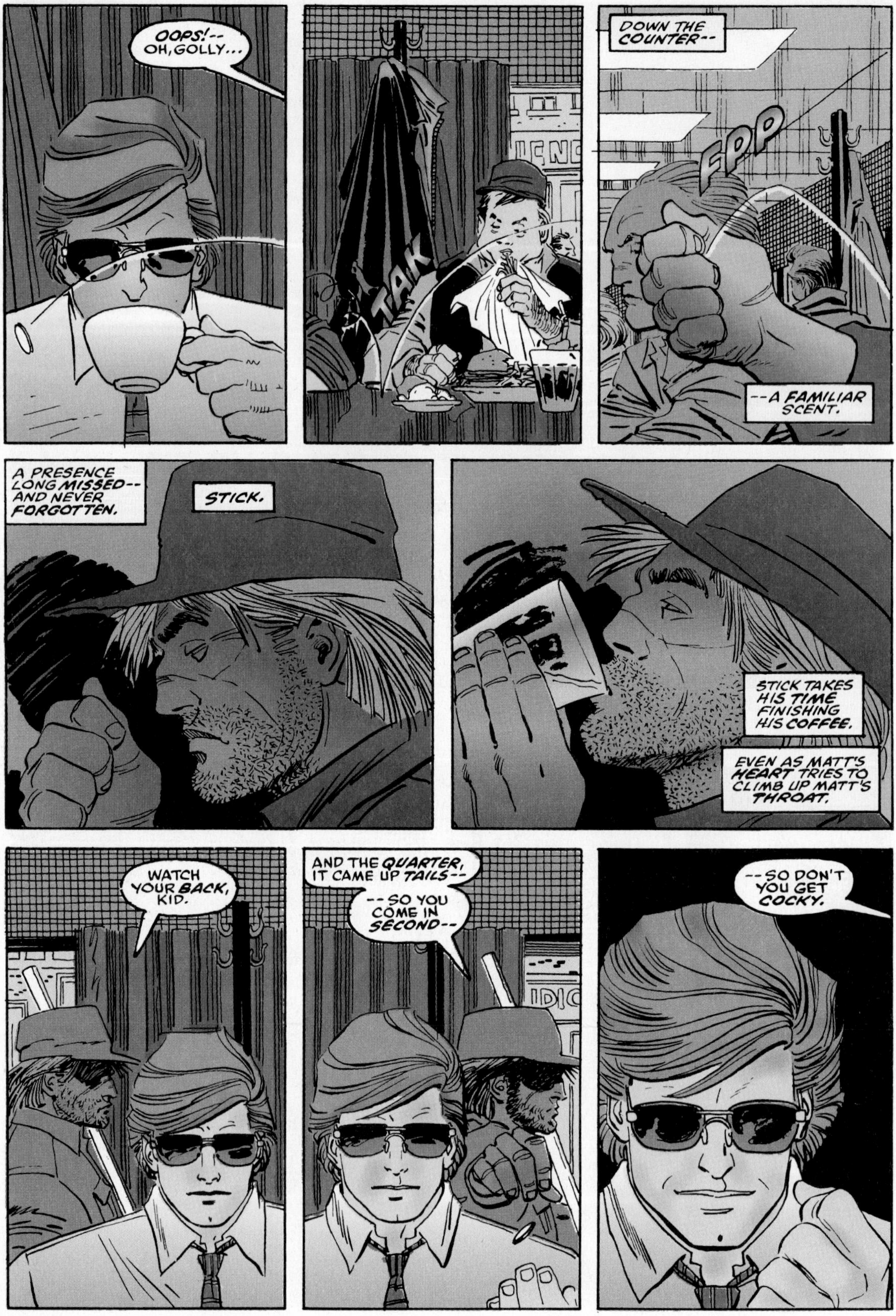
OOPS!-- OH, GOLLY...
DOWN THE COUNTER--
FPP
--A FAMILIAR SCENT.
A PRESENCE LONG MISSED-- AND NEVER FORGOTTEN.
STICK.
STICK TAKES HIS TIME FINISHING HIS COFFEE.
EVEN AS MATT'S HEART TRIES TO CLIMB UP MATT'S THROAT.
WATCH YOUR BACK, KID.
AND THE QUARTER, IT CAME UP TAILS--
--SO YOU COME IN SECOND--
--SO DON'T YOU GET COCKY.

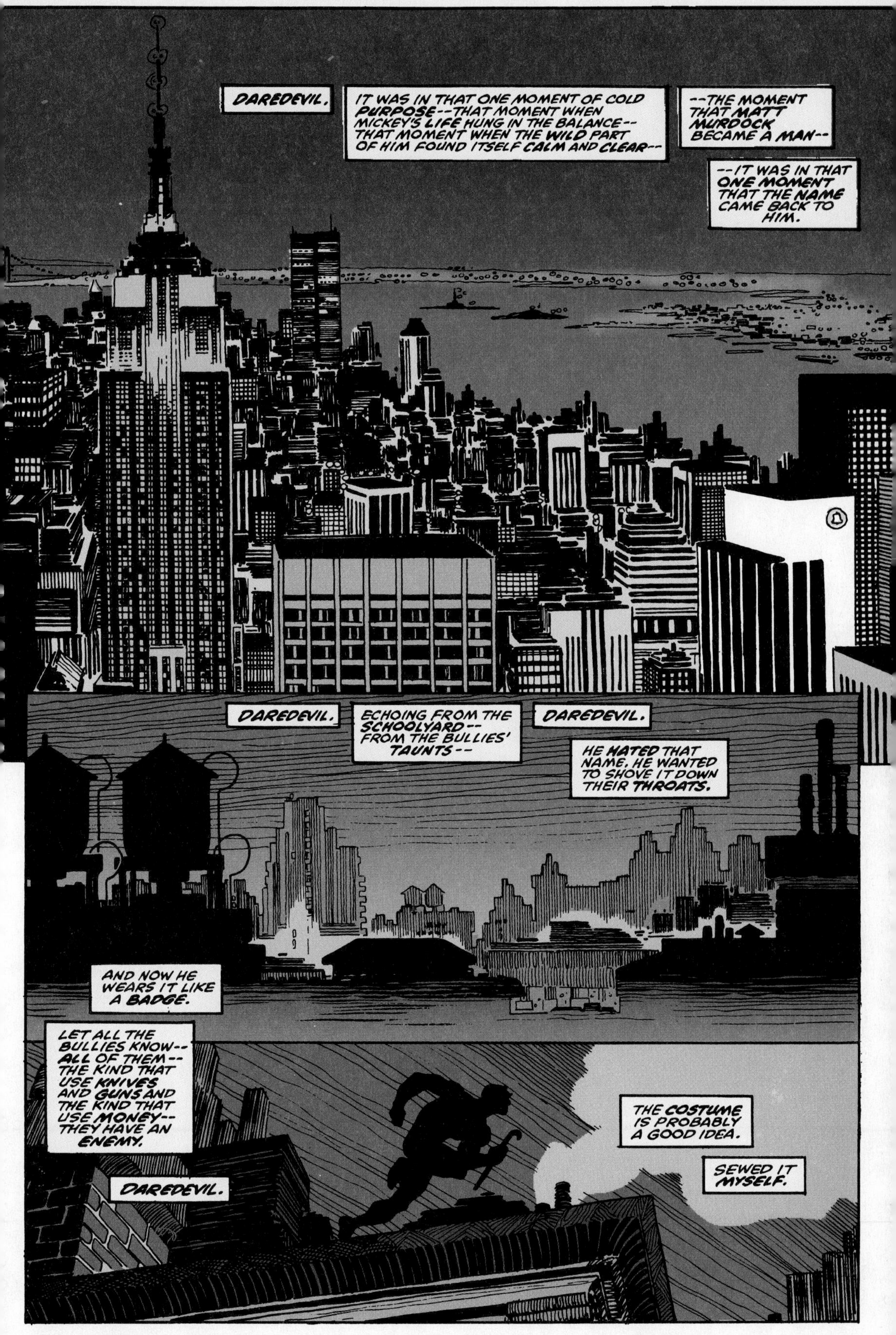
DAREDEVIL.
IT WAS IN THAT ONE MOMENT OF COLD PURPOSE--THAT MOMENT WHEN MICKEY'S LIFE HUNG IN THE BALANCE--THAT MOMENT WHEN THE WILD PART OF HIM FOUND ITSELF CALM AND CLEAR--
--THE MOMENT THAT MATT MURDOCK BECAME A MAN--
--IT WAS IN THAT ONE MOMENT THAT THE NAME CAME BACK TO HIM.
DAREDEVIL.
ECHOING FROM THE SCHOOLYARD--FROM THE BULLIES' TAUNTS--
DAREDEVIL.
HE HATED THAT NAME. HE WANTED TO SHOVE IT DOWN THEIR THROATS.
AND NOW HE WEARS IT LIKE A BADGE.
LET ALL THE BULLIES KNOW--ALL OF THEM--THE KIND THAT USE KNIVES AND GUNS AND THE KIND THAT USE MONEY--THEY HAVE AN ENEMY.
DAREDEVIL.
THE COSTUME IS PROBABLY A GOOD IDEA.
SEWED IT MYSELF.

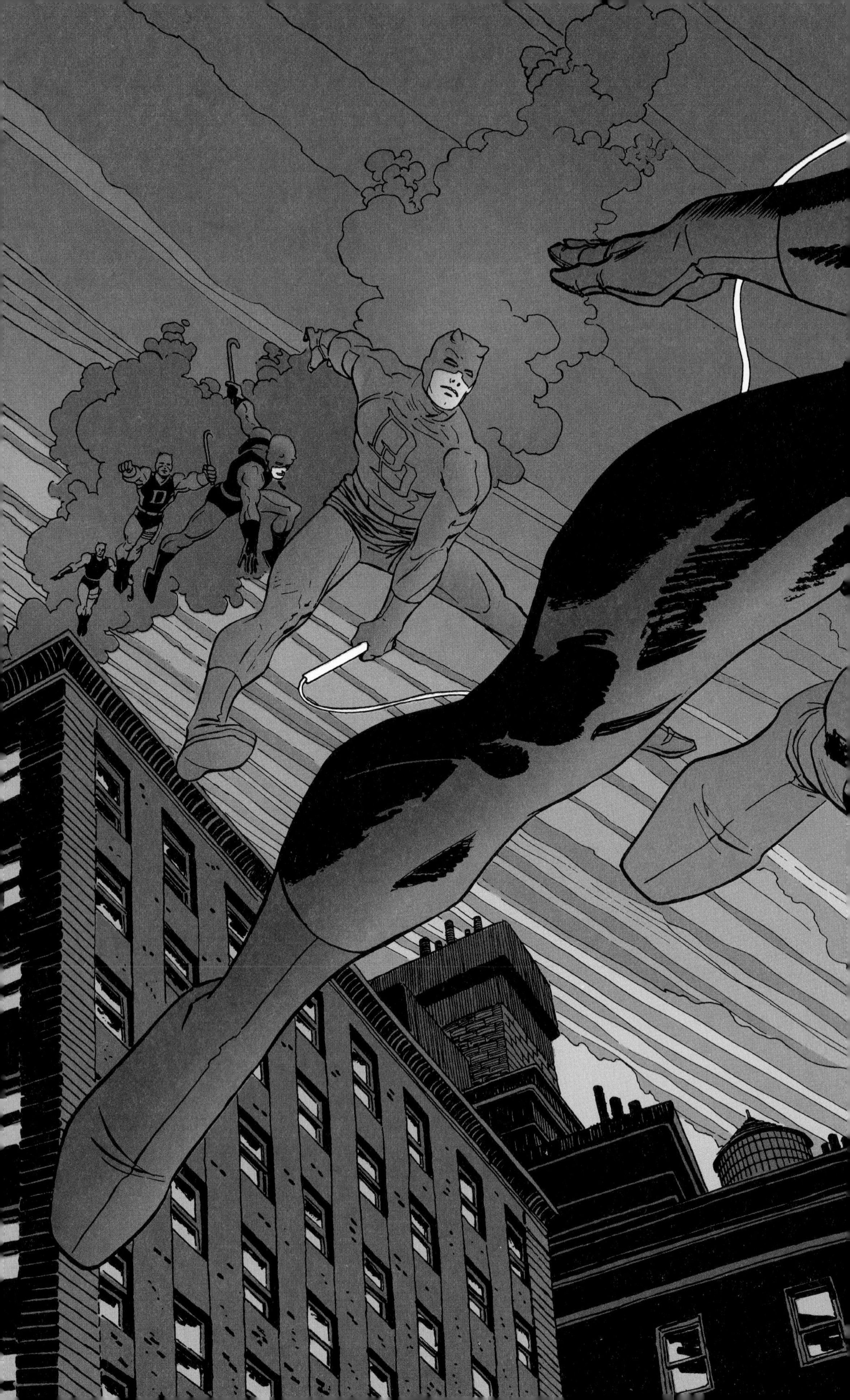

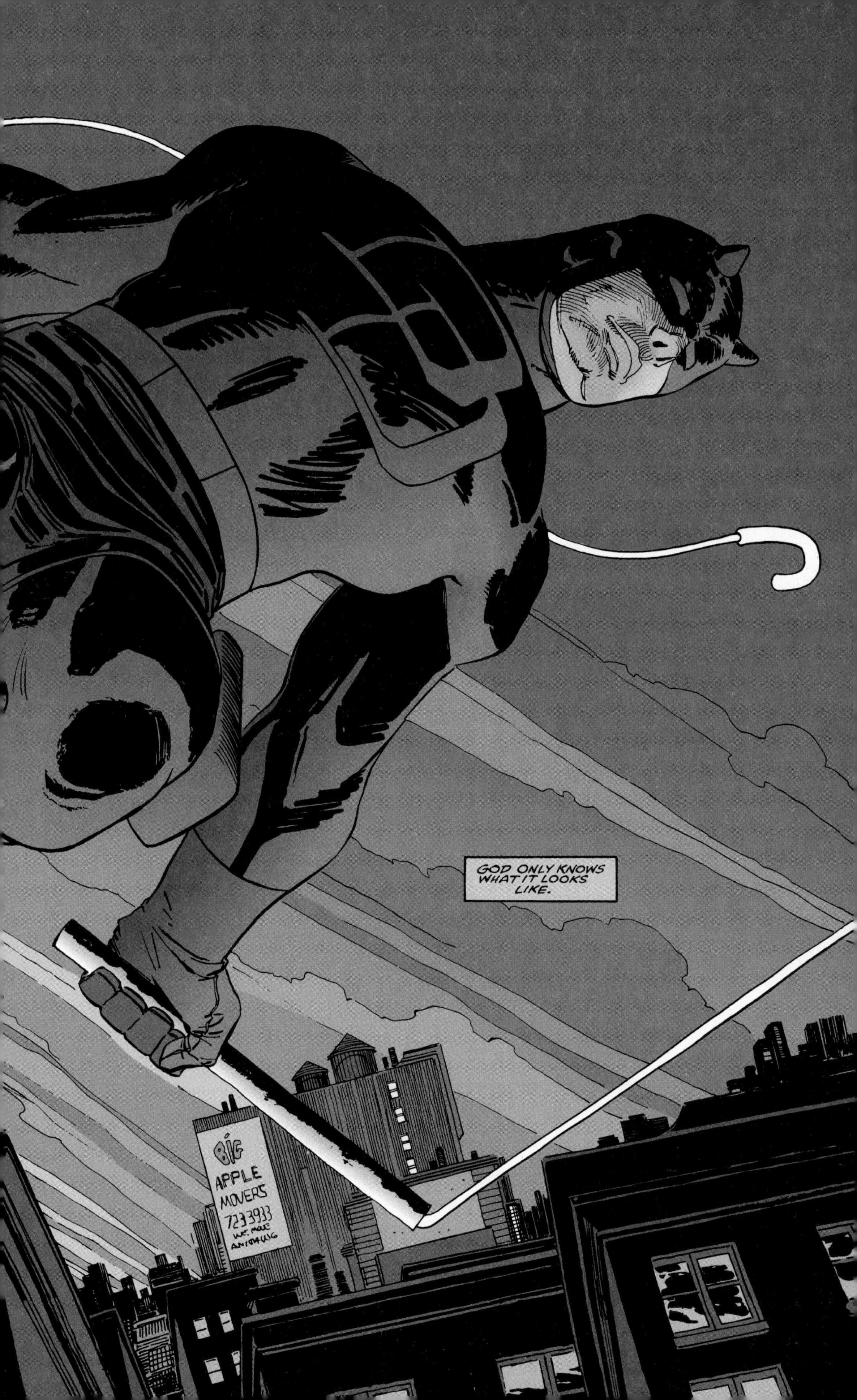
GOD ONLY KNOWS WHAT IT LOOKS LIKE.
BIG APPLE MOVERS
723 3933
WE MOVE ANYTHING

BLIND JUSTICE
A Marvel Graphic Novel

Story by
Frank Miller

REVISED DRAFT #2
6/2/88

***

ACT ONE

At age eight, **Matt Murdock** is a dirty-faced little terror. His hair is an overgrown weed, bright orange in color. His eyes are green and wild. The impoverished neighborhood of **Hell's Kitchen** is his home; its sunbaked streets and rattling fire escapes form his playground.

Matt plagues fat **Patrolman Itkowitz**, who'd throw Matt into Juvenile Court if it weren't for the black ski mask Matt wears to conceal his identity. Itkowitz is left puffing and red after Matt's boldest stunt, one sweltering summer afternoon : Matt steals Itkowitz' night stick, right from his belt, right in front of **Julio** and **Rachel** and the other neighborhood brats Itkowitz had caught playing about an open fire hydrant. Itkowitz doesn't have a hope of catching Matt, the way the boy flies down the street on his skateboard and scrambles to the rooftops like a monkey.

Matt hides the billy club in a rusty locker at **Fogwell's**, a dilapidated old gymnasium. The gym's walls are cracked, aging -- and covered with posters featuring Matt's father, **Jack Murdock**.

Jack Murdock is a heavyweight boxer. Years ago, he was considered a possible contender for a national title. He never quite made it, though, and the years of taking punches have not been kind. Nor has the bourbon.

The bourbon he drinks alone, at night. Young Matt pretends to sleep and tries not to listen as Jack whispers of his love for Maggie, Matt's mother. When Jack gets

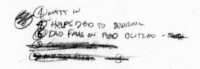 

helplessly drunk, and Matt has to guide him to his bed, Jack speaks of Maggie as if she were still alive.

He's not the man he used to be, and he knows it. His fists are still quick, but his mind is slow and easily confused.

"Battlin'" Murdock has two lives. Neither of them brings him any pleasure.

In the gym, during his bouts with neighborhood longshoreman, Murdock never loses, but at least the fights are fair -- or so he thinks. But the purses are small, hardly enough for him to sponsor Matt's education.

He's paid better for roughing up locals who welch on bets. It makes him sick to do it -- it cost him his wife -- but his own life, his own dignity, mean little to Jack. Matt is all that matters.

The stocking mask and cap don't fool anybody. They know who he is, just as they know he's carrying that baseball bat mainly for show. Mostly he'll just slap a welcher around a bit, or smash a window. The welchers aren't likely to complain to the top neighborhood mobster, the **Fixer**.

For the nastier jobs the Fixer uses a hulk named Slade.

Jack is determined to spare Matt a life of poverty and violence. A thousand times he sits in that overstuffed chair, his hand on Matt's shoulders, telling Matt that he must never fight; a thousand times Matt protests, saying how much he adores his Dad, how much he wants to be just like him. He doesn't yet understand where his father goes with his baseball bat, who that "somebody else" is that Dad says he has to be. Jack can't bring himself to explain.

One day, when Matt comes home, triumphant from an encounter with local bullies, Jack screams at him, and slaps

him, leaving Matt bloody-nosed and terrified. Matt runs
off, to sit at the top of the Brooklyn Bridge until dawn.
His father had never struck him before, not once. It was
bad. Matt keeps thinking that people need rules to live by.
Dad says he's going to be a doctor or a lawyer or something.
Maybe he can help make people obey the rules. Maybe he'll
be a lawyer.

Matt bites his lip and obeys his father's wishes,
studying every night, ignoring the endless taunts. The
bullies torment him with a sarcastic, damning nickname:
Daredevil.

He hears them chanting it when Julio slaps him, and
beats him, revelling in his rival's humiliation. The word
rises from them again and again as Julio's fists force the
back of Matt's skull and spine to test the strength of the
old schoolyard's chain link fence.

The worst of it is when Matt sees Rachel, turning away,
walking away, humiliated by Matt's cowardice.

Matt's rage explodes only in secret, only in the old
gym, only when the sound of his fists striking the large,
worn punching bag echoes like machine gun fire.

In the darkness of the gym, silent, unnoticed by Matt,
a strange old blind man named **Stick** listens, and waits. He
has noticed Matt's courage, Matt's restlessness. He has
great hopes, and many fears ...

At age sixteen, Matt tackles an old wino from the path
of an out of control truck. Drums filled with radioactive
waste tumble from the back of the careening truck.
Punctured, one sprays a glowing blue rivulet across Matt's
eyes. Matt is blinded for life.

Blinded, and transformed into something more than
human.

***

ACT TWO

At first, Matt thinks he's hallucinating. The world becomes impossibly loud, and filled with impossible odors. It takes an effort of will to shut out the bass drum pounding of his own heartbeat.

The doctors from the corporation that produced the radioactive waste are pleasant and friendly. But when they whisper about mutated nerve centers and experimental surgery, Matt hears them, and learns to keep his amplified senses a secret.

Everyone pities him. Everybody wants to help him cross the street.

Only Stick understands.

Stick has been blind since birth, and an orphan since he was a baby. He has suffered every cruelty the city inflicts upon the helpless, and survived them, learning to use his remaining senses in extraordinary ways.

He speaks to Matt for the first time when Matt is curled on the floor of the old gym, crying in frustration, his body bruised from attempt after futile attempt to use the parallel bars. He orders Matt to get up.

In the filthy basement of an abandoned tenement, Matt's training begins. Stick teaches Matt to recognize people and objects by scent, to sense movement by feeling the touch of displaced air. Matt learns to fight, sparring with Stick, tracking Stick's heartbeat, hearing the rush of blood through veins that signals movement.

Strangely, Stick insists Matt practice with bow and arrow. Matt thinks it's idiotic -- his hearing can't help him find the target -- until Stick fires three arrows, each striking the bullseye. Matt misses at first, many times. Stick shouts at him, won't let him give up. Matt keeps firing arrows past the target, till dawn. Then, exhausted and teary, Matt feels the shape of the target, as if touching it from across the room. Matt fires an arrow, striking the target off center. Matt gives out a yelp. Stick swings his walking stick across Matt's backside. "Monkey with a typewriter," he says. "You just got lucky." Matt aims again, and fires, striking the target at its center. His next arrow splits the last.

Jack Murdock knows nothing of all this; he's simply thrilled by Matt's good grades, and more determined than ever to see Matt go to college.

Stick also has his own secret plans for Matt, though he rarely speaks of them. It's just as well; Matt is doomed to fail his training.

The Fixer orders Jack to throw a fight.

Seeing his son in the audience, during the sweaty, exhausting bout, Murdock fights to win with everything he has. His opponent is younger, faster, and meaner than he, but Murdock wins.

That same night, he is cornered in a back alley by five of the Fixer's men. They take their time with him, slapping him, beating him brutally. The Fixer watches, smiling, smoking a cigarette. When Murdock is no longer able to rise, the Fixer shoots him through the head.

In the morgue, Matt touches the cold thing that had been his father's face. Something colder happens in his gut.

Hell's Kitchen has the best cops money can buy. They call it a mugging, but everyone in the neighborhood knows who killed Jack Murdock.

Two of them are staggering home, blind drunk. They pause to take a swig, balancing themselves on a streetlight.

A baseball bat, dragged across pavement, echoes from the shadows.

They stare into the darkness. A frightfully calm voice speaks to them. One curses, drawing a switchblade. The other smashes the end from his bottle and staggers forward, in a clumsy charge ...

... a few moments later, a police cruiser screeches to a stop. The two lie beaten to within an inch of their lives. One, barely conscious, mutters about Jack Murdock and begs to be arrested. "We killed the bastard ... but he's back ..."

Slade works out at the big bag, wearing shorts, a sweaty sleeveless t-shirt, and boxing gloves. He's in a good mood; he took a lot of pleasure flattening Murdock's face. He chats with slick little **Marcello**, who's got the jitters and can't stop playing with his stiletto.

Marcello shrieks when the lights go out, then babbles uncontrollably, fearfully. Slade orders him to shut up. Marcello stops in mid-word, lost in the darkness. Slade calls out to him, stumbles about in the darkness, trying to find him. What he finds is sticky wet and barely breathing.
From behind him, a voice says, "take your gloves off."

A single spotlight strikes the boxing ring at the center of the gym's main room. Matt wears his father's hat, jacket, and stocking mask. Matt tosses his bat aside and gestures Slade toward him. Slade laughs, and climbs over

the ropes. He towers over Matt, a full foot taller and wider than Matt. "Small for the job," says Slade.

"Sit down," says Matt.

Matt pivots, kicking Slade in the knee, breaking bone. Slade's leg gives way. He drops to one knee, looks up at Matt, snarling. Matt punches Slade three times in the face, in the space of one second. His nose broken, his lip split, Slade curses, still unafraid. He sees Matt's feet step backward, as if dancing. One foot draws far back, then moves forward, a blur. Slade's ribs flex inward. He tumbles backward, over the ropes.

The Fixer shows up for the last of it, and runs like Hell to his limousine. As the limo tears down the street, Matt takes to the rooftops, bat in hand.

He leaps into space, flips on a flagpole, and lands on the hood of the car. The Fixer fires his pistol from a side window just as the driver panics, wrenching the wheel. Matt tumbles from the limo. The limo crashes into a subway entrance.

The Fixer stumbles from the car, runs into the subway station. His driver runs away. Matt rises from the street, his knee scraped and bloody, and follows the Fixer into the station.

Matt hears the Fixer's heart race -- until an express train roars through the station, deafeningly loud for Matt. The Fixer wheels, panting, grinning, aims his pistol at Matt. The train leaves the station, clicking off down the tunnel. The station is silent except for the Fixer's gun as he cocks it -- and the Fixer's heart, beating fast, too fast. The Fixer almost pulls the trigger before he drops dead of a heart attack.

Matt leaves the station. There's still the driver to catch.

32
(1) HOSPITAL ROOM
(2) DETECTIVE CLOSE
(3) MATT ON ROOF WATCHES WHOREHOUSE
(4) DRIVER ON COUCH SCARED - WHORES AROUND
(5) MATT IN GRABS DRIVER
(6) GIRLS ATTACK MATT

In a hospital, surrounded by cops, the two Matt left by the streetlight are both babbling now, one trying to shut the other up. A plainclothes detective grinds out his cigar and tells one of his men to wake up the judge. They'll be needing some warrants.

Using his senses to pick the sputtering, cursing driver from a sea of noise, Murdock hunts him to a whorehouse and attacks him. The whores come to the driver's aid, confusing Matt. In his struggle to break free, Matt kicks one of the whores.

She stumbles backward, crashing through a window, to her death.

Matt hears the scream, the crunch of bone many stories below, the pitiful last sound, half cough, half gurgle.

***

33
(1) MATT STRUGGLES
(2) MATT ACCIDENTALLY SHOVES GIRL
(3) THRU WINDOW -
(4) MATT LISTENS TO IT HORRIFIED
(5) ONTO ROOF
(6) RUNS - SIRENS

ACT THREE

Matt barely escapes arriving policemen.

Bloody, his fury turned to horror and shame, Matt makes his way back to the old gym. He calls out to Stick again and again. There is no answer.

Matt cannot find Stick. He never learns what Stick had planned for him. He only knows that he has failed, and failing, killed an innocent woman.

Haunted, Matt becomes obsessed with obeying his dead father's command. He studies incessantly. He sails through Pre-Law at Columbia. He does his best to forget the old gym.

His roommate, **Franklin "Foggy" Nelson**, a chubby, affable fellow, is Matt's only friend. Foggy is the butt of constant taunts and practical jokes from a sadistic frat boy named **Brad**. Matt hears, in Brad's laughter, that of Julio and all the other bullies of his childhood.

When Brad is found, naked and bound, face down on the tennis court, he doesn't tell any of his friends how he got there. But he remembers Matt's voice, whispering, and leaves Foggy alone.

At age twenty-four, Matt is a quiet, driven man – and an outstanding graduate student on a full scholarship at Harvard Law School.

In New York, in Matt's old neighborhood of Hell's Kitchen, a monster comes to power. He is a huge, bald man, tremendously strong. He has never spoken.

(37) (1) HANDS ON SHOULDERS (2) ON HEAD (3) SNAP (4) BOSS DEAD (5) GRABS CARNATION

He is an aging gangleader's bodyguard. After calmly listening to the old Mafioso argue against horrifying suggestions from his lieutenants, he murders the gangleader by breaking his neck, and takes the leader's place. When he speaks, his voice is smooth and cultured.

They call him the **Kingpin**. You might say he's the biggest bully of them all.

(38) BOSSES

***

ACT FOUR

Soon the Kingpin's gang is larger and more profitable. Unlike his predecessor, there is no crime that is too terrible for him. He caters to every vice imaginable. He engineers the wholesale production of every form of pornography, including films of torture and murder. Kidnapped children disappear into soundproofed warehouses. Drug traffic flourishes. The Kingpin rules with a Satanic relish, and a bookkeeper's precision.

He recruits a group of mercenary soldiers led by a cadaverous old demon named **Slaughter**. They become his private Gestapo, and the terror of rival gangs.

A nameless man, whose face has been made lifeless by repeated plastic surgery, is the Kingpin's personal assassin. He silences dissent and punishes inefficiency within the Kingpin's organization. They call him **Larks**, after the cigarettes he constantly smokes.

Smoking is the least of Larks' vices. The Kingpin provides for all of them.

Matt graduates Harvard and goes to work for a respectable law firm in Boston. He plans never to return to New York. He protests when his boss orders him to Manhattan on a research assignment. But Matt is new to the firm, in no position to refuse.

Back in New York, Matt is drawn inexorably to the nightmare of his past.

Unable to sleep, Matt walks, late at night, his white blind man's cane tapping garbage-strewn sidewalks, every corner bringing some fresh, buried memory. He's running his fingers across the chain link fence that surrounds his old schoolyard, hearing the chant of his hated nickname, when he realizes that he has returned to Hell's Kitchen.

13

He hears the group of punks whispering to each other, sizing him up, as they approach from down the street, behind them. He has plenty of time to run away, but his feet won't obey. He turns, facing them.

One of them wastes no time, swinging his blade at Matt's face. Matt kicks, and the knife clatters across the street. The other four draw weapons and snarl at Matt, cursing him.

They don't say the name, but Matt hears it.

"Daredevil."

Matt snaps his blind man's cane in two, throws it away, and attacks, spinning, punching, kicking.

Soon they lie at his feet, crumpled, moaning, whimpering. One rises, and runs off. Matt chases after him, a wild man.

***

ACT FIVE

The next thing Matt knows his knuckles are bleeding and the youth is whimpering for mercy.

Matt's the bully now.

Sickened with himself, he staggers down the street.

When he calms down, he's at the old gym. It's now abandoned, its shattered windows covered with wooden planks. Matt pulls a plank free and slips inside.

He walks past yellowed, cracked posters of his father.

He hears equipment creak, and the frantic breathing of a child.

She tries to hide. She fires a ball bearing at him from a slingshot. She gasps when he catches it in one hand, smiling.

She's a scruffy little girl. She's found the old gym and made it her hideout.

She says her name is **Mickey**. She says she's an orphan. She's lying both times.

The two meet nightly after that. They work out together. Matt never touches his old locker, which is now caked shut by rust.

One night, Mickey asks Matt about a crinkled poster of Jack Murdock dressed in a cheap, wrinkled scarlet devil's costume. The poster announces a wrestling match between "Devil" Murdock and "Destroyer" Donovan. As she describes the poster to Matt, he scowls in distaste. "Local kids loved that. Kidded me about it a lot," he says, his voice low, "Dad had to do a lot of things to keep us going."

Matt pulls on his boxing gloves. "I've always wanted to throw that nickname back in their faces," he says.

"What nickname?" asks Mickey. Matt's response is lost in the shotgun blast of his fist striking the bag.

Matt runs across his old roommate, Foggy, at a restaurant. Foggy's wrestling with a tough legal assignment. Matt helps him, working late with Foggy at Foggy's apartment.

The Kingpin makes a mistake that will cost him dearly. He sends Lark to pressure the head of his Film Department to reduce overhead costs.

The Film Department becomes extremely budget conscious.

One of the department's dispatchers, feeling the heat, gives two junkies named **Roberto** and **Alice** a break.

Matt's working with Foggy when Roberto and Alice find Mickey. She fights hard and well before Roberto pins her down and Alice brings the chloroform-soaked cloth over her face.

Matt's called back to Boston by his boss for an urgent new assignment. On the way to the airport he goes to the gym to say goodbye to Mickey.

Matt finds Mickey's change purse on the alley floor outside the gym. He finds a student ID card in it, pries its plastic lamination off, and reads Mickey's real name and address by touch.

Roberto and Alice don't get paid on delivery. Frantic, Roberto calls Mickey's parents, and demands a ransom. Matt hears the call, from outside the parents' window, perched on a ledge.

Matt punches in the rusty door of his old locker and tears it loose. He grabs his billy club.

Mickey must not die.

***

① BIG SHOT - MATT ON LEDGE
② PUNCHES IN LOCKER
③ BILLY CLUB

ACT SIX

Terrified of the Kingpin and frantic for a fix, Alice sells Roberto out. Very soon, the Kingpin sends Larks in to clean things up.

Larks kills the dispatcher who hires Roberto and Alice, and stakes out the hotel room, waiting for Roberto.

Matt's amplified senses serve him well, as he follows Mickey's father back and forth across town like a ping pong ball, from phone booth to cab to phone booth, for yet another of Roberto's directions.

But Matt's senses are anything but an asset on the subway, where, as before, screeching brakes and blasting horns overwhelm Matt's supersensitive hearing, making him helpless when Mickey's father mistakes him for a cop and attacks him.

Matt barely keeps the trail from the desolate South Bronx where Roberto gets his money, to downtown, where Roberto gets his heroin, to Roberto's hotel room, where Roberto gets a bullet through his brain.

Matt dodges bullets himself, then tracks Larks to the waterfront. During his encounter with Matt, Larks is astonished by Matt's abilities. From his limousine, Larks calls the Kingpin. The Kingpin calls in Slaughter to turn the waterfront into a deathtrap for his mysterious new foe.

In the warehouse, they wash Mickey's hair, scrub her down, make her up, and put her in a party dress. They lock her in a cubicle the size of a closet, one of dozens, she notices. She knows there's only one man who can save her, and she knows he has great ears, so she begins singing, her voice pure and beautiful. Other voices, from other cubicles, join in.

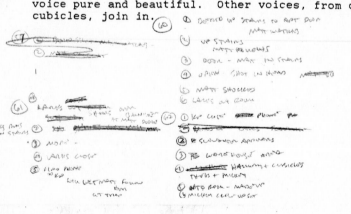

The children's chorus is the last thing Matt hears,
after detecting Slaughter's men waiting for him on the
warehouse roof, among crates piled on the dock, crouched on
the deck of a rusty old steamer overlooking the warehouse.

***

ACT SEVEN

Larks has been promised a bonus, .and takes his time making his selection. He looks over each of the children in turn, taking time to compliment the manager on getting them to sing.

Silent as a ghost, Matt glides, running along a power line to the warehouse roof. The men on the roof are noisy hearts and lungs, startled gasps, splintered jaws and ribs as he moves from one to the next, demolishing them with his fists and his club.

He leaps to the side of the warehouse, pulls the spark plugs from the cars and trucks in the lot. He pushes through rotten planks on the docks.

He swims to the steamer, crawls into a porthole near water level, and makes his way to the steamer's deck, his sneakers, sweat pants, and sweat shirt soaking wet.

He brings his club up across the neck of the first, choking him to unconsciousness. As he fells the second with a spinning kick to the jaw, his wet snaker slips on the wet deck, and he stumbles, not gaining his balance in time to avoid the last of them, who tackles him. They tumble from the side, to the water.

Under water, the man holds a bayonet to Matt's throat. Matt twists his wrist, driving the blade between the man's ribs.

He grabs the man's grenade belt and ties it to a piling under the dock. He pulls the grenade pins.

He climbs to the dock, leaps across crates, tracked by gunfire from Slaughter's men. The grenades explode, the dock lurches, and Matt is everywhere, springing from behind tumbling crates, striking with his club, his fists, and his feet.

The warehouse wall bursts outward. Slaughter attacks Matt with an urban assault vehicle. Matt dodges machine gun fire and runs right into the path of arriving police cruisers.

Larks made his selection before the shooting started. He drags Mickey to his limousine. The engine won't start. Cursing, he drags her down the street.

Matt falls beneath a dozen cops. They cuff him, shove him in a cruiser, and the cruiser drives off.

Mickey screams.

***

ACT EIGHT

There are three cops in the cruiser, and Matt's hands are cuffed behind his back.

Matt kicks the one next to him and the driver, slams his skull against the skull of the remaining one. The cruiser crashes against an elevated highway support column.

Mickey screams again. The cabbie barely has a chance to curse before Larks' silenced shot strikes him between the eyes. Larks throws Mickey into the taxi and drives off, taking time to shove the dead cabbie to the street.

Matt kicks out the windshield of the cruiser and drives it, chasing Mickey's scream.

The open windshield isn't enough. Matt has never driven before, and he's blind. There isn't much he doesn't hit, and he can't tell a red traffic light from a green one. He's caused three accidents and there isn't much left of the cruiser when it careens into Larks' cab.

The rest of the chase is on foot. It ends in a small, smoky saloon. Larks holds his pistol to Mickey's temple when Matt appears at the doorway, club in hand.

Larks shoots Matt in the calf. Matt doesn't retreat. Larks takes aim and fires again, at Matt's head.

Matt swings the billy club. Its end splinters. The bullet strikes the floor near Larks' foot.

Larks gasps, astonished, terrified.

"Who are you?"

Matt says the nickname, not hating it.

"Daredevil."

Larks shrieks and aims again. Matt's voice is soft, pleading.

"Don't."

Larks fires. Matt swings his club again. The bullet shatters the wood of the club, revealing its steel shank, and flies backward, to strike Larks between the eyes.

Matt's gone by the time the cops arrive.

It's the largest bust of its kind in the city's history. The net of evidence begins to close about the Kingpin. The Kingpin flees the country, leaving evidence to falsely incriminate one of his lieutenants, never knowing the name of the man who nearly exposed him.

Matt's boss screams at him over the telephone, that morning. Matt loses his job in Boston. Matt can't help but laugh. Nothing could make him leave New York, not now.

Matt's having coffee with Foggy at a Chock Full O'Nuts, a few days later. Foggy's got this big idea about the two of them starting a firm of their own, in partnership. Foggy flips a coin into the air, to decide who's name will come first. He flips it too far. It sails across the counter.

A few stools away, Stick catches it. He knocks back the last of his coffee, and walks past Matt, dropping the coin on the counter. He nods at Matt and walks off.

The low tenements of Hell's Kitchen, black silhouettes, squat beneath a steely, moonless sky.

Somewhere a police siren wails. Its light rises from the street, crawls around the side of a rotting old water tower, casting the shadow of a running man.

Mickey made the thing. Says she based it on that old
wrestling poster. Says Matt can throw the name back at them
now, finally.

God knows what it looks like.

Steam blasts forth from a roof vent. Daredevil rises,
in mid-leap, his club raised.

                    THE END

DAREDEVIL GRAPHIC NOVEL
Story Addenda
by Frank Miller
6/8/90

PRELIMINARY NOTE:

John, Ralph--

As we've discussed, this book offers a few more
opportunities than those taken in my original story.
Elektra in particular should be spotlighted.

Looking over the pages I have (1-39), I've discovered
a few more places I'd like to expand the narrative,
spots where scenes would embroider Matt's history or
underscore the importance of particular phases of his
life. So I'm going to hell with myself, and hope
you'll join me.

I also hope that page count isn't a concern at this
stage. One great thing about this format is that it
can allow for greater detail and depth. Let's take the
term "novel" seriously and not worry if we turn out a
thick one; this story covers two decades in time and a
hero's rite of passage. The character and the fans
deserve a full, rich story.

Besides, it's so much fun getting those gorgeous
Romita pages in the mail.

John--on the Elektra stuff: keep in mind that Elektra
is psychotic. Her craziness didn't start when her
father died. Her expressions should be frequently
inappropriate, matter-of-fact when she confesses to
murder, almost amused at her father's grave,
businesslike as she murders. This is a major aspect of
her character and gets across the craziness without
beating the reader over the head with it.

Also, the dialogue accompanying some of these scenes
is by no means complete or final. It's just me
thinking on paper, trying to communicate my intent.

Okay, here we go...

AFTER EXISTING PAGE 4:

(1)

EXT. GYM - NIGHT

(5)

(1) GYM
(4) FIXER CLOSE
(5) JACK CLOSE
(6) MATT IN SHADOWS

Establishing shot (to accommodate SOUND EFFECT: WHUKK)

INT. GYM - NIGHT

JACK MURDOCK is on his knees, the wind knocked out of him. SLADE stands over him, sweaty, holding his head up by the hair. The FIXER smiles.

FIXER
That's enough, Slade.

FIXER explains to Murdock where he stands: he's got to do the Fixer's dirty work, or he'll get no fights--he's a loser and his brat will end up a loser or a corpse if Jack doesn't play along.

JACK fumes, defeated--not only by Slade's fists.

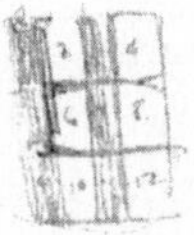

In the shadows MATT listens, tearful, angry. If only he wasn't just a kid...

(2)

AFTER PAGE NINE:

(9)

(A1) BLACK
(A2) AMBULANCE
(A3) BLACK
(A4) MATT INSIDE
(A5) BLACK
(A6) ON CART - CORRIDOR
NURSES + INTERNS
(A7) BLACK
(A8) MATT CLOSE WRITHES IN AGONY
(A9) BLACK
(A10) FINGERS ON SHEETS
(A11) BLACK
(A12) SURGERY

JOHN: The plan here is to add pages that recount Matt's discovery of his senses during his hospital stay. Exactly this material was covered using black panels only in DD#229, and I'd like to use the same script, ending page 9 with the line "Is it radioactive?" and beginning the first new page with Matt's narrative on a black panel--then proceeding with pictures of, among whatever else you think best corresponds with the text:

- Matt's ride in the ambulance as PARAMEDICS try to anesthetize him and the RADIOACTIVE GOOP sizzles across his face;

- MATT rushed on a CART down a hospital corridor; NURSES and INTERNS everywhere;

- MATT, his face bandaged, writhing in agony, discovering that it's just the sheets that feel like sandpaper;

- A SURGICAL TEAM at work on MATT'S FACE;

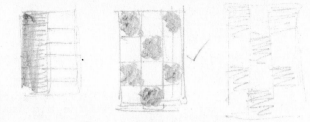

- MATT alone in his hospital bed, at night;

- JACK MURDOCK, distraught, trying to encourage Matt;

- MAGGIE's visit and her conversation with Matt, including his fingers touching the small gold CROSS at her breast and her tearful exit;

- and Matt's second hospital conversation with his father.

Please spot black panels between scenes to aid me in the transitions of time.

This is a CRUCIAL sequence. Give it the room it needs. And please take your cue from the DD#229 script--I'd like to keep it as it is, not just for continuity's sake, but because I really killed myself on those pages and I'd hate to change them. I hope this isn't too much of a pain in the ass--I believe it could be extremely dramatic. It's at this point in the story that we introduce the whole PREMISE of Daredevil.

AFTER EXISTING PAGE 17:

Speaking of pains in the ass, here I think we need a DOUBLE PAGE SPREAD of STICK and MATT dashing across rooftops against a PANORAMA of Manhattan at night. A moment of joy before what follows.

BETWEEN PANELS 3 AND 4, EXISTING PAGE 34:

INT. GYM - NIGHT

CONTINUING PREVIOUS SCENE: Here ends a major phase of Matt's life, and we could use a couple of shots not only to punctuate it, but to explain it as well. Start with a LARGE PANEL of the GYM FLOOR, MATT tiny in shot, curled on the floor, horrified and scared. I suggest you take the rest of the page with it.

EXT. FLEABAG HOTEL - NIGHT

Words come from a cracked, darkened WINDOW:

                    STICK (VO)
          I SCREWED up. All there
          is to it. The kid looked
          GOOD...

INT. FLEABAG HOTEL ROOM - NIGHT

STICK sits cross-legged, facing a SHADOWED FIGURE--a
fellow member of the SEVEN, STONE, who is huge.

                    STICK
          ...He had everything it
          TAKES to be one of us. If
          it weren't for that
          TEMPER of his...
                    (2)
          I was wrong about him.

                    STONE
          How much does he know?

CLOSE UP--STICK.

                    STICK
          Not enough to compromise
          us. No, he'll never find
          us...

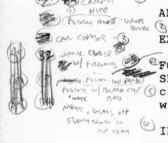

AFTER EXISTING PAGE THIRTY-FOUR:

EXT. CAMPUS - NIGHT

FOGGY runs, terrified, across LAWN, pursued by by a
SPORTS CAR driven by the JERK who picked on him in
class. JERK'S FRIENDS are with him, drunken, howling
with laughter. FOGGY is dropping BOOKS.

INT. DORMITORY - NIGHT

MATT tends to FOGGY, who's been beaten, one EYE closed
in a bruise.

COLUMBIA
CAMPUS -
CARS- ✓

FOGGY tells MATT to forget about it. MATT removes his
GLASSES, tells Foggy everything will be okay.

And here's the big one...

(9) ~~BETWEEN PANELS 4 AND 5~~, EXISTING PAGE 35:

AFTER TENNIS COURT SCENE:

EXT. CAMPUS - DAY

The JERK left bound and gagged by MATT apologizes to a
startled FOGGY. Passing STUDENTS take it in, hiding
smiles. MATT listens in quiet satisfaction. A pair of
GIRLS--one of them lovely hispanic PATRICIA DeJESUS,
view the scene with amusement.

JERK exits. FOGGY shakes his head with a "Golly, Matt.
How do you figure THAT?"

PATRICIA sidles up to MATT, flirtatious, requesting
help with her studies. Checking his watch, MATT puts
her off. Late for class.

MATT walks off with FOGGY as PATRICIA and her friend
HILDY confer. PAT's got a crush on MATT; he doesn't
seem to notice.

HILDY doesn't understand the attraction. A blind guy.
PAT says she's never met anybody so intense as Matt.

THAT NIGHT - INT. DORMITORY ROOM

FOGGY's on his bed, asleep in front of a small
portable TV that sits between his splayed legs,
snoring, BOOKS and JUNK FOOD scattered. MATT turns the
TV off.

MATT lies in bed, eyes open, staring at the ceiling.

FOGGY snores.

MATT won't get any sleep tonight.

It's not Foggy's snoring.

EXT. ROOFTOPS - NIGHT

It's not Foggy's snoring. It's the WIND, whipping a TV ANTENNA on a rooftop. The SNOW does little to muffle the sound.

It's the WIND, scattering Autumn LEAVES across campus SIDEWALK.

It's the WIND, gusting a forgotten NEWSPAPER, making it lurch across the street like a wounded dog.

It's the WIND, carrying the comforting smell of fresh baked BREAD from a BAKERY as the BAKER opens the door just wide enough to hand an old WINO a free LOAF...

It's a pack of STRAY DOGS, scattering angrily before an onrushing CHECKER CAB.

One DOG raises its HOWL to the MOON.

MATT'S SILHOUETTE flips upside-down across the MOON.

Wearing his Converse All-Stars and sweatshirt&pants, MATT lands at a run on a rooftop.

Leaps into space, a humming POWER LINE the only thing between him and a six-story drop to the unforgiving pavement.

Cartwheels along the POWER LINE.

Bounds to another ROOF, scaring a flock of PIGEONS.

A WOMAN'S MOUTH opens involuntarily, breathing deep, excited, her lips full and sensuous.

MATT hears it, whirls.

A HEARTBEAT quickens as her breast heaves against light fabric.

MATT tracks the sound.

A WOMAN'S FEET--wearing expensive designer RUNNING SHOES--break into a run.

MATT runs after a shadowy figure as she dashes past a WATER TOWER. (Yes, of course it's Elektra--but keep her mysterious and don't show her full face until the end of the Central Park sequence.)

He's almost caught up with her.

She plummets from the ROOF into an ALLEY.

MATT leaps after her.

INT. ALLEY - NIGHT

MATT soft-lands in BAGS OF GARBAGE piled ten high.

MATT scans the alley. No sign of her.

Whirls at a sudden SCREECH from a scrawny STRAY CAT.

Somewhere HER MOUTH chuckles an invitation.

EXT. STREET - NIGHT

MATT rushes to the STREET just as a UPS TRUCK roars around the corner, headed right at him. CENTRAL PARK sprawls at the other side of the street.

TIRES slide on SLUSH.

MATT somersaults out of the TRUCK'S path. Inches to spare.

MATT rises, angry now, his pant leg torn at one knee, his knee bleeding.

He hears LAUGHTER from CENTRAL PARK.

IN CENTRAL PARK

MATT explodes through SNOW-COVERED BRANCHES, furious, entranced. In heat.

MATT stumbles across her RUNNING SHOES.

Holds one up, gathering her scent. Now he can't lose her.

MATT'S FEET run past her SHIRT, on the ground.

Then her PANTS.

MATT stops. Her PANTIES hang from a BRANCH in front of him.

A SCREAM splits the night.

MATT whirls, lit by HEADLIGHTS.

A POLICE CRUISER stops in front of him, two COPS leaping from it, PISTOLS trained on MATT.

Hesitation. He could disarm them...

...in his mind the HOOKER crashes through the WINDOW.

Falls forever...

...MATT holds out his wrists in surrender.

COPS cuff MATT and yell "WHERE IS SHE, YOU BASTARD?" as ELEKTRA, face lit with glee, sits out of sight behind a WALL, pulling her SHOES on, fully dressed. (This should be our first clear view of her.)

One COP looks through Matt's WALLET, stares at his DISABILITY CARD, confused.

                    COP
          CARD says you're BLIND.
          What the hell you doing
          in CENTRAL PARK at two in
          the MORNING?

                    MATT
          Taking a WALK.

says Matt, frustrated, humiliated, furious.

EXT. CAMPUS - DAY

MATT steps reflexively backward at a CURB, dropping his BOOKS, as ELEKTRA screeches to a stop in a sleek convertible, almost hitting him. FOGGY is livid, shouting. SNOW falls. She's got the top down anyway. She wears a thin summer dress.

FOGGY stares aghast as MATT hops into the seat next to ELEKTRA, his books forgotten.

CONVERTIBLE roars away. FOGGY picks up Matt's BOOKS.

EXT. FREEWAY - DAY

CONVERTIBLE cuts off a huge SEMI, that takes out a few GUARD RAILS avoiding collision. SNOW falls, harder now.

EXT. MOUNTAIN ROAD - DAY

CONVERTIBLE rockets along a narrow DIRT ROAD. SNOW is a blizzard.

MATT suggests ELEKTRA put the top up. "Why?" she asks, spinning the wheel; he's holding on for dear life.

CONVERTIBLE leaps from the ROAD.

Tears between TREES.

BRANCHES cut at the two as the Convertible rockets along. ELEKTRA is laughing silently.

CONVERTIBLE cuts across an open stretch toward a CLIFF.

Slides to a stop inches from a hundred foot fall.

Her hair drenched and her summer dress clinging to an impossibly perfect, lithe body, still laughing, ELEKTRA stands at the cliff's edge.

Quite a drop. A river POOL covered in ICE, tiny below.

She stares at it, fascinated. MATT approaches her from behind.

She turns to him. Touches a hand to his chest.

Her lips brush his.

She steps backward from the cliff.

She falls.

The HOOKER falls...

HOOKER is now inches from the pavement, mouth open in a SCREAM...

ELEKTRA cuts the ICE like a knife.

The WATER calms.

MATT'S FEET leave the cliff.

UNDERWATER

MATT plummets in a perfect dive. ROCKS form the walls
of the pool. There's no sign of Elektra.

Give me a CLOSE UP of MATT, scanning, holding his
breath. He's not sensing her, but his senses don't
serve him very well underwater, either.

MATT'S HANDS grope rocks; his radar's useless.

It's getting hard to hold his breath.

AT THE SURFACE

MATT explodes from underwater through thin ice,
breathing deep. Hearing that LAUGHTER and the
Convertible engine ROARING to life.

AT THE TOP OF THE CLIFF

ELEKTRA drives off. She's genuinely happy.

THAT NIGHT - IN THE DORMITORY

MATT enters the room. Angry, worried FOGGY rushes to
the door, his PIZZA forgotten. MATT is not in a great
mood; his clothes are still drenched.

                    FOGGY
          Where've you BEEN?

                    MATT
          Taking a SWIM.

LATER - IN THE BATHROOM

FOGGY stands at the DOOR. MATT has his shirt off,
draped over the shower curtain. He's unbuckling his
drenched PANTS.

                    FOGGY
               So what's with you and
               that ELEKTRA?

                    MATT
               Is that her name?

As MATT dresses:

                    FOGGY
               Yeah, I checked her out.
               Exchange student from
               GREECE. Everybody says
               she's pretty weird.
               Better WATCH yourself,
               Matt. I mean, I KNOW
               she's BEAUTIFUL, but...

                    MATT
               I'll bet she is.

Intense, fierce:

                    MATT
               Tell me where to find
               her, Foggy.

LOOKING THROUGH A FENCE - DAY

SEQUENCE OF PANELS, SAME ANGLE--from inside a WROUGHT
IRON FENCE at the street as:

- a tough-looking MAN in a black suit walks by the
fence, talking to a WALKIE-TALKIE;

- MAN exits frame, revealing MATT in b.g., emerging
from behind a PARKED CAR;

- MATT is at the FENCE, straining as he tries to
squeeze through a narrow space between BARS of the
fence (narration will explain it's a trick that Stick
taught him--though a difficult one);

LOCATION - ESTATE

- MATT is most of the way through--still straining, but he's going to make it;

- MATT is gone; ANOTHER MAN with a WALKIE-TALKIE passes.

EXT. MANSION - DAY

Whoever lives in this place has got to be a millionaire a few dozen times over. MATT runs, low to the ground, past PARKED LIMOS.

MATT scrambles behind well-groomed BUSHES outside the mansion, out of the line of sight of ANOTHER GUARD who passes by. Still no weapons visible on guards.

SAME ANGLE--MATT'S FEET are airborne as he leaps upward. GUARD doesn't notice.

MATT climbs the mansion's SIDE, FINGERS gripping BRICKS.

MATT moves along a narrow LEDGE toward an open WINDOW, his balance faultless, his back to the wall.

CLOSE UP--MATT hears pretty piano music. Classical. He can't identify it.

He catches her scent.

INT. BEDROOM - DAY

It's hers. MATT enters through WINDOW.

Passes her BED. Neatly made. Everything tasteful and expensive.

Passes a full-length MIRROR. Her scent is everywhere. Driving him nuts.

MATT'S HAND runs across a KARATE TROPHY. A SWIMMING TROPHY and a dozen others sit beside it on a shelf.

Another scent. A dog. Coming this way. That's okay. Dogs like him.

INT. HALLWAY - DAY

MATT steps from DOORWAY as a lean DOBERMAN charges.

                    CAP
          Must be her dog. It's got
          her charm.

MATT flattens the DOBERMAN with a spinning kick as a
MAN in a BLACK SUIT rushes behind him, reaching for a
WEAPON.

MATT continues the spin of his kick, knocking an UZI
from the man's hand.

MAN swings a FIST--MATT ducks under it, body-blocking
the MAN.

MAN falls backward through an intricate Oriental
SCREEN.

INT. ENCLOSED GARDEN - DAY

Lit by a SKYLIGHT. Utterly lovely. GUESTS in white tie
dress. Fountains. Flowers. ELEKTRA at a huge PIANO,
dressed in a lovely virginal-white GOWN, wearing
circulare wire-rimmed schoolgirl GLASSES. A DOZEN MEN
IN BLACK SUITS drawing UZIS as the MAN Matt kicked
comes crashing over an AWNING on the second story.

MAN sprawls across the PIANO. ELEKTRA has moved her
glass of mineral water out of the way just in time.

CLOSE UP--ELEKTRA looks up, mouth parting slightly in
surprise--and arousal.

MATT at the AWNING.

MEN firing UZIS.

MATT dives away as BULLETS tear at AWNING.

ELEKTRA continues playing the PIANO.

FINGERS dancing across KEYS.

Breast heaving, mouth loose and sexy as she breaks a
fragrant sweat, eyes closed as she listens to the
gunfire...she's switched from the lilting notes of
Vivaldi to haunting, driving Mahler...

                    DOGS

(34)

Her FATHER--stately HUGO NATCHIOS--shrugs off the black-suited CIA AGENTS who are trying to move him away.

HUGO stands behind ELEKTRA, his hand on her shoulder as she continues playing and the gunfire becomes more distant...

One CIA AGENT listens to a WALKIE-TALKIE.

Clicks it off.

     CIA AGENT
   The assailant has
   escaped. He's fast.
   Leaped the FENCE like it
   was NOTHING. My men are
   sure he took a bullet or
   two.

ELEKTRA stops playing, turns to CIA AGENT. Cool as dry ice. HUGO studies her.

     ELEKTRA
   Where?

     CIA AGENT
   Caught one in the ARM.
   That we're sure of.

EXT. ROOFTOP - DAY

MATT'S FEET stumble on a CONDUIT bolted to a rooftop.

MATT hunches, holding his upper arm, in pain.

CLOSE ANGLE--the wound really hurts. There are times when his heightened senses are not a blessing. That's why he tripped; he can barely think straight.

BLOOD streams across his HAND from inside the sleeve. He's never taken a bullet before.

CLOSE IT OFF, Stick told him, years ago. IT'S ONLY PAIN. CLEAN THE WOUND--STOP THE BLEEDING--and IGNORE IT.

MATT rises, running again. Stick also told him he was an asshole, and that's true too, thinks Matt...

EXT. DORMITORY - SUNSET

MATT stumbles toward the entrance, getting a glance
from a jogging CO-ED.

INT. DORMITORY - NIGHT

MATT stumbles in, hurting, taking his jacket off,
heading for the bathroom. ~~Asshole.~~ ~~Asshole.~~ ~~Asshole.~~

IN THE BATHROOM

BLOOD SPLATS on tile FLOOR.

MATT rummages the MEDICINE CABINET.

Grabs a bottle of HYDROGEN PEROXIDE and a roll of
BANDAGING TAPE. Thank God Foggy's out at the movies.
Thank God the bullet went right through.

MATT finally hears--

--the SHOWER running.

A HAND emerges from behind the SHOWER CURTAIN, pulling
it open. It's not Foggy's hand...

INT. DORMITORY - A HALLWAY

outside the room Foggy and Matt share. FOGGY hunts his
pockets for his keys.

KEYS in hand, he unlocks the DOOR.

DOOR opens an inch, held by a CHAIN LOCK within.

FOGGY calls for Matt.

Waits impatiently.

MATT appears at the DOOR, hair tousled, nervous as all
get out. Can't help smiling, though.

He asks FOGGY to wait a little while.

EXT. DORMITORY - NIGHT

Bored FOGGY sits on the steps. JOGGER passes.

FOGGY checks his WATCH.

FOGGY stares in awe as ELEKTRA exits the building.

INT. DORMITORY - NIGHT

FOGGY stands aghast at the DOORWAY, looking at the
utterly devastated ROOM. A BOOKSHELF has been knocked
over; A LAMP lies across the floor, shattered; SHEETS
from Matt's bed are scattered; FOGGY'S TYPEWRITER lies
on its side. MATT lies on his bed, wearing a bathrobe,
exhausted.

FOGY sits on his BED, removing his SHOES. MATT stares
blissfully upward.

                    FOGGY
          ...so what do you KNOW
          about her, Matt?

                    MATT
          She seems nice...

EXT. TIMES SQUARE - NIGHT

SNOW. Wearing a sleek TRENCHCOAT, high heels and
circular, wire-rimmed schoolgirl glasses, ELEKTRA
saunters past various lowlifes, hookers, and winos.
Members of a STREET GANG check her out, one gesturing
"check THAT out" to the next.

STREET GANG falls in behind ELEKTRA as she turns into
a NARROW ALLEY. There's five of them.

ELEKTRA stands, facing the BACK WALL that makes the
alley a blind one, her back to the approaching STREET
GANG. A WINO sprawls, BOTTLE in hand, curled at the
base of the wall. ALLEY is, again, very narrow.
Figures close to each other throughout this scene.

ELEKTRA'S FEET remove her shoes. No hands.

ELEKTRA whirls, facing the STREET GANG, shrugging her
TRENCHCOAT from her shoulders.

She wears a skimpy LEOTARD that displays her body to
them. She also wears short DRIVING GLOVES.

They're stunned, lustful.

Imperious:

                    ELEKTRA
          Come and get it.

GANG LEADER produces a SWITCHBLADE, gestures with it.

TWO GANG MEMBERS move to either side of ELEKTRA,
grabbing her arms, shoving her back against the wall
as GANG LEADER advances, SWITCHBLADE in hand.

CLOSE ON ACTION--TWO PANELS: GANG LEADER brings the
SWITCHBLADE to Elektra's LEOTARD, about to cut it away
at her breast. SAME ANGLE--he's dropping the
SWITCHBLADE as, off-panel, Elektra's knee is causing
serious damage to his groin. She's pitched forward a
bit with the action.

PULL BACK--GANG LEADER clutches his groin as ELEKTRA
kicks him in the head, nearly taking it from his
shoulders. The two GANG MEMBERS who aren't holding
Elektra are reaching for weapons: one a CHAIN, the
other a PISTOL.

PISTOL GANG MEMBER fires as ELEKTRA wrenches one
holding her into the bullet's path. He's hit.

ELEKTRA heaves the SHOT GANG MEMBER. He sprawls across
PISTOL GANG MEMBER, knocking him from his feet.

CHAIN GANG MEMBER swings his CHAIN, hitting bare WALL
as ELEKTRA ducks low, driving her free HAND into the
side of the GANG MEMBER who holds her.

Her gloved hand comes free, covered with GANG MEMBER'S
blood, as GANG MEMBER staggers away, clutching his
side and CHAIN GANG MEMBER swings his CHAIN backward
for another try.

ELEKTRA's gloved HAND neatly catches CHAIN in mid-air.

ELEKTRA kicks GANG MEMBER in the chest, lifting him
from his feet, making him let go of CHAIN, as PISTOL
GANG MEMBER shoves the guy atop him aside and takes
aim. Close quarters; they're all very near each other.

46

CLOSE--CHAIN whips around PISTOL GUY's wrist--his
fingers are releasing PISTOL.

CLOSE--ELEKTRA'S HAND, open, slams its palm to the
base of PISTOL GUY's NOSE (driving bone into his
brain).

ELEKTRA turns as the guy whose CHAIN she has begins to
lurch away.

CLOSE--CHAIN whips around the lurching guy's FACE.

FULL FIGURES--ELEKTRA wrenches CHAIN, lifting the poor
bastard aloft, sending him toward the WALL.

WINO still sleeps as SICKENING SOUND EFFECT is heard.

EXT. STREET - NIGHT

ELEKTRA stands across the street from a COMMOTION,
hand raised, hailing a CAB. SQUAD CARS and CIVILIANS
stand about the alley entrance. COPS hold CIVILIANS
back.

INT. ALLEY - NIGHT

COPS and a CORONOR inspect sprawled GANG MEMBER
BODIES. The one ELEKTRA swung on the chain is face-
first against the WALL, BLOOD splattered from where
his face used to be. One COP is holding WINO by the
collar, shouting a question. WINO has no idea what's
going on. LT. MANOLIS stares at the WALL; I♡NY is
written in blood on it.

If only the dojo had allowed full contact combat. Then
she wouldn't have to practice on the streets...

INT. GYMNASIUM - DAY

It's a private gym, well-equipped. They've got it to
themselves. ELEKTRA and MATT move like gods at play
across the equipment.

Flip through the air at each other, bodies almost
brushing.

They lie on the gym FLOOR, sweaty, entwined. ELEKTRA
casually confesses to MATT that she killed five people
in Times Square. He laughs it off.

47 48

INT. CLASSROOM - DAY

FOGGY casts MATT a worried glance as Matt fails to
answer a question from a furious PROFESSOR. Matt's
smiling, day-dreaming.

EXT. DORMITORY - NIGHT

SNOW falls.

INT. DORMITORY - NIGHT

FOGGY lies asleep in bed, mouth open in a snore. MATT
stares blindly at STICK, who crouches on his bed, the
end of his STAFF pressed to Matt's throat.

STICK tells MATT to stay away from ELEKTRA.

                    STICK
          She's not lying when she
          tells you she kills
          people. She's got the
          TALENT, just like you do.
          Only she's worse than
          you. A lot worse. You're
          just a FAILURE. She's
          POISON.

A jab of the STAFF. MATT's eyes roll back.

                    STICK
          Don't do any more damage
          than you already have.

MATT jerks awake. No sign that Stick was ever
there...except that unwashed scent of his.

Senses must be fooling him. Just a dream.

EXT. SLOPE - NIGHT

Two figures in skiing gear somersaulting in mid-air,
ELEKTRA and MATT are equally graceful.

They ski into WOODS, a couple alone together amidst
white BIRCH TREES.

They ski toward a small LOG CABIN.

INT. LOG CABIN - NIGHT

They are naked by a roaring FIREPLACE.

She touches her fingers to his forehead and glares at him, surprised. Stick...

She tells him he should listen to Stick.

She tries to explain what she is to him. He thinks she's kidding, or crazy. She's not kidding.

She talks about the HAND, how they're out to kill her father. He thought the old coot was just paranoid.

She shakes her head. Says he'll never understand.

He tells her he loves her. Realizes she's asleep.

EXT. GRAVEYARD - DAY

SNOW falls. MOURNERS exit. MATT stands with frightfully calm ELEKTRA.

                    ELEKTRA
          He had to die. I was part
          of him. He had to die.

EXT. AIRPORT - NIGHT

MATT with ELEKTRA as she moves toward a small PRIVATE PLANE. A CIA AGENT carries her small SUITCASE.

                    ELEKTRA
          Never. No. We will never
          meet again.

She kisses him passionately.

MATT stares after it as the PLANE flies away.

...HOOKER crashes to the pavement.

END OF ADDENDA

Daredevil: The Man Without Fear #1 pinup by John Romita Jr.

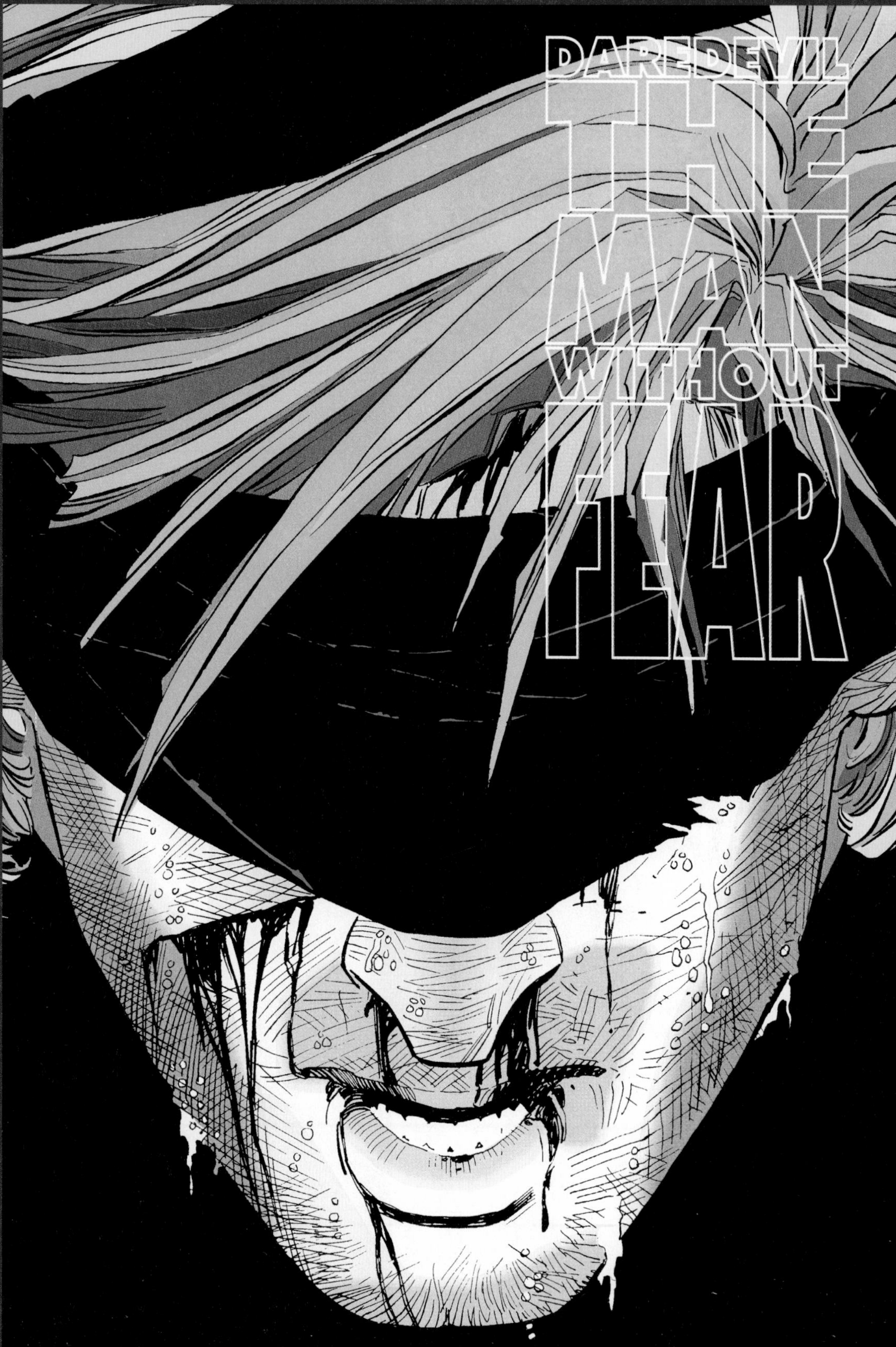
DAREDEVIL
THE
MAN
WITHOUT
FEAR

Daredevil: The Man Without Fear #2 cover pencils by John Romita Jr.,
as shown on the inside-back cover of issue #1

NEXT ISSUE

DAREDEVIL® THE MAN WITHOUT FEAR Vol. 1, No. 1,
October, 1993. Published by MARVEL COMICS, Terry
Stewart, President. Stan Lee, Publisher. Michael Hobson,
Group Vice President, Publishing. OFFICE OF PUBLICA-
TION: 387 PARK AVENUE SOUTH, NEW YORK, N.Y. 10016.
Published monthly. Copyright © 1993 Marvel Entertainment
Group, Inc. All rights reserved. Price $2.95 per copy in the
U.S. and $3.75 in Canada. GST #R127032852. No similar-
ity between any of the names, characters, persons, and/or
institutions in this magazine with those of any living or dead
person or institution is intended, and any such similarity
which may exist is purely coincidental. This periodical may
not be sold except by authorized dealers and is sold subject
to the condition that it shall not be sold or distributed with any
part of its cover or markings removed, nor in a mutilated
condition. DAREDEVIL (including all prominent characters
featured in this issue and the distinctive likenesses thereof)
is a trademark of MARVEL ENTERTAINMENT GROUP, INC.
Printed in CANADA

Daredevil: The Man Without Fear #3 cover pencils by John Romita Jr.,
as shown on the inside-back cover of issue #2

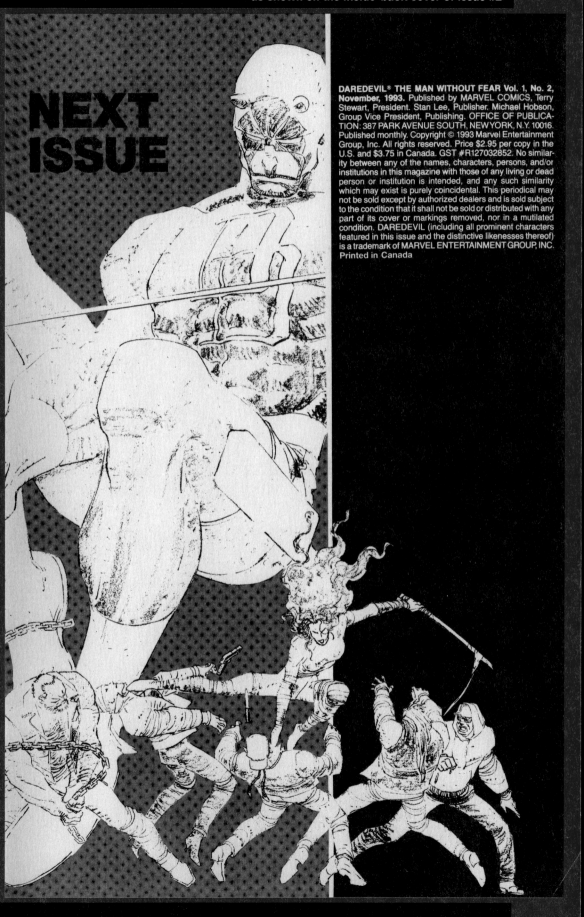

NEXT
ISSUE

DAREDEVIL® THE MAN WITHOUT FEAR Vol. 1, No. 2, November, 1993. Published by MARVEL COMICS, Terry Stewart, President. Stan Lee, Publisher. Michael Hobson, Group Vice President, Publishing. OFFICE OF PUBLICATION: 387 PARK AVENUE SOUTH, NEW YORK, N.Y. 10016. Published monthly. Copyright © 1993 Marvel Entertainment Group, Inc. All rights reserved. Price $2.95 per copy in the U.S. and $3.75 in Canada. GST #R127032852. No similarity between any of the names, characters, persons, and/or institutions in this magazine with those of any living or dead person or institution is intended, and any such similarity which may exist is purely coincidental. This periodical may not be sold except by authorized dealers and is sold subject to the condition that it shall not be sold or distributed with any part of its cover or markings removed, nor in a mutilated condition. DAREDEVIL (including all prominent characters featured in this issue and the distinctive likenesses thereof) is a trademark of MARVEL ENTERTAINMENT GROUP, INC. Printed in Canada

***Daredevil: The Man Without Fear #4* unused cover by John Romita Jr.**

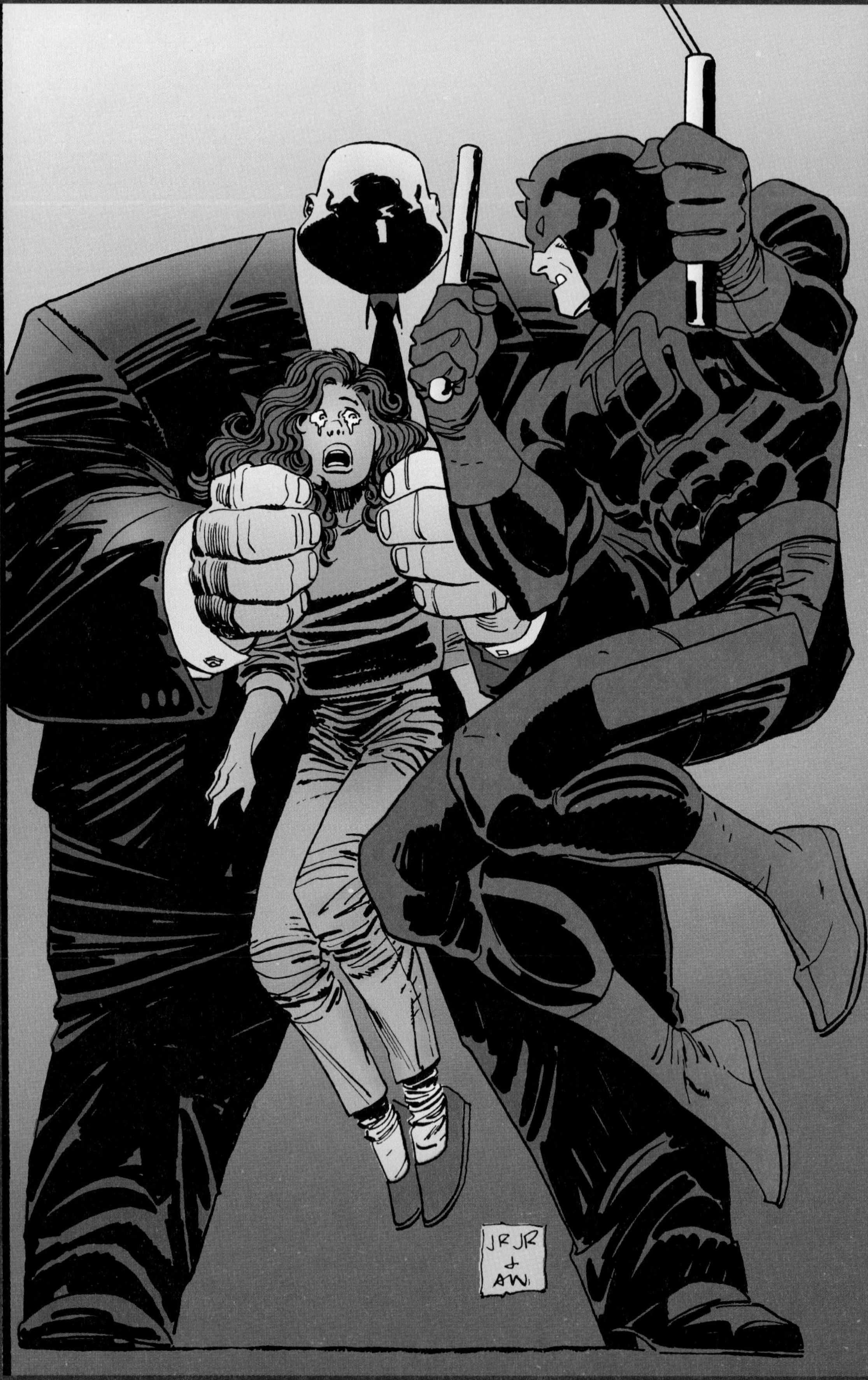
JRJR
+
AW

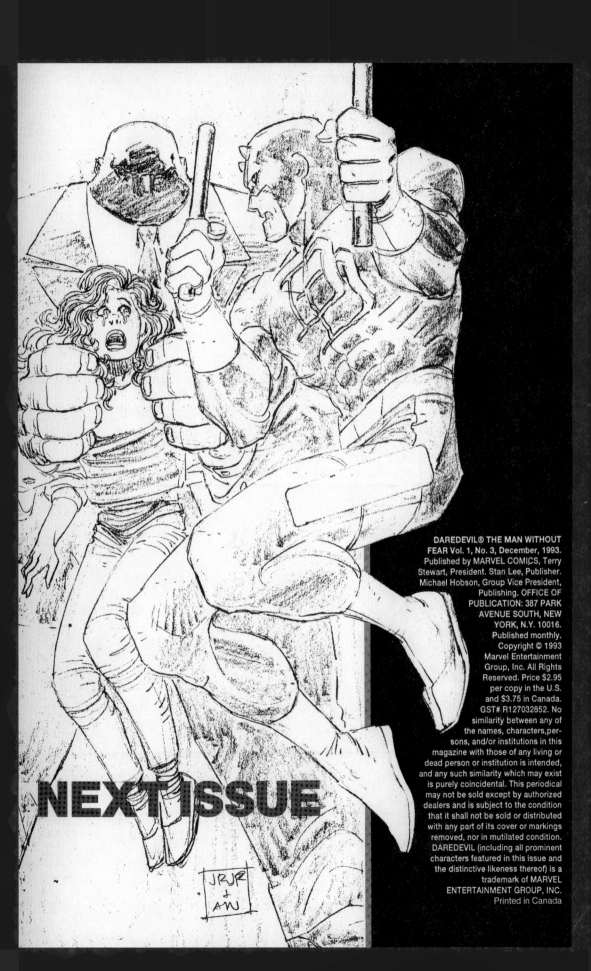

NEXT ISSUE

DAREDEVIL® THE MAN WITHOUT FEAR Vol. 1, No. 3, December, 1993. Published by MARVEL COMICS, Terry Stewart, President. Stan Lee, Publisher. Michael Hobson, Group Vice President, Publishing. OFFICE OF PUBLICATION: 387 PARK AVENUE SOUTH, NEW YORK, N.Y. 10016. Published monthly. Copyright © 1993 Marvel Entertainment Group, Inc. All Rights Reserved. Price $2.95 per copy in the U.S. and $3.75 in Canada. GST# R127032852. Printed in Canada

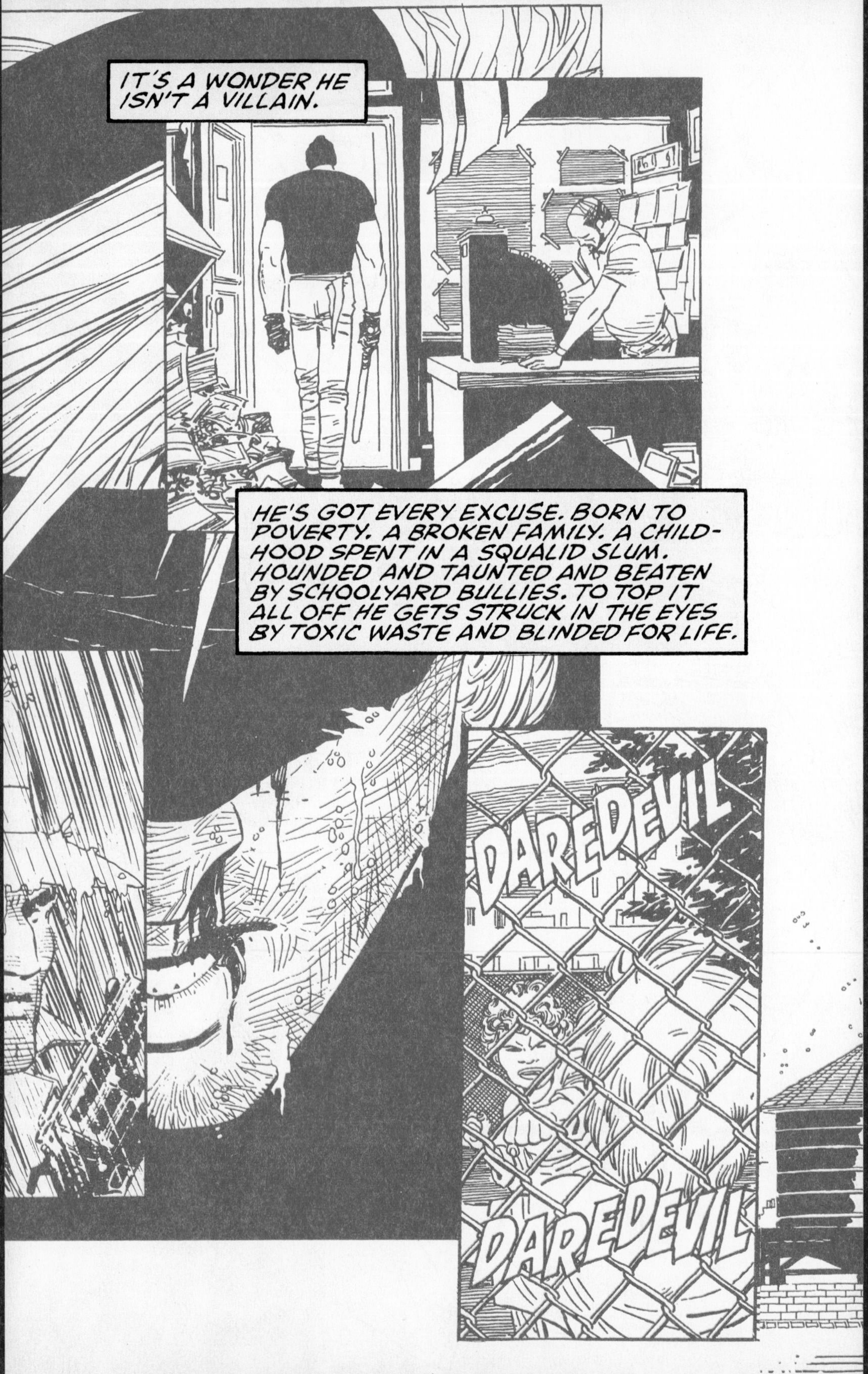
IT'S A WONDER HE ISN'T A VILLAIN.
HE'S GOT EVERY EXCUSE. BORN TO POVERTY. A BROKEN FAMILY. A CHILDHOOD SPENT IN A SQUALID SLUM. HOUNDED AND TAUNTED AND BEATEN BY SCHOOLYARD BULLIES. TO TOP IT ALL OFF HE GETS STRUCK IN THE EYES BY TOXIC WASTE AND BLINDED FOR LIFE.
DAREDEVIL
DAREDEVIL

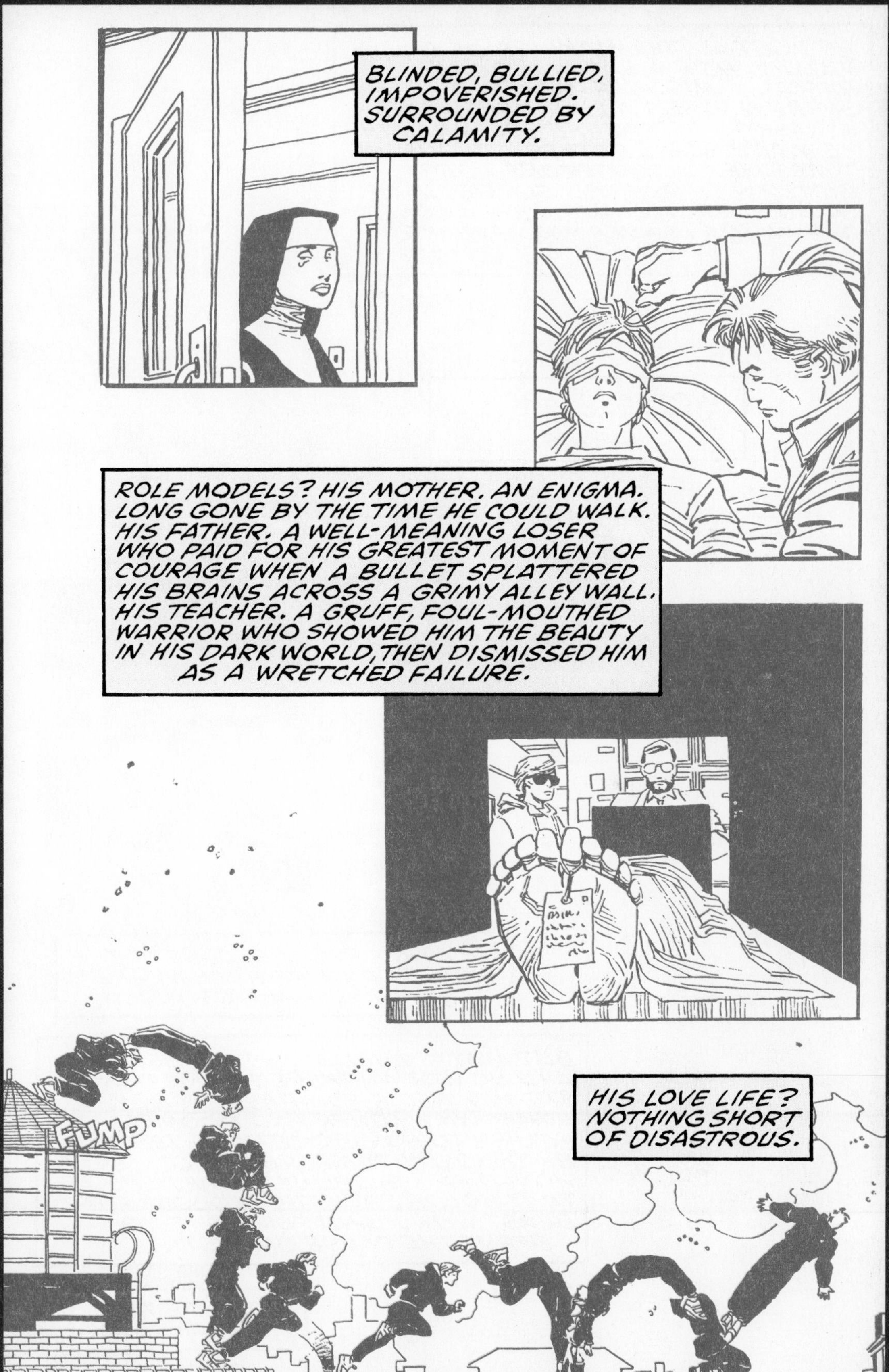
BLINDED, BULLIED, IMPOVERISHED. SURROUNDED BY CALAMITY.
ROLE MODELS? HIS MOTHER. AN ENIGMA. LONG GONE BY THE TIME HE COULD WALK. HIS FATHER. A WELL-MEANING LOSER WHO PAID FOR HIS GREATEST MOMENT OF COURAGE WHEN A BULLET SPLATTERED HIS BRAINS ACROSS A GRIMY ALLEY WALL. HIS TEACHER. A GRUFF, FOUL-MOUTHED WARRIOR WHO SHOWED HIM THE BEAUTY IN HIS DARK WORLD, THEN DISMISSED HIM AS A WRETCHED FAILURE.
FUMP
HIS LOVE LIFE? NOTHING SHORT OF DISASTROUS.

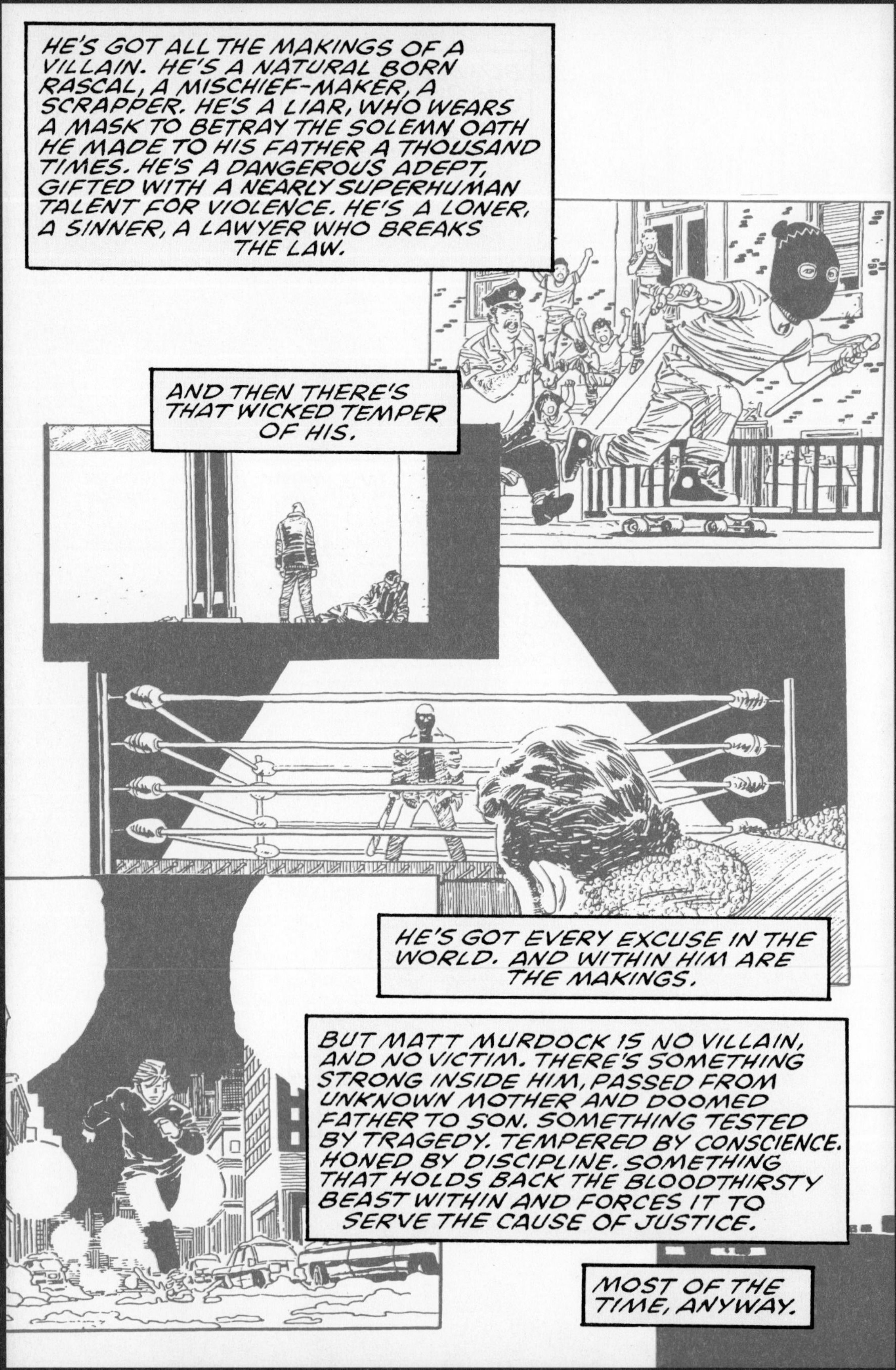
HE'S GOT ALL THE MAKINGS OF A VILLAIN. HE'S A NATURAL BORN RASCAL, A MISCHIEF-MAKER, A SCRAPPER. HE'S A LIAR, WHO WEARS A MASK TO BETRAY THE SOLEMN OATH HE MADE TO HIS FATHER A THOUSAND TIMES. HE'S A DANGEROUS ADEPT, GIFTED WITH A NEARLY SUPERHUMAN TALENT FOR VIOLENCE. HE'S A LONER, A SINNER, A LAWYER WHO BREAKS THE LAW.
AND THEN THERE'S THAT WICKED TEMPER OF HIS.
HE'S GOT EVERY EXCUSE IN THE WORLD. AND WITHIN HIM ARE THE MAKINGS.
BUT MATT MURDOCK IS NO VILLAIN, AND NO VICTIM. THERE'S SOMETHING STRONG INSIDE HIM, PASSED FROM UNKNOWN MOTHER AND DOOMED FATHER TO SON. SOMETHING TESTED BY TRAGEDY. TEMPERED BY CONSCIENCE. HONED BY DISCIPLINE. SOMETHING THAT HOLDS BACK THE BLOODTHIRSTY BEAST WITHIN AND FORCES IT TO SERVE THE CAUSE OF JUSTICE.
MOST OF THE TIME, ANYWAY.

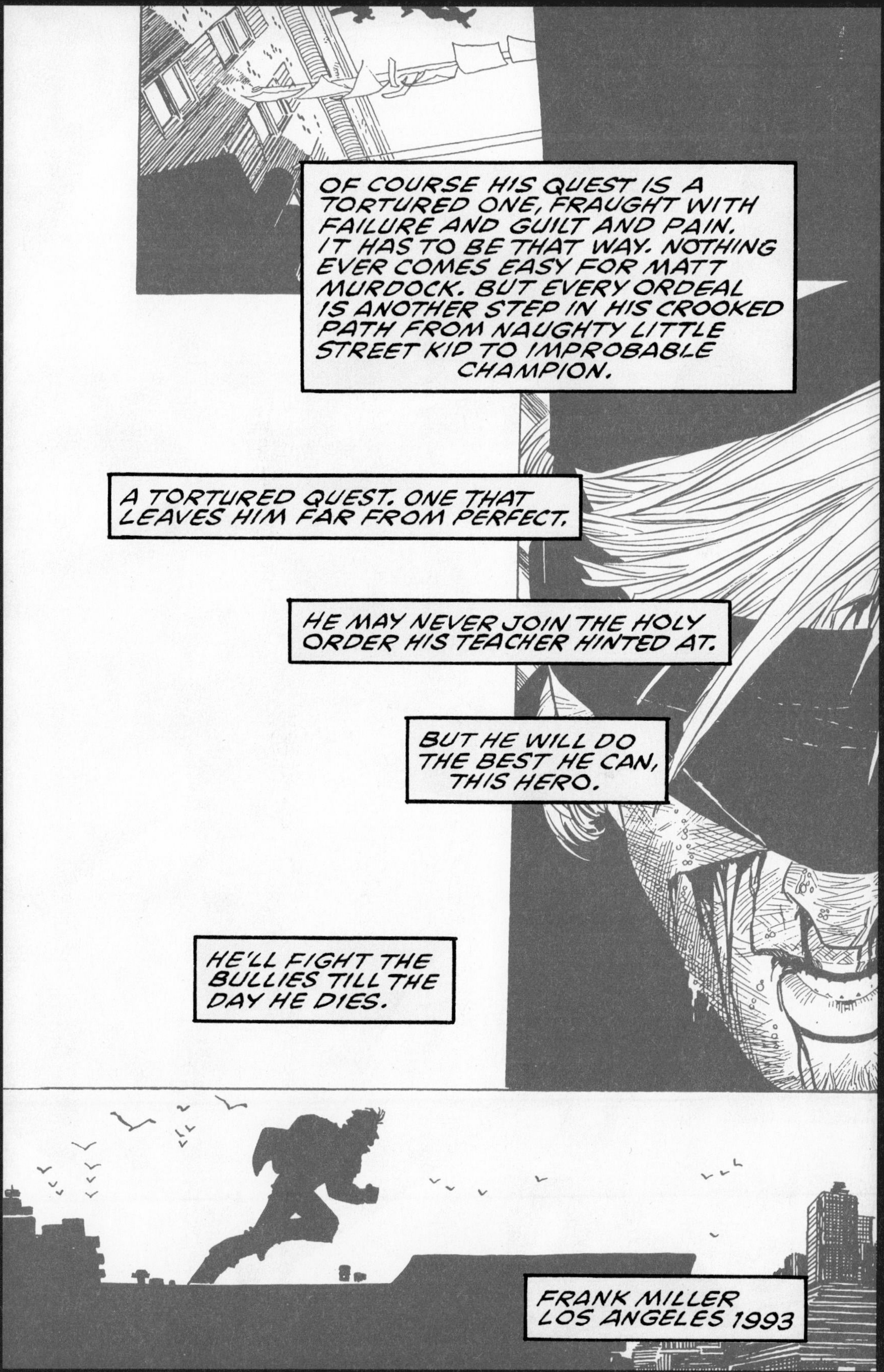
OF COURSE HIS QUEST IS A TORTURED ONE, FRAUGHT WITH FAILURE AND GUILT AND PAIN. IT HAS TO BE THAT WAY. NOTHING EVER COMES EASY FOR MATT MURDOCK. BUT EVERY ORDEAL IS ANOTHER STEP IN HIS CROOKED PATH FROM NAUGHTY LITTLE STREET KID TO IMPROBABLE CHAMPION.
A TORTURED QUEST. ONE THAT LEAVES HIM FAR FROM PERFECT.
HE MAY NEVER JOIN THE HOLY ORDER HIS TEACHER HINTED AT.
BUT HE WILL DO THE BEST HE CAN, THIS HERO.
HE'LL FIGHT THE BULLIES TILL THE DAY HE DIES.
FRANK MILLER LOS ANGELES 1993

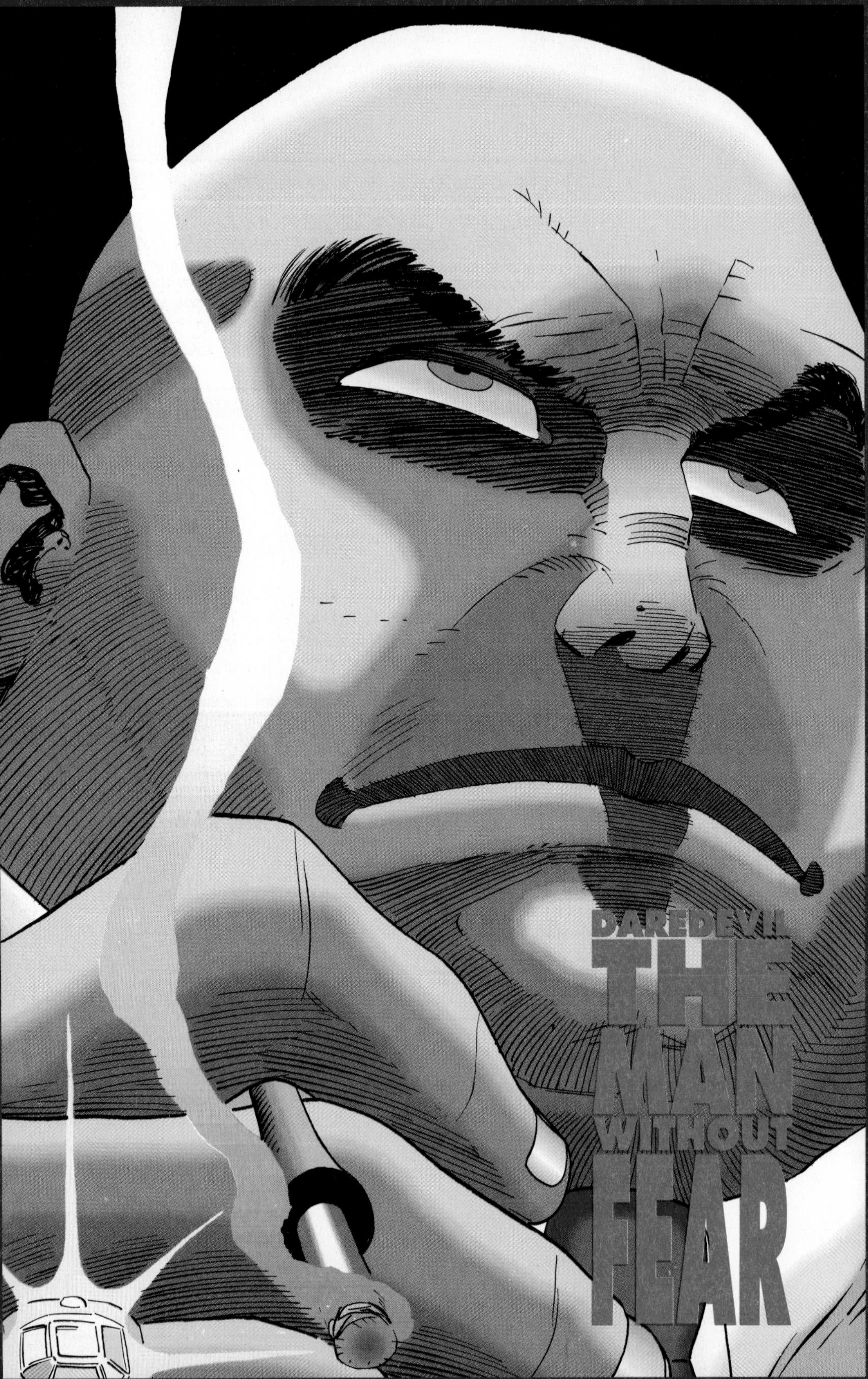
DAREDEVIL
THE MAN WITHOUT FEAR

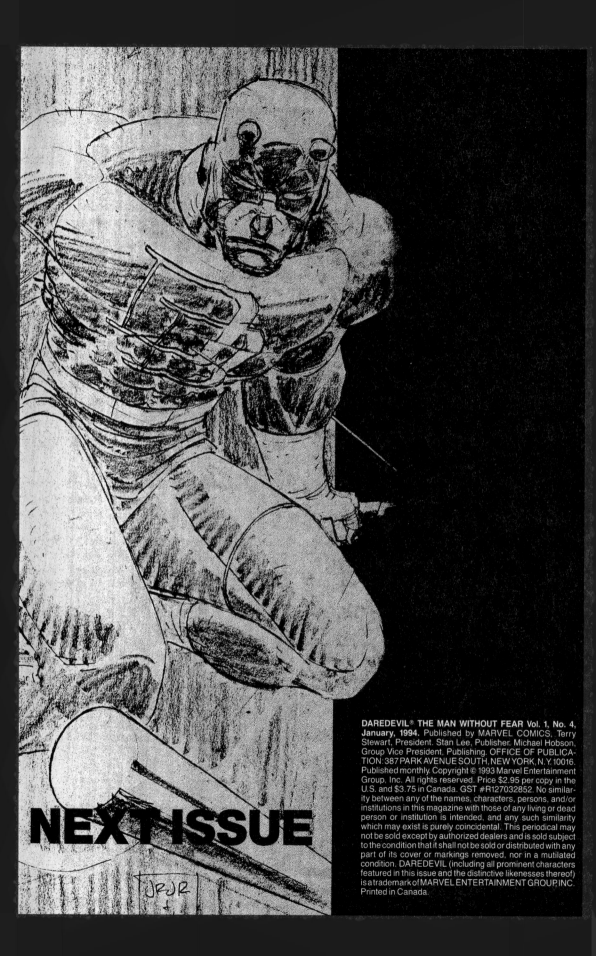

NEXT ISSUE

DAREDEVIL® THE MAN WITHOUT FEAR Vol. 1, No. 4, January, 1994. Published by MARVEL COMICS, Terry Stewart, President. Stan Lee, Publisher. Michael Hobson, Group Vice President, Publishing. OFFICE OF PUBLICATION: 387 PARK AVENUE SOUTH, NEW YORK, N.Y. 10016. Published monthly. Copyright © 1993 Marvel Entertainment Group, Inc. All rights reserved. Price $2.95 per copy in the U.S. and $3.75 in Canada. GST #R127032852. No similarity between any of the names, characters, persons, and/or institutions in this magazine with those of any living or dead person or institution is intended, and any such similarity which may exist is purely coincidental. This periodical may not be sold except by authorized dealers and is sold subject to the condition that it shall not be sold or distributed with any part of its cover or markings removed, nor in a mutilated condition. DAREDEVIL (including all prominent characters featured in this issue and the distinctive likenesses thereof) is a trademark of MARVEL ENTERTAINMENT GROUP, INC. Printed in Canada.

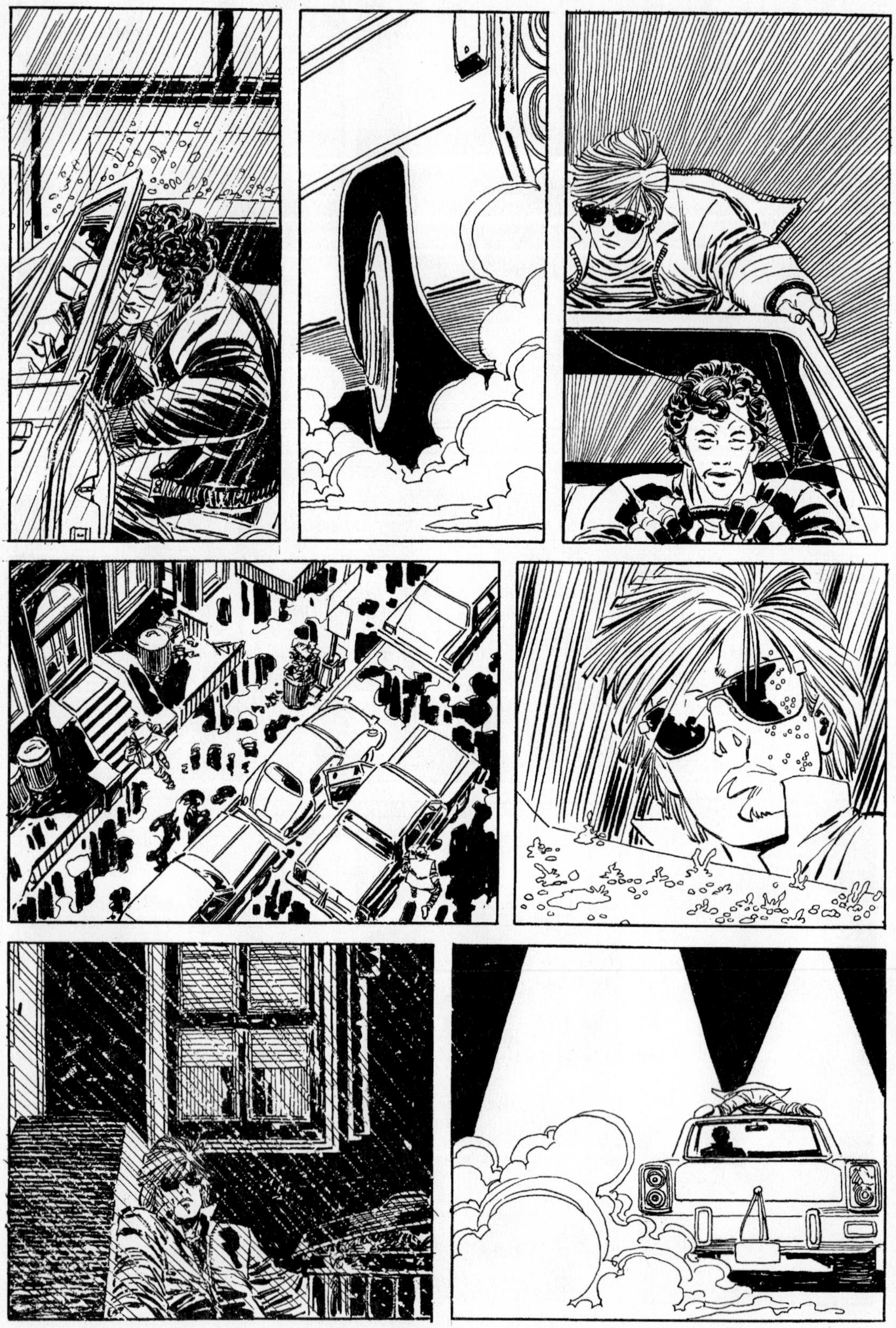

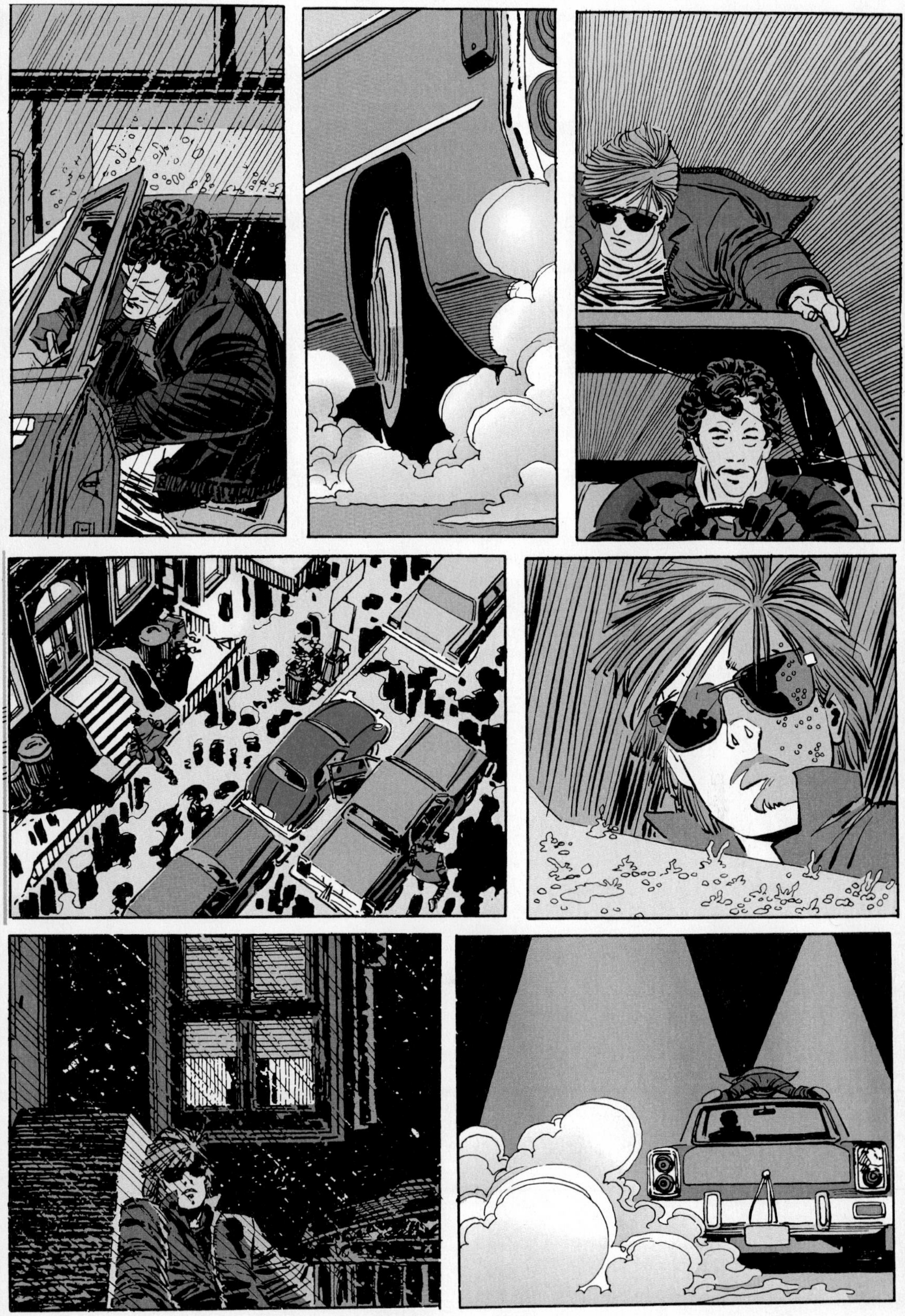

It's no secret. *Daredevil: The Man Without Fear* was supposed to have been published as a graphic novel. When John and I sat down over the phone and broke up the story into five volumes, we knew we'd have pages to fill.

My first reaction was, "Uh, John, don't we have extra art, um ya know, uh… lying around or something?"

Yeah, a whole two pages! Two beautiful pages of Matt chasing Mickey's father and her kidnapper around New York City taken from issue #4.

And then…I had JR redo the cover to issue #4 — ouch! Add one more page of art to our filler material. That's three…wait-a-minute — just how were we ever going to fill ten comic book pages (between issues #4 and #5) with material that fans would want to see and read?

Well, last issue you heard from Frank. This issue it's JR's turn. He's got a story to tell. Have fun. We did.

(Frank, please excuse Johnny's artistic license and vernacular!)

———————————

Circa 1987

"Frank?"

"Yeah."

"John Jr."

"Hey—how's it goin'?"

"Great—how 'bout you?"

"Great, but busy as hell!"

"Yeah, I know—you superstars."

"Hah—what's up?"

"Well, I was wondering if you wanted to get together on a job?"

"I've got a ton of stuff on my desk, but what didja have in mind?"

"Actually I'm embarrassed to say, I'd like to make as much money as humanly possible and retire to the south of France—so how's 'bout a Wolvy graphic novel or something?"

"South of France sounds good, but everyone's doing a Wolverine project lately—there's gotta be five or six slated for next year."

"Yeah?"

"Yeah."

"Well, I'd still like to work on something with you—something big—y'know something that kicks a**!"

"Yeah, me too, but um… HEY, wait a minute! I've got an idea—there's this Daredevil story that I have—it was supposed to have been a movie treatment, but it never happened. It's kind of a 'Daredevil: Year One' type of thing—would you be interested in something like that?"

"Yeah—sure. I've been doing DD for a while."

"I know—this could be great if I can get it worked into plot form—let me get back to you."

"Sure, see ya."

"Okay, bye"

———————————

"Johnny?"

"Yup."

"Frank."

"Hey, what's up?"

"I think I've got this thing ready to go. I'm gonna send it to Ralf, see what he sez, and we'll go from there!"

"Great—I already spoke to Ralf 'bout it and he's as excited 'bout it as I am."

"Great—I'll talk to you soon."

"Okay, thanks, see ya."

"Bye"

———————————

"Ralf?"

"Yo."

"John Jr."

"Heeeeey, Johnny, how're you doin', how's it…"

"RALF, WHAT THE HELL ARE YOU DOIN'! I'M DYIN' OVER HERE! GET ME THAT PLOT OR I'LL BLOW UP YOUR HOUSE!!!"

"Easy, John, I've got to get this thing right. There's a lot of stuff here and it's got to be true to the character—you know, it was a movie treatment so there are a couple of 'adjustments'."

"A couple? This'll be the fourth version—if you tick Frank off and jeopardize this job I'll blow up your house!"

"You already said that."

"Okay, got any relative with houses?"

"Yeah, lots."

"I'll blow up there houses too!"

"Okay, okay, it's on the way!"

"Great, Ralf, have a nice day."

"Nice day? Does that mean no bombs?"

"I dunno, make me rich, and I'll forget it!"

"Gotcha, bye."

"See ya!"

———————————

"Frank—John Jr."

"Hey."

"I read it—I love it—I'm gonna start on it like… yesterday."

"Great, listen, I'll clear my desk of some of these projects, and by that time you'll be done, and I'll script it, and it'll be fantastic!"

"Sure—sixty-four pages—six months—start to finish."

"Yeah."

"See ya."

"Right, bye."

———————————

"Ralf."

"Johnny, what's up."

"Well—you know that addendum that Frank sent me—y'know the 'Elektra' stuff?"

"Yeah?"

"Well, I thumbnailed it out, and it's ninety pages!"

"NINETY—not too bad. We've had some novels go 84 pages so I guess we could…"

"Ralf! Shut up. THE ADDENDUM IS NINETY PAGES!"

"What?"

"Yeah!"

"Oh boy."

"Oh boy? Is that all you can say, oh boy? An educated man like you, oh boy?"

"What do you want me to say? What do you want me to do?"

"I'LL TELL YOU ONE THIN TO DO—LOOK FOR A BOMB SHELTER—AND TELL FRANK 'CAUSE HE'S NEXT!!"

"Down, boy, can you handle this?"

"Yeah… I guess… I can drop *Iron Man* and *Daredevil* for a while, and I'll just work on this. Then I'll put on my cape and tights and my big red 'S'—no problem."

"Yeah right. Bye, Johnny."

"Bye."

———————————

"Johnny."

"Johnny?"

"Uhhhnnn…"

"Johnny, it's Ralf!"

"Uhhhnnn…"

"Johnny, the pages look great, only fifty more to go—it's great!! Johnny?"

———————————

"Ralf?"

"Johnny—what's up?"

"Where the hell is Frank!?!"

"I don't know—last I heard he was working on ROBO II—he wrote the screenplay, y'know!"

"SCREENPLAY—HE'S WRITING A *&#@@*% MOVIE!?!"

"Yup."

"Yeah, but Ralf—this is important! This is not some cheap sequel—this is my novel—this is important! I've been done for months! 144 pages of work! I killed myself on this…"

"Yeah I know, but he's 'incommunicado'."

"Where's that—in Texas?"

"Uhhnn."

"If he doesn't write those pages soon…"

"You'll blow up his house?"

"No—his car—he's a Californian—he's always in his car!"

"Uh, right, bye!"

"Bye."

———————————

"Johnny."

"Yeah."

"It's Ralf—it's in—the script is in! Joe is lettering it as we speak—Al is ready and willing, so is Christie—it's on the schedule—we're done! We're there!!—one thing though, we're gonna break it up into 5 parts, first, so we'll need some cover sketches and covers and some splashes and a byline by you, of course, whaddaya thing?"

(pause)

"Johnny?—Johnny?"

"Oh God, Pat—I think he's dead—I think we killed him—oh God!!"

"No, Ralf, I'm okay—I'm just reading these detonator directions

JRJR
Circa 1993

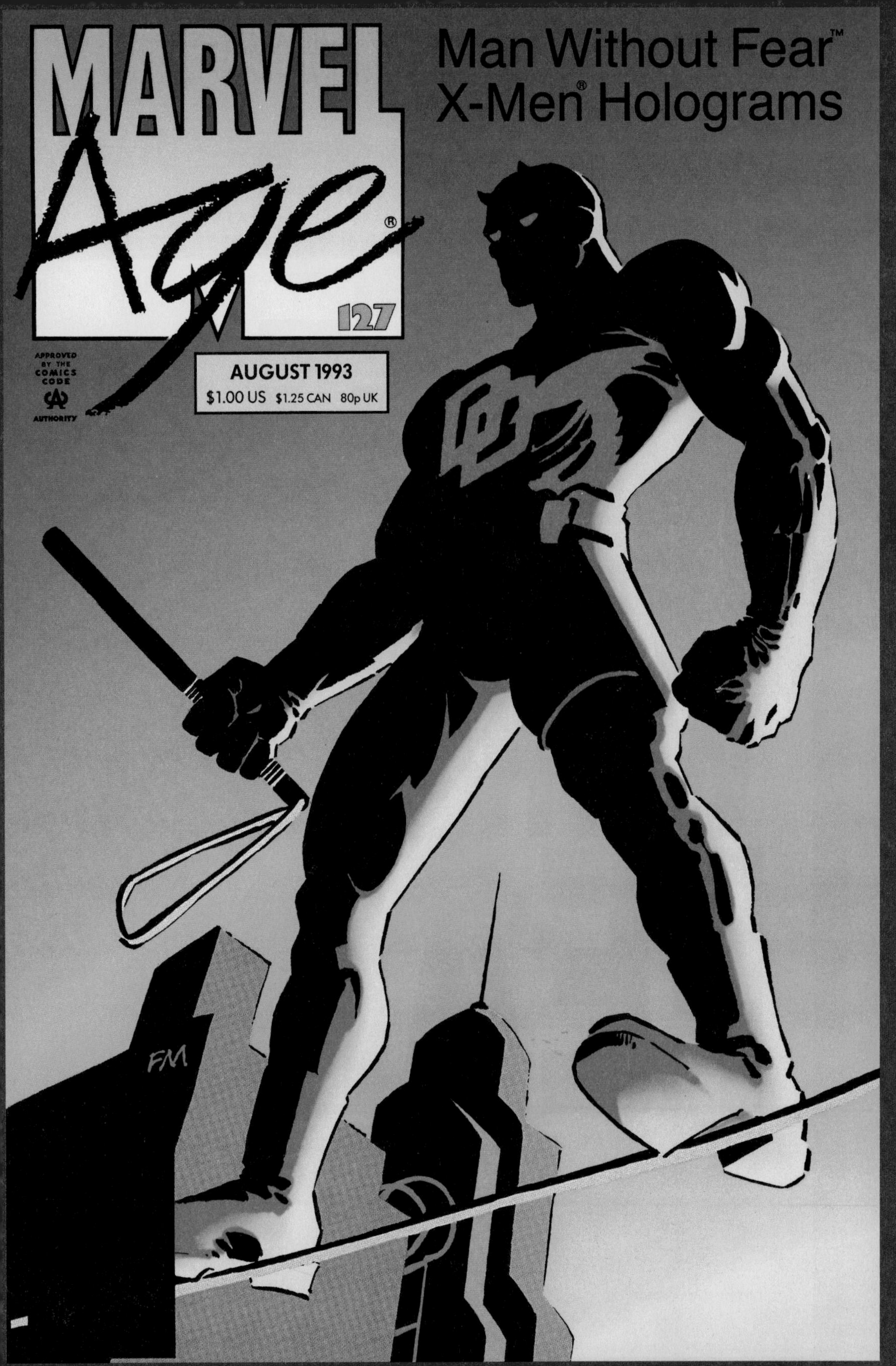

MARVEL Age®
127
Man Without Fear™
X-Men® Holograms
APPROVED BY THE COMICS CODE AUTHORITY
AUGUST 1993
$1.00 US $1.25 CAN 80p UK
FM

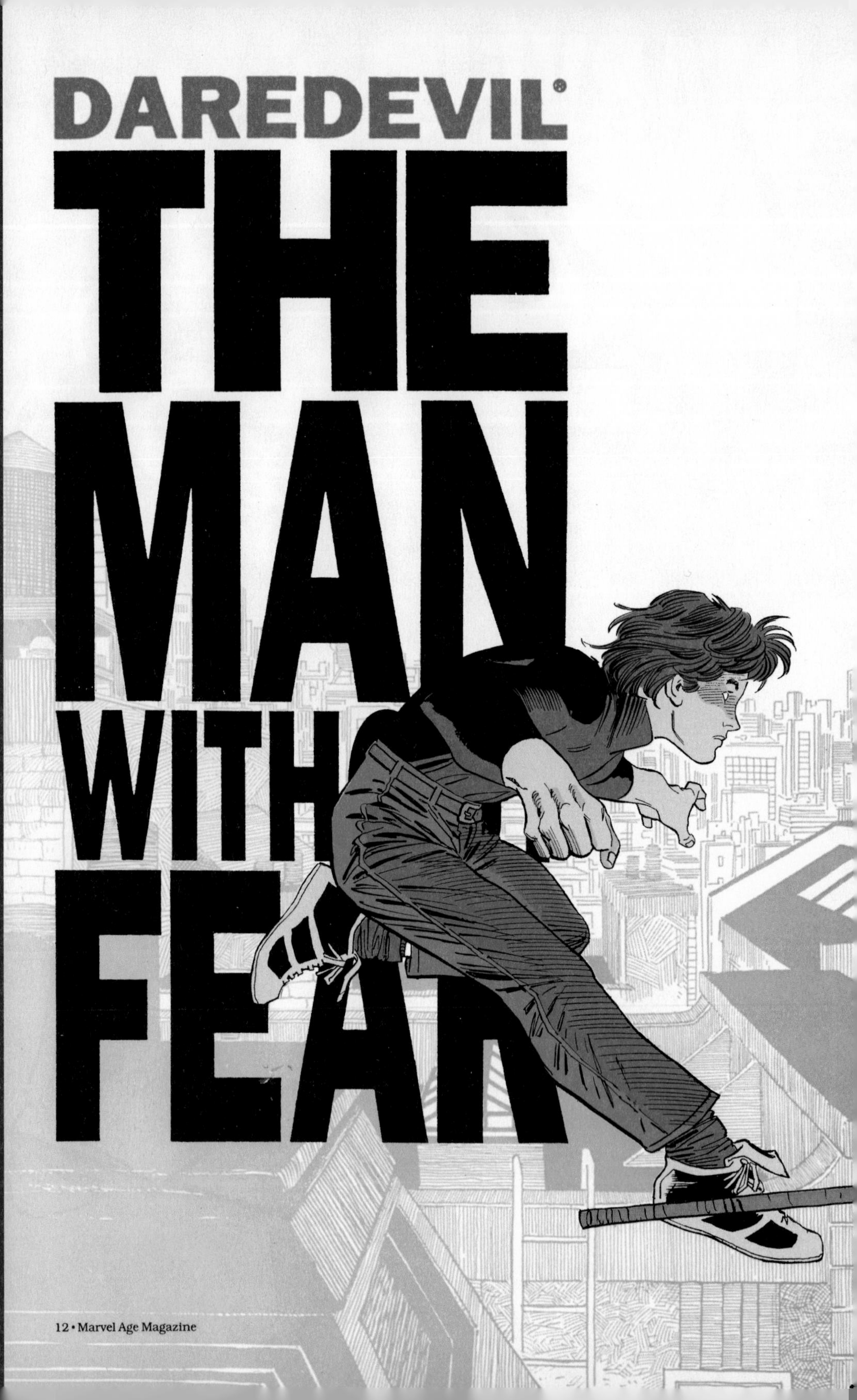
DAREDEVIL®
THE
MAN
WITH
FEAR

A tomcat shrieked.

"Please ignore the howling in the background." Frank Miller paused to apologize for the constant interruption. "It's my old cat. He's deaf, and in the past few years, he's been screaming like crazy."

He returned to the subject of the telephone interview — another old friend who is missing a sense — Matt Murdock, also known as Daredevil. "Back when I was drawing DAREDEVIL, I always saw him as a good vehicle for super hero crime comics that bring in more of the feeling of a crime novel or movie."

So simple, so straightforward. Like Bruce Wayne, Matt Murdock pledged to avenge his father's death by dedicating his life to fighting crime as a costumed super hero. Unlike Bruce Wayne, Matt was born on the wrong side of the tracks in New York's Hell's Kitchen, and after age fifteen or so he couldn't rely on all his senses because he had been blinded.

Five years before Frank Miller shook the foundation of the *Batman* legend with *The Dark Knight*, he delved deep into the psyche of the Man Without Fear and redefined the moral ground upon which that urban vigilante must tread. But Miller wasn't satisfied when he left the series. Why had Matt become Daredevil? What moral torment had

he weathered through the loss of his father and of his sight? When was his first encounter with Kingpin? How had he met Elektra?

While Miller had touched upon Matt's youth in some issues, this summer, he'll answer these questions more fully than ever in THE

are rites of passage in the origin and growth of a hero, whether he's a samurai or a super hero or a gunfighter. It's very faithful to the continuity all the way back to #1, but there's just a much bigger story to be told."

The project's own origin story

"At first, the heightened senses are a complete and absolute nightmare…"

MAN WITHOUT FEAR, a giant 144-page, five-part limited series penciled by John Romita, Jr., and inked by Al Williamson, slated for an August debut.

"It's an epic," Romita unabashedly described Miller's concept. "It's War and Peace. It's *Gone With The Wind*. It spans years and it reaches levels that most comic books don't."

"It's about all things Matt Murdock goes through and the decisions he makes, including entire episodes that have never been in DAREDEVIL comics before," Miller offered. "It'll be a book that you can hand to somebody, and they'll know who he is, *why* he does what he does and *what* he can do. What I was after was putting Matt through the paces that a classic hero goes through. There

took more than seven years. Back in 1987, Romita's wife, Patty, convinced him to call Miller and invite him to collaborate on a project. While Romita's famous father had penciled DAREDEVIL back in 1965 when The Man Without Fear was still being penned by Stan Lee, Romita, Jr. suggested a Wolverine tale.

Miller politely declined the character but not the offer. "He said everybody's doing Wolverine, but I do have this idea, let me send it to you," Romita said.

What Miller put in the mail was a plot synopsis he had developed for a Daredevil TV movie that had fizzled even before pre-production. Romita was so excited that he contacted Marvel Editor Ralph Macchio, who

immediately gave the collaboration an enthusiastic thumbs up. It was to be a 64-page retelling of Daredevil's origin story in a graphic novel format. Then Miller had proposed some 90 extra pages — more than enough for a complete additional book.

"Frank had mentioned a couple of times that he wanted to add some stuff to it," Romita remembered. "He felt there were so many things that had gone by the wayside with DAREDEVIL when he worked on it, he didn't want to leave anything out. 'Let's make this the DAREDEVIL bible,' he said."

Thrilled about the new material, which included an extensive Elektra segment, Romita tried to contact Miller. But Miller, then working on the *Robocop 2* movie script, seemingly, had disappeared off the face of the earth. So Romita called Macchio to find out if a 144-page book would be OK.

"I told Frank and John that I trusted their instincts," Macchio said, obviously certain now he made the right decision. "What they gave me [initially] was far too long to publish as one thing. But it included *everything* that these guys wanted to say about the character's origin. There was a lag time in which it languished in my drawer for about a year while Frank wrote *Robocop 2*. Then Frank went back to it and did a brilliant script, and John's art is brilliant."

Indeed, MIller was excited to work with Romita, particularly because they share a love of crime noir fiction and film. As should come as no surprise to Miller's *Sin City* fans, he wanted this origin tale to be grounded in its own unique texture, not necessarily the one the average super hero fan would expect. Miller shares Walter Mosley, his favorite noir writer with President Bill Clinton. Raised on his father's love for '30s and '40s film crime thrillers, Romita preferred Mickey Spillane, what he describes as not necessarily "noir" per se, but certainly "that rainy back alley, collar up feeling."

"This is going to be unusual for some super hero readers in that sense, but I thought that would be a very good way to play this out because it can be as exciting and dramatic as dozens of guys in tights," Miller explained. "In comics, it's so easy to lose focus, for it just to become the 'villain of the month' and for the hero just to be someone who can punch people out. There has to be a compelling emotional core and a sense of the world they inhabit."

In the limited series, Miller uses these elements to create a Kingpin in an earlier stage of criminal empire-building than readers have ever seen before. While reluctant to provide too many details, he confirmed that the Kingpin, while he doesn't fight Daredevil face-to-face in this series, plays the major villain in its second half.

"What the Kingpin really is to New York City," he guaranteed, "that's scary stuff."

The pungent urban scent of crime, though, surrounds Matt Murdock from page one when Miller introduces him as a mischievous boy growing up in the slum of Hell's Kitchen, wearing a mask in play and "doing things he wasn't supposed to do." Miller also promised "surprising revelations" about Matt's ex-prizefighter father, whom he described as "a very tortured man" and the source "of much of Matt's quest for redemption."

"We get to see Matt in combat at virtually every stage of his early life," he continued. "We get to see him at the mercy of bullies because his Dad won't let him fight. As a teenager, we get to see just how formidable he is up against the gangsters who killed his father. That's the first time he really turns into the super hero of the story. It's always in him, but the horrible revenge he takes out forever changes him. I don't want to ruin pieces of the story, but he makes a very bad mistake early on, and for most of the rest of the story, he's trying to come to grips with that."

In dealing with the circumstances of Matt's blindness, Miller verified that up until recently, bins of toxic waste were regularly trucked through Manhattan, adding a certain degree of plausibility to Stan Lee's original premise. More important, though, to Miller, were the psychological ramifications of the accident.

"At first, the heightened senses are a complete and absolute nightmare, and one of his earlier tests of character is to be able to adjust to them. At first, even though he can smell, and hear, and all of that, better than anybody who ever lived, he's in constant pain, and it doesn't make him any better at doing anything. That's when Stick comes in. Stick is a crusty old goat. He drives the kid very hard."

He added that Matt's training with Stick will be a key part of the story.

"There's more told about Stick in this book than ever has been before. There's more description about where he comes from — that he was born blind and on the street and taught himself to function as a warrior."

The next stage in Matt's life story is college, friendship with Foggy Nelson, and law school. But of course, nothing prepared Matt for his first encounter with love. "He's out one night gallivanting around because he can't sleep, and he smells this woman, feels her presence," according to Romita, who added that the Elektra scenes were

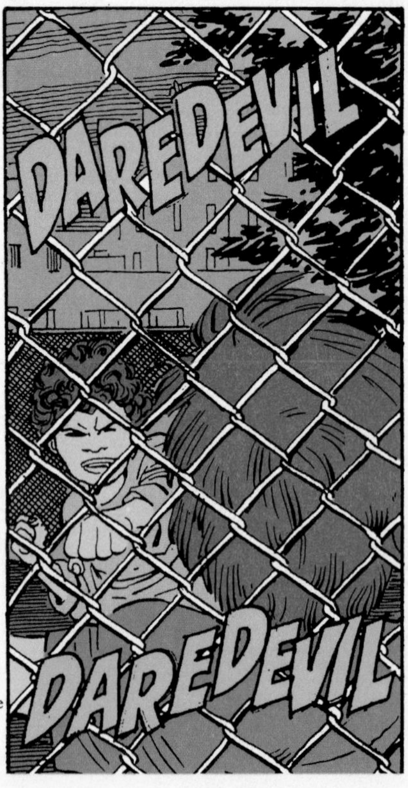
DAREDEVIL
DAREDEVIL

among his favorite to draw. "I did this series of panels where he smells, feels, hears and then he suddenly sees her. He watches her running away from him, then all of a sudden she jumps off this building. He follows her, gets to the alleyway, lands in the garbage, and realizes she's gone. And it suddenly occurs to him that there's somebody else in this world like him."

Miller's next plot twist confirmed for Romita that the woman was, in his words, already "wacko." She pulls up to Matt in a blizzard with the top down on her convertible, offers him a ride, and they end up swimming in an icy lake. "This is the first time we see beyond a very few panels of what Elektra was like when Matt met her," Miller added. "That's always been very sketchy. We see in this that she is kind of nuts, but she and Matt are almost two creatures that are different from the rest of us. The attraction between the two is instantaneous and ferocious."

> "'Let's make this the DAREDEVIL bible,' he said."

Childhood, Stick, Elektra, The Kingpin: all of this could suggest that Miller had covered every aspect of Matt Murdock's character that he'd like to explore, but, according to Miller, he would like to return to the character again.

"The weird thing about these characters is that there's always one more, and it's usually scribbled on a notepad somewhere. And there is one, but it's just a matter of when it germinates and the time is right. I've returned to this character so many times it makes my head spin. Matt's like an old friend. There always seems to be another corner he can take."

And Elektra stories?

"The answer's the same. Obviously, they would have to happen in the past, but she's nearer and dearer to my heart because I created her. But the story would have to be just dead on perfect."

A cat screams somewhere beyond Miller's voice as if it senses the synchronicity.

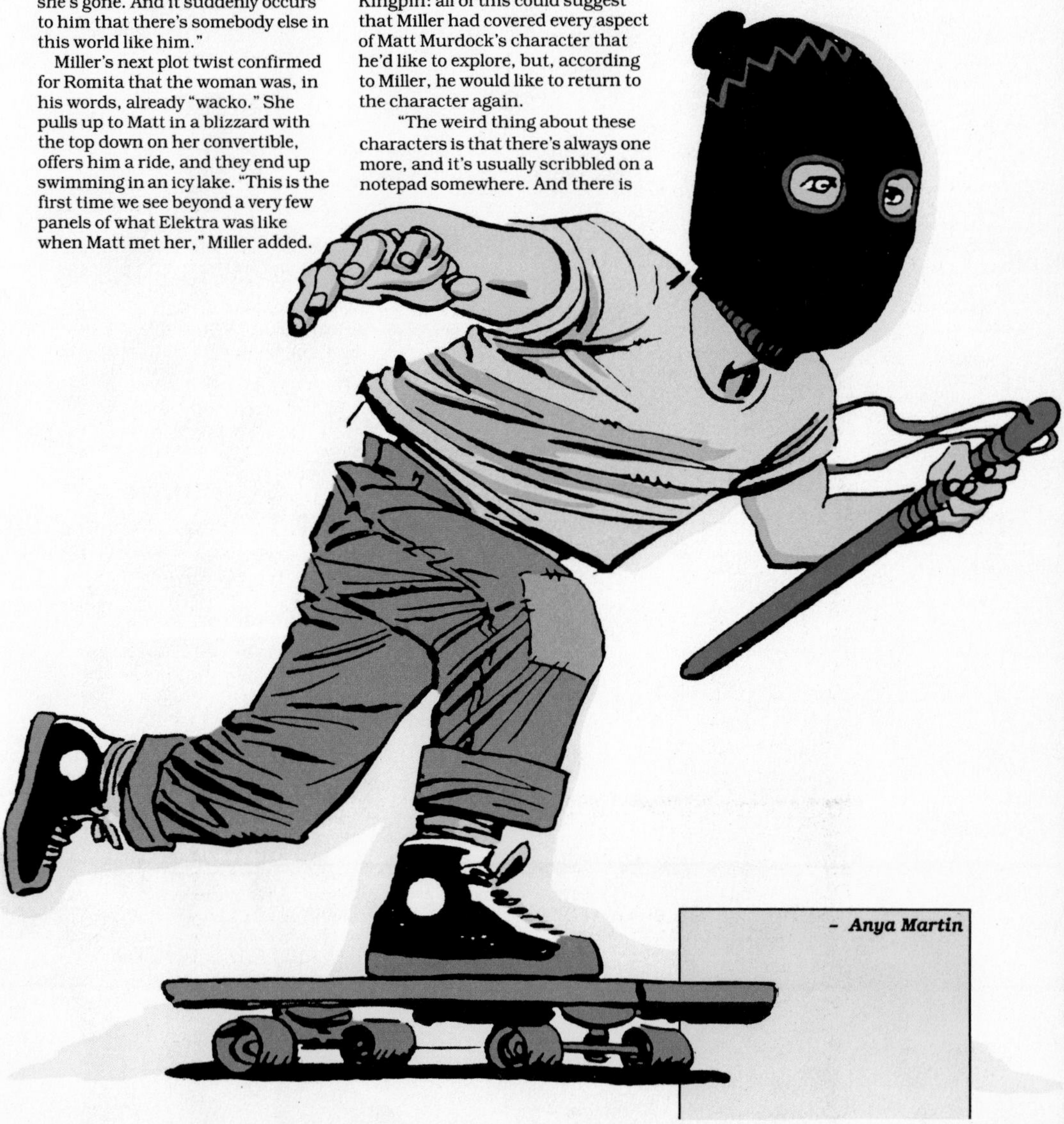

– Anya Martin

***Daredevil: The Man Without Fear* TPB** **(October 1994) cover by John Romita Jr.**

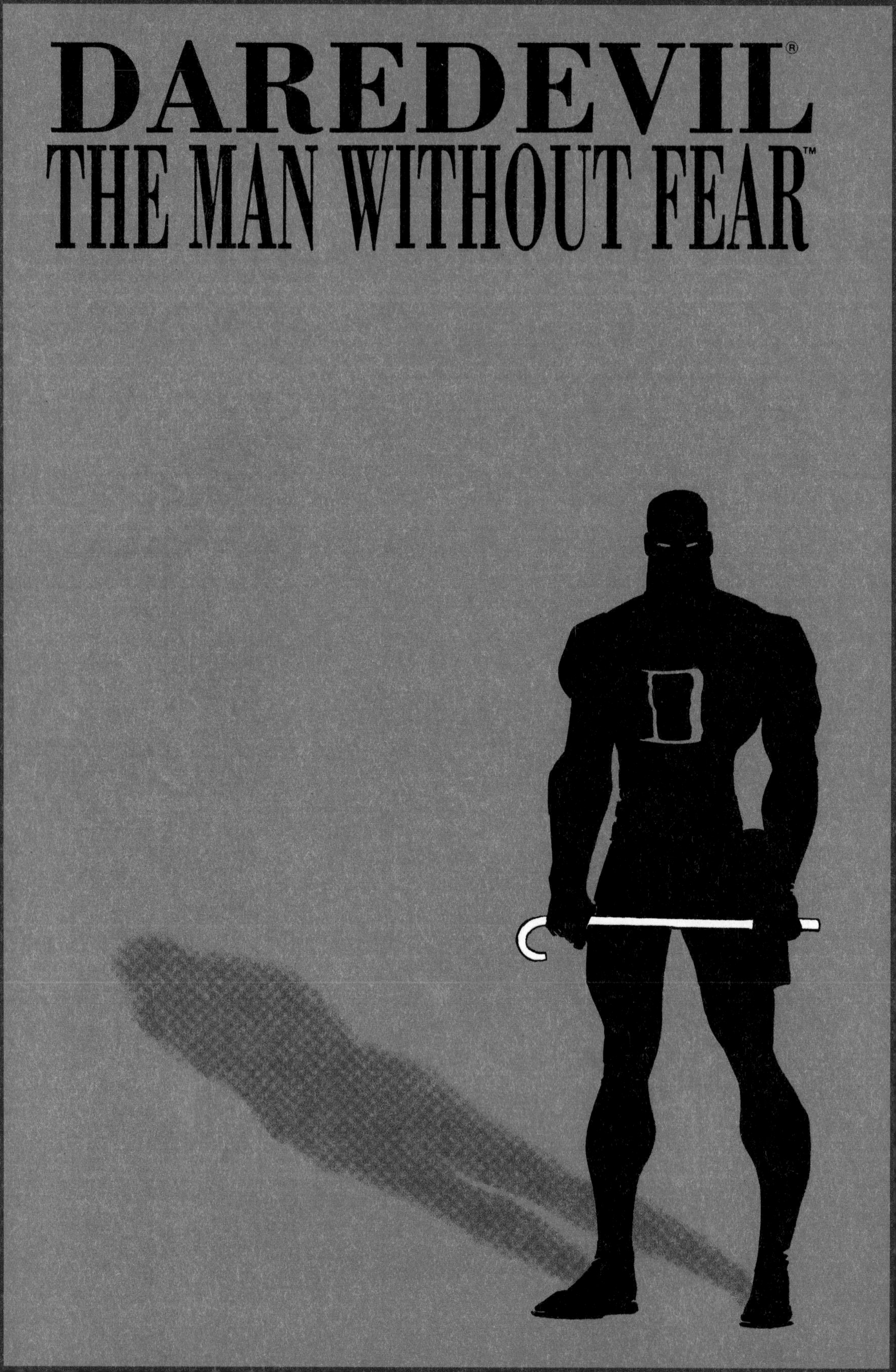
DAREDEVIL®
THE MAN WITHOUT FEAR™

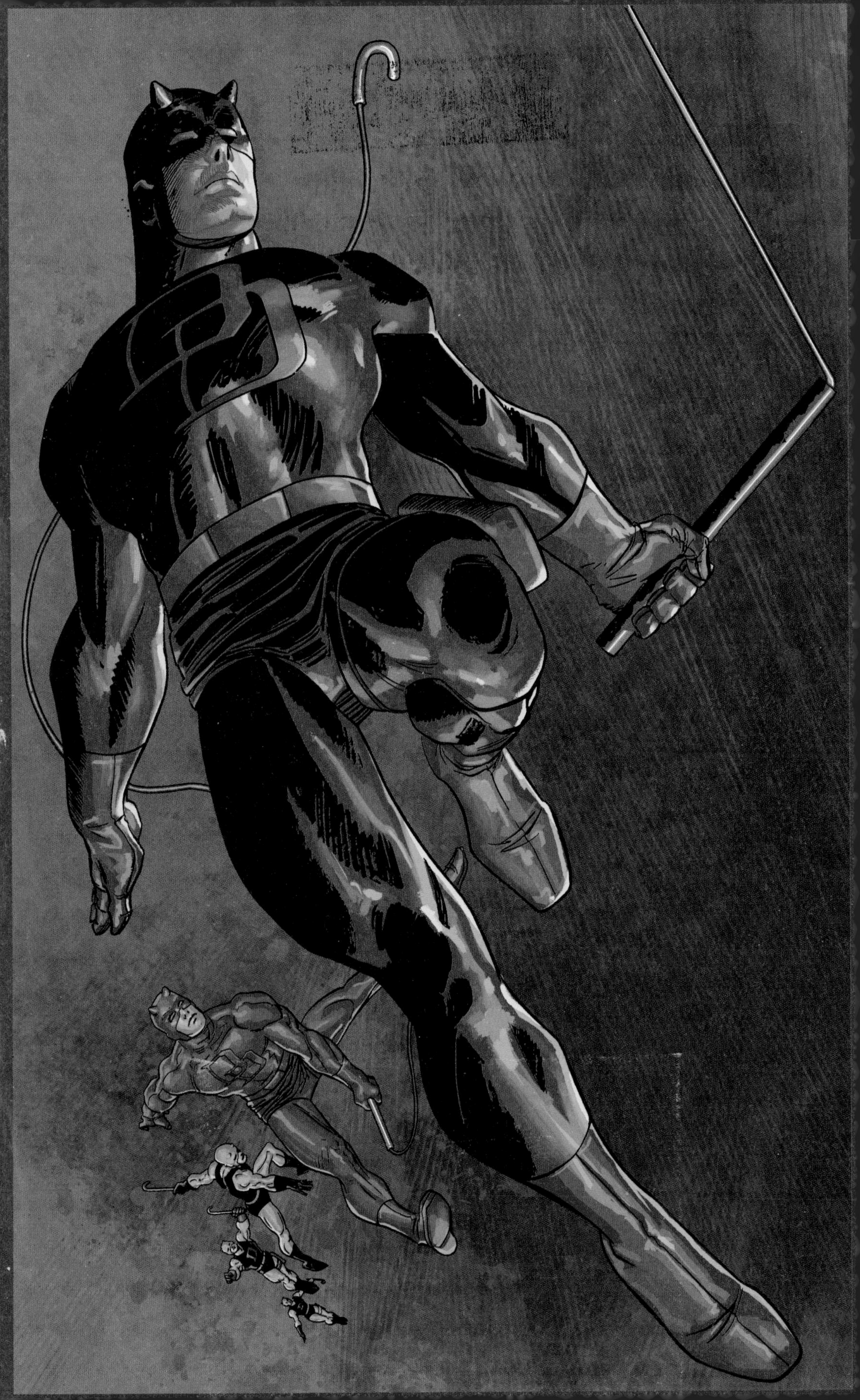

Daredevil: The Man Without Fear TPB (4th Printing: 2003) cover by John Romita Jr.

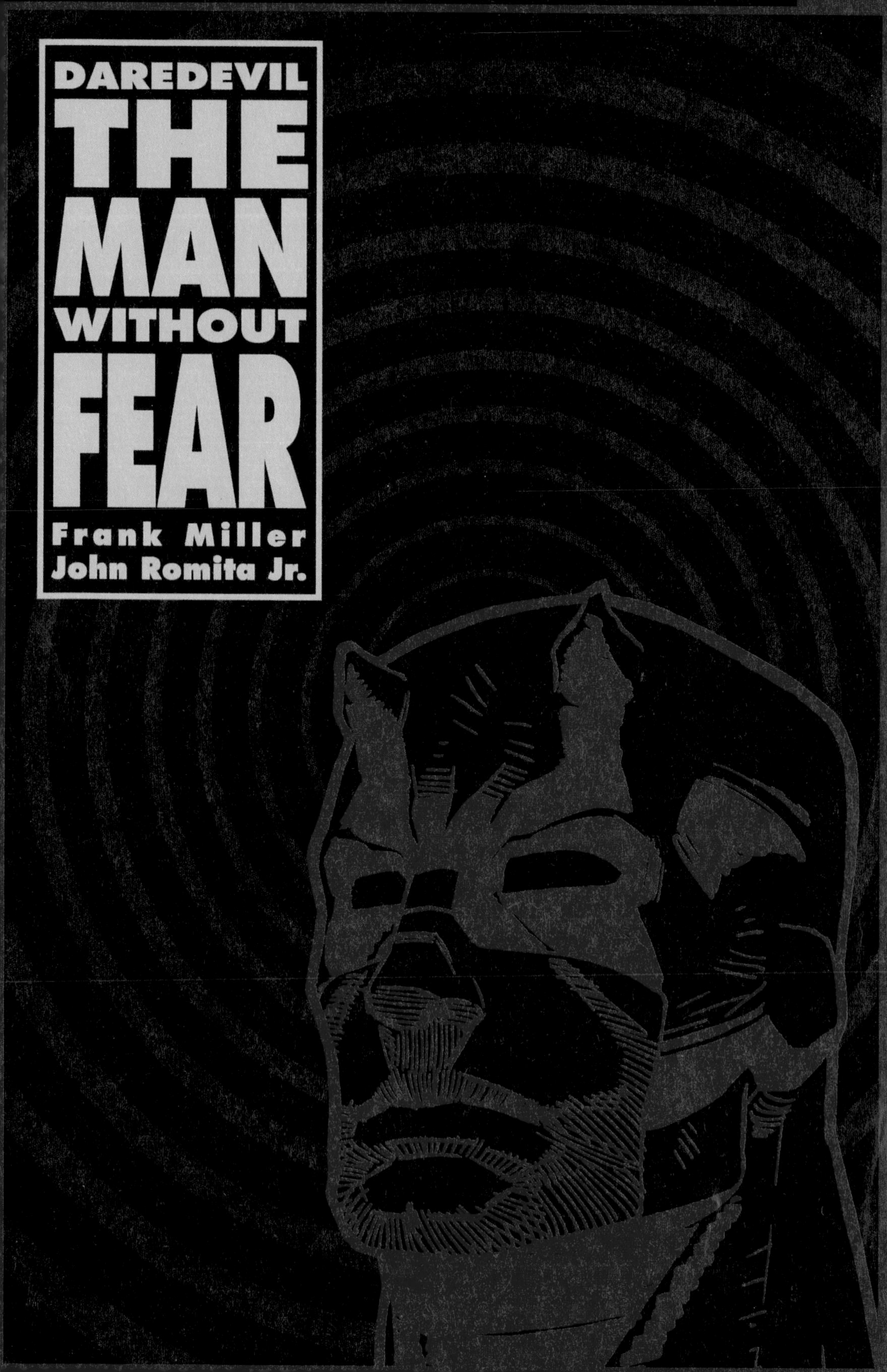
DAREDEVIL
THE MAN WITHOUT FEAR
Frank Miller
John Romita Jr.